Left of Poetry

SARAH EHLERS

Left of Poetry
Depression America and the
Formation of Modern Poetics

The University of North Carolina Press *Chapel Hill*

This book was published with the assistance of the Authors Fund of the University of North Carolina Press.

© 2019 The University of North Carolina Press
All rights reserved
Set in Arno Pro by Westchester Publishing Services
Manufactured in the United States of America

The University of North Carolina Press has been a member of the Green Press Initiative since 2003.

Library of Congress Cataloging-in-Publication Data
Names: Ehlers, Sarah, author.
Title: Left of poetry : Depression America and the formation of
   modern poetics / Sarah Ehlers.
Description: Chapel Hill : University of North Carolina Press,
   [2019] | Includes bibliographical references and index.
Identifiers: LCCN 2018042307| ISBN 9781469651279 (cloth : alk. paper) |
   ISBN 9781469651286 (pbk : alk. paper) | ISBN 9781469651293 (ebook)
Subjects: LCSH: Poetics—History—20th century. | American poetry—
   20th century—History. | American poetry—20th century—
   History and criticism.
Classification: LCC PS324 .E35 2019 | DDC 811/.5209—dc23
   LC record available at https://lccn.loc.gov/2018042307

Cover illustration: Detail of *Stamped-Tin Relic* (1929, gelatin silver print) by Walker Evans. Digital image courtesy of the Getty's Open Content Program.

A portion of chapter 3 was published as "What's Left of Lyric: Genevieve Taggard and the Redefinition of Song," in *Lineages of the Literary Left: Essays in Honor of Alan M. Wald*, ed. Howard Brick, Robbie Lieberman, and Paula Rabinowitz (Ann Arbor: University of Michigan Press, 2015), 20–37.

A short excerpt from chapter 5 was published as "Communism for Kids: Martha Millet, the New Pioneer, and the Popularity of the Old Left," on Mike Chasar's *Poetry and Popular Culture* blog, posted 18 April 2013.

For Jason and for Jonah:
"The universe is made of stories, not of atoms."
—Muriel Rukeyser, "The Speed of Darkness"

It has now become plain that the economic crisis is to be accompanied by a literary one.
—Edmund Wilson, "The Literary Class War"

Contents

List of Illustrations ix
Acknowledgments xi

Introduction: The Poetic Front 1

Part I
Documentary

CHAPTER ONE
Photography and the Development of Radical Poetics:
Langston Hughes in Haiti, Mexico, Alabama 27

CHAPTER TWO
Fusing an Alloy: Muriel Rukeyser at the
Limits of Poetry/Documentary 65

Part II
Lyric

CHAPTER THREE
Lyric Effects: Singing the Futures of Poetry with
Genevieve Taggard and Edwin Rolfe 105

CHAPTER FOUR
Lyric Internationalism: Jacques Roumain and His Committee 143

Part III
Rhythm

CHAPTER FIVE
The Left Needs Rhythm: Popular Front Poetry, Antifascism,
and the Counterarchives of Modernism 181

Epilogue 219

Notes 223
Bibliography 253
Text Credits 273
Index 275

Illustrations

1. Langston Hughes, contact sheet labeled "Langston Hughes in Haiti with Zell Ingram," ca. 1931   35
2. Langston Hughes, loose page from Haiti Scrapbook, ca. 1931   40
3. Langston Hughes, loose page from Haiti Scrapbook with photograph labeled "Poor Homes," ca. 1931   41
4. Langston Hughes, page from Haiti Photograph Album with photographs of the Citadel, ca. 1931   42
5. Langston Hughes, first page of Haiti Photograph Album, ca. 1931   43
6. Photographic print of Scottsboro Boys in jail at Birmingham, undated   57
7. Manuel Álvarez Bravo, *Los agachados* (The crouched ones), 1934   61
8. Muriel Rukeyser, page from the photo-text "Adventures with Children," *Coronet*, September 1939   79
9. Genevieve Taggard, scansion marks on poems by E. E. Cummings, Carl Sandburg, and Kenneth Fearing, 1942   134
10. Langston Hughes, "Free Jacques Roumain," on the cover of *Dynamo*, May–June 1935   152
11. Teenage Martha Millet featured on the cover of *Labor Defender*, January 1936   182
12. Martha Millet, pages from "Pioneer Pied Piper," *New Pioneer*, May 1931   188

Acknowledgments

My critical interest in the poetic culture of the Depression-era left grew from uncritical attachments. As a first-generation college student from a rural, working-class background, I have often felt out-of-place, if not unwelcome, in academia. During difficult years as a graduate student, the writers, artists, and activists of an earlier era provided a language for various forms of anger, and my love for their poetry a means to disidentify with institutions of art and criticism codified by people in positions of privilege. The study I eventually pursued would have been impossible without Alan Wald, a peerless thinker and generous mentor who sets the example for committed scholarship.

Yopie Prins and June Howard taught me to read rigorously and encouraged me to trust my instincts; their brilliant methodological insights mark every page. My teachers from the University of Michigan are sustaining influences—especially Howard Brick, Joshua Miller, Gillian White, John Whittier-Ferguson, and Sara Blair, to whom I owe my abiding interest in visual culture. Paula Rabinowitz's scholarship was an inspiration before I met her in person, and she has been an encouraging force since my first years as a graduate student. Perhaps my greatest debt is to Victoria Harris. Because of her, my first lessons in poetry were also lessons in politics.

At the University of South Dakota, John Dudley and Emily Haddad fostered my early career and, along with my first-rate colleagues Sarah Townsend and Skip Willman, offered incisive and generous feedback on early drafts. I am energized continually by the dynamic intellectual and creative communities at the University of Houston. The people to thank for support, conversation, and advice are too numerous to name. Nonetheless, I would be remiss if I did not acknowledge my American Studies and Poetics colleagues Lauren Brozovich, Sally Connolly, Amanda Ellis, Elizabeth Gregory, and Michael Snediker for their comments on chapter drafts, as well as Wyman Herendeen and James Kastely for material support. I have also benefited from interactions with an incredible cohort of graduate students, especially Erika Jo Brown, Niki Herd, Alexandra Naumann, Henk Rossouw, and the inimitable Rhianna Brandt, who saved the day. One could not ask for a better colleague than Roberto Tejada, whose dazzling intellect improved these pages in the final rounds. For feedback as well as friendship, my thanks to Julie Tolliver and

Cedric Tolliver. Cedric has been a true department comrade from day one—may our long hallway conversations about the literary left continue.

It has been a pleasure working with the University of North Carolina Press, an institution whose long-standing commitment to scholarship on literary radicalism is well alive. I would like to thank Mark Simpson-Vos for his early interest in the project, and I am especially grateful to Lucas Church for his support of the book and for ushering it to completion. The insightful commentary offered by the press's two anonymous readers pushed my thinking and made *Left of Poetry* a far better book.

A number of individuals generously shared information and granted permission to reproduce archival materials. I owe particular gratitude to Jerri Dell, Alex Garlin, Emily Garlin, Judith Benet Richardson, the late Perry Robinson, William Rukeyser, and Ronald Sauer as well as Craig Tenney and Alex Smithline at Harold Ober Associates. Selections from chapter three and chapter five appeared previously in slightly different form, and I thank the University of Michigan Press and Cambridge University Press for permission to reprint them here.

Librarians at the University of Michigan Labadie Collection, the University of Chicago Special Collections Research Center, the Yale University Beinecke Rare Book and Manuscript Library, the New York Public Library, the Newberry Library, the University of Pennsylvania Kislak Center, and the Library of Congress helped to locate and reproduce essential unpublished materials. John Durham welcomed me to Bolerium Books and provided a space to rifle through papers. Funding for research trips was generously provided by a fellowship from the University of Chicago Libraries as well as grants from the University of Michigan English Department, the University of South Dakota College of Arts and Sciences, and the University of Houston College of Liberal Arts and Social Sciences.

Conversations with colleagues in left literary studies and modernist poetry studies have enlivened my thinking. Thanks to Benjamin Balthaser, Mike Chasar, Cheryl Higashida, Walt Hunter, Robbie Lieberman, Julia Mickenberg, and Chris Vials as well as my Michigan comrades Konstantina Karageorgos and Nate Mills. For invaluable exchanges about modern poetics, a special shout out to Caroline Gelmi, Melissa Girard, and Erin Kappeler. A now dispersed cohort of beloved friends from Ann Arbor—Katie Brokaw, Nan Da, Asynith Palmer, and Sheera Talpaz—sustained me along the way. Sara Lampert was a lifesaver during the coldest winter. Rachel Feder and Rebecca Porte find the right words and put them in the right order; they have always made everything dance.

My parents, Byron and Janine Ehlers, labored to support my education, and I am forever grateful for the love that they and my brother, Gavin, have given over the years. The memory of Orlu Kleber has stuck with me at every turn. James and Deborah Berger, indeed the entire Berger crew, were always ready with encouraging words. David Michael Jones should only find his name in the paragraph reserved for thanking one's family.

My son, Jonah, has infused these words with joy from the beginning. And what is left to say to Jason Berger, whose brilliance is not even a match for the care with which he spins our life world and with whom the smallest gestures of love transform to revolutionary acts.

Left of Poetry

INTRODUCTION

The Poetic Front

Which side are you on?
—Florence Reece

What We Talk About

In "What We Talk about When We Talk about Poetry," a short story embedded in David Buuck and Juliana Spahr's collaborative prose experiment *An Army of Lovers* (2013), four Bay Area writers pass a bottle of gin around a table while discussing the "subject of poetry" and whether it has anything to do with politics. Mel, a curly-haired poet-professor and former union organizer, disagrees with Terri, his second wife, that Louis Zukofsky was a political poet. Embarrassed that he once loved a Mary Oliver poem and possibly drunk, he begins to explain to his companions why they should be ashamed of talking like they know what they are talking about when they talk about poetry and politics. Mel retells the story of the 1984 Bhopal disaster to prove his point that poems make nothing happen:

> Years before all this, in West Virginia, the same Union Carbide dug a three-mile tunnel under a mountain. So the workers hit a, what's it, a silica deposit. They're not given any masks, even though everyone knew that the miners needed masks. But Union Carbide doesn't bother. So, surprise, most of the workers are all dead within a year. Okay, so, Muriel Rukeyser, now here's your political poet, Muriel Rukeyser writes a poem about it. The poem is fucking beautiful, full of clear language, so no need to quote Marx to get the point across. It opens with the poet going down into the valley. She takes the words of the wives of the dead miners and she turns it into this lyric song. There's your "sings an impulse to action" or whatever. It is impossible not to be moved by this poem. It is a clear, strong poem. A famous poem. People read it. And it did nothing. Fifty years later, Union Carbide, Bhopal, boom, nothing.[1]

The thing I want to talk about is how Mel's impromptu explication illuminates the distance between contemporary debates and practices and the debates and practices emerging in Rukeyser's interwar communist milieu. When Rukeyser's *The Book of the Dead*, the poem sequence she wrote in response to the West Virginia disaster, appeared in her 1938 volume *U.S. 1* it was lambasted as much as it was praised. For one thing, few thought it got its point across clearly. The folk singer Lee Hays wrote to the U.S. Communist Party (CPUSA)–affiliated magazine *New Masses* to complain that Rukeyser wrote nothing that had anything to do with real life. He had "worked in many a cornfield" and wondered if she "ever came near one."[2] For another, as poets and critics grappled with finding terms to describe the sequence, they found in it little lyricism or song and were confounded by its strange mixture of poetic language, journalese, and left intellectualism. Critics who liked the sequence, such as William Carlos Williams, suggested that it aspired to be something other than a poem.[3]

"What We Talk about When We Talk about Poetry" stages elements of ongoing debates about the relationships among poetic form, political commitment, and actual social and economic transformation. An overarching premise of this book is that such debates remain incomplete without a reexamination of the communist-influenced poetic culture that flourished in the United States in the 1930s and 1940s. During the Depression years, literary leftism became a "mainstream affair."[4] As Alan Wald makes clear, in the thirties and forties, "Communist institutions, ideology, and committed cadres 'gave voice' in variously effective ways" to diverse writers "radicalized" by extreme changes in the economic system and in international relations.[5] In what follows, I excavate (to turn another of Rukeyser's phrases) buried, wasted, and lost remains of the procommunist presence in modern American poetics. I am interested in the conditions that prompt us to recognize a generically hybrid sequence such as *The Book of the Dead* as a poem, the processes by which all poems become either exemplary "lyric songs" or their opposites, the complex ways poetic forms get equated to political positions or actions, and how poetry writing and reading are defined as modes of political resistance.[6] My chapters tell a part of the cultural history of political poetry in the United States, and in so doing, they devise alternate models for comprehending the interwar literary imagination. This historical and analytical work has significant consequences: first, it indicates the importance of historical revolutionary imaginative work for reevaluations of modernist poetic formations; and second, it provides different terms and parameters for understanding the logics of socially engaged poetries across the twentieth and twenty-first centuries.

Since the 1960s and 1970s, scholars of U.S. literary radicalism have challenged canonical literary histories and evaluative methods by recovering and interpreting complex variations of 1930s poetic practices. *Left of Poetry* is indebted to that tradition, one that has been propelled by a collective commitment to studying and teaching suppressed authors and texts that make up an emancipatory archive of American literary study.[7] New work in left literary studies has built on earlier groundbreaking recovery projects by retrieving the variegated artistic and intellectual fronts of the early-twentieth-century international communist movement in order to reconceive labor struggles, black liberation, intersectional feminism, and anti-imperialist solidarity against formations of Cold War liberal capitalist modernity.[8] The present study contributes to these efforts by returning to the poetic as a vital site of inquiry. My chapters expand knowledge of the historical and political terrain on which leftist writers of the 1930s both composed socially engaged poetry and waged struggles over the meaning and function of poetry as an object (a body of poems) and an ideal (a set of claims about what poetry might do for individuals or for the social worlds in which they live). At the same time, I leverage the rich poetic legacy of the interwar U.S. communist movement and its international connections to intervene in current discourses about the relationships among aesthetic forms, processes of economic and racial dispossession, and movements for social justice.

This is all to say that many of the issues at stake for poetry and poetry criticism within our current volatile economic and political terrain are not new.[9] Analyzing the Asian American left writer Carlos Bulosan's Depression-era story about Filipino migrant workers, "The Romance of Magno Rubio," Sarita See juxtaposes past and present economic crises in order to uncover new forms of knowledge relevant to understanding the 2008 subprime mortgage crisis as well as broader paradigms of obligation and debt. See argues, "It is only through the terms of a different system of valuation that it becomes clear that *foreclosure is another form of enclosure.*"[10] In the context of this study, See's line of argument suggests how a consideration of marginalized interwar poetries might alter the logics of contemporary social poetics, especially as scholars work to productively disorganize long-standing debates about the alignments of poetic forms with political positions and to uncover the dynamics of institutional power influencing and sustaining the very terms of those debates.

Left of Poetry rethinks the literary history of modern poetry and criticism by recontextualizing and retheorizing fundamental ideas about poetics from the perspective of the interwar procommunist left. Tracing alternative historical conceptions of poetic genres and tropes, interpretive categories, and notions about how poems do or do not do political work, I work in the vein of recent influential scholarship fitting under the rubric of "historical poetics" and "poetry and cultural studies" that has, in different ways, called for more contextually specific analysis of writing and reading practices.[11] The poets and texts that I examine destabilize the claims that modern and contemporary critics have made for poetry as well as the claims that historical poetics scholars have made for history. In an era that witnessed an unprecedented growth of the organized left in resistance to economic inequality, racial injustice, and military and financial imperialism, there was a demand for poems that were deeply imbricated in immediate conditions. Through a set of literary and theoretical analyses based in archival scholarship, I demonstrate how the changed relationship between the political and aesthetic realms during the interwar period forced writers to think anew about the relationship between poetry and other material, economic, and political registers—including the category of history itself.

My chapters thus seek more than a simple restoration of text to context. To put it in the terms of this introduction's opening anecdote: it does not really matter if I can prove or disprove Mel's explication of *The Book of the Dead* with historical research and analysis. Either way, a poem about how the Union Carbide Corporation was responsible for one of the worst industrial disasters in American history did nothing to stop the Union Carbide Corporation from facilitating one of the worst industrial accidents in Indian history. What does matter is how the compositional practices and poetic discourses of the interwar communist left illuminate the ways that, at a particular moment of crisis, writers imagined history and poetry as mutually constitutive. Jodi Dean has argued for a reconsideration of "the party form unfettered by the false concreteness of specific parties in the contingency of their histories" that would allow for a reflection on communist "modes of association in the abstract."[12] I evoke Dean's arguments not to route around the specificities of the communist cultural milieu during the interwar period but rather to suggest that, if we put pressure on how the matter of history manifests itself as a poetics, we might push beyond historical-empirical epistemologies and toward alternative modalities that enliven desires for radical collectivity and create opportunities for politics. As Kenneth Fearing implored in his 1935 poem "Denouement," "Desire of millions, become more real than warmth and breath and strength and bread."[13]

Left of Poetry thus combines a literary-historical thesis about the central role of communist poetic culture in the development of modern American poetics with a set of theoretical questions about how poetry both abstracts and enacts different versions of history and politics. While the texts and contexts I consider span from the onset of the Depression in late 1920s to the beginnings of the "high" Cold War in the early 1950s, my primary focus is the so-called red decade of the Great Depression. In making this period demarcation, I do not intend to reentrench the received wisdom that the heyday of U.S. communism began with the 1929 Wall Street crash and ended with the 1939 Hitler-Stalin pact. To the contrary, my analyses of poets such as Genevieve Taggard and Jacques Roumain look at shifts in conceptions of lyric that bridge late-thirties Popular Front and early-forties antifascist discourses. My closing chapter, a recuperation of the communist poet and labor journalist Martha Millet, considers how communist writers attempted to intervene in discourses about modern poetics throughout the fifties and sixties.

Nonetheless, as this introductory chapter demonstrates, the historical and economic crisis of the Depression coincided with a complementary crisis in the literary that socially engaged poets would worry over across the thirties. The historical schematic that views artistic production across the decade according to the shift from the Comintern's revolutionary "third period" to the "Popular Front" provides a useful frame, not least because the prescriptions for making art that attended party policy had a hand in shaping writing and reading practices. At the same time, the poetic culture of the period is constituted by a rich and aesthetically diverse matrix of schools and movements that emerged in the early Depression years and that would continue to influence poetic discourse. While the impact of communist political and cultural formations extends beyond the red decade, the thirties is a crucible for understanding both the history of poetics and the role of poetic thought in conceptualizing historical change.

Linking Caroline Bird's notion that the Great Depression is an "invisible scar," an "absent presence that has driven American culture," to the problems of memory associated with the ascendancy of the institutional and literary left during the "red decade" of the 1930s, Paula Rabinowitz avers, "The 'invisible scar' of the Left serves as a point of obsessive rumination—for worrying over, the way one fingers an unseen blemish unconsciously, almost ritualistically, until it erupts into prominence.... The 1930s appear simultaneously as the most remembered and most forgotten decade in American cultural history."[14] If the economic dislocations of the present prompt the need to construct a prehistory of anticapitalist poetics, it would only be a matter of time before we would have to confront the thirties—a return of the depressed, so to speak.

Poetic Affronts

To say that 1930s radical poetry has been understudied or misunderstood is perhaps to belabor the obvious. The reduction of "the thirties" to an icon for a certain brand of political art has long obscured the intricate relationships among poetic practice, literary-critical discourse, and political thought in the era. Unsympathetic and sympathetic readers alike have committed follies: holding onto categories, concepts, paradigms, and battle lines that have failed to account for the depth and complexity of Depression-era poetic culture.[15] As such, while the poetry of the 1930s has not necessarily been forgotten, it remains largely unknown.

Efforts to recover Depression-era poetry have either attempted to save it in the name of mainstream versions of modernism or tried to revalue it using evaluative schematics suitable to various political ideologies. Scholars of early-twentieth-century radical poetry thus have relied on the same paradigms about poetry that guide reactionary studies: one entrenches sacrosanct modernist versions of art, and the other reduces poems to historical symptoms. In other words, even when "high modernism," "New Criticism," and/or "the canon" have been targeted as the enemy of left poetry, it remains unclear how to theorize radical poetics outside of ideas about modernism, poetic expression, and formal mastery that are themselves products of what Gillian White has described as "a diffuse New Critical discourse by now so thoroughly absorbed so as to seem natural."[16] While it would seem that scholars have collectively debunked New Criticism, many New Critical assumptions remain operational, though they might go under different names or function in different ways. White, for example, describes how contemporary discourses about experimentalism are themselves defined by a repudiation of New Critical discourses. In the field of left literary studies, scholars often acknowledge how New Critical biases have distorted knowledge of modern poetics, yet they continue to employ New Critical exegetical practices based on, for example, the centrality of the poetic speaker.[17] At the same time, the codification of Language Writing in the 1970s as "an explicitly anticapitalist project" produced a narrow set of possibilities for understanding the politics of poetic form, especially in relation to class, race, and gender identities.[18] With a few exceptions, the poetic has remained as conspicuously absent from more recent influential scholarship on literary radicalism as it was from Michael Denning's field-defining *The Cultural Front*. One result is something like a remark I heard during a Q&A following a conference session on the radical novel: "I just don't know what a communist poetry would look like."

This offhand comment reminds me of a moment in Doris Lessing's 1962 novel *The Golden Notebook*, when the British ex-communist Anna Wulf admits that "the really deadly skeleton in the Communist closet" is that "everyone had that old manuscript or wad of poems tucked away." She muses, "Isn't it terrifying? Isn't it pathetic? Every one of them, failed artists. I'm sure it's significant of something, if only one knew what."[19] For Anna, and arguably for scholars of literary radicalism, the skeleton in the communist closet is a wad of poems. For critics and historians of U.S. poetry, the dreadful wad of communist poems is the proverbial skeleton in the closet. Such statements, which act to divide radical left literary production produced in the orbit of the Communist Party from "poetry" itself, have implications not just for studies of U.S. poetry and literary radicalism but also for critical studies of modernism. As I will explore in more detail later, *Left of Poetry* reconfigures prevailing views of modernism, including the legacies of the modernist avant-garde, through the lens of Depression-era art and politics.

The poetic culture of the 1930s is the product of the major cultural shifts occurring during the Depression and in the buildup to World War II. The 1929 Wall Street crash and what followed it—mass unemployment, mass hunger, mass strikes, bank failures, drought, industrial disaster, Jim Crow, the colonial occupation of Haiti/Korea/Libya, the rise of fascist dictatorships in Europe—created, as Malcolm Cowley put it, "a new conception of art" that replaced "the idea that it was something purposeless, useless, wholly individual and forever opposed to the stupid world."[20] These historical, political, and cultural changes did not just shift the ground on which individual poems were produced and evaluated. They also changed the terms of what would be recognized as a "poem" and altered notions of "poetry" as an ideation.

Langston Hughes's 1928 poem "Johannesburg Mines" thinks through these shifts. The content of "Johannesburg Mines" is documentary fact; its lineation prompts us to read it as a poem:

> In the Johannesburg mines
> There are 240,000 natives working.
> What kind of poem
> Would you make out of that?
>
> 240,000 natives working
> In the Johannesburg mines.[21]

"Johannesburg Mines" cleverly and poignantly offers a provisional answer to its own question—"What kind of poem / Would you make out of that?"—merely by existing. What is more, Hughes suggests that the very existence or status of the poem changes when it attempts to represent the violence of capitalism's uneven development. While "Johannesburg Mines" was penned just before the 1929 Wall Street crash, it demonstrates how the imperative to make art that addresses the inequities of capitalism was opposed to a conception of poetry also forming in the early twentieth century in which "poetry" became synonymous with "pure expressiveness" and "absolute literariness."[22] This latter conception of poetry, which associated it with high culture, individual achievement, and the modernist cult of the poet-genius, was viewed by Depression-era literary radicals as the refuse of a crumbling economic system and defunct bourgeois literary order. Interwar poets sought to write poems that did not aspire to poetry qua absolute literariness. As they debated what such poems might look like, they altered the ideation of poetry in the early twentieth century by soldering it to ideals of collectivity and of collective political action.

The historical record abounds with accounts of how the political crises of the 1930s were related to crises in the literary scene, perhaps most succinctly encapsulated in Edmund Wilson's line, "It has now become plain that the economic crisis is to be accompanied by a literary one."[23] Looking back on the Depression in *On Native Grounds*, Alfred Kazin wrote, "The crisis of the nineteen-thirties, . . . whether interpreted as a breakdown of capitalism or a visitation from on high, a temporary failure of institutions or the epilogue to America's participation in the First World War, . . . imposed with catastrophic violence what other national experiences had induced slowly and indirectly—a new conception of reality."[24] Kazin's retrospective was shaped by later disillusionments, but the basic point remains: under unprecedented historical pressures, that which had gone by the name "poetry" for so long had to be rethought and, ultimately, called into question as a form of expression and as a material part of social life. I argue that this process entailed both encounters with the "unthought" of poetic practice and attempts to change the historical and political parameters for the production of poetry itself.[25] During the 1930s, narratives about "poetry" confronted a new sense of "history" marked by urgency and crisis. At this intersection of poetry and history, left-leaning poets encountered not merely a social poetry—that is, a renewal of poetry's engagement with mass audiences and social movements—but a sense of poetry's alterity and its alternatives.

In order to make these arguments, I offer new ways of interpreting poems that served what might be considered doctrinaire politics or dogmatic prescriptions for what a revolutionary poem should look like, revealing the complexity and importance of these poems when understood as part of the fabric of social life. Denning's *The Cultural Front* opened possibilities for understanding interwar cultural production outside of a narrow focus on party policy and state institutions. Nonetheless, a utilitarian view of political poetry is still commonly associated with Old Left writing practice. In the introduction to

Proletarian Literature of the United States (1935), Joseph Freeman declared that "art, as an instrument in the class struggle, must be developed by the proletariat as one of its weapons," and Shaemas O'Sheel described the poems collected in the antifascist anthology *Seven Poets in Search of an Answer* (1944) as a resumption of "the great tradition of poetry as a sword against evil."[26] The imperative that poems serve a utilitarian purpose in fights against imperialism, fascism, and race and class oppression was accompanied by a distinct set of aesthetic criteria: poems should privilege the public over the private, the collective over the individual, the accessible over the obscure, hope for the future over despair of the present. As Stanley Burnshaw put it in his 1930 "Notes on Revolutionary Poetry," "Let him [the revolutionary poet] remember that if literature is to be a weapon it must not be a thin, shadowy, overdelicate implement but a clear, keen-edged, deep-cutting tool."[27]

The glut of poems written to be weapons were made to serve a political function that cannot be discerned through the modes of interpretation to which most literary critics and historians are accustomed. Indeed, the poem-cum-weapon presents problems beyond the manifest political ones: weapons are meant to be stockpiled, handled, or fired—they are not meant to be read.[28] As a result, scholars have, when not overlooking these poems altogether, presented them as more or less interesting historical specimens while turning their interpretive gazes to works that blend revolutionary politics with modernist aesthetic principles that conform more easily to evaluative standards. In more recent criticism, the evaluative "double bind" faced by left poetry scholars wanting to convince "skeptical modern poetry specialists that the Old Left produced more than ... verse rightfully consigned to oblivion" is, it seems, in the process of being replaced by a vein of modernist poetry scholarship that, while attentive to left political theory and ideology, concentrates on how a narrow set of aesthetic strategies registers the contradictions of modern capitalism and the revolutionary spirit of communism.[29]

I return to poems written in a range of genres in order to track the social relations they attempted to make possible.[30] Left poets, critics, and readers theorized the criteria for useful or weapon-like poems by crafting alternative histories for traditional verse genres (especially variations of the song and ballad) as well as poetic tropes (particularly voice, the speaker, and rhythm) and categories (primarily the opposition between accessibility and difficulty). Such critical work often involved reframing the relationships among nineteenth- and twentieth-century verse cultures as well as between the so-called high and low. What is more, many artists in the communist milieu imagined themselves as part of a diverse international formation, and in consequence, generic experimentation was underwritten by thinking about racial and national formations.[31] The aim of such experiments was literary as well as social. What kinds of poems would circulate most widely? Or be the most convincing? Or even unite the amorphous masses?

My task, then, is to interpret the Depression as a moment of historical crisis that is coupled with crises in genre. At a time when the political horizon changed at a rapid pace—when the moment, itself, became radicalized—old, even perhaps anachronistic, genres were stretched and used in new ways. What poetry meant and the kinds of claims that could be made for what it does were thus recast according to models for what poetry was said to represent or inscribe. This is especially the case when considering how poems wrestle with the tensions inherent in the seeming opposition between communism, on one hand, and an essentially lyric poetry, on the other. In a 1931 *Rebel Poet* editorial, Philip Rahv declared of lyric poetry that "there's nothing more up that street."[32] Statements such as Rahv's assume a New Critical definition of "lyric" as an expression that stands outside of history and is, therefore, contradictory to the social and historical orientation of the communist project. Considering lyric and communism in relation rather than in opposition to each other, however, generates a new ground for understanding the lyric as a mode for representing and processing history and, at the same time, puts pressure on the very idea of history itself. As I will detail shortly, a more historically and culturally specific look at the development of left lyric reveals that left poets, rather than eschewing the lyric, actively worked to reinvent its contours, especially in the internationalist context of communist commitment. In the process, they actively theorized notions of liberal subjectivity, coherent personhood, and the subject's relationship to history *through* the lyric rather than against it.

Discourses and debates about the forms of Depression poetry also remain inseparable from the major shifts in technological reproduction and consumer culture that occurred during the decade. Media forms such as photography, film, and radio shaped how communist poets approached problems of political representation as well as how they thought through issues of circulation and accessibility. Poetic experiments were mediated by modern technologies in ways that altered nominal definitions of poetry and the poem and relocated questions of authorship. While my chapters are particularly attuned to the cultural emergence of documentary photography during the thirties, especially as it relates to the development of documentary poetics, I also demonstrate how radio and film influenced theorizations of poetic form and of poems' social uses.

Radical Historical Poetics

To repeat Mike Gold heralding the proletarian literary movement in the January 1929 *New Masses*, if you've got the guts, come left. Gold's "Go Left, Young Writers!" column has become a tagline for the leftward migration of U.S. writers during the thirties. In it, he outlines the "historic task" of developing a literature from knowledge of working-class life and a "hard precise philosophy of 1929 based on economics." Gold effectively demystifies creative work, defining it as "one of the products of civilization like steel or textiles." Literature "is not a child of eternity, but of time. It is always the mirror of its age. It is not any more mystic in its origin than a ham sandwich."[33] Gold's provocation to "go left" takes place in relation to the influence of Third Period policy and the attendant reaction to the so-called high modernist literature of the 1920s. Equating literature to steel or textiles—even a ham sandwich—strikes an instrumentalist tone while debunking sacrosanct modernist versions of art. Gold reminds his readers, as Kenneth Fearing does in a 1935 poem in his "American Rhapsody" sequence, that high literature is a commodity that can be exchanged on the market like everything else:

> Closing prices: Is This Really a Commercial Age?
> —100. That Anguished Soul of Marcel Proust—
> 150. Liberty or Dangerous Freedom, Which?
> —210. That Unknown Patriotic, Law-abiding
> Corpse—305.[34]

Gold's "ham sandwich theory of literature" was, of course, more provocation than serious theory, his attempt to give control of the writing scene to the "common people." While Gold's views of literary production might seem hopelessly reactionary, they open up pivotal questions that cut across emerging debates in the field of poetry studies. In order to define literature as political, Gold makes recourse to the forces of history (literature as "a child . . . of time"). But is a materialist or historical impulse ipso facto a political one? Or does the reduction of, say, a poem to a product (something like "steel or textiles") foreclose political desire and thus possibility by harnessing it to base conditions? Are the politics of poetry located in the poem itself or in the way that we choose to read it?

Recent influential work fitting under the rubric of "historical poetics" has called for renewed attention to the historical and social conditions in which "readers recognized and poets produced various verse genres."[35] Much of this work has coalesced around the arguments of Yopie Prins's *Victorian Sappho*

(1999), Virginia Jackson's *Dickinson's Misery: A Theory of Lyric Reading* (2005), and Jackson and Prins's *The Lyric Theory Reader* (2014). These studies delineate processes by which specific verse genres and their historical functions came to be interpreted in terms of an idea of "lyric" that is abstract and ahistorical. While this line of argument might appear to be common sense and thus uncontroversial, historical poetics approaches have been the subject of formative criticisms. On one hand, scholars of poetics have taken the "historicizing inclinations" of this brand of criticism to task for failing to notice "continuities" in "conceptions of genres" across periods.[36] On the other hand, scholars of modern and contemporary poetry argue, from a different angle, that historical poetics scholarship would "benefit" from a "more capacious" sense of the historical vista. Oren Izenberg claims that while his study *Being Numerous* (2011) is historical—in the sense that it "seeks to retell a portion of the history of twentieth-century poetry" on the "changed conceptual grounds" of "a philosophical concept of personhood"—it has a different "theoretical disposition" than the "relentlessly nominalist and localist" historicisms prevailing in the current moment.[37] In Jackson's own response to *Being Numerous*, she praises the book's local arguments and then asks, "But please don't call it history."[38]

I agree with Jackson that Izenberg's study "is not a history of poetics but a fabricated tradition of poetics, a fiction (partially rehearsed, partially original) of what poetry does or can do."[39] But the question of how history is defined within historical poetics methods persists. Contemplating a similar question— "What is historical poetics?"—Prins suggests that the "contestation" over how to define "historical" and "poetics" is productive because "different approaches give form to radically different reading practices, research projects, aesthetic claims, and political agendas."[40] In Prins's view, historical poetics is a contestatory though widely applicable methodological rubric that creates diverse opportunities to counter (rightly) the dehistoricizing tendencies of modern poetry scholarship. Despite the possible diversity of approaches, however, there seems to be some implied definitional consensus across historical poetics projects, at least where the term "history" is concerned. For example, Sonya Posmentier has pointed out that central historical poetics claims about "lyricization" are based implicitly on Euro-American literary-historical narratives and conceptions of history, and she proposes Édouard Glissant's notion of "nonhistory" as an alternative historical conceptualization.[41] Along these lines, influential historical poetics scholarship, so far largely situated in the nineteenth-century Anglophone world, has taken up shifting ideas about the poetic in relation to flashpoint moments when notions of national identity and belonging were up for grabs. The purview of these studies, however, seems predicated on a diachronic notion of history, whereby various transitional moments and crises in question tend to fit within existing narrative trajectories and ultimately liberal models of reality.[42] Following Prins's invitation to forward a "different approach" that gives rise to new practices, I argue that thirties communist poetic cultures provide new discourses for thinking about "historical" and "poetics" as well as how those two terms relate to and inform each other.

In *Left of Poetry*, historical poetics methods act as a staging ground for considering the contours of political poetry as well as the politics of reading and interpretation, thus invoking the several possible permutations of what we might call "radical historical poetics": the radicalization of poetic culture at specific historical moments, the use of the poetic to conceive of radicalism and its history, the place of radicalism in histories of poetry, the importance of a radical historical framework to understand the nature of the poetic, and the potential radicalization of broad methodological interests consolidated under "historical poetics." *Left of Poetry* is thus a historical book. But I am very careful about saying so. I reveal how 1930s poets' conceptions of the dynamic interaction between artistic production and processes of historical change challenge the positivist assumptions about history undergirding historical poetics scholarship.

In this sense, *Left of Poetry* reveals how the possibilities of 1930s poetry were irreparably shaped by the specific historical horizons of the moment. Through historical work, I illuminate aesthetic and political formations that have been obscured by dominant literary-historical paradigms; but I trace another lineage too, in which ideas about poetry provide the coordinates of radical imagination. Robin D. G. Kelley, in his study of black radicalism, *Freedom Dreams*, gives the name "poetry" to the imagination of "something different," the "realization that things need not always be this way." "Poetry," he continues, "is not what we simply recognize as the formal 'poem,' but a revolt: a scream in the night, an emancipation of language and old ways of thinking." I am interested in how, for thirties left writers, the formal poem both traced and imagined the idea of revolt.[43]

Left of Lyricization

Discussions of the state of lyric studies have been coextensive with discussions of the state of poetry (as part of social life) and poetry studies (as a facet of academic discourse or production).[44] Within this line of questioning, scholars have brought renewed attention to the ways in which discourses about race and imperialism intersect with discourses about lyric as both a mode and a form.⁴⁵ *Left of Poetry* approaches these broader methodological interests by addressing a set of questions about the historical and theoretical development of the poetic lyric. The poetic culture of the 1930s left is crucial for illuminating alternative "motives for the materialization of lyric," to employ Rei Terada's useful phrasing, that emerge concomitant with and against the discourses about lyric that would become, by the end of World War II, the accepted models for defining, reading, and teaching poetry.⁴⁶ To be clear, this book is not focused exclusively on the lyric mode; however, the historical and analytical problems I approach constellate around debates about lyric as a mode of expression as well as of interpretation.

The innovations, lyric and otherwise, of the interwar period have more or less fallen through the cracks in histories of lyricization that have deconstructed the codification of New Criticism in the 1940s and 1950s in order to reinterpret nineteenth- and early-twentieth-century poetic practices. For radical poets and critics, the lyric and the claims about the individual associated with it were part of the wreckage of the historical crises of the 1930s. For poets influenced by communist and cultural front formations, modernist poetics and their romantic inheritance were premised on models of political identity that could not possibly represent the forms of subjectivity and community that might be produced from new economic and political alignments. The new "credo" undergirding radical artistic practice was, as Edwin Rolfe wrote in 1931, for "the mind" to "renounce the fiction of the self."⁴⁷ While some thirties communist poets rejected wholesale the terms of lyric, others attempted to articulate new possibilities for identity and community formation via experimentations with and analyses of the lyric mode.

Each of my chapters seeks to add to a range of studies that explore the social implications of lyric by examining the dialectical relationship between the abstraction that goes by the name lyric and the histories producing that abstraction. Stathis Gourgouris describes how clichés about lyric poetry and communism represent a basic antagonism between "the force of history and the force of the human imagination" that translates to "an uncompromising conflict between an ethical impulse and an aesthetic impulse." Against such easy distinctions, Gourgouris locates in communist poetries (his examples come from the Greek context) an "ascription of lyric subjectivity to the demands of historical materiality [*matter-reality*]," in which "poets saw the ethical demand of communism's historical intervention as a poetic task and, conversely, their poetic project as a chance to hone history's materiality into a language that metabolizes itself in turn to an actual historical praxis."⁴⁸

Such an approach provides a means to reorient the antagonism in poetry studies between the historicist critique of lyric and the insistence that lyric is a generic category that transcends historical specificity. Just as important, this approach reframes the division between lyric and antilyric discourses that were codified in the latter half of the twentieth century, especially as they have coalesced around questions of political critique and activism. With regard to the recent history of poetry criticism, the Language-school critique of the "traditional" or "expressive" lyric that took hold in the 1970s and 1980s has produced the assumption, still prevalent in poetry reading today, that the "lyric tradition" is a "liberal tradition." Within this framework for reading, the lyric poem, insofar as it connotes a political project, functions as a means for subjects to establish recognition within a centrist democratic system.[49] Conversely, specific forms of linguistic experimentation, such as parataxis, are treated as expressive of anticapitalist politics. Such reading practices make generalized assumptions about which forms are best suited for articulating radical politics.[50] If New Criticism dismissed the poetic culture of the 1930s in the name of an apolitical formalism, then the avant-gardists of the next generation erased a significant part of it in the name of a legacy that skipped from Gertrude Stein to the "New American Poetry" to the "New Sentence." The "innovation paradigm" that has governed accounts of modern and contemporary poetry, one that has no use for lyricism, sentimentality, or the didactic, obscured significant elements of the left literary tradition that I seek to illuminate here.[51]

In the wake of the 2008 financial crisis and mass political mobilizations such as Occupy and Black Lives Matter, poets and critics disrupted these long-standing divides and, in so doing, challenged the assumption that "formal strategies ... might bear some self-evident political content."[52] These considerations joined a scholarly tradition that, in viewing experimental writing from feminist and antiracist perspectives, has questioned assumptions about the political content of experimental forms, especially as they relate to concepts of identity formation.[53] Subsequent to the 2008 recession, a number of poetry scholars have provided welcome critiques of a literary-critical milieu that eschews Marxist hermeneutics, and their rigorous interpretive practices have demonstrated how poetry is a potent site for Marxist inquiry.[54] Christopher Nealon's *The Matter of Capital: Poetry and Crisis in the American Century*, for example, offered a pathbreaking survey that considered how North American poets "attempt to understand the relationship between poetry and capitalism, most often worked out as an attempt to understand the relationship of texts to historical crisis."[55]

The growing body of scholarship on poetry and capitalism has focused primarily on more recent poetry—from about 1970 on—perhaps because the argument that poetry is "uniquely suited" to represent "the ontology of capitalist disaster" is also suited to aesthetic and political debates and practices of that era.[56] The questions that arise out of the post-1970s milieu, however, have perhaps obscured the political and aesthetic regimes of earlier eras. For instance, Ruth Jennison's welcome and rigorous account of how 1930s poems and poetic movements registered "the variegated geographical, social, and cultural landscapes of capitalist modernity" focuses solely on the formal experimentation of the Objectivist movement; and Nealon's chapter on the 1930s in *The Matter of Capital* centers on two canonical modernists, Ezra Pound and W. H. Auden, who are first introduced by way of two experimental midcentury poets, Robert Duncan and Jack Spicer.[57]

I offer these examples to introduce areas for further consideration and to emphasize how the broad literary culture of the Depression remains an aporia in scholarly takes on the relation of poetry to historical capitalist crisis and to the revolutionary imagination. Returning to the specific milieu of the CPUSA requires that we move past the notion that the leftism evident in thirties poems was, to borrow a phrase from Nealon, "preening and damaging."[58] At the same time, it necessitates a recalibration of the relationship between evaluative claims about poems and analytical claims about the politics of poetry. By arguing for an attention to lyric and documentary forms, as well as sentimental schlock and worked-over nursery rhymes, I am suggesting that further investigation of Depression-era communist poetic culture provides a means to open current interpretive practices to a broader range of genres as well as figures, forms, and tropes.[59]

My chapters uncover sites where Depression-era poets developed alternative generic, aesthetic, and political forms. I expose and explore the processes whereby ideas about political representation—representations both of capital and of those subjects who have been dispossessed by it—are attached to specific genres and tropes. In the literary culture of the Depression, a diverse array of poetic practices posed as abstractions for political work, and debates about the forms poems should take stood in for a range of shifting political and cultural concerns. Conceiving leftist poetics this way means making different kinds of claims for "experiment," whereby experiment does not merely mean breaking from old forms but also conceiving of old forms in new ways.

The Radical Unread

Left of Poetry seeks to complicate those narratives that have been erected to make Depression-era poetic culture easy to understand and, in many cases, easy to move past. Roughly, critics assume that the aesthetic innovations of the 1920s were curtailed by a dogmatic, even hostile, left front that valued simple, accessible poems that toed the Communist Party line.[60] All of these assertions, which act to divide radically left literary production from "poetry" itself, have implications for studies of political poetry, modernism, and literary radicalism.

Left of Poetry seeks to challenge as well as move past such easy assertions about 1930s poetry. At the same time, I hope that my work will reiterate the substantial interventions of scholars working within the field of literary radicalism. Oftentimes Cary Nelson's foundational *Repression and Recovery* appears in requisite qualifying clauses and endnotes as a stand-in for the collective efforts of scholars studying U.S. left poetry and its international connections. For instance, Nealon cites Nelson's "career-long effort" to "broaden the canons of American poetry to include poems written from in and around the American labor movement" as one of the few, if only, attempts to discern "the persistence of capitalism as a subject matter for American poetry."[61] In this quick gesture, the variegated landscapes of left literary and scholarly production are reduced to "labor movement poetry" and to a singular effort to expand the canon. I do not mean for this to sound like a nitpicky complaint. But such innocuous critical moves suggest just how invisible certain strands of left poetic traditions and scholarship have become—even at a time when matters of financial crisis, working-class representation, the perils of individualism, and the possibilities for global connectedness outside the flows of capital are at the forefront of thinking in the humanities.

In a sense, I take my cues from the poet Walter Lowenfels, who, in his 1934 elegy for Hart Crane, imagined Crane's skull buried at the bottom of the sea while stocks move, a strange image of a dead poet resting within the oceanic flows of economic crisis. Lowenfels writes that Crane's "acts of revelation" are "like an ocean in an empty shell, / and his religions / oil in a wound / we are bound to tear open."[62] So I imagine my task as ensuring that the wounds are, in fact, "bound to tear open" by cutting back through again to keep open the possibilities that inhere in a disruption. In retrospect, "the thirties" might have been a failure in several senses. But our critical paradigms have, in many ways, failed them too. As I have already begun to suggest, the story of New Critical repression has loomed too large over studies of early-twentieth-century radical poetry: obscuring the various ways that slightly left-of-center and even Marxist paradigms have left untold the story of Depression-era radical poetics and, in consequence, an important story about the intersections of poetry with politics and history. So we have all ended up a little bit like the widow whom the communist poet Alfred Hayes described in a 1935 *Partisan Review* statement on poetry—the one who would join her husband in heaven only if the deity promised to haul up her weather-beaten house, scrawny pigs, and barren plot of ground too. As Hayes tells it, "the angel transported all. And then the wife was happy in Heaven, for it was like the earth she had always known, as vile, as old, as barren, as ever."[63] In what follows, I establish a new ground for thinking about Depression-era poetry and poetics and, through this work, a different means to consider the critical traditions that superseded it. This entails both accounting for critical traditions and histories and breaking from them: reinventing the old and inventing the new.

It is common knowledge that the history of American poetry since modernism has been divided into two camps: the traditional line that views modernism as continuous with romanticism, and the experimental avant-garde tradition that traces a lineage from the experiments of Stein, Pound, and Williams to the development of the "New American Poetry" at midcentury and, eventually, to the Language writing of the Vietnam era. Such divides have been consequential for the study of radical poetry, with scholars finding themselves in the crosshairs of debates they cannot seem to win. When we value the hackneyed and the sentimental, we side with those who would exclude left writers from the front lines of the modernist avant-garde. When we illuminate left writers' engagements with literary modernism, we aggrandize the very narratives that have obscured our subjects. When we place value on the political spirit in which the work was written, we are accused of being poor readers—or, worse, of skirting what Wald has called the "Janus-faced juggernaut" of Soviet Communism.[64]

And so one might think of 1930s radical poetics as occupying the same troubled position Louis Zukofsky did in 1935, just after he had "at last decided to cut himself off from Ezra Pound" and was left with "no God, no Ezra, no nothing." As Marya Zaturenska described it, Zukofsky was "going to try communism and has gone around humbly to C.P. headquarters asking for guidance. The cultural directors . . . gave him a lot of proletarian poetry, but naturally it was difficult to swallow after Ezra who is after all a craftsman. Life is very hard for those who can't face it without guidance from an inspired source."[65] The legacies of literary modernism have, indeed, made proletarian poetry a hard pill to swallow. On one hand, the entrenchment of the New Critical version of modernism, as Jennison has recently argued, is part of a long history of anticommunism that "continuously constructs, clips, redeploys, and refashions the historical record of the politics, causes, and aesthetics" of global economic crisis.[66] If for most of the 1930s there was little regard for the New Critical pronouncement that poetry and politics do not mix, by the end of the decade the spoils had fallen to those on "the side of the eternal verity of purportedly apolitical art."[67] New Critical values ascended during the Cold War, cementing ideas about form and literary value that devalued and denounced poetry produced by authors associated with the ideologies and institutions of the procommunist left.[68]

In our current moment, scholars have attempted to replace a monolithic concept of "modernism" or "modern poetry" with a range of "new modernisms" or plural "poetries." Such studies make room for multiple conceptions of what poetry might mean, especially as it occupies different roles in different reading communities. Such historical and theoretical reexaminations of modernism are welcome, especially because they have made room for marginalized writers.[69] And yet, it remains imperative that, as scholars expand the purview of modernism, they eschew forms of expansion and compromise that, while suitable to current neoliberal politics, potentially cover over deep historical antagonisms.[70] I take a cue from V. F. Calverton, who, in the inaugural issue of *The Left: A Quarterly Review of Radical and Experimental Art* (1931), put it this way: "*Industry respects no traditions; bows to no customs; slowly but steadily it destroys differences and establishes resemblances. The similar becomes dominant, and diverse traditions very soon become one tradition.* . . . The battle in American literature today, therefore, is no longer between traditions. . . . It is impossible to revive a tradition that is based on a way of life that is already dead."[71] I, for one, am an advocate for taking sides, especially in a contemporary moment, however newly politicized, where many scholars shy away from the sort of side-taking required for "*a ruthless criticism of everything existing*."[72]

By way of explanation, I want to turn briefly to Genevieve Taggard, the subject of chapter 3. Taggard was a prolific poet and critic, but her importance as a radical woman writer and public intellectual has remained relatively obscure. When Cary Nelson included a selection of Taggard's poems in the first edition of the *Oxford Anthology of Modern American Poetry* (2000), Marjorie Perloff questioned the choice:

> Why is Genevieve Taggard in the anthology? According to the headnote, she worked for various Communist causes in the twenties and in 1934 married Kenneth Durant, "who headed the American office of Tass, the

Soviet News Agency. This placed her at the center of left politics in the 'red decade' of the 1930s. Tass would employ several Spanish Civil War vets, including poet Edwin Rolfe, in the 1940s, and Taggard came to know them well," and so on. What precisely, are the undergraduates of 2001 [one of the supposed audiences for the anthology] to make of these facts? Are they to admire the "radicalism" of what were at best idealists duped by one of the more repressive and violent totalitarianisms of modern times? Are they to believe that this is "poetry" despite its reductive ideology? Or conversely that its poetic blunders aside, this poetry carries an "important" message?[73]

While Perloff's assessment seems dated (at one point she references her three-pound Dell laptop), it remains pertinent. Indeed, her critique of Taggard is continuous with her troubling criticism of Nelson's inclusion of contemporary poets of color in the volume, and is just one part of Perloff's career-long defenses of the white avant-garde. In her review of Nelson's anthology, Perloff cites Taggard's 1940 "Ode in a Time of Crisis," which is about the United States' refusal to accept refugees from Nazi Germany during World War II, as an exemplary bad poem that defies "every notion of the *mot juste* that had prompted and animated the revolution of Modernist poetry." Perloff ultimately decides that Taggard appears in the Oxford anthology only because Nelson values poems that wear their radicalism on their (red, hammer-and-sickle-stitched) sleeves. The whole anthology is a "forced feeding" she concludes, citing Frank O'Hara: a book-as-middle-aged-mother "trying to get her kids to eat too much cooked meat, and potatoes with drippings."[74]

What would Taggard's poems have had to look like for her to deserve inclusion in the anthology? Would the poems have to look modernist in the strict sense, with all of the right words in the right order? And, even if they looked right, would Perloff forgive her for being a so-called dupe of the left? I will save my specific arguments about Taggard for that chapter. For now, I want to reiterate the point that *radicalism does matter* to our understanding of the history of poetry and criticism, as it mattered for the undergraduates of 2001 and the undergraduates of today. As has been well documented, poets associated with the institutions and ideologies of the communist left during the Depression worked in multiple forms and genres, and they welded their political convictions to their aesthetics in diverse ways.

What I seek to reveal is an aesthetic that emerged on the left—a *poetics*—that Jacques Rancière describes vis-à-vis James Agee's *Let Us Now Praise Famous Men* as developing from the inevitability that the realities of the Depression would exceed, even explode, preexisting guidelines for making art. For Agee, this meant creating a poem—and it is no accident that Rancière calls *Let Us Now Praise Famous Men* a poem—that would simultaneously see "each thing as a consecrated object and as a scar," an "image of the beauty of others" that becomes "a scar on a wound," an artistic program that "demands description that makes sensible at the same time both the beauty present at the heart of misery and the misery of not being able to perceive this beauty."[75] Against the easy dismissal of Depression-era writing as hack propaganda and resistant to the notion that Depression-era writing can be salvaged according to mainstreamed rubrics for "modernism" or "innovative writing" that emerged following the Cold War, *Left of Poetry* offers an alternative approach to 1930s radical poetics: considering how, in an era of economic depression, U.S. writers conceived of poetry as a means to imagine new models of political representation, modes of agency and resistance, and possibilities for international community formation. Poetry was thus much more than a simple "weapon" in anticapitalist, antiracist, and anticolonialist struggles. Radical poets, by responding to their volatile historical terrain, rethought traditional genres in ways that reformulated the contours of aesthetics. Bringing to light a range of Depression-era poetries as well as theories about poetry that emerged at the same time, I argue their importance for poetry theory and criticism, American and modernist literary histories, and twentieth- and twenty-first-century traditions of "political poetry."

Chapter Outline

Left of Poetry is at once an in-depth study of interwar poetry and part of a cultural history of the idea of poetry. While my chapters focus largely on single figures, each examines a literary-historical problematic in order to illuminate how the 1930s is a moment crucial to our understanding of the history of poetry—and crucial to our understanding of poetry's assumed role in historical and political change. The book is divided into three sections, each of which takes up a mode of writing that predominated thirties discourses and that has stakes for the current landscape of poetic interpretation and left literary-historical practice: documentary, lyric, and rhythm.

The first two sections focus, respectively, on documentary and lyric: modes that were significantly reimagined during the interwar period but that became clichéd stand-ins for the poles of history and poetry. Indeed, if in the twentieth century "lyric" became synonymous with "the essence of poetry, the poem at its most poetic," then "documentary" became a signifier for a counterinsurgent mode that ground down the poetic under the weight of historical fact.[76] Placing documentary and lyric next to each other, I treat the confrontations and slippages between the two as points of orientation from which to understand both.

Part I turns to two canonical Depression-era poets, Langston Hughes and Muriel Rukeyser, in order to explore how radical poets' engagements with other media allowed them to address questions of representation in their interwar political poems. Chapter one, "Photography and the Development of Radical Poetics: Langston Hughes in Haiti, Mexico, Alabama," examines Langston Hughes's overlooked archive of photographs and scrapbooks from his 1931 trip to Haiti. I argue that Hughes's photographic encounter with Haiti reveals significant aspects of how he imagined the poem in relation to other technologies for representing political subjectivity. Chapter two, "Fusing an Alloy: Muriel Rukeyser at the Limits of Poetry/Documentary," charts the historical formation of the documentary poetry tradition vis-à-vis a consideration of Rukeyser's *The Book of the Dead* and her subsequent efforts to adapt the poem sequence into a documentary film. I demonstrate how Rukeyser pushed the boundaries of genre and media in order to imagine modes of expression that resisted traditional notions of liberal subjectivity and embodied modes of self-expression.

In part II, I explore how radical writers reinvented the parameters of the lyric subject. Genevieve Taggard, one of the poets at the center of chapter three, "Lyric Effects: Singing the Futures of Poetry with Genevieve Taggard and Edwin Rolfe," wrote that she considered herself a poet who "could never stop experimenting with lyric effects."[77] The chapter explores the formal and rhetorical strategies that Taggard and Rolfe used to reconstitute lyric and provide a competing "lyric ideal." Their work speaks to a prevailing suspicion on the left that romantic and modernist versions of the poetic lyric and the lyric subject ran counter to radical utopian visions of revolutionary community and, in many ways, to poetic attempts to document scenes of working-class, antiracist, and anti-imperialist struggles. In chapter four, "Lyric Internationalism: Jacques Roumain and His Committee," I consider the work of the Haitian communist poet Jacques Roumain and his reception in the United States. I argue that the distinct version of internationalism that Roumain posited in the 1930s and 1940s provides a means to interrogate what it meant for poetry to circulate globally and to represent conditions of human life. Analyzing the production, circulation, and reception of Roumain's writings and his authorial persona in the United States, I explore several connected variants of a communist internationalism that is imagined through the idea of "lyric" or "lyricism," and I demonstrate how these international imaginaries are tied to developing conceptions of history.

In part III, I turn to the role of the archive in left literary studies through a recovery of the Jewish American communist poet Martha Millet. Chapter five, "The Left Needs Rhythm: Popular Front Poetry, Antifascism, and Counterarchives of Modernity," extrapolates Millet's claim that the left "needs rhythm in all its implications, in order to combat the profit system in its latest manifestation, the totalitarian state."[78] For artists such as Millet, rhythm was an essential formal component of revolutionary art because it was at the root of human experience and, as such, contained new possibilities for collective representation. As the chapter unfolds, I use materials from Millet's previously unknown archive to reiterate the claim that the history of American poetry—and criticism about it—cannot be fully understood without fuller knowledge of poets who were marginalized on the basis of politics, gender, and ethnicity.

Before moving into chapter one, I want to suggest the relationship between the methods I pose here and what might be considered the debts we owe to the hopes of a radical past. Projects that emphasize recovery, more often than not, are premised on the notion that we might owe missing work to the historical record. While such methods and the resulting scholarship are an important part of our critical history, I argue that considering this missing work more on its own terms might complicate the logic of history to which many scholars tend to genuflect. The archive of left poetry has been destroyed alongside the destruction of lives and careers. It has been suppressed by political formations, modes of interpretation, and the fears of the writers themselves. It is a brittle puzzle that, even as we try to put it together, breaks into more pieces at our very touch. Putting the story back together means looking for some sort of coherence out of that which is dispersed, fractured, broken. So on one level, we must, to paraphrase Jack Halberstam's introduction to Stefano Harney and Fred Moten's *The Undercommons*, learn how to live with brokenness without blindly following the fantasies of respectability and recognition that deny rights to those who have been disenfranchised or forgotten. But, at the same time, we must ask if, out of that brokenness, we can establish what Halberstam describes as "another sense of that which is owed that does not presume a nexus of activities like recognition and acknowledgment, payment and gratitude."[79] Or maybe Agee says it best, when he asks in *Let Us Now Praise Famous Men*, "Who are you who will read these words . . . and through what cause, by what chance, and for what purpose, . . . and what will you do about it?"[80]

But then again, as Agee would also say, this is only a book at best.

Part I
Documentary

CHAPTER ONE

Photography and the Development of Radical Poetics
Langston Hughes in Haiti, Mexico, Alabama

But how many people have really listened to this photograph?
—Fred Moten, *In the Break*

What Kind of Poem Would You Make?

For Langston Hughes, the "red decade" began with a trip to the Caribbean. During the spring and summer of 1931, Hughes and the African American artist Zell Ingram traveled to Cuba and Haiti. The trip came at a formative moment for Hughes, when the "personal crash" engendered by his break with patron Charlotte Osgood Mason intersected with the effects of the 1929 stock market crash. As he later described it in his autobiographical *I Wonder as I Wander*, which opens with his 1931 travels, "When I was twenty-seven the stock-market crash came. When I was twenty-eight, my personal crash came. Then I guess I woke up."[1] Whether or not Hughes's contemporary readers specifically reference his travels to the Caribbean, they also mark the early 1930s as a significant moment of personal and artistic transformation. Hughes had been involved in left political and cultural institutions prior to the 1930s (as a high school student, he supported the Russian Revolution, and he had been writing for Communist Party publications throughout the twenties), but his participation in the left increased exponentially during the Depression and had a "marked impact" on the form and content of his poetry.[2] Hughes's experiences in the Caribbean, and in Haiti specifically, were influential on the construction of his political persona and his radical poetics during the Depression. In U.S.-occupied Haiti, Hughes witnessed the exportation of Jim Crow, and what he saw there intensified his outrage at systems of race and class oppression. At the same time, his travels in the country engendered a connection to histories of black rebellion, which he linked to present international struggles against racial and economic imperialism.[3] His 1932 poem "Always the Same," for instance, evokes the "coffee hills of Haiti" in order to articulate the struggle of black laborers in the Americas at the same time that it uses documentary lists to demonstrate how those "coffee hills" are connected to "the docks at Sierra Leone" and the "cotton fields of Alabama" in ways that disrupt U.S. nationalist-populist discourses about left struggle.[4]

Thirties political poems such as "Always the Same" can be better understood, in both historical and theoretical terms, when one considers that Hughes traveled to the Caribbean in 1931 with the Kodak camera that his friend Amy Spingarn gave him as a graduation present. The extent to which Hughes used his handheld camera to document Haitian people, landscapes, and monuments is proven by his extensive visual archive from the trip, which contains several contact sheets of photographic prints, picture postcards, a photograph album, and "loose pages" from a scrapbook. At first glance, Hughes's snapshots from Haiti, along with the albums and scrapbooks where he carefully arranged and captioned them, might appear as unremarkable personal ephemera. This is perhaps why, despite the continued critical interest in discerning the literary-historical and political import of Hughes's travels in Haiti, almost every story told about them either leaves out the fact of Hughes's Kodak or mentions it only in passing.

Hughes's experience of taking photographs in Haiti, along with the process of organizing them in albums and scrapbooks, generated questions about the politics and practices of representation that he pursued in his subsequent political poetry. He did not snap pictures as merely a hobbyist or awed tourist. Hughes's practice of visually documenting Haiti occurs in the context of his increasing involvement in left political and literary organizations during the early 1930s, and his photographs of barefoot children, fishermen, and women selling wares in crowded marketplaces demonstrate his concerted, if vexed, political effort to make visible the Haitian peasant class as well as his desire to comprehend the experiences of black diaspora subjects in relation to the totalizing effects of capitalism and imperialism. Hughes's oft-cited accounts of Haiti—"The People without Shoes" (1931), "Whites Shadows in a Black Land" (1932), and the first chapters of his autobiography *I Wonder as I Wander* (1956)—indicate how he saw the country through the lens of intersecting racial and class struggles, and they emphasize the connections he made between what he witnessed in Haiti and the conditions of subaltern groups in other parts of the world. Hughes's photographic encounter with Haiti is part of the construction of a transnational vision that starts in the Caribbean but then moves through the U.S. South and Mexico. Across these sites, Hughes utilizes documentary imaging as a resource in the construction of an anticapitalist, anti-imperialist countervisuality, one that is enacted in the interference between photography and writing.[5] The photographic image is fundamental to Hughes's attempts to map the connectedness of persons and locales in a capitalist world system as well as to imagine the formation of international political communities in resistance to that system.

The two chapters that compose this first section examine closely the nexus between documentary and poetic genres, demonstrating how Depression-era writers fused the two as part of their efforts to grasp historical experiences of capitalist crisis. Documentary techniques and objects reveal significant aspects of how left writers imagined the poem in relation to other technologies for representing political subjects. Even though Hughes was not publishing actively in photo-textual or photojournalistic modes during the thirties and forties, he, like his comrade Richard Wright, was attuned to the form and politics of the documentary photograph, and his experiments with emergent proletarian aesthetics were informed by the possibilities of photography.[6] Indeed, it was a photographer, Henri Cartier-Bresson, who reminded Hughes in 1935, "You're a child of the proletariat first."[7] Unlike poets discussed in chapter 2, such as Muriel Rukeyser, Ben Maddow, and Archibald MacLeish, Hughes did not overtly incorporate or theorize visual objects in his poems. Nonetheless, he described his early-thirties poetry as "*documentary*, journalistic, and topical."[8] The interactions between Hughes's Haiti photography and his early Depression poems are conceptually complex: exemplifying Rukeyser's call to "extend the document" and, as I will discuss later in the chapter, to "photograph and extend the voice," in ways that explicitly address the international black proletariat and multiracial communist coalitions. The range of Hughes's engagements with documentary imaging—from his own photographs of Haiti to his relationships with photographers such as Manuel Álvarez Bravo and Cartier-Bresson—push beyond the bounds of New Deal initiatives as they employ documentary in the shaping of an international public sphere.

Opening Hughes's visual archive from Haiti recontextualizes the development of his radical poetics in terms of a documentary modernist tradition and, in so doing, reframes his political poems in relation to black experimental writing traditions. When Hughes's 1930s poetry is recuperated, it is often idealized as a conduit for "common" or "vernacular" speech.[9] Even recent efforts to demonstrate how the internationalist impulse of Hughes's social poetics was mediated by modern technologies such as the radio cling to fantasies of "representative voices" that "could speak for all" through the ideal of a "universalized" expressive subject.[10] Such analyses partake in an interpretive practice that Anthony Reed terms "racialized reading," a "particular kind of misreading" that "locates texts within a preemptive black tradition or black social location," and as a result they foreclose alternate possibilities imagined through experimental writing. Hughes's engagements with photography, insofar as they complicate the notion that his poems are sites of authentic or unmediated expression, provide an alternate interpretive context that also allows for a "radical unlearning" of the predetermined understandings of black social life on which racialized reading practices rely.[11]

Complicating current understandings of Hughes's career as a radical poet, this chapter further illuminates how African American writers' engagements with photography enable "an altered understanding of the literary field" as well as a renewed understanding of "photography as a practice and cultural resource."[12] The movement between Hughes's visual archive and his thirties poems also reorients conceptions of the relationship between the historical and the expressive. Created out of the interference between the visual and the verbal, Hughes's radical verse interrogates how the speaker of a poem exists in a gap between lived history and representation, and it enacts a mode of expression that is not authentic or private but mediated by technology and history. Thus, there is more at stake in Hughes's contemplation of the relationship between the photograph and the poem—or image and text—than figuring how the poem might match the photograph's ability to render visible subaltern populations. What struck Hughes about photographs was not their evidentiary power but their unique temporality: the photograph's capturing of an immediate situation provided Hughes with a template for representing new global political realities and networks of relation. Even if the photograph per se vanishes from Hughes's interwar radical poetry, it remains as part of his conceptual and formal imagining of an international revolutionary community. In this sense, Hughes's interwar political verses, far from being merely "ham-fisted" or "didactic," are historical exemplars of, and precursors to, contemporary multimedia experiments that negate the conservative ideological parameters of the expressive subject.[13]

I begin by examining Hughes's overlooked archive of photographs and scrapbooks from Haiti, demonstrating how Hughes's photographic encounter with Haiti reveals significant aspects of how he imagined the poem in relation to other technologies for representing political subjects. In subsequent sections, I extend these considerations to Hughes's interwar radical verse, including his 1931 verse play *Scottsboro Limited*, showing how Hughes's encounters with visual objects on an international scale continued to influence his poetic compositions during the interwar period. The chapter closes by demonstrating how Hughes's contemplation of the relationship between the practices of photography and poetry writing opens up new readings of James Agee and Walker Evans's canonical documentary modernist text, *Let Us Now Praise Famous Men* (1941), notably Agee's statements about the status of the poetic.

Hughes's early radical verses, like Agee's experimental prose, attempt to translate the truth claims of the photograph into language and, in so doing, gesture toward an unrealizable whole through a concentration on the particular. To put it in Jacques Rancière's terms, Hughes's writings, like Agee's, are built on the notion that "beyond science and art, beyond the imagined and the revisive, the full state of consciousness that perceived the 'cruel radiance of what is' must still pass through words."[14]

"Paradise for a Kodak": Hughes and Caribbean "Image Environments"

In the logbook that Hughes kept while traveling in the Caribbean, he jotted a series of notes for a "winter article" on the "warm lands of the South." In an undated entry, he urges,

> Go To The Black Countries
> Cuba—Haiti—West Indies, Brazil, Africa
> Rates and Means
> No passports to C. & H.
> Hotels
> South by Car
> Spanish & French at your very door
> Cultural & racial advantages
> Invaluable contacts—to see one's own people in banks, shops, fine clubs, high positions
> Negro artists—Exchange of ideas
> musicians & painters, new rhythms, new colors, and faces. Poets and writers—new backgrounds & basis for companions.
> A paradise for Kodak camera . . .
> Sunrise in a new land—a day that will be full of new brownskin surprises, strange dark beauties, and hitherto unknown interesting contacts in a world of color.
> Beer, wine, & liquors
> Tropical fruits you've never heard of before[15]

Hughes's journal passage highlights the significance of travel networks for African Americans between the United States and the Caribbean in the middle part of the twentieth century, pointing out how cross-cultural "exchanges" were made easier by the fact that one did not have to secure a passport or visa to visit Cuba or Haiti.[16] Important for my argument is that, within such networks,

Hughes refers to the Caribbean as "a paradise for [a] Kodak camera." The litany of reasons to "go to the black countries" is a documentary artifact that approximates the list-like poems that Hughes penned during the thirties and forties: moving from the opening directive to directions for travel to the image of a sunrise promising "hitherto unknown interesting contacts in a world of color." The promise of snapping a sunrise or tropical plant is secondary to the prospect of encountering "one's own people" in "high positions," suggesting the camera's importance for capturing what has already been made visible by Haiti's and Cuba's "cultural & racial advantages."

But what "paradise" constituted was also complicated to figure given the effects of military and financial imperialism in the Caribbean. The "cultural and racial advantages" afforded by seeing "one's own people in banks, shops, fine clubs, high positions" was undercut by what Hughes observed of class and color lines in Cuba and Haiti. The idealistic tenor of Hughes's journal notes was retranslated in published essays such as "White Shadows in a Black Land," in which the imagination of Haiti as "a new world, a darker world" is quickly destroyed by the realization that the Haitian people were caught in the hands of foreign economic oppression and that the U.S. marines effectively imported Jim Crow.[17]

Hughes's plan to turn the journal notes into a "winter article" on the "warm lands to the South" belies how he actually encountered and made "contact" with Haiti via his Kodak.[18] Most all of the images Hughes chose to collect in his scrapbooks depict the lives of the Haitian peasant class, providing a counternarrative to the "paradise" he describes, including touristic descriptions of Haitian women as "strange dark beauties" and his evocation of the landscape as ripe with "tropical fruits you've never heard of before." While Hughes's collection of photographs includes images that suggest a tourist gaze, his archive demonstrates that he was more interested in the people and environments he described in his journalistic accounts. His scrapbooks and albums are filled with snapshots of workers, milk women, and fishermen as well as of crowded marketplaces and peasant huts[19] (see figure 2). The scrapbooks, in this sense, fit with the rejection of tourist spots that Hughes makes central to his recollections in *I Wonder*.

Hughes's collection of snapshots, personal scrapbooks, and vacation albums is part of the forgotten history of what Geoffrey Batchen has called "vernacular photographies"—those sundry "ordinary photographs" made and collected by "everyday folk."[20] However, as Shawn Michelle Smith theorizes, such popular forms serve as potent sites of resistance.[21] The immediately personal nature of Hughes's albums obscures how cannily his photographs comment on the broader contexts in which images of the Caribbean and Haiti circulated. During the late nineteenth and early twentieth centuries, photographic imaging was a predominant means by which the Caribbean was imagined for white tourist consumption. Representations of the islands created for tourists, by making the natural landscape into an image, were "intrinsic to social and spatial control of the islands" as well as the disciplining of its subjects.[22] Popular cultural representations of Haiti in the United States during the interwar period, from sensationalist travel narratives such as William Seabrook's *Magic Island* (1929) to zombie movies, "stabilized images of black primitivism," feeding the narrative that Haiti was in need of U.S. intervention and effectively "recruit[ing] the public into the project of empire building."[23]

The postcards and guidebooks that Hughes collected in Haiti remain in his archive as evidence of his encounters with touristic images of the country and its citizens. Hughes's photograph albums, not unlike his 1932 illustrated children's book *Popo and Fifina: Children of Haiti* (written with Arna Bontemps and featuring illustrations by E. Simms Campbell), move out of the realm of the private album, demonstrating Hughes's attempts to dignify the lives of lower-class Haitians through documentation. In contrast to, for instance, the picture-postcard that Hughes saved that depicts a naked Haitian woman standing in a lush grove, seemingly blending into the natural landscape, Hughes photographed Haitian women leaning in door frames and sitting on the steps of their homes. His images of Haitian streets depict multiple realities of Haitian life rather than, as in another postcard he kept, a street scene featuring a line of cars and men in suits that was likely meant to frame Caribbean cities as safe for white tourist consumption. The point of view in Hughes's photograph of a "street scene" (see figure 2) tries to look with the subjects it depicts rather than at them. In this context, his photographs can be read as a revision of the colonizing tourist gaze, or what Krista Thompson calls a "tropicalizing gaze," evident in other visual materials he collected and kept.[24]

Reading Claude McKay's dialect poetry in relation to widely circulating images of Jamaica in the early twentieth century, Leah Rosenberg argues for the importance of considering photography with writing, demonstrating how similarities in "subject matter" combined with differences "in the manner of representation" challenge "the tropicalizing iconography of early tourist photography" and offer "empowering" alternatives.[25] Hughes's writings from Haiti should thus be understood in the context of the images of Haiti he both resisted and attempted to create. In addition to revising the tourist gaze, Hughes's images also have a distinctly proletarian flavor that relates to changes in his poetry and essays. Hughes's photographs of the Haitian peasantry depict the very scenes he would describe in his reports from Haiti for the Left Press. Both his photographs and his journalism are concerned with the plight of "the people without shoes," who, as he wrote in *New Masses*, do "all of the work that keeps Haiti alive, pay for the American Occupation, and enrich foreign traders."[26] In this way, Hughes's visual archive from Haiti gives significant insight into his thinking about representations of the Caribbean as well as his broader concerns with representing the "common people" that would continue to occupy him during the Popular Front period.

The intersections between Hughes's photographic practice and his writing practice are further evident in his use of visual tropes and metaphors, especially his continued evocation of the "white shadow." The conceit of the white shadow appears in the title of Hughes's aforementioned essay "White Shadows in a Black Land," one of his more well-known writings about Haiti, and in 1931 he penned a poem titled "White Shadow" (it was later retitled "House in the World") that addresses, though more subtly, issues central to "White Shadows in a Black Land." While the poem does not appear to be about Haiti specifically, the imagery of the white shadows, coupled with the year of its composition, suggests direct links between the poem's content and Hughes's experiences in Haiti:

> I'm looking for a house
> In the world
> Where the white shadows
> Will not fall
>
> *There is no such house,*
> *Dark brothers,*
> *No such house at all.*[27]

The meanings and importance of "White Shadows in a Black Land" and "House in the World" alter slightly when read in the context of Hughes's photographs of Haitian domestic spaces. Two of Hughes's photographs from Haiti stand out as complements to "House in the World," both because they depict scenes of being "at home" and because they each are marked formally by light and shadow. The first photograph is of a woman sitting in a window frame (see figure 1). The woman is completely surrounded by darkness, but a brilliant light shining through the window illuminates her figure. The photograph captures its subject in the space between the inside and the outside—the house and the world—emphasized by the contrast of light and dark as well as by her position at the edge of the building. One cannot help but wonder if

FIGURE 1 Langston Hughes, contact sheet labeled "Langston Hughes in Haiti with Zell Ingram," ca. 1931. Langston Hughes Papers, James Weldon Johnson Collection, Yale Collection of American Literature, Beinecke Rare Book and Manuscript Library, Yale University, New Haven, CT.

Hughes recalled this photograph when, four years later, he commented on the walls in some Henri Cartier-Bresson photographs and described the "clash of sun and shadow."[28]

Read alongside "House in the World," the substance of light and shadow in Hughes's scrapbook photographs demonstrates how he positioned himself as a documentarian in and of the Caribbean as well as how he thought through his experiences as a raced subject in relation to complex racial formations within and across national boundaries.[29] In poems such as "House in the World," the "white shadow" is a metaphor for the diffuse violence of Jim Crow and U.S. economic and military imperialism. But how is a "white shadow" portrayed in the documentary photograph? Is it displayed as the intensity of the sunlight or the shade cast by the wall? The "house in the world" where "white shadows will not fall" does not exist in the present of the poem. But in Hughes's photograph, the "clash of sun and shadow" contains another possibility. The image of the solitary woman sitting in the window frame suggests his attempts to create what Hughes later described as "pictures more than pictures"—that is, photographs that are "not only reproductions of the people taken, but a comment upon their lives—or more still, a comment upon the social order that creates their lives."[30] The play of light and shadow illuminates the wall between house and world at the same time that it refuses such borders, and the subject of the photograph appears in the space between inside and outside, dark and light.

Such attempts by Hughes to document Haitian life contrast contemporaneous documentary accounts of the Caribbean steeped in the anti-imperialist politics of the CPUSA, notably the Latin America journalist Carleton Beals's documentary book *The Crime of Cuba* (1933), which included a series of photographs by Walker Evans. In the book's opening section, "Contrast," Beals uses the black-and-white photograph as a literary trope for dramatizing how U.S. economic exploitation instantiated Cuba's racialized caste system. Employing the term "tone," in photography the range of the lightest to the darkest part of an image, Beals right away draws sharp distinctions that rely on binary logics: "The major tones of Cuba are black and white. The sharp blade of the sun divides the world. High-noon brilliance, as I gaze over the indigo Caribbean Sea, lifts the waters like a black wall. The horizon recedes; the sky-space is sliced by expanding steel-white disks. Chalky palm-trunks, dazzling sands, low calcium buildings transform Cuba into a shell-white island floating on a black ocean."[31] Both Hughes and Beals harness proletarian aesthetics in their documentary productions in order to expose the atrocities of the U.S. empire and to envision alternate forms of national identification. Hughes activates the camera to suggest a border perforated by the commingling of sun and shadow. But Beals, who presumes his "I" is the camera's eye, sees only a "black wall" dividing the world. John A. Gronbeck-Tedesco points out that, despite Beals's political intent, his "desire to ocularize" his experiences of Cuba results in the imposition of "a racialized language that preserves the conventional social locations of white and black" and ultimately preserves "the supremacy of white U.S. subjectivity."[32] More apt, and perhaps more in line with Hughes's own techniques, is one of Evans's accompanying photographs of a wall displaying the graffiti phrases "APOYEMOS LA HUELGA DE LOS CIGARROS" ("Support the Cigar Maker Strike") and "ABAJO LA GUERRA IMPERIALISTA" ("Down with Imperialist War"). Hughes saw the walls in Cartier-Bresson photographs as "painfully human," able to "live and talk about themselves."[33] The writing in Evans's photograph is something that does not love a wall; it is an insurgent act that allows the wall to speak.

Hughes's attention to light and shadow, literally envisioned in his photographs and thematically pursued in his poems, unsettles rather than reaffirms knowledge of a place and of the systems that govern it. The house and its walls are not just metaphors but spaces made and lived in. Here we might consider briefly a second photograph from Hughes's scrapbooks, labeled "Poor Homes," that depicts a long wooden building with three entranceways (see figure 3). A woman stands in the door frame on the far right of the photograph, a small child next to her. This photograph is especially compelling because the photographer's inability to penetrate the interior space of the home with his camera demonstrates that he is prohibited from full knowledge of his subject. While "House in the World" suggests that the poet can speak for those who wish for a place "Where the white shadows / Will not fall," the photograph suggests the impossibility of such acts of speaking for or speaking as another.

Scaling the Citadel

"House in the World" demonstrates how focusing solely on Hughes's journalistic accounts obscures the significant place of the photograph in his attempts to represent Haitian people and landscapes as well as in his thinking through the politics and processes of such acts of representation. The snapshot provided a means to capture, in a photographic instant, the richness of Haitian history, the effects of the U.S. occupation, and the complex relationship between the peasant and elite classes. The ways Hughes contemplated the historical effects of the "white shadow" over Haiti are also apparent in his contemplation of the nineteenth-century slave rebellion leader Henri Christophe's mountaintop fortress, the Citadel La Ferrière.

While Hughes was in Haiti, he climbed the Citadel three times. Perhaps on each climb he paused at Christophe's burial spot and stopped to read his epitaph: "Here lies Henri Christophe, King of Haiti. I am reborn from my ashes."[34] It would be fitting, for Hughes had come to Haiti in the wake of what he called his "personal crash." As the Hughes biographer Arnold Rampersad explains, what the poet "needed" most in Haiti was to "heal himself" through a "temporary erasure of his identity."[35] And yet the biographical fantasy that views Hughes's trip to the Caribbean as a moment of erasure or as an empty time of Romantic self-reconstruction is complicated by his Kodak. The Citadel is the most photographed object in Hughes's visual archive from Haiti: he placed snapshots of the site throughout his scrapbooks; he saved several postcards and negatives of images of the monument; and he dedicated an entire page of his photograph album to "views of the Citadel" (see figure 4).

According to Rampersad, Hughes experienced the Citadel both as a tourist and "as a prodigal son who, having wasted his birthright in a foreign clime, had now limped home for forgiveness."[36] But he also encountered the monument as a left-leaning travel reporter and amateur documentary photographer. Hughes's copious photographs counteract the fantasy of "erasure" engraved on Christophe's tombstone and embedded in biographical accounts. His camera work functioned as an experiment in self-exploration and self-presentation, and his resulting visual documentation indicates how his self-conscious reconstruction of his identity in Haiti contained political and formal concerns. Perhaps it was as an awed tourist that Hughes snapped photographs and collected picture postcards. But he also used his camera to explore feelings of personal and historical dislocation that he would continue to negotiate in his 1930s political poems.

At the Citadel, Hughes was situated uneasily between the promises of Haiti's revolutionary past and the present conditions of the U.S. occupation. In "White Shadows in a Black Land," Hughes employs the figure of the Citadel to express his disappointment with a Haitian elite that, according to him, forsook the "splendid history" of the 1791 slave rebellion by giving Haiti over to foreign interests. He writes of "that Citadel today, standing in lonely majesty against the clouds twenty miles from the city of Cape Haitien."[37] In this syntactic construction, the deictic "that" distances the historical Citadel from the conditions of present-day Haiti, where everywhere there is evidence that the legacies of Christophe, Jean-Jacques Dessalines, and Toussaint L'Ouverture had been betrayed. As if to illustrate the point, the misty and scenic photographs of the monument collected in Hughes's scrapbooks seem to capture *that* Citadel—the Citadel that "glories in the splendid history" of the nineteenth-century revolution. The photographs Hughes selected for an album page dedicated to "views of the Citadel" attempt to convey the size and dignity of the monument as well as its contemporary "loneliness." He includes mostly wide views of the monument's exterior. In the singular photograph giving a close-up view of the fortress, the interior details (a stone wall, an entranceway, and the foot of a stairway) are so bathed in light that the scene takes on an almost ghostly quality. While Hughes's snapshots attempt to harness an idyllic or mythic past, the photographs also seem flat, in Roland Barthes's sense of the term: necessarily arresting time and interpretation rather than opening up to utopian futurity. The flimsiness of the scrapbook pages and paper snapshots effectively "renounce," to again borrow from Barthes, the grandiosity of the monument even as they bear its trace.[38]

Hughes's photographs of the Citadel thus illustrate Nicole Waligora-Davis's point that "occupied Haiti supplied fecund ground" for reimagining "both the semantic contours of a 'dream deferred' and the world he dreamt."[39] Hughes's imagination of Haiti in the early 1930s takes place in the context of, to borrow a concept from Roberto Tejada, the United States and Haiti's "shared image environment" as well as the larger historical role of the Haitian Revolution in, as Nicholas Mirzoeff argues, "producing modern visuality" and the "counter-visuality of antislavery."[40] While popular images of Haiti circulating in the United States during the occupation reinforced paternalistic attitudes, cultural workers such as Hughes and Zora Neale Hurston produced alternative images in hopes that they might play a role in shaping black cultural identity. Haiti thus served as a "visual laboratory" for Hughes at a crucial moment in the development of his politics *and* his poetics.[41]

Scrapping History, Making Poems

The construction of Hughes's photograph albums and scrapbooks allow for further contemplation of the importance of visual objects for Hughes's writing practice. Hughes's photographic practice does not just open up questions about the forms of his political poems. His political poems allow for a reconsideration of the critical purchase of the documentary photograph during the early 1930s. As I have already suggested, Hughes's attempts to visually document Haitian people and landscapes correlate to his poetic efforts to provide portraits of subaltern persons and to represent shared political and historical realities. Along these lines, the images that Hughes included in his albums and

FIGURE 2 Langston Hughes, loose page from Haiti Scrapbook, ca. 1931. Langston Hughes Papers, James Weldon Johnson Collection, Yale Collection of American Literature, Beinecke Rare Book and Manuscript Library, Yale University, New Haven, CT.

FIGURE 3 Langston Hughes, loose page from Haiti Scrapbook with photograph labeled "Poor Homes," ca. 1931. Langston Hughes Papers, James Weldon Johnson Collection, Yale Collection of American Literature, Beinecke Rare Book and Manuscript Library, Yale University, New Haven, CT.

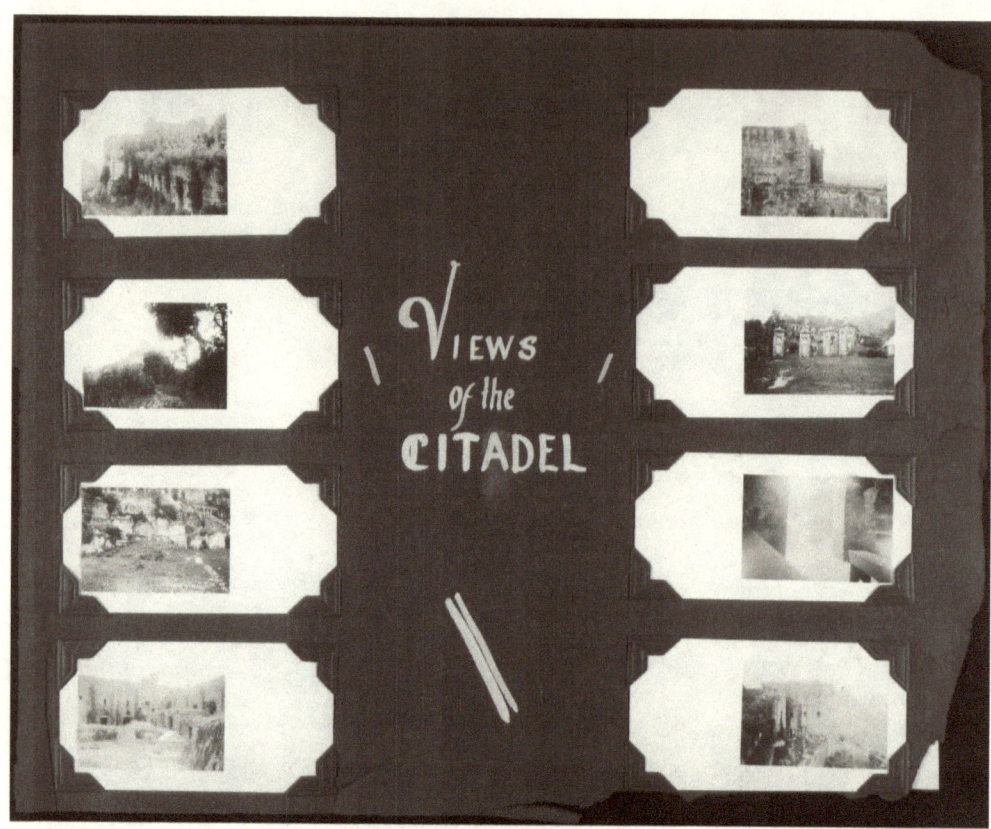

FIGURE 4 Langston Hughes, page from Haiti Photograph Album with photographs of the Citadel, ca. 1931. Langston Hughes Papers, James Weldon Johnson Collection, Yale Collection of American Literature, Beinecke Rare Book and Manuscript Library, Yale University, New Haven, CT.

FIGURE 5 Langston Hughes, first page of Haiti Photograph Album, ca. 1931. Langston Hughes Papers, James Weldon Johnson Collection, Yale Collection of American Literature, Beinecke Rare Book and Manuscript Library, Yale University, New Haven, CT.

scrapbooks from Haiti further demonstrate his interest in and knowledge of widely circulating representations of the black peasantry and of Caribbean landscapes. At the same time, the materiality of the books suggests that the process of taking pictures and captioning and arranging them also facilitated new thinking about how the representational capacities and limits of the photograph intersected with possibilities for politically effective writing. Through the practice of scrapbooking, Hughes contemplated how the photograph could represent a historical reality in an instant, and he subsequently crafted poems that could simultaneously harness the temporality of photographic representation and describe complex processes of subject and community formation.

To understand how Hughes's engagements with visuality facilitate new ways of reading his radical poetics, we must examine his archive of photographs, albums, and scrapbooks as complex sites where practices of personal record keeping, public history, and multimodal experimentation overlap. As Rachel Feder suggests, because commonplace objects such as travel journals and scrapbooks "imitate public forms while serving private functions," they make possible "cross-genre and cross-textual conversation, and invention" and provide "an alternative origin story for modern experimental poetry that dramatizes the overlapping public and private spheres represented by [their] literal and theoretical materiality."[42] The photograph albums and scrapbook pages that Hughes made to document his time in Haiti evince his engagement with the popular custom of accumulating personally meaningful objects and arranging them in books. His photographs and scrapbooks are as much the visible record of a place and time as they are the story of a subject's relationship to them.

This is evident on the first page of Hughes's Haiti photograph album, where he placed a typed caption amid three photographs of himself (one depicts him standing waist deep in the ocean; in another he is posing beside a woman in a white dress; the third is missing). The caption reads, "Langston Hughes in Haiti." The year, "1931," is scrawled in pencil below, almost as an afterthought (see figure 5). As one opens Hughes's album, this arrangement perhaps seems unremarkable. Hughes was, after all, just one among many early-twentieth-century Americans who "turned to the scrapbook as a vehicle for chronicling personal histories and negotiating identity in an increasingly pervasive mass print culture."[43] Given the contexts surrounding Hughes's visit to Haiti, however, it is worth examining Hughes's scrapbooks as something more. To start, the fact that he used his full name, "Langston Hughes," might indicate that he was not just recording his travels for personal memory but that he was, even if subconsciously, preparing a record for history.[44] In any case, the scrapbook blurs the line between Hughes's private experiences and his developing interest in sociopolitical struggles at home and abroad. Read as a tourist's vacation album, a "souvenir," the collection of photographs in the scrapbook "moves history into private time."[45] But history moved into "private time" is history nonetheless: exhibiting public commitments and attesting to Hughes's new thinking about the transfiguration of isolated local communities into global revolutionary collectives. If, as Sara Blair suggests via Barthes, "photographs shape the historical narrative and alter the experience of history" as well as "make sharply visible the elusive experience of history," then Hughes's visual archive stages the powerful experience of the subject in history vis-à-vis the image.[46] The scrapbook, in this context, acts as both a material object that brings the viewer closer to the moment or person it represents and a medium for contemplating the act of representation itself.[47]

Hughes's interest in preparing a more public record of Haiti is evident in the "loose pages" from another of his scrapbooks. In contrast to the bound photograph album, most all of the snapshots pasted to the loose pages depict scenes from Haitian peasant life, and each is captioned in Hughes's hand. Some of the captions mark specific sites or landmarks, such as "rue Bord de Mer" or the "Prow of the Citadel," but others are generic and nondescript (see figure 2). Hughes also affixed captions—such as "sun on water," "fishing boats," and "children bathing"—to several of the photographs. At first thought, this may seem inconspicuous, especially because the snapshots and captions appear in a vacation album. But this practice seems to be more than a mere idiosyncrasy. On a basic level, the placement of linguistic representations next to pictorial ones further suggests how carefully Hughes meditated on the different possibilities for rendering visible the effects of racial and economic dispossession. Approaching Hughes's loose scrapbook pages as something like a vernacular photo-text, the captions seem to *interfere*, forming a dialogue that the "reader or observer enters into and sponsors, and which with other dialogues forms part of a more general conversation."[48] And yet, because the photographs that Hughes includes already clearly make visible people such as the "workmen" or objects such as "fishing boats," such a conversation remains static. Fastening the word to the photographic representation of the object is a way of figuring out how language can work not just in relation to but also in the face of the photograph's power to evince people and places.[49] In Haiti, Hughes's Kodak bestowed a power of direct and immediate representation that prompted him to rethink the role of language in the unfolding of violent historical realities.

Before moving into a consideration of how Hughes's interest in the ontology of the image influences the interpretation of specific poems, I want to briefly explain the relationship between my reading of Hughes's scrapbooks and poetry and other recent scholarship that studies scrapbooks in order to reframe the literary history of modernism and the development of modernist aesthetics. As Mike Chasar elucidates, poetry scrapbooks constructed by "everyday readers" proffer alternative stories about modern poetics while also acting as a "vernacular counterpoint to modernist writing."[50] Taking scrapbooks seriously also, Bartholomew Brinkman argues, influences the ways in which we understand and interpret the material form of the modernist poem.[51] While such studies productively craft alternative histories of modernist canonization and avant-garde forms, my aim here is to explore how Hughes conceptualized the political work of the poem in relation to the ontology of the photograph. While it is nearly impossible to reconstruct a "site of composition"—a story about how Hughes crafted his 1930s poems with his photographs and scrapbooks also spread out before him on his writing desk—there are discernible relationships between Hughes's thinking about processes of visual and linguistic representation.[52] The photograph acts something like a "vanishing mediator," an important influencing factor that is forgotten or erased once its purpose has been achieved. In addition to contemplating language's ability to represent a given historical reality in the face of the indexical photograph, Hughes also considered the position of the speaker within these attempts at representation. The personal nature of the scrapbooks denaturalizes the "photograph's aura of objectivity" at the same time that it proffers a new means to consider the relationship of the speaker in a Hughes poem to the positions he attempts to represent.[53]

Wait!

Hughes's 1933 poem "Wait" provides an important link between his photographic and scrapbooking practices and his writing practices in the 1930s. The poem pursues questions of how to represent dispossessed political subjects and the totalizing effects of capitalism through an innovative format influenced by Hughes's early thinking about the visual. The poem's attempts to apprehend the formation of historical class consciousness and, relatedly, to map possibilities for utopian coordination cannot be fully understood absent

Hughes's contemplation of the interference between photography and written language. The photograph's presumed ability to arrest time and, in so doing, make visible in new ways subjects and scenes provides Hughes with the conceptual foundation to craft a poem that imagines a reorientation of the relationships between individuals and collectives, localities and the world.[54]

"Wait" was originally published in the first issue of *Partisan*, the magazine of the John Reed Club in Carmel, California, where Hughes lived for a year in the early 1930s. The center of "Wait" is a first-person poem with traditional lineation. The poem's speaker, named "the Silent One," is dispossessed within current systems of economic and colonial domination and is

> Saying nothing,
> Knowing no words to write,
> Feeling only the bullets
> And the hunger
> And the stench of gas
> Dying.

Despite present subjection, the Silent One warns that "someday" the moment for fighting back will arrive. "I shall raise my hand / And break the heads of you / Who starve me," the speaker admonishes. "I shall raise my hand / And smash the spines of you / Who shoot me."[55] The expression of the unnamed "Silent One" is bordered on all four sides by a catalogue of specific sites and groups. These lists of names designate the groups that form the revolutionary class ("pickers," "strikers," "negroes," "farmers"), geographic areas of oppression ("Alabama," "Johannesburg," "Haiti"), zones of international conflict ("Chapei," "Japan"), and major sites of labor uprisings in the United States and abroad ("Meerut").

While the Silent One's expression begins with a singular "I" addressed to a "you," it soon becomes evident that these pronouns denote political collectives rather than individual subjects, especially when the poem outlines the Silent One's plan of action:

> I shall take your guns
> And turn them on you.
>
> Starting with the bankers and the bosses
> Traders and missionaries
> Who pay the militarists
> Who pay the soldiers

>   Who back the police
>   Who kill me—
>   And break my strikes
>   And break my rising—[56]

The poem (and the gun) addresses networks of persons and groups that participate in forms of militarism and capitalism. The "I" is similarly plural as it encompasses the multifarious revolutionary collectives named in the borders of "Wait." And yet the presence of the specific names prevents reading the central "I" of the poem as a melding of these groups and sites into a singular "One" or, as expression in Hughes's thirties poems is often described, as a "universalized" "I" that purports to "speak in the name of the black millions."[57] The specific names remain as part of the poem, so that even as the first-person speaker seems to draw disparate populations and locations together by casting them in the position of the Silent One, that "I" is still necessarily linked to sites and communities that are historically and politically contingent. Perhaps like Wright's later *Twelve Million Black Voices*, Hughes's early-thirties poems experiment with "a first-person plural that convenes and divides groups along lines of class, race, and region."[58] The disparate groups, locations, and events listed in "Wait" are united by a common horizon of economic dispossession, but they are not unified by a common experience of its effects. The central first-person poem thus should be read from the vantage of a propositional "I" that suggests multiple combinations and recombinations of the nouns in the border.

Against the logic of racialized reading, which in the case of Hughes's reception is twinned with narrow ideas about procommunist poetry as merely reactive, I argue that "Wait" does not attempt to represent the conditions of silenced subjects so much as it sets out to cognitively map experiences of capitalism and imperialism at a particular moment in time. The process of "cognitive mapping" allows for a conceptualization of the self in space, or a "practice of orientation," that Fredric Jameson identifies as necessary to "any socialist project."[59] According to Jameson, in the historical phase of late capitalism, the "truth" of an individual subject's experience "no longer coincides with the place in which it takes place."[60] In other words, there is a disconnect between "limited daily experience" and the global and economic system that "determines the very quality of the individual's subjective life."[61] The experimental format of "Wait" approaches a possible "aesthetic of cognitive mapping" that, as Alberto Toscano and Jeff Kinkle explain, would "enable individuals and collectivities to render their place in a capitalist world-system intelligible."[62] By presenting specific sites of conflict and uprising in no particular order or pattern, "Wait" provides a matrix of potential coordinates that may be mapped and that might lead to new conceptions of political reality.

Hughes's engagements with documentary photography during the early thirties is crucial to analyzing "Wait" as an aesthetic of cognitive mapping, especially because documentary culture was so integral to efforts to understand capitalist crisis. A 1936 *Life* article on postcrash photojournalism expressed, "depressions are hard to see because they consist of things not happening, of business not being done."[63] Within this context, photography emerges as an effort to concretize the abstractions of economic relations, an abstraction suggested in the very term "depression," which carries an affective buzz that is at once everywhere and impossible to envision. Hughes's experiments with photographs and photo books undergird his experiments using poetic form to represent social and economic forces while problematizing the aims of representation as such.

On the simplest level, the layout of "Wait" invites a comparison to the format of Hughes's scrapbook pages, specifically the pages on which Hughes wrote brief captions next to his snapshots. With regard to format, the lists of names on the sides and bottom of the page align with the poem in much the same way that Hughes's captions align with his snapshots from Haiti. What is more, the act of captioning suggests an effort to make visible subjects that have been rendered invisible within the capitalist world-system that Hughes evokes in "Wait." Here, too, the photographic image acts as a template for Hughes. While I will not go so far as to suggest that in "Wait" the photograph dissolves and the captions remain, the individual nouns forming the margins of "Wait" might be read as a series of snapshots. Each word, in essence, evokes a snapshot of a person or place. Read as snapshots, the words in the lists illuminate the processes and violence of capitalism by freezing moments and spaces where such violence takes place.

If we read the words forming the borders of "Wait" as palimpsests of photographic images, then we might also see how the poem resists forms for representing capital, such as modeling and diagramming, that break with models of representation, such as the photograph, where there is a "correlation between signifier and signified, index and referent."[64] Reading Hughes's poems with regard to paratextual elements, as Cary Nelson encourages, "Wait" stands in contrast to the "economic review" article that appeared next to it in *Partisan*, which includes a line graph juxtaposing increases in worker production to decreases in wages.[65] Models and diagrams might give the appearance of "seeing" economic relations and processes, but they also render their own forms of invisibility. The social totalities that Hughes attempts to portray in "Wait" are suppressed by the graph's concern with wages. The graph suggests instead a "general 'ungrounding' of representation, from floating currencies to floating signifiers."[66]

Hughes evokes economics, or the transnational exchange of money and commodities, by adding "BONUS" to the lists of nouns in the poem's border, along with goods such as grapes, beets, and sugar. "BONUS" could refer to the Bonus Army marchers who, in 1932, marched in Washington, D.C., to demand cash payment for military service certificates earned for service in World War I. Given the poem's other references, however, "bonus" more likely suggests the processes by which commodities become money and vice versa. The photographic takes on yet another meaning in this context, as the "picker" or "miner" can be read in relation to either signifiers of revolutionary action ("communists," "strikers") or the commodities with which they are identified (the word "grape" always appears next to "pickers"). Allan Sekula makes a link between photographs and money in his reading of Oliver Wendell Holmes's 1859 essay "The Stereoscope and the Stereograph," which compares the "cheap" and "transportable" stereograph to "banknotes." For Holmes, Sekula points out, the photograph is "like money": it is "both a fetishized end in itself and a calibrated signifier of value that resides elsewhere, both autonomous and bound to its referential function."[67]

The Silent One's speech, which is also speech withheld, represents a possible way out of such systems of circulation by the very act of occupying an impossible position. In "Wait," the presence of nouns is also a transmogrification of the photograph's arresting of time into the medium of language. Thus, we might play on Donald MacKenzie's assertion that representations of capital are "an engine, not a camera"—asserting instead that Hughes's "camera view" is an attempt to halt engines of capitalist accumulation.[68] This political and conceptual ideal does not yet coalesce in the poem; it is still in the future. The Silent One is "saying nothing" and "Knowing no words to write," but there are still words on the page. At the end of the poem, Hughes intimates that the Silent One will not speak until it successfully overthrows capitalist and colonialist regimes:

> I, silently,
> And without a single learned word
> Shall begin the slaughter
> That will end my hunger
> And your bullets
> And the gas of capitalism
> And make the world

My own.
When that is done,
I shall find words to speak

Wait!⁶⁹

Ultimately, the Silent One is a subject that has not yet been formed. It is silent because its various components—the participants in the revolutionary class struggle represented in the lists of common and proper nouns—have yet to conceptually merge. Thus, the Silent One is not merely an "I" unifying disparate political communities and promising that it will "find words to speak" for them. It is, perhaps more radically, an entity that represents historical class consciousness in the process of formation. The silence in the poem is not an absence of action, or an absence of "voice," but rather a fierce withholding implied in the title's threat: *Just you wait.*

"I Said, Me": Listing the Subject

"Wait" is perhaps unique in Hughes's oeuvre; it is his only poem that uses nouns to form a graphic border. This is not to say that Hughes did not continue to experiment visually with his compositions during the thirties. He composed a series of dramatic monologues that used a vertical line to separate "The Poem" from what Hughes designated as "The Mood," using page space in order to suggest two different yet intersecting registers for thinking about the work. Poems associated with radical left causes, such as "Come to the Waldorf Astoria" and "Addressed to Alabama," a collection of three poems about the Spanish Civil War, were published with visual borders reminiscent of the ballad broadside. While "Wait" might be read in relation to these experiments with how poems look on the page, I am more interested in interpreting "Wait" in relation to a strategy that Hughes employs over and over in his thirties poetry—the use of documentary lists. Such poems, like "Wait," continue to demonstrate how Hughes's photographs and scrapbooks facilitate alternate interpretations of how Hughes constructed his radical interwar poems.

Put another way, even if few of Hughes's interwar poems look like "Wait," many of them are structurally similar. Hughes's 1930s poems often feature a central speaker as well as lists of nouns that indicate a relationship between the speaker and specific groups, events, and places. This strategy is perhaps most obvious in poems such as "Open Letter to the South," "Always the Same," and "Good Morning, Revolution" but can also be seen, albeit in more subtle ways, in poems such as "Let America Be America Again," "A New Song," "Kids Who Die," and "Roar, China." For example, the first line of "Open Letter to the South" addresses "White workers of the South," and that line is followed by a list of the different types of workers that might fall under the umbrella of white southern laborer. Only after each group has been listed does the poem indicate the speaker:

> Miners,
> Farmers,
> Mechanics,
> Mill hands,
> Shop girls,
> Railway men,
> Servants,
> Tobacco workers,
> Sharecroppers,
> GREETINGS!⁷⁰

The extended greeting that opens the poem is followed by an assertion of the poem's speaker, who asks the white worker to "listen." This short introduction is followed by yet another list, this time of the spaces where black and white laborers interact:

> I am the black worker,
>   Listen:
> That the land might be ours,
> And the mines and the factories and the office towers
> At Harlan, Richmond, Gastonia, Atlanta, New Orleans;
> That the plants and the roads and the tools of power
> Be ours:⁷¹

While one could certainly interpret "Open Letter to the South" in relation to what James Smethurst has described as the dialogic folk speaker that characterizes many of Hughes's thirties poems, it is worth considering different possibilities for how the lists of nouns function in relation to the poem's speaking persona. What "Wait" helps us see about poems such as "Open Letter to the South" is that, while Hughes's thirties poems are often spoken in a "folk voice," his mouth is always full of nouns. It would seem logical that this tendency owes to the influence of Walt Whitman and Carl Sandburg. William Stott, in his landmark study of documentary expression in the United States, links thirties documentary culture to forms of poetic expression, arguing that the Depression era "produced so many counterfeit Walt Whitmans ... in part because no other time so prized the Whitmanian 'I'—able to see, incorporate, and give voice to all human experience."[72]

The formation of Hughes's "I" is informed by his thinking about documentary expression, but it is no Whitmanian one. Hughes's attempts to render what he observed in Haiti intersect with his desire to represent global affiliations and to articulate the possibility of an international revolutionary community. Hughes's interest in photography provides a new lens through which to view his radical poetic experiments, one that is linked to broad shifts in media culture during the Depression era. As Mark Goble points out, late modernist authors did more than incorporate multiple media in their writing during the early twentieth century. They also thought deeply about the differences that such mediations make. More specifically, Goble identifies a struggle between "database" (what Lev Manovich describes as a "structured collection of data" in which history takes the form of "information") and "narrative" (historical information presented in the form of story).[73] By the 1930s, the demand to accumulate information into the form of story would seem impossible to meet, as demonstrated by Walter Benjamin's 1936 meditation on information culture, "The Storyteller." In the same way that Hughes's scrapbooks accumulate pieces of information—places, objects, persons, and the words that one might attach to them—his poems present the strain of managing the things and histories that continue to accumulate. The speaker of Hughes's poem is not so much a coherent subject but rather what Tejada describes as a "proposition, a reason we ascribe belatedly to a sequence of effects."[74]

We might, then, turn to Hughes's poem "Always the Same," which invokes the "coffee hills of Haiti" alongside the "docks at Sierra Leone," the "cotton fields of Alabama," the "diamond mines of Kimberley," the "banana lands of Central America," the "streets of Harlem," and the "cities of Morocco and Tripoli" in order to describe how "it is the same everywhere" for the speaker of the poem, who is

Black:
Exploited, beaten and robbed,
Shot and killed.
Blood running into

   Dollars
   Pounds
   Francs
   Pesetas
   Lire[75]

The blood that runs into multiple national currencies is rerouted; it is, the speaker claims, "Better that my blood / Runs into the deep channels of Revolution." This action is described in the rest of the poem, first as the speaker is driven away from his countries of origin (which necessitates another list) and struggles with all "workers in the world" against various forms of exploitation (again, represented in list form). The poem ends with yet another list, this one describing the "faces, black, white, olive, yellow, brown" of the "Red Armies of the International Proletariat" united "to raise the blood-red flag that / Never will come down!"[76] The abundance of lists in "Always the Same" reinforces the point that modernist poems struggle against the accumulation of historical information, which is for Hughes embedded in a narrative of capitalist accumulation, represented here by money made from blood. At the same time, however, the politics of Hughes's poem demonstrate his concerted effort to configure this historical material into a new version of political subjectivity, a story about networks of oppression as well as solidarity. Tejada describes this as a "power of storytelling" wherein the experimental work of art might "provide us with scripts of action so we can navigate the intangible space of so much unprocessed information."[77] In other words, the poet does not so much present himself as exhausted by the accumulation of information in a modern age as, rather, he attempts to map information in ways that represent or provoke radical political formations.

Hughes's engagement with photography provides a new understanding of how he imagined both the formation of revolutionary subjectivity and the conceptual merging of international political communities. In speeches and essays written during the late thirties, Hughes further articulates the imperative to comprehend the relations between specific political communities and sites of antagonism. In his June 25, 1938, speech before the International Writers Association for the Defense of Culture, "Writers, Words and the World," he writes, "Because our world is like that today, so related and inter-related, a creative writer has no right to neglect to understand clearly the social and economic forces that control our world. No matter what his country or what his language, a writer, to be a good writer, cannot remain unaware of Spain and China, of India and Africa, of Rome and Berlin. Not only do the near and far places influence, even without his knowledge, the very subjects and materials of his books, but they affect their physical life as well, their actual existence and being."[78] In poems such as "Wait," "Open Letter to the South," and "Always the Same," such "relatedness" and "interrelatedness" is conceived as a dialectical relationship between diverse local spaces and histories and an ideal political community. In the poem, Hughes attempts to reassemble various forces that have been divided by economic and imperial violence by plotting out single words and connecting them to a narrative of revolutionary uprising. The subject formed (or in the process of formation) is a conglomerate of persons, groups, places, and actions something like the "new guy" he "makes way for" in "Goodbye Christ": "A real guy named / Marx Communist Lenin Peasant Stalin Worker ME." "I said, ME!" he reiterates in the poem.[79]

But if he said it, do we hear it? Can we see it too? In the next section, I turn to Hughes's writing about the Scottsboro case in order to explore the relationship in his poems between the visual and the sonic. For what if we could see the sound of a radical poem? Or hear the sound by seeing?

Listen Up! (The Voice of the Photograph)

For all that Hughes asks us to see, how can we shake his commands to *listen*? I account for the sound of Hughes's poetry not by suggesting that it resists or opposes the role of the photograph in his early work; rather, I demonstrate how an interdynamic photographic-poetic mode discernible in Hughes's political poems manifests itself in his 1932 collection *Scottsboro Limited*. Hughes visited the Scottsboro defendants, the eight young black men who had been accused of rape in Alabama in 1931 and unjustly sentenced to death, in 1932 while on a public reading tour through the South. That same year, he put out the thin volume of poems *Scottsboro Limited* and donated proceeds from the book to the Scottsboro defense fund as well as published the essay "Southern Gentlemen, White Prostitutes, Mill-Owners, and Negroes" alongside his poem "Christ in Alabama" in the magazine *Contempo*.

While Hughes's imaginative work responding to the Scottsboro trial is relatively well known, no one remarks on the fact that Hughes possessed a snapshot of the defendants and penned a journalistic account of his visit with them in Kilby prison. Hughes later attributed his decision to pursue the southern reading tour to a realization that he had in Haiti: "I determined to ... [take] poetry, my poetry, to my people."[80] A closer look at Hughes's visit with the Scottsboro defendants, however, challenges this statement. His reflection on the scene in the prison, where he read his poems to eight men doomed to die, suggests that he was deeply anxious about the function of the poem in the face of violent political realities. Hughes's article "Kilby Prison: Scottsboro Boys" evinces how his visit made him doubtful of poetry's ability to speak to human and political problems: "As I read my poems, standing at one end of the corridor opposite the guard, I could not see the dark faces of those condemned to die peering at me from the narrow cells on either side. But I felt their presence.

And my poems seemed futile and stupid in the face of death. I spoke about the past of our race, and how I had tried to put its glories and sorrows into poetry—but with the feeling that what I was saying meant little to men doomed never to mingle with the living world again."[81] The undated snapshot of the Scottsboro defendants was probably taken during the same visit in which Hughes realized how "futile and stupid" his poems seemed "in the face of death." Perhaps he snapped it with his own Kodak.[82] Coupling Hughes's snapshot of the Scottsboro defendants with his journalistic commentary provides an alternate context for reading his early-1930s radical verse. These two archival objects indicate that the poems Hughes composed in response to the Scottsboro case are marked by doubts about the ability of the poem to represent political subjects as well as about the role of language in shaping the political landscape.

In the photograph (see figure 6), six of the men are seated; they look away from the camera and past one another. The other two stand facing the camera, leaning almost casually against the bars of the cell. A white warden on the other side of the bars peers over their shoulders. A caption that looks to be written in Hughes's hand is affixed to the upper right-hand corner: "The Scottsboro Boys in jail at Birmingham." The frontal view of the prison cell, intensified by the two men who gaze straight into the camera, complicates Hughes's narrative of "I could not see the dark faces of those condemned to die peering at me from the narrow cells on either side." Perhaps in his memory of reading and speaking to the men, Hughes can only "feel their presence," and so the photograph he possesses supplements or fills this absence. This confusion—between what is visible and what is invisible, between what is seen and what is unseen but felt—ultimately becomes a question about how to evoke the "presence" of a political subject in political art.

Readers of Hughes's 1930s radical verse find such presence in his poems by interpreting his experiments with rhythmic patterns and popular genres as attempts to render an authentic voice. This version of Hughes's interwar radical verse is readily apparent in criticism of his one-act play *Scottsboro Limited*, which, like the photograph and newspaper article, depicts the Scottsboro defendants in their prison cell awaiting death. The play is textbook agitprop. In one scene, the Scottsboro "Boys" battle the injunction that they must die in the electric chair as "mob voices" from the audience shout for their death. At the end, one of the "Boys" asserts that he should be heard even from the "death house." He is joined by "red voices" from the audience who urge on the "Boys" as they refuse "death in the chair"; and these disparate voices eventually meld so that the "Boys" declare, "the voice of the red world / Is our voice, too."[83] *Scottsboro Limited* ends with a vision of the white and black working class join-

Photography and the Development of Radical Poetics 57

FIGURE 6 Photographic print of Scottsboro Boys in jail at Birmingham, undated. Langston Hughes Papers, James Weldon Johnson Collection, Yale Collection of American Literature, Beinecke Rare Book and Manuscript Library, Yale University, New Haven, CT.

ing together to fight for "new life" under the banner of a red flag and, if the audience chooses, the singing of the "Internationale."[84]

Many critics highlight how the dialogue in *Scottsboro Limited* combines verse and prose, a formal feature apparent in the play's opening exchange between the "White Man" and two of the "Black Boys." As all of the "Boys" make their way from the back of the auditorium to the stage, chained together at their ankles, the "Man" rises from the audience and twice asks, "What are you doing here?" When he receives no response, he follows them to the stage and asks again,

> MAN: What the hell are you doing in here, I said?
> 1ST BOY: (*Turning simply*)
>   We come in our chains
>   To show our pain.
> MAN: (*Sneeringly*) Your pain! Stop talking poetry and talk sense.
> 8TH BOY: (*As they line up on the stage*)
>   All right, we will—
>   That sense of injustice
>   That death can't kill.[85]

The Scottsboro Boys continue to "talk poetry"—their speeches employing rhyme and repetition—while the white characters speak in prose sentences. In a simple sense, the opposition between the revolutionary class and the oppressor is cast in terms of the opposition between poetry and prose. The "Man" does not want to hear poetry and opposes it to "sense"; but in Hughes's play, the only characters "talking sense" in political terms are those who are also "talking poetry." William J. Maxwell argues that, by writing the "Boys'" dialogue as poetry, "Hughes points to poetry as the distillation of the sensible, demotic speech of black workers." Maxwell casts the "Man" as the "prosaic enemy of verse and Communism," who wants to "disassociate poetic diction, black vernacular language, and a drama of black proletarian expression" but who "never succeeds in squashing the boys' 'talking poetry.'"[86] Smethurst also suggests that the speech "marked as poetic" in *Scottsboro Limited* is linked to speaking "the unvarnished truth about race and class oppression."[87] Michael Thurston picks up on Smethurst's and Maxwell's readings, relating the "transformative space" of the theater to the "transformative media of rhythm, rhyme, and repetition" in order to posit that these two elements come together to forge a collective of "workers of all colors under the Red flag."[88]

Maxwell's and Thurston's arguments in many ways replicate cultural fantasies about the social uses of poetic genres that circulated on the left during the Depression, particularly the idealization of "rhythm" as a means to represent the speech of the masses. Hughes's engagements with multiple media and modes of cultural production criticize such idealizations. During the 1930s and 1940s, "rhythm" was frequently invoked in left discourses about poetics, especially those that called for a return to traditional verse genres and away from modernist formal experimentation. Left cultural workers idealized rhythm as a medium for representing the speech of the "common people." As I examine in chapter 5, interwar debates about the social usefulness of popular genres such as ballads, songs, and chants turned on this notion that rhythm was a conduit for speech, and these debates aligned rhythm with authentic expression as well as political efficacy. The idealized or "uplift" version of what poetry can accomplish within the space of *Scottsboro Limited*—support the struggles of black workers, create an interracial political coalition, trump the prosaic enemy—relies on a similar notion of rhythm qua poetry that conflates political subjects, their manner of speech, and the speeches they make.

Scottsboro Limited destabilizes the alignment of poem and speech, or poem and voice, rather than invoking it. On the surface level, the verse sections of the drama seem to combine rhymed verse, chant, and song in a way that suggests that poetic rhythms and verse genres have the power to quilt together political communities by making heard the voices of the oppressed. But, as Michael Cohen has demonstrated, such paradigms for reading enable poems to "mediate cultural fantasies about oral, pre-modern culture" in such a way that "abstractions of genre" are substituted for "persons and personal voices."[89] And yet the desire remains to access or represent—to make present—a personal voice in the same way that the photograph bears the trace of a body's presence.

It is here that the fact of the photograph adds another coordinate to readings of Hughes's radical verse. Looking at Hughes's photographs, journalism, and poems addressing Scottsboro together, and within the established framework of Hughes's photographic practice in Haiti, one can discern something like what Fred Moten describes as the "phonographic content" of the photograph. This "phonic substance" is a sound or music that Moten codes as both the photograph's contextual meaning (that is, what came before the decision to create and display the photograph) and its ability to contain an excess of meaning. Moten thus argues for the act of "listening" to the photograph and, in so doing, approaches a reconceptualization of the relationship between speech, writing, and photography. He writes,

> So that speech is broken and expanded by writing; so that hieroglyphics is affected by phonetic script; so that a photograph exerts itself on the alphabet; so that phonographic content infuses the photo. And this movement doesn't mark some orbital decay in which signification inevitably returns to some simple vocal presence; rather it's the itinerary of the force and movement of signification's outside. The implications of this aural aesthetic—this phonographic rewriting of/in the photograph—are crucial and powerful then, because they mark something general about the nature of a photograph and a performance—the ongoing universality of their absolute singularity.[90]

Moten's suggestion that a photograph might be interpreted according to an "aural aesthetic" and thus rewritten according to its "phonographic" content helps one to see how photography is mediating the purpose and construction of Hughes's early-thirties radical poems. Moten's conception of a "phonographic content" uses both the visual and the sonic metaphorically and thereby blurs the boundaries between photographic analysis and sound studies. Moten allows us to move toward the possibilities for reading Hughes's poems for sound that both account for Hughes's interest in the visual and also chafe against expected methods of reading visual culture.

Hughes troubles the document's claims to objectivity, and he approaches the "crisis" inherent in any attempt to represent a political collective.[91]

Specific to Hughes, the photograph offers a site to dialectically transcend an essentialist construction of voice—one that has been read back into *Scottsboro Limited*, as well as Hughes's thirties radical verse in general, at the moment of its initial reception and in moments of its critical recovery. Hughes's 1930s poems are, indeed, the product of a conversation between image and text. But this is not a "mutual dialogue," as most readers of documentary photo-texts would have it, nor do his writings emerge in the utopian space *between* the linguistic and pictorial, to use Michael North's formulation.[92] It is here that we might return to Hughes's amateur snapshots and their banal captions. If, in Hughes's scrapbooks, image and word represent two modalities of representation, then his 1930s political poems emerge out of the indiscernibility between these two practices. At a critical moment in the development of Hughes's radical poetics, he encounters photography as part of the "unthought" potential of poetic language.[93] To put it in Moten's terms, Hughes does not attempt to write the photograph; rather, he is trying to write, or represent, its phonographic content. Refusing to "neutralize the phonic substance" of the photograph, Hughes attempts to rewrite the symbolic coordinates of the image in a poem that calls up the pain of the past at the same time that it opens up to potential futures.[94]

A Piece of the Body Torn Out at the Foot

In the preceding readings, the temporality of the photograph, an aspect of the photographic image that is linked to its indexical nature, allows for a reconsideration of how Hughes imagined local political collectives as well as global networks and relationships. As much as Hughes's work from the 1930s was concerned with accumulating and then arranging information—pasting it in scrapbooks, jotting it in lists—he also paid close attention to singular and specific images. I would like, then, to begin this section by considering one particular image that resonated with Hughes, Manuel Álvarez Bravo's *Los agachados* (see figure 7). Hughes wrote about the image in his essay "Pictures More than Pictures" (1935), which accompanied an exhibition booklet for a joint show featuring photographs by Álvarez Bravo and Henri Cartier-Bresson. His description evinces his thinking about light and shadow as well as his attention to how bodies are photographed: "Whereas the sun in a Bravo photo almost always has a sense of humor, one cannot be sure about the shadows. The iron curtain is partly down, and the heads of the customers are in the shadow—so one can laugh about the feet."[95] The meaning of the heads in the shadows is significant, as the play of light demonstrates how "all sub-

FIGURE 7 Manuel Álvarez Bravo, *Los agachados* (The crouched ones), 1934, gelatin silver print, 7 × 9⅜ in. © Archivo Manuel Álvarez Bravo, S.C. Courtesy of J. Paul Getty Museum, Los Angeles, CA.

jects are inflected by labor, regardless of whether it can be readily cast in the shadows."⁹⁶

Perhaps not surprisingly, Hughes is interested in the feet. In Haiti, it was the appearance of a bare foot (as opposed to a shoe) that became the imagistic marker of the peasantry, those persons he described as "the people without shoes." Years later, a focus on feet added "documentary flavor" to his Jesse B. Simple sketches. Blair cites one particular sketch as evidence of Hughes's continuing engagement with documentary imaging. In it, Simple sits on a bar stool (another coincidental link to Álvarez Bravo's image) and blows "the foam from the top of a newly filled glass." "If you want to know about my life," he tells the bartender, a stand-in for the reader, "don't look at my face, don't look at my hand. Look at my feet and see if you can tell how long I've been standing on them."⁹⁷

The ways that Hughes's thirties poems incorporate the language of the documentary image, so ubiquitous at the time, are often obscured by a concentration on the "folk voice" of Hughes's radical poems and his interest in popular verse genres such as the song and ballad. Thus, one might be tempted to gloss over imagistic poems such as "Negro Ghetto," which was included in *A New Song* (1938), published by the International Workers Order with an introduction by Mike Gold. The poem is, from start to finish, about the act of looking and recording what one sees:

> I looked at their black faces
> And this is what I saw:
> The wind imprisoned in the flesh,
> The sun bound down by law.
> I watched them moving, moving,
> Like water down the street,
> And this is what moved in my heart:
> Their far-too-humble feet.[98]

In the context of the poems included in *A New Song*, it would seem that Hughes is here describing a labor march or protest. The poem, not unlike a photographic image, is formally constrained. The single stanza looks like a tight square, and the lines are bound together by the end rhymes (saw/law and street/feet), all in ways that reinforce the controlling of natural elements in the images of "wind imprisoned in the flesh" and a "sun bound down by law." The poem travels the length of a body, from the speaker's first gaze at the "black faces" to the "far-too-humble feet."

Of course, the iconography of the New Deal is all about shoes and the feet that go in them, as demonstrated by one of the most enduring New Deal photographs, Walker Evans's portrait of Floyd Burroughs's work boots. But Hughes's poem is more like the painstaking prose efforts in the thirties along the lines of Agee's own attempts in *Let Us Now Praise Famous Men* to describe persons and their social realities in ways that answer the representational power of the photograph. Hughes's attempts to conceptualize the photograph's relation to language align his thirties poetry with experimental photo-textual projects such as Agee and Evans's *Let Us Now Praise Famous Men* and place him squarely in a documentary modernist tradition several years before his well-known collaborations on photo-texts such as the 1955 *Sweet Flypaper of Life* (with Roy DeCarava) and the 1956 *A Pictorial History of the Negro in America* (with Milton Meltzer).

Hughes's scrapbooks, in their contemplations of the relationship between photography and writing, are homologous to Agee's fraught attempt to provide text to accompany Evans's photographs of Alabama tenant farmers in *Let Us Now Praise Famous Men*. In the first pages of *Let Us Now Praise Famous Men*, Agee imagines an alternate form for his and Evans's book that would include no writing. "If I could do it, I'd do no writing at all here," he writes. "It would be photographs; the rest would be fragments of cloth, bits of cotton, lumps of earth, records of speech, pieces of wood and iron, phials of odor, plates of food and excrement.... A piece of the body torn out at the root would be more to the point."[99] The pages of meandering prose that follow Evans's photographs constitute Agee's effort to make the medium of language perform the work of the camera. But for Agee, the photograph does not necessarily expose the limits of linguistic representation: it illuminates his desire to move beyond such limits and to push the capabilities of language into another realm. While *Let Us Now Praise Famous Men* is a "paean to the power of vision,"[100] it is also a book that speculates how photography might produce a new modality of language. In other words, it is an attempt to make language slip into, and pass through, the domain of the photographic image in order to become something else.

Despite the fact that *Let Us Now Praise Famous Men* is chock-full of prose, Agee's desire to arrive at a new modality of linguistic representation via the interference between text and image ultimately emerges as a desire for poetry—or, at the very least, it is labeled as such. For Agee, poetry approaches photography because it avoids "description," and the poet "continually brings words as near as he can to the illusion of embodiment."[101] Agee's estimation that poetry might come close to doing the work of the photograph is illustrated by two passages in which he equates the persons and places he attempts to document with poems. At one point, on the heels of asking if things are "beautiful which are not intended as such," he asserts that "the partition wall of the Gudgers' front bedroom *is* importantly, among other things, a great tragic poem."[102] In a later passage describing Mrs. Gudger's wedding hat, he imagines the woman at sixteen and concludes that she was "such a poem as no human being shall touch."[103] In both moments, Agee returns to the fantasy that he began with: objects he would have preferred supplant his writing (a wall, a hat, a human body) are named poems. However, no poem ever manifests itself in those pages; a poem is there in name only, arrived at through images of a room and a woman arrested in time.

Agee and Hughes share in the desire to create an aesthetic that can make visible as well as beautiful a localized presence. However Hughes's contemplation of the interference, or cross-fertilization, of photograph and poem opens up potentials outside the immediate present in ways that Agee's does not. In keeping with Moten's theorization of the visual object, phonographic content generates multiple meanings out of a single body and time. The phonic substance interrupts the presumed silence of the static image, creating new coordinates for understanding the relationship between the particular and universal—or, in the case of Hughes, localized sites of oppression and the potential for revolutionary political networks. Photographs, flimsy papers like money, mark something like what Moten calls, at the end of *In the Break*, "a rematerialization of value" associated with a coming communism.[104] The image becomes for Hughes a way to demonstrate how a singular moment, arrested in time, carries echoes of past longing at the same time that it acts as a passageway to future potentials.

CHAPTER TWO

Fusing an Alloy
Muriel Rukeyser at the Limits of Poetry/Documentary

That is the legend of our buried poetry.
The dead children and the singing bones.
—Muriel Rukeyser, *The Life of Poetry*

A Refusal

In March 1936, Muriel Rukeyser traveled to Gauley, West Virginia, with the radical documentary filmmaker Nancy Naumburg to visit the site of one of the worst industrial accidents in U.S. history. In 1930, under the auspices of the Union Carbide Company, construction began on a tunnel that would divert water from the New River in Fayette County, West Virginia, to a hydroelectric power plant that would provide energy to a metallurgical plant in the nearby town of Alloy. The tunnel was also mined for silica, a compound valuable to the production of steel. To save time and money, the engineers overseeing the mining of the tunnel did not take basic precautions to protect workers from inhaling silica dust, and as a result, more than seven hundred men died from the pernicious lung disease silicosis. While lawsuits were filed on behalf of the workers as early as 1932, it was not until the midthirties that the incident received national coverage.[1] Rukeyser constructed the poem sequence *The Book of the Dead* from materials she gathered in West Virginia, and the sequence was first published in her 1938 volume *U.S. 1*. The twenty sections that constitute *The Book of the Dead* lay bare the catastrophic events at Gauley Bridge by drawing on prevalent modes of thirties documentary expression that sentimentalized subjects in efforts to appeal to middle-class audiences.[2] At the same time, the poem sequence experiments with prescribed genres and conventions in ways that call into question the structures and assumptions of documentary rhetoric.

The proverbial center of *The Book of the Dead* is the section "Absalom," which tells the story of the Gauley resident Emma Jones losing her husband and three sons to silicosis. The depiction of Emma, a mix of straightforward testimony with descriptions of her pained efforts to obtain money and medical care while supporting her family, is comparable to iconic Depression-era photographs such as Dorothea Lange's *Migrant Mother*, which garnered empathetic effect and, in consequence, support for liberal government programs, by portraying maternal bodies coiled in pain. If "anyone with even a passing interest in the [1930s] references it through the images of hungry migrants caught by the Farm Security Administration's (FSA) photographers," then Rukeyser's poem-portrait of Emma is as much a part of New Deal iconography as a photograph of some California pea picker or Alabama sharecropper is.[3] But Rukeyser also resists the kind of sentimental framing that presumes to lock suffering in time. Averting the attention of another, the Joneses are positioned more like the Italian immigrant woman who cradles a child in Jacob Riis's *How the Other Half Lives* and who refuses the camera's gaze.

Midway through "Absalom," the portrait of the bereaved Emma is coupled with the request of her youngest son, Shirley, to be "opened up" and thus transmogrified into evidence that could indict the Union Carbide Company. Emma recounts how Shirley did not go to the doctor to have x-rays (called "lung pictures" in the poem) made. At first, there was not enough money to pay a doctor. Then, once the x-ray money had been "begged" for, Shirley was not strong enough to make the trip to the Charleston hospital. Jones remembers how her youngest son "lay and said, 'Mother, when I die, / I want you to have them open me up and / see if that dust killed me.'"[4] His plea, situated in a poem sequence in which the x-ray camera is figured "as a penetrating medium that could retrieve emancipatory truths from Gauley tunnel," seems motivated by the then-pervasive belief in the power of facts proved visually.[5] In this reading, the medical autopsy is invoked to perform an institutional function like that of the documentary photograph and, perhaps more forcefully, the radiographic image: publicizing industrial abuses and making an argument for compensation. Medical technology is conjured as a validation for Shirley's testimony, as if validation for his suffering depends on the recognition of state structures expected to administer justice.

But could we also read Shirley's request to "open me up" as a political act of refusal and, in consequence, as a key complication to understanding how Rukeyser negotiates documentary representation in *The Book of the Dead*? Jones's youngest son is asking that his life not be reduced to a single image of the death inside him—the silicotic lung—and he resists being captured by the empirical knowledge produced by a "lung picture." While he invites us to "look inside" for proof, his deathbed wish also forgoes any promises made for mechanical reproduction, especially as such promises are related to claims for political recognition or reparation. The reader, rather than take immediate comfort in liberal sentiment, is forced to consider potentials that exist outside of the present situation and out of that body's refusal to be captured on film at a particular moment in time. Shirley imagines that his hard-breathing body is proof of a right to trial after his death, when his cadaver will testify that the dust killed him (habeas corpus / habeas corpse). In Rukeyser's rendering of the scene, the act of "opening up" also transcends such instances of representation, expressed in her appropriation of a line from the Egyptian *Book of the Dead*: "*I open out a way, they have covered my sky with crystal.*"⁶

"Absalom" thus is a text that attempts to exceed the representational possibilities available in documentary and poetry alike. Those who are familiar with the critical conversation around *The Book of the Dead* will notice "exceed" as an alternative to "extend." A single line from Rukeyser's "Note" on *U.S. 1*—"Poetry can extend the document"—has been used often as a rubric for understanding the incorporation of and experimentation with documentary materials in her poems.⁷ And yet, as a rubric, "extension" does not capture fully the ways Rukeyser negotiates modes and metaphors for representation. The argument that Rukeyser draws on the resources of the poetic to "extend the document" implies that the apparent neutrality of documentary objects cannot be called into question on their own terms. What is more, such arguments presume to discuss "poetry" as an object when they really mean it as an ideation, an assumption about how words on the page can and will do work in the world. Overextending the definition of "poetry" in this way has a reverse effect: pulling the work of the poem away from the material historical realities documented rather than folding it back into them.

The broad aim of this chapter is to examine the importance of how poems and documents as objects and poetry and documentary as abstract ideas interfere in *The Book of the Dead*. At the close of chapter 1, I used James Agee's breaking of documentary convention in *Let Us Now Praise Famous Men* to expand my arguments about how Langston Hughes developed his radical poetic practice through engagements with documentary arts. Comparing Hughes's and Agee's writings, I suggested that the closest Agee got to naming his attempt to represent "human actuality" was to call it a poem, where the sign "poem" emerged not as an object but as a desire to recognize the reality of another without doing violence to it (to see Mrs. Gudger as a "great poem," impossible to touch). The vexed relationship between poetry and documentary in the Depression demonstrates the very breakdown of generic categories that would prompt Agee to use the noun "poem" to name a body that could be captured neither on camera nor in experimental prose. As Christopher Nealon notes, poets such as Rukeyser "developed genre-mixing forms of documentary poetics to capture the costs and the violence of industrial capitalism," and *The*

Book of the Dead "begins an attempt to foreground both the media of perception that risk glossing over the miners' tragedy, and the generic pressures that urge both reader and writer to take the political situation and rewrite it in generically recognizable terms."[8]

Contemporary takes on documentary poetry often originate in readings of Rukeyser's poems, and *The Book of the Dead* is treated as a documentary poem par excellence because, in addition to incorporating technologies associated with documentary culture, it tests the limits of subjective poetry and objective documentary. I want to resist the temptation to interpret Rukeyser's sequence on these terms, which map supposed tensions between "poetry" and "documentary" onto ideas about the "subjective" and "objective," or "lyric" and "narrative." In the sections that follow, I reorient the conceptions of political subjectivity and expression that are at stake in these predominant rubrics for interpretation. The chapter begins with a brief account of the historical, definitional, and theoretical concerns that have shaped documentary poetry, and then it moves on to examine how *The Book of the Dead* plays at the limits of recognizable genres in order to shift conceptions of human experience as well as the relationships between political subjects and economic and historical materials. My analyses examine the impact of industry on subject formation in order to demonstrate how Rukeyser experimented with literary and visual genres, as well as poetic tropes and themes, to devise alternate modalities of personhood that interface the human with the materials of history and industry. While my analyses are concerned primarily with how documentary and poetic forms mediate conceptions of history and political agency, my readings of *The Book of the Dead* also have stakes for contemporary ecopoetics scholarship that demonstrates how poems responding to the environmental damages wrought by capitalist acceleration engage uniquely with "the problem of human agency and the limits of individual perception and ethical response."[9] Facing the fact that the silica dust is everywhere—in the tunnel, on the trees, on the tips of boots, in the lungs—forces an encounter with alternate modalities of being that integrate the human with the debris of economic development at the same time that they potentially engender creative forms of resistance.

The Book of the Dead does not make documents poetic, nor does it poeticize documentary; rather, the very materials of "poem" and "document" dissolve into particles as finely grained as silica dust. To read *The Book of the Dead*, we must, like Agee, begin with the materials: scraps of paper, shards of glass, photographs, water, clumps of earth, a wooden table, millions of dust particles. Doing so, we understand that the poem is not merely multigeneric or multimedia but a complex fusing of elements that becomes a speculation on the ontology of the poem itself—in a word, an *alloy*. Alloy, of course, names the West Virginia town that the silica-ridden tunnel supplied with water. Alloy also has a broader historical and formal resonance. In the 1934 essay "Author as Producer," Walter Benjamin used the metallurgical alloy as a figure for the newly charged relationships among art, politics, and media forms registered in *The Book of the Dead*. "Alloys begin," Rukeyser writes in one of the sequence's final stanzas,

> : certain dominant metals.
> deliberate combines add new qualities,
>   sums of new uses.

Rukeyser deploys an industrial process to imagine "new processes, new signals, new possession" for political agency and collective resistance.[10] As I explore in the chapter's conclusion, Rukeyser's efforts to adapt *The Book of the Dead* into a documentary film demonstrate a combination of formal and technical resources that further illuminate how the alloy might function as a principle of composition.

Next to the materials from West Virginia, the most important source text for *The Book of the Dead* was the Egyptian *Book of the Dead*, which Rukeyser viewed when it was displayed at the Metropolitan Museum of Art. But like her nineteenth-century precursor Henry David Thoreau, Rukeyser had little use for monuments, museums, or archives, for such institutions could only preserve death.[11] Through processes of composition and production, Rukeyser attempted to bring back the dead and to create materials that vibrated with different life. (Agee again: "Is anything more marvelous or more valuable in the state of being we distinguish as 'life' than in the state of being a stone, the brainless energy of a star, the diffuse existence of space?")[12] And so we might cut from Rukeyser standing in the Metropolitan Museum of Art observing the scrolls of the *Book of the Dead* to the water flowing through the New River Gorge to Shirley Jones breathing hard in his small room. And when "all that is solid melts into air," we have to face the corpse on the bed filled with dust. Will it get up and walk the earth among the living? And will it speak with us?

In the Same Breath: Poetry/Documentary

Turning to the initial reception of *The Book of the Dead*, this section rearticulates the Depression era as a nodal point for definitional and theoretical reappraisals of documentary poetics, while pointing to women's innovative writing as the core of the documentary poetic tradition. A modality with seemingly no singular historical or national origin, "documentary poetry" has described a diverse range of poetic projects that either make use of documentary materials or narrate historical events.[13] Pursuing the question of what makes a poem documentary, Joseph Harrington asserts that documentary poetry is poetry that (1) "contains quotations from or reproductions of documents or statements not produced by the poet" and (2) "relates historical narratives, whether macro or micro, human or natural."[14] Critical concern with defining documentary poetry has been tied up with debates about what counts as "poetry" and what does not; and conversations about documentary poetics index shifting historical concerns about the relationship between poetry and other historical and political registers. A reconsideration of thirties discourses about the relationship of poem to document, especially as they coalesced around *The Book of the Dead*, reorients both definitional debates about documentary poetry and theoretical debates about documentary poetics as a form of social action.

In the U.S. context, the tradition of the "documentary" or "nonfiction" poem "including history" emerged in the late 1920s and coalesced in the 1930s in conjunction with advancements in documentary film and the heightened cultural relevance of documentary photography. In the immediate postwar period, poetry was sharply opposed to documentary in order to reify a "normative conception of poetry" as "an art form that expresses the current thoughts and emotions of the individual."[15] As part of the backlash against New Critical ideologies in the 1960s and 1970s, the incorporation of historical and documentary matter into the field of the poem became a means to assert revolutionary poetic models. In a significant 1975 treatise, the poet and social activist Ed Sanders coined the term "investigative poetics," a mode of "history-poesy" inspired by Charles Olson, Ezra Pound, and Allen Ginsberg that included techniques such as creating "high energy verse grids" and "data clusters." The future of poetry, for Sanders, depended on a "voyage into the description of *historical reality*."[16] While experiments with documentary, or investigative, poetry were a feature of innovative poetries across the twentieth century, the terms "documentary" and "poetry" were, according to the poet and critic Jill Magi, first consistently "used in the same breath" in the mid-1990s when the journal *CHAIN* published a special issue on the topic of documentary; the poet Susan Howe taught a class on "documentary and poetry" at the University of Buffalo; and feminist and leftist scholars recuperating Rukeyser's work began to describe her poetry as "documentary." Despite a varied and contested history, by 2007 the editors of *American Poets in the Twenty-First*

Century: The New Poetics could use the terms "documentary poetry" and "documentary poetics" as if they needed no explanation.[17]

The Vietnam War–era reemergence of documentary poetics within left-leaning poetry circles was accompanied by a renewed attention to documentary rhetoric in scholarship on left cultural production. William Stott's pathbreaking study *Documentary Expression and Thirties America* (1973) returned to the documentary impulses of the Depression decade from the perspective of the seventies. For Stott, *Let Us Now Praise Famous Men*, though widely dispraised in its time, had become "*the* thirties classic" because it harnessed documentary convention while transcending it through its innovative style.[18] At roughly the same time, the feminist proletarian writer Tillie Olsen published her Depression novel *Yonnondio*, framing it as an archival discovery "from the thirties" that had been deciphered and pieced together from "38 to 41 year old penciled over scrawls" in order to present a document of "the consciousness and roots" of the thirties, "if not its events."[19]

Scholars of the cultural left point to the reemergence of documentary rhetoric in the 1970s as symptomatic of the 1960s obsession with documentary and folk culture, including folk and blues purism in music, new journalism, and cinema verité. Michael Denning, for example, argues that during the 1960s and 1970s, Depression cultural production was recast in a documentary mold, and in consequence, questions about realism, authenticity, and propaganda that are associated with documentary culture were overemphasized in subsequent accounts of the period.[20] Indeed, postwar discourses about documentary have obscured knowledge about Depression experiments with the genre. By ignoring the poetic, however, Denning and others miss how Stott's elevation of Agee's experimental style, and even Olsen's reframing of her novel as fragmented and incomplete, fits with predominant postwar discourses about modernist aesthetics that placed a high value on linguistic experimentation and cross-media collaboration.

Absent from both of these literary and critical trajectories, one related to the history of poetry and one to the history of the procommunist left, is a full accounting for Depression engagements with what now goes by the name documentary poetics. Recuperative readings of early-twentieth-century documentary poetry has delimited thirties experiments to oppositions between subjective and objective, or lyric and antilyric, that have underwritten much poetry scholarship since midcentury. As Magi puts it, "It might be the case that those who are interested in documentary poetry define it as 'other' to lyric poetry and find that difference satisfying enough."[21] Insofar as readers have addressed the significance of Rukeyser's marginalization for postwar accounts of documentary poetics, *The Book of the Dead* has been understood within the purview of a lyricism, sometimes coded as humanist and sometimes as feminist, whereby the insertion of the personal into the field of history reenvisions the presumed objectivity of documentary poetics composed in the (white, male) modernist tradition.[22] Even Magi's statement that 1990s poets and critics used the terms "documentary" and "poetry" "in the same breath" evokes aspiration and therefore an utterance that originates in the body but that, apropos Olson's "Projective Verse" (1950), may or may not be "lyrical."[23]

In *The Book of the Dead*, every breath taken is filled with the detritus of industrial capitalism. As such, the sequence challenges readers to imagine the poem as a conglomeration of materials that refuses familiar parameters of poetic and, consequently, political subjectivity. While I will have more to say about this feature of the poem in later sections, for now I wish to underscore how *The Book of the Dead* registers the newly charged relationships among art, politics, and media forms that Benjamin described in his contemporaneous essay "The Author as Producer" as a metallurgical alloy. "We are in the midst of a vast process in which literary forms are being melted down," he wrote in 1934, "a process in which many of the contrasts in terms of which we have been accustomed to think may lose their meaning."[24]

Readers of *The Book of the Dead* approached the dissolution of the poem into document (or, to return to Agee's exhaustive lists, hats and tables and clothes and cows and stardust) with greater trepidation than did Rukeyser, often misrecognizing the ideological effects that her sequence advanced.[25] Nonetheless, the responses to her volume are instructive—not least because we find that "poetry" and "documentary" were perhaps first used "in the same breath" in 1938 when the poet and screenwriter Ben Maddow (writing under the pen name David Wolff) published a review of *U.S. 1* under the title "Document and Poetry." Popular Front artists such as Maddow were interested in how multimedia experiments might open up the revolutionary potentials of existing forms. Nonetheless, when Maddow set out to parse the combination of document and poetry in *The Book of the Dead*, he was unsure how to do so. Such confusion is evident from the review's title, which does not posit the relationship between two forms (document and poem) but between a form (document) and an idea (poetry). *The Book of the Dead* clearly unsettles Maddow's own definitions of poetry:

> Miss Rukeyser desired to utilize the records of questions and answers, discovering the extraordinary movement of factual document, which proceeds almost dully, then turns and strikes at you with the abrupt violence

of the event itself. Documents, skillfully cut, do have a poetic force. But the poet has made an error, this reviewer feels, in not marking off the documents clearly from the body of the poem. Instead, they are divided into lines as if they were poetry—badly phrased poetry, for their internal rhythms conflict with the more rapid and pulse-like beat of poetry; or, very often, the poem itself is converted to factual uses.[26]

Maddow seems much more comfortable with the notion that documents could have a "poetic force" than he is with the idea that the poem could be reduced to the status of document. He praises Rukeyser's technique, but his praise does not derive from those hybrid poems that stage conflicts between the "personal" or "internal" and "the 'immense street' outside." Singling out more loco-descriptive and meditative poems such as "Alloy," "Power," "A Child Asleep," and "The Dam," Maddow highlights Rukeyser's "technical range" and the "precision of epithet which convinces one, for a moment, that poetry is the most exact of the arts." Ultimately, Maddow roots Rukeyser's achievements in the mind of the poet: lauding her for the ways that she "faced her own conflict, the tragic necessity of the artist to record our bloody era without flinching."[27] The best record of a "bloody era" is poetic expression; and exactitude is the encapsulation of a felt truth, not the accuracy of documented fact.

As Maddow's review indicates, Depression-era readers of *U.S. 1* were vexed by the relationship between poem and document, but their responses are also based in historically specific understanding of the two terms. Here it is worth noting that, in the Anglophone context, the idea of "documentary" always already contained within it an idea of "poetry." When the Scottish filmmaker John Grierson coined the term "documentary" in his 1926 review of Robert Flaherty's film *Moana*, he leapt from documentary to poetry. Translating the French *documentaire*, designating travel or expedition films, to "documentary," a descriptor he later defined as "all films made from natural material," Grierson described Flaherty's film as having "documentary value." The review, however, quickly asserted that *Moana* achieved "greatness primarily through its poetic feeling for natural elements."[28] It was precisely this "poetic feeling" that readers found missing from *U.S. 1*. Reviewing Rukeyser's volume for *Poetry* magazine, the communist poet Willard Maas took issue with the absence of a "subjective voice." An admirer of Wallace Stevens, Maas admitted that he favored "subjective poetry rather than that modeled after leaflets," not least because leaflets and "poetry trying for the same effect" are "immediate and transitory" rather than aiming for "permanence." While he was sympathetic to Rukeyser's aims, Maas pushed her on "the larger question of the most appropriate means by which the poet can make effective use of propaganda."[29]

But Maas's criticisms of U.S. 1 were not simple denunciations of documentary as propaganda, and his preference for the "subjective" and the "permanent" was not tantamount to a New Critical ideal of the lyric poem uttered by a solitary speaker and lifted from historical contingency. Maas shared with Rukeyser the sense that poems could transmogrify into industrial elements, perhaps by melding with other media such as film. His Depression writings called for poems built of "girders" and described lyrics as "metallic songs." He also went on to imagine avant-garde film techniques as a means to make poems, through collaborations on "film poems" such as *The Mechanics of Love* (1955) and *Narcissus* (1956) that combined sequences of suggestive images with voice-over narration. Nonetheless, when assessing Rukeyser's experiments, Maas appealed to the "subjective" for fear that combining poem and document would divest poetry of its timelessness.

The Book of the Dead divests from ideas about subjective, and relatedly affective, expression that animate how Maddow, Maas, and Grierson conceptualize the role of the poetic. Rukeyser does not, as Grierson's gesture toward the poetic "value" of documentary would suggest, attempt to infuse "natural material" with exacting expressions of "feeling." Rather, she imagines conglomerations of materials—bodies, histories, languages, texts, textiles—that constitute human subjects and lay the ground for alternative modalities of representation and expression. In this sense, of all the reviewers of U.S. 1, William Carlos Williams perhaps came the closest to comprehending the volume's stakes: "Rukeyser's material, *not* her subject matter but her poetic material, is in part the notes of a congressional investigation, an x-ray report and the testimony of a physician under cross-examination. . . . She knows how to use the *language* of an x-ray report or a stenographic record of a cross-examination. She knows, in other words, how to select and exhibit her material. She understands what words are for and how important it is not to twist them in order to make 'poetry' of them."[30] Placing quotation marks around the word "poetry," Williams almost echoes W. H. Auden's statement that "there are events which arouse such simple and obvious emotions that an AP cable or a photograph in *Life* magazine are enough and poetic comment is impossible."[31] His review prompts us to consider the ethics of twisting violent historical fact into "poetry" at the same time that its praise hints at new models for composition, in which poems are ground down to basic elements.

Stubborn Representations

"The Road," the first section of *The Book of the Dead*, summons the materials at the poet's disposal to make her way to West Virginia and, in effect, to an understanding of the disaster there: maps, statistics, newspapers, a friend's advice, headlights illuminating "future of road." As the roads taken by the poet become the mountain passes that lead to the New River Gorge, a photographer appears as coauthor.[32] The photographer, perhaps a figure for Naumburg,

> unpacks camera and case,
> surveying the deep country, follows discovery
> viewing on groundglass an inverted image.[33]

Readers of *The Book of the Dead* generally agree that the modalities of representation that Rukeyser experiments with and, in turn, theorizes rely on her poems' implicit critiques of visual documentary forms. Walter Kalaidjian points out, for example, that the "inverted image" viewed on the groundglass in "The Road" suggests how "camera work" serves as "a key metaphor for ideological representation" throughout the sequence. Drawing on Marx's figuration of the camera obscura as a metaphor for ideology, Kalaidjian argues that the camera "at once projects a visual image of middle-class American prosperity *and* exposes it as the inverted 'other' to Gauley Bridge's particular historicity of class conflict and ruthless labor relations."[34]

Certainly, *The Book of the Dead* questions the role of documentary photography and cinema as the go-to media for representing the social realities of the Depression. Reading the sequence with regard to its negative relation to documentary, however, reasserts the notion that poetic language (and especially poetic language read as lyric) can represent an interior space unavailable in the documentary image. I suggest that *The Book of the Dead* might be understood in relation to competing ideas of visuality that structured New Deal portraiture and that, in turn, influenced a number of multimedia literary experiments, including Archibald MacLeish's poetic photo-text *The Land of the Free*, published in the same year as *U.S. 1* and reviewed negatively by Rukeyser. Rukeyser and MacLeish, though their approaches differed, were, like popular photographers such as Margaret Bourke-White and Dorothea Lange, interested in the potential of camera work as a means to reveal an inward reality.

MacLeish's *The Land of the Free* attempted to document the crises of the Depression by combining a long poem with eighty-eight photographs taken under the auspices of the FSA and Resettlement Administration (RA).

MacLeish described his poem as a "soundtrack" to accompany documentary images by venerable photographers such as Walker Evans, Dorothea Lange, Arthur Rothstein, and Ben Shahn. As he explains in his note on the text, what began as a poem to be illustrated by photographs ultimately became its opposite:

> "Land of the Free" is the opposite of a book of poems illustrated by photographs. It is a book of photographs illustrated by a poem. The photographs, most of which were taken for the Resettlement Administration, existed before the poem was written. The book is the result of an attempt to give these photographs an accompaniment of words. In so far as the form of the book is unusual, it is a form imposed by the difficulties of that attempt. The original purpose had been to write some sort of text to which these photographs might serve as commentary. But so great was the power and the stubborn livingness of these vivid American documents that the result was a reversal of that plan.[35]

Louis Kaplan points out that MacLeish finds the "livingness" of photography in the "direct and indexical connection of these images to their referents in lived reality" and thus "downplays their status as representations and their artificial and constructed nature."[36] The lines of text on each page too appropriately match the images alongside them and therefore render artificial whatever MacLeish hoped to illustrate. To give one example, early in the book the line "We're wondering" is placed adjacent to a photograph of a woman sitting on the edge of a bed, chin in hand and eyes downcast, presumably "wondering" about her future. As MacLeish finds the "livingness" of photographic documents, he relegates the poem to a separate soundtrack, itself a telling misnomer for a print text, and consequently forecloses possibilities for representation that, as I argued in chapter 1, might be opened by interdynamic photographic-poetic modes.

When *The Land of the Free* was first published, Rukeyser also took issue with how MacLeish theorized photographs. In a review, Rukeyser praised MacLeish's sequencing of images—which begins with "individual portraits," then moves to "wide memorable views of mountain range and prairie," then turns to "house and farm and face again"—but she criticized the way he balanced the images with the text of the poem. "MacLeish has acknowledged the 'stubborn inward' life of these pictures and subordinated his text to the position of illustration to the photographs," she wrote. "But there is a great lack of balance there." The task of writing text for photographs is not to provide accompaniments or illustrations but *translations*. MacLeish fails at this because, according to Rukeyser, he "has taken these people's faces and translated (or rather failed to translate) the inarticulate physical life seen in them to a lost periodless quality."[37] Even though Rukeyser praised the arrangement of images in *The Land of the Free*, a similar flatness is to be found in the book's predictable movement from individual portraits to landscape photographs to individual portraits and, finally, to closing portraits of crowds. Each image seems captioned, in a way, by the one preceding it, making the succession of photographs as predictable as the adjacent lines of text are.[38]

Rather than harness on Rukeyser's criticism of *The Land of the Free*, I would like to trace out the possibility that the images in the volume hold an "inarticulate physical life" that could somehow be successfully translated. Some Depression documentarians resisted the idea that text could express the inner life of the subject photographed. Dorothea Lange and Paul Taylor's *American Exodus: A Record of Human Erosion* (1939) combined documentary photographs with quotations from the subjects pictured; but Lange and Taylor wanted the quotations to "adhere to the standards of documentary" and offer a "report" of "what the persons photographed said, not what we think might be their unspoken thoughts." Lange imagined that the quotations would "fortify" the image "without directing the person's mind."[39] For others, however, the surface of the photograph could possibly convey interior depths. Tellingly, the title of Erskine Caldwell and Margaret Bourke-White's famous photo-text *You Have Seen Their Faces* (1937) is a reworking of the title for Hallie Flanagan and Margaret Ellen Clifford's drama *Can You Hear Their Voices: A Play for Our Time* (1931), an adaptation of Whittaker Chambers's *New Masses* story "Can You Make Out Their Voices" (1931). Bourke-White's "Notes" to *You Have Seen Their Faces* provides a compelling take on the relationship between subjects' faces and their interior thoughts. She recalls how Caldwell would talk with their subjects for up to an hour: until "their face or gestures gave us what we were trying to express." The camera flash, she concludes, provides "the best means I know, under poor light conditions, of letting your subject talk away until just that expression which you wish to capture crosses his face."[40] Bourke-White's recollection suggests that a subject's interior life could be captured, somehow, on the surface. This effect is greatly exaggerated in *You Have Seen Their Faces*, a volume that features mostly close-up, frontal portraits of its subjects.

In *The Book of the Dead*, as in much other New Deal portraiture, the camera often is an authoritative instrument representing and therefore shaping a lived reality. At different moments in Rukeyser's sequence, the camera controverts the authority of the poetic speaker: asserting the power of the instrument while also undermining the fantasy that poetic language expresses unseen interiority. For example, at the start of the fourth section, "Gauley Bridge," the camera is given the first word as its "eye" replaces the "I-witness" and provides a picture of the town. The first line reads, "Camera at the crossing sees the city."[41] Throughout the poem, the town of Gauley Bridge is refracted through multiple "panes of glass" analogous to the camera lens: post office and plate-glass windows, movie-poster frames streaked with rain, beer glasses held to the lips. Viewed through glass, the "one street town" that looks like "any town" becomes something like the special toy that Benjamin recalls from his Berlin childhood, also made of glass: "the large glass cube, containing a complete working mine, in which miniature miners, stonecutters, and mine inspectors, with tiny wheelbarrows, hammers, and lanterns, performed their movements precisely in time to a clockwork." Unlike the toy, which Benjamin remembers "did not begrudge even the child of a wealthy bourgeois household a view of workplaces and machines," the glass surfaces displaying Gauley Bridge begrudge.[42] The panes of glass in "Gauley Bridge" glimpse the workings of a mining town, but they also separate the onlookers from the scene by keeping them behind the glass, so to speak. The poem ends with an interrogation of looking: "What do you want—a cliff over a city? / A foreland, sloped to sea and overgrown with roses? / These people live here."[43]

Rukeyser's portrayal of the town and the valley around it, as well as the persons who inhabit and work in those landscapes, is informed by an expanded conception of the face-to-face confrontation that took place between photographer and subject. A focus on the meaning of face-to-face encounters usefully connects Rukeyser's thirties documentary poetics to her later analyses of the photographer Berenice Abbott. More specifically, Rukeyser's observations about the concept of the face in her 1960 foreword to Abbott's *Photographs* informs, and seems informed by, Rukeyser's earlier documentary experiments. The foreword begins with references to the faces in Abbott's portraits, but it quickly extends the concept of "face" to include nonhuman landscapes and objects: "These faces look out at us with the clarity of extremes. They are human faces, yes; but they are also human bodies looking out at us, with their pride, their deep gifts, their magnetic strangeness asking for response. They are also buildings, streets, shopwindows, a cart and a clock, all seen by this photographer as human faces, with their expressive power entire. They are also a penicillin mould and a bouncing metal ball, watched with the attentiveness and grave joy that let them speak to us."[44] Rukeyser turns attention away from the face as directly connected to a singular human body, conceiving of whole bodies and buildings as potential loci of expression. Abbott's genius lies in the fact that she "sees" every object—"buildings, streets, shopwindows, a cart and

FIGURE 8 Muriel Rukeyser, page from the photo-text "Adventures with Children," *Coronet*, September 1939, featuring a photograph of an Ozarks cabin by Carl Mydan, 1936. Farm Security Administration / Office of War Information Collection, Library of Congress, Washington, D.C.

a clock"—as human faces that invite the response of the viewer. Scholars of Rukeyser's documentary engagements have suggested that Rukeyser significantly revised the "facial encounter" characteristic of thirties documentary portraiture in ways that portrayed ethical modes of relation. Such analyses, however, potentially link the concept "face" to a liberal construction of personhood hewed to an abstract body and thus miss how and why Rukeyser transposed the human face onto material objects. By supposing that a building or cart might "speak," Rukeyser suggests a more complex thinking about the parameters of personhood in relation to the terrain of history and economics.

This line of thinking is indicated in "Adventures of Children," one of two photo-text sequences Rukeyser created for the magazine *Coronet*. One of the images Rukeyser selected for the sequence shows a young girl standing against the wall in her home, and it is composed so that the child seems to blend in with the backdrop (see figure 8). Rukeyser provided the caption: "she backs against the wall, she is lost in her past and her family; against this kind of decoration, against this life, she is hardly distinguishable from the furniture."[45] Rukeyser's caption intimates the ways in which children in poverty, handed lives they have not asked for, are reduced to objects both in the economic system that impoverishes them and in the photographs that seek to represent their realities. The photograph that Rukeyser selects, however, also resists liberal-humanist presumptions about political recognition. The viewer of the photograph is drawn to the center image of the girl's hat, perfectly mirroring a scrap of newspaper tacked to the wall. Such mirroring reinforces the girl's reduction to object of study or sympathy. But it also, perhaps, makes the newspaper something of a subject. Turning from this image to *The Book of the Dead*, we might reconsider where faces appear and how they "speak to us," thus illuminating how Rukeyser rethought the constitution of persons in relation to the scraps of news, industry, and history.

Landscapes

In *The Book of the Dead*, Rukeyser attempts to portray the experiences of specific persons without reducing their representation to the logics of liberal reform undergirding New Deal portraiture.[46] Nonetheless, interpretations of Rukeyser's sequence often replicate the assumptions of documentary portraiture rather than challenge them. The persona poems included in the sequence are often read as lyric expressions, where the assumption of lyric expressivity in the poems overlaps with the idea that a portrait photographer might express the "inward life" of her subject.[47] By this logic, sections of *The Book of the Dead* such as "Face of the Dam: Vivian Jones," "George Robinson: Blues," and "Mearl Blankenship" ostensibly function as documentary portraits of persons affected by the tunnel disaster. But these poems also resist the logics of both documentary portraiture and subjective expression. In them, Rukeyser reimagines the body of the tunnel worker in relation to the landscape.[48] In so doing, she exposes the limits of available modes of representation as well as the terms of generic recognition: pointing to the inability of these predetermined modes to capture the totality of the events at Gauley Bridge.

The fourth section of *The Book of the Dead*, "The Face of the Dam: Vivian Jones," recalls the conventions of documentary portraiture by undoing them: the "face" in question is not Jones's but the dam's, and Rukeyser uses a colon to suggest a reciprocal relationship between the industrial landscape and Jones's visage. While the poem follows Jones, a locomotive worker, over the course of an hour—his movements out of town, to and across the dam, and back to town are marked at quarter-hour intervals—the title conditions the way we read his perceptions. Thus, when Jones observes the dam's "great wall-face" with its "immense and pouring power," we understand the "face of the dam" as something that is seen by Jones as well as something that signifies the person "Vivian Jones." The way the landscape produces the figures that inhabit it is reiterated in Jones's observations of the men working the ground below. He looks down, and

> There, where the men crawl, landscaping the grounds
> at the power-plant, he saw the blast explode
> the mouth of the tunnel that opened wider
> when previous in the rock the white glass showed.[49]

The syntax of the line, "the men crawl, landscaping the grounds," conflates the work the men do (landscaping) with their status as part of the landscape (they landscape the grounds in the same way that a plant might). Intrinsic to this image is the dissolution of the borders between the people and the place, iterated in more explicitly economic terms later in the poem when Jones imagines how "hundreds breathed value, filled their lungs full of glass."[50] Considering Jones's perspective in the poem, which approximates a bird's-eye view of the industrial and natural scene, we might read these images of work in keeping with the title itself, in which the coherent expressive subject signified by the "face" is transposed onto the landscape. The image of the explosion opening the tunnel mouth, which bears its glass-white teeth, is an unnatural one that replaces the romantic and humanist logics underscoring the concept of the "face."[51]

A later section of *The Book of the Dead*, "Mearl Blankenship," similarly uses the figure of a "landscape with a face" to examine the relationship between the subjects of Gauley Bridge and the places they work. Against standard conceptions of the "lyrical," the Blankenship poem is not expressive. In the poem, he has "no words," and the reader only knows his thoughts through quotations from his letters. Blankenship speaks no more than the tunnel itself, as shown in a description of a dream that is quoted in his letter:

> I wake up choking, and my wife
> rolls me over on my left side;
> then I'm asleep in the dream I always see:
> the tunnel choked
> the dark wall coughing dust.

While we might read Blankenship's description of his dream as a fragmented recollection of choking in the tunnel—a splicing of images (the tunnel, the dark wall) and actions (choking, coughing)—in light of the foregoing, it is more fitting to understand the tunnel and the wall as actors that, themselves, choke and cough. As in the "Vivian Jones" section, when Blankenship surveys the scene at the river the landscape and his body are conflated,

> He stood against the rock
> facing the river
> grey river grey face
> the rock mottled behind him
> like an X-ray plate enlarged
> diffuse and stony
> his face against the stone.[52]

Michael Thurston writes that this scene "is Blankenship himself writ large" and that Blankenship's body functions as "a metonymy for the region itself."[53] Thurston's reading is apt, but it also falls back on humanist conceptions that Rukeyser resists in her poem sequence. When the gorge becomes "Blankenship writ large," it too becomes invested with the "lyricism" that readers ascribe to Rukeyser's monologues.

The image of the "X-ray plate enlarged" conjures the complex interplay of inside and outside that structures many of the poems and images in *The Book of the Dead*. The x-ray is a picture of the dust inside the lungs, a testament to how deadly earthly minerals were incorporated into the body of the worker. This image provocatively challenges John Wheelwright's criticism that *The Book of the Dead* "attacks the exressencies [sic] of capitalism, not the system's inner nature."[54] Indeed, one of the main conceits of the sequence is that the excrescence of capitalism grows on the inside. In "Mearl Blankenship," this dynamic relation between inside and outside, human and landscape, is projected onto the surface of a rock. The enlarged radiographic image not only shifts representation away from a concern with the individual but also shifts individual expression and experience to a terrain of historical material symptoms and realities.[55]

As David Kadlec points out, the radiographic image is also central to the imagination of racial identity in *The Book of the Dead*. Placing Rukeyser's composition in the context of then-emerging x-ray technologies and state-sponsored photography, Kadlec argues that the reification of x-ray proof in the sequence erases the visual markers of racial difference that influenced working conditions and access to health care. One of the signal moments for thinking about how racial difference is articulated in relation to cross-race working-class solidarity is "George Robinson: Blues," a first-person poem rendered from the official testimony of George Robison (Rukeyser may have gotten the name wrong), a black migrant driller. The final stanzas describe how thoroughly the silica dust covered the work camps:

> Looked like somebody sprinkled flour all over the parks and groves,
> it stayed and the rain couldn't wash it away and it twinkled
> that white dust really looked pretty down around our ankles.
> As dark as I am, when I came out at morning after the tunnel at night,
> with a white man, nobody could have told which man was white.
> The dust had covered us both, and the dust was white.[56]

For Kadlec, the final image of the poem demonstrates how, in line with the x-ray technologies that erased racial difference and therefore structures of racial inequality, Rukeyser's George Robinson poem "restored a universalizing whiteness to the blackened workers" and sacrificed "race to class interests."[57] The image of black and white workers equally covered in the lethal materials of heavy industry also suggests the practical politics of imagining cross-racial alliances characteristic of Rukeyser's Popular Front milieu.[58] Through the image of twinkling silica dust sticking around the workers' ankles like a ball and chain, Rukeyser also calls attention to the spectacular violence of the dust as white matter. This image informs the closing image of a black man and a white man covered in silica; the final phrase "and the dust was white," as well as the repetition of "white" at the end of last two lines, emphasizes rather than obscures how any imagination of working-class solidarity must be built on an acknowledgment of the racial character of capitalism.

"George Robinson: Blues" evokes the *longue durée* of historical experience that produced the unequal social relations dividing Gauley Bridge's working class; and it activates the blues as a means to suggest that this field of relations is not reducible to a present appearance of racial difference. "George Robinson: Blues" begins with Robinson's tongue-in-cheek account of Gauley Bridge as a "good town for Negroes":

> Gauley Bridge is a good town for Negroes, they let us stand around,
>   they let us stand
> around on the sidewalks if we're black or brown.
> Vanetta's over the trestle, and that's our town.

This up-front recognition of racial segregation and the precariousness with which black and brown workers "stand around on the sidewalks" of Gauley Bridge condition the meaning of the two stanzas that follow:

> The hill makes breathing slow, slow breathing after you row the river,
> and the graveyard's on the hill, cold in the springtime blow,
> the graveyard's up on high, and the town is down below.
>
> Did you ever bury thirty-five men in a place in back of your house,
> thirty-five tunnel workers the doctors didn't attend,
> died in the tunnel camps, under rocks, everywhere, world without end.[59]

These stanzas are derived from Robison's accounts of mass burials. In his testimony before a congressional subcommittee, Robison related that when men became too sick to work, they were run out of the tunnel camps, but they were too weak to go far and so died in the camps, in hospitals, and under rocks. While Rukeyser does not use a traditional blues stanza, she embeds Robinson's blues testimony within a series of temporal dislocations and displacements that are characteristic of blues structures. The "slow breathing" that marks the walk up the hill extends temporally beyond the walk itself as the poem suggests the ongoing cycles of a "world without end."[60]

Insofar as the blues has been a site for lyrically rendering collective historical experience—as in Ralph Ellison's description of blues as "an autobiographical chronicle of personal catastrophe expressed lyrically"—George Robinson's blues expressions are voiced from a collective of persons and particles. Rendering Robison's recorded testimony as a "blues," Rukeyser seems to equate black experience with blues expression, thereby abstracting race into a predetermined form.[61] At the same time, however, as particles penetrate drinking water, camps, tree groves, clothing, skin, and lungs, the terms of agency in the poem shift away from bodies as singularly recognizable or readable entities. In the space of the tunnel, laboring bodies, precious metals, natural landscapes, tent homes, and towns and their histories and economic systems fused with one another in ways that depended on different histories of racialization but that nonetheless transformed human agents.[62]

Sections in *The Book of the Dead* organized around a singular persona, such as "Face of the Dam: Vivian Jones," "Mearl Blankenship," and "George Robinson: Blues," demonstrate Rukeyser's reconceptualization of the relationship between persons and landscapes. As I move into the next section, which takes up assumptions about voice and representation in Rukeyser's work, I want to suggest how the fusion of political personhood with historical material and economic reality that I have described here works on another plane. In sections such as "Face of the Dam: Vivian Jones," the body of a specific worker is projected onto the landscape; in sections such as "Alloy" and "Power," the landscape is imagined as having its own body. "Alloy," a section describing the steel factory and the town named for it, renders the factory site in terms of human anatomy: the "hill of glass" slopes "as gracefully as thighs." Rukeyser also connects the hills to the factory furnace that she imagines as a "brick throat" that "speaks" with "severe flame." It is through this "crucible" that the tunnel workers must pass:

> Forced through this crucible, a million men.
> Above this pasture, the highway passes those
> who curse the air, breathing their fear again.[63]

If the landscape of "Alloy" is first posited as a lure through the image of "graceful thighs," then this desire is quickly shot through with the image of "a million men" being forced through its "crucible." Similarly, in "Power," the poem immediately following "Alloy," the poet compares her experience of the landscape to a sexual encounter, in which the "quick sun" and the "green designs" bring "sex up under all the skin" and "the entire body watches the scene with love."[64] The power plant is a body, and the speaker descends its "ladder mouth." While the "mouth" of the plant is open, the mouths of the workers are covered with a "cage of steel."

Critics have suggested that throughout *The Book of the Dead*, Rukeyser uses a "panorama of voices and perspectives" to call attention to, and even correct, the presumed objectivity of documentary representation.[65] But, in juxtaposing the open ladder-mouth with the steel-covered mouth of the welder in "Power," Rukeyser suggests that ladder-mouths and brick throats are the loci of voice in the poem, and in this way she supplants the expressive voice that comes from a singular subject. In this sense, we might read *The Book of the Dead* as somewhere between Oren Izenberg's recent claim that "'poetry' names an ontological project: a civilizational wish to reground the concept and value of *the person*" and Mark Nowak's description of documentary poetry as "labor history with line breaks."[66] Rukeyser's poems are neither transcendent philosophical meditations on the concept "person" nor mere histories. Rather, they are attempts to represent political personhood fusing with historical material and economic reality: a "history that hurts" sung from a brick throat.[67]

Who Speaks?

Rereading the acts of expression in *The Book of the Dead* as complex alloys that destabilize the dichotomies between inside and outside, subjective and objective, and, therefore, poetry and documentary allows for a reexamination of the question of voice, which, in North American poetry studies, is at once contested and taken for granted.[68] Arriving at the question of voice from the perspective that I have established so far, this section reorients predominant arguments about *The Book of the Dead* that presume Rukeyser employs voice as a subjective counterpoint to the objectivity of the document. Such readings depend on a figurative connection between "voice" or "speech" and political agency and, in so doing, reinforce modes of liberal subjectivity and representation that *The Book of the Dead* often actively subverts.[69] Indeed, the reception of *The Book of the Dead* registers enduring ideas about voice in poems, and Rukeyser's documentary poetic practice therefore has ramifications for current scholarly attempts "to theorize as well as historicize alternatives to the assumption of voice" in contemporary reading practices.[70]

From a historical standpoint, *The Book of the Dead* articulates thirties ideas about voice. The impulse to record was not relegated solely to photography: Depression-era writings in a range of genres including ethnography, oral history, folklore, and journalism evince an "unprecedented concern with recording the speech of disinherited and marginalized Americans."[71] In addition to oral histories such as John Neihardt's *Black Elk Speaks* (1932), ethnographies such as Zora Neale Hurston's *Mules and Men* (1935), and nonfiction books such as the hard-boiled writer Benjamin Appel's *The People Talk: American Voices from the Great Depression* (1940), to give just three examples, state agencies published volumes such as *Lay My Burden Down* (1945), an oral history of slavery, and *The Disinherited Speak* (1936), a collection of sharecroppers' letters. Embodying John Dos Passos's assertion that "mostly U.S.A. is the speech of the people," these publications were driven by an urgent need for dispossessed persons to be "heard" and therefore "known."[72] "Somehow they must be given representation," W. T. Couch insisted in his preface to the oral history collection *These Are Our Lives* (1939); "somehow they must be given voice and allowed to speak, in their essential character."[73]

As Couch's quotation suggests, it was through the printed text that marginalized persons could presumably "speak" and might be "heard." On the Depression left, the poem became a particularly privileged site for conveying the human voice, evoked in MacLeish's aforementioned assumption that his poems functioned as a "soundtrack" to a photographic montage. But manipulations of poetic forms and tropes also made visible the mediation of voice and thereby disrupted, or at least called attention to, the notion that voice was a means to garner political recognition. The idea that voice is something that can be possessed—and then given over from one person to another via a literary record—is based in a metaphysic of presence that leftist women's documentary poetics disentangled. In an analysis of Tillie Olsen's "I Want You Women Up North to Know," a documentary poem adapted from a *New Masses* letter by the Texas garment worker Felipe Ibarro, Paula Rabinowitz demonstrates how left women writers employed poetic techniques to enact complicated processes whereby the voice of another is translated across media as well as across differences of place, class, and race. Insofar as "speech inaugurates politics," it does so through a desire that exceeds documentary representation. The highly mediated transference of "red love" that Rabinowitz describes accounts for material conditions and thus does not aspire to the universalized lyric communication that Susan Stewart describes as poetry's "voice," whereby the "music and meter of poetry" have meaning insofar as they allow for processes of "being spoken through as well as speaking." The "new processes, new signals, new possession" that Rukeyser points toward in *The Book of the Dead* might also thus be read as an evocation of new parameters for Stewart's linking of poetic voice with "possession," as Rukeyser attempts to make subjects present in a way that resists liberal modalities of self-identity or self-sufficiency.[74]

It is from this vantage that I want to return to "Absalom" and to the politics of refusal that I identified in the chapter's opening. Shirley's refusal of the empirical knowledge captured by the "lung picture" is one of a number of moments in Depression-era writing when subjects refuse the gaze of another. Surveying Depression-era fiction, Denning formulates the category of the "proletarian grotesque" as a refusal of aesthetic response to industrial catastrophe, poverty, and racial violence. He reminds us that Tillie Olsen, in her thirties novel *Yonnondio*, puts her description of a catastrophic mine explosion on hold to taunt the reader: "And could you not make a cameo of this and pin it onto your aesthetic hearts?"[75] In a scene from *Jews without Money*, Mike Gold narrates how East Side kids refused to be scenery for liberal sightseers: "Then a big sightseeing bus rolled down. A gang of kids chased it, and pelted rocks, garbage, dead cats and stale vegetables at the frightened sightseers. 'Liars, liars'; the kids yelled, 'go back up-town!' Joey and I joined in the sport. What right had these stuckup foreigners to come and look at us? What right had that man with the megaphone to tell them lies about us? Kids always pelted these busses. The sport is still popular on the East Side."[76] Photographers, despite the technology at their service, lie like the man with the megaphone. So the chin turned slightly or the eye averting the camera's gaze in certain documentary portraits suggests a refusal to be represented through the smallest gesture. (Could we imagine an archive of photographs never taken? The refusal to pose for the camera as a refusal to labor for the photographer?) Roy Stryker, the director of the FSA's documentary photography program, refused thousands of photographs produced under the auspices of the program by punching holes in them. James Agee, already self-conscious about enforcing a camera-like gaze, felt his "reflexes . . . twitching in refusal" of the food offered up to him by the families he studied.[77]

In "Absalom," Shirley's spoken request—"I want you to have me cut open"—is a refusal to be photographically captured that, in another potential development of the photographic negative, transforms into a desire that can be heard alongside the sounds of hard breathing. "Absalom" is central to *The Book of the Dead* because, in that poem, Rukeyser performs the ritual of restoring speech to the dead. The request to "open me up" anticipates not just the autopsy but the burial rite, and the poem articulates the "opening of a way" through transcriptions of the Egyptian *Book of the Dead*. The incorporation of italicized refrains from the Egyptian *Book of the Dead* augment Emma's testimony, elevating her account to ritualized invocation and transforming Shirley's deathbed scene into a religious ceremony. The refrains are rewritten in a first-person voice, so that the reader attributes them to either Emma or Shirley. While all of the refrains seem to be Emma's expressions, the final one is ambiguous:

I open out a way, they have covered my sky with crystal
I come forth by day, I am born a second time,
I force a way through, and I know the gate
I shall journey over the earth among the living.

He shall not be diminished, never;
I shall give a mouth to my son.[78]

Here, Shirley's existence exceeds the temporality of a single image or moment because he is always moving forward: he "open[s] out a way"; he "force[s] a way through"; and his "journey over the earth among the living" is cast in the future tense. The "opening" suggests a confluence between "opening out a way" and "opening his body" and therefore determines that transcendence is shaped by the historical and material realities of the industrial accident. His sky is covered with "crystal," a reference to the silica dust that he breathed in and that will come forth when he is cut open.

At the end of "Absalom," Emma promises, "I shall give mouth to my son." The line, though not italicized, is a reference to the "opening of the mouth" ceremony outlined in the Egyptian *Book of the Dead*. The ceremony restored "the power of speech" to the dead; once this power was regained, the dead were free to leave the underworld and roam the earth among the living.[79] By re-creating the ancient Egyptian ritual through the contemporary mother-child relationship, Rukeyser shifts the terms of agency and collectivity employed in the poem; in so doing, she also reorients the terms by which we understand the poem's representation, its documentation, of Gauley Bridge's living and dead. Shirley is possessed and possessing: he is the ghost that haunts the poem, "roaming the earth among the living" in order to imagine a form of collectivity that transcends bourgeois fantasies of subjectivity and political alignment. But he is also dispossessed: a roaming victim who prompts the reader to imagine collective forms of injustice. When Emma Jones "gives mouth" to her son, he ceases to become a political subject and becomes instead a political tool.

The ritual of giving speech to the dead is extrapolated throughout *The Book of the Dead* in the many instances when the landscape testifies to events at Gauley Bridge. For example, a line in "The Cornfield," a section about unmarked mass burial sites, describes "Abel America calling from under the corn, / Earth, uncover my blood!" and therefore lends additional meaning to Rukeyser's assertion that "the whole valley is witness" to the tragedy.[80] Such instances of imagined speech are, I argue, a contrast to the actions of the committee members who reflect "the will of the people." While the committee stands in for the parameters of political agency typically associated with democracy, the workers' voices are expressed in the poem as something like what Rukeyser describes in *The Life of Poetry* as the "ground music" of "buried voices."[81] While voice, especially as it is related to political speech and therefore recognition, is a physical mechanism for pronouncement, in Rukeyser's hands it becomes a way of describing a passage between a living body and history.

For example, in the section "The Disease: After-Effects," Rukeyser begins with "the life of a Congressman" but then pans out to larger political contexts. As the poem lays out "the proportions of war," it develops the x-ray into a map of the country:

No plan can ever lift us high enough
to see forgetful countries underneath,
but always now the map and X-ray seem

> resemblent pictures of one living breath
> one country marked by error
> and one air.⁸²

The picture of the breath and voice mapped onto "one country marked by error / and one air" expands the parameters of voice and its origin from an individual body to a corporeal totality that includes the "map" of the entire country and its "errors." Colleen Glenney Boggs describes how voice opens up "a more expansive register of representation that takes us beyond the visual and verbal to the aural and the physical."⁸³ While Boggs is specifically interested in the slippages between human and animal sounds, her arguments are relevant to the ways that the sounds of human labor, such as coughing and heavy breathing, translate to the voice of the poem. In moments such as the foregoing one, Rukeyser both visualizes the mechanism of voice and distributes voice across the body. The landscape resembles the x-ray, and both are pictures of "one living breath." Marked by the rhymes "error" and "one air," the stanza highlights how one of the aspirations of the poem itself is a totalizing vision that is indelibly marked by the events in West Virginia. In so doing, Rukeyser emphasizes that the plane of expression is a complex material assemblage, another form of the alloy, that has historical meaning but that also exceeds existing representational boundaries. In a landscape where "a gradual scar formation" will eventually "block the air passageways," a new mechanism for voicing must be discerned.⁸⁴

The final section of *The Book of the Dead*, also titled "The Book of the Dead," describes the body of the worker as integrated into the landscape—"a landscape mirrored in these men"—and it articulates their actions in terms of breathing and coughing. In this culminating poem, the act of reconstructing history does not rely on documentary evidence or records, whether visual or oral, but on the fact of the flesh itself:

> Half-memories absorb us, and our ritual world
> carries its history in familiar eyes,
> planted in flesh it signifies its music
>
> in minds which turn to sleep and memory,
> in music knowing all the shimmering names,
> the spear, the castle, and the rose.
>
> But planted in our flesh these valleys stand,
> everywhere we begin to know the illness,
> are forced up, and our times confirm us all.⁸⁵

Rukeyser changes the terms of "speech" and "representation," altering the way that we think about the relationship between vocalization and political recognition. By distributing "voice" spatially across the body of the worker, as opposed to locating a physical utterance in time, Rukeyser links voice to body by creating a history told through singing body parts. In *The Life of Poetry*, Rukeyser writes that "the legend of our buried poetry" is the "dead children and the singing bones."[86] But Rukeyser does not merely ask what kind of history would be told *by* singing body parts. Rather, she seeks to write a history *of* bones and lungs.

What ultimately "speaks" in the poems is the unthought of history. In the last stanza of "The Book of the Dead," the "urgent need" to resurface repressed histories is described in terms of the documentary photograph as well as the voice. Rukeyser writes of the need to

> Carry abroad the urgent need, the scene,
> to photograph and to extend the voice,
>   to speak this meaning.
>
> Voices to speak to us directly. As we move.
> As we enrich, growing in larger motion,
>   this word, this power.[87]

The closing poem indicates that the documentary object is a means to "extend the voice." But it also suggests that the work of extending the voice and speaking "this meaning" takes place outside of, or beyond, the boundaries of the documentary object, what Rukeyser describes as the "unmade boundaries of acts and poems." While *The Book of the Dead* seems to end lyrically, with "desire, field, beginning . . . communication to these many men," its communiqués do not exist within the present parameters of political subjectivity but rather within "seeds of unending love."[88] The sense of recognition, named "seeds of unending love," is a desire not for liberal recognition but for a community that exists across the boundaries that separate the living and the dead.

"Film into Poem": The Matrix for a New Form

This chapter has tried to discover how *The Book of the Dead* imagines poems, and the idea of poetry that attends them, ground to dust. When William Carlos Williams described *The Book of the Dead* for Depression readers, he intimated that Rukeyser knew better than to violently twist the materials of an industrial disaster to make "poetry" out of them. At the same time, "poem" is the word Agee used in *Let Us Now Praise Famous Men* to describe a human body "impossible to touch"; and so "poem" also glances a possible ethical relation, one in which another might be made present but not subjected to representation. If *The Book of the Dead* carries a desire for what poems can do, that desire is nothing short of rousing the dead to strike out against history and walk the earth among the living. For Rukeyser, the inclusion of the dead as part of the material reality of the living engenders expansive notions of collectivity and history that change the scale of politics.

My arguments about Rukeyser's efforts can be concluded, at least for now, by examining her planned adaptation of *The Book of the Dead* into a documentary film. Rukeyser worked on plans for the film, to be titled "Gauley Bridge," from 1938 to 1940, though she never completed a full script. She sent scene sketches to Paramount and Columbia Pictures, but both studios turned down the project. She eventually published an extensive story outline in a 1940 issue of *Film*, and additional notes for the script titled "Story Outline for Gauley Bridge," along with letters to filmmakers, remain in her Library of Congress archive.[89]

The planned adaptation of *The Book of the Dead* into the documentary film "Gauley Bridge" is perhaps the most concrete extant example of Rukeyser's assertion in *The Life of Poetry* that film could be a means to realize "a new appropriate poetry, now unborn": "To understand the possibilities of language moving against, as well as with, a flow of images, will be to understand new values in film as well as in poetry," she explained. "The combination of narrator, the voices of dialogue, music, sound, and beyond these voices from anywhere . . . will give us a new function. We are at the age to develop this function, and the film is a matrix for the new form."[90] Rukeyser proposed that "Gauley Bridge" would tell "a chapter of the great American migration" that was "a new phase of the old story" of the "struggle for power." As in the poem sequence, the history of the landscape was an important factor in understanding present events, but she also sought to rethink how historical realities are constructed and represented, as well as how these new realities transform human agents. The planned film illuminates how the formal innovations of the poem sequence generate new possibilities for bearing witness to historical catastrophe while also amplifying her conceptualizations of historical experience and political representation in *The Book of the Dead*. Rukeyser's process of adapting her documentary poem sequence into a documentary film is also a meditation on the changing function of poetry, especially as the labor of poetic production and the mediating capacities of the poem alike are transmogrified by film.

As suggested in this chapter's earlier discussion of Ben Maddow and Willard Maas, Rukeyser was one of a number of writers and visual artists interested in combining the techniques of poetry and film. Her *New Masses* review of the Frontier Film group's *China Strikes Back* gives a partial account of this milieu. Published at some point between the composition of *The Book of the Dead* and the planned film adaptation, Rukeyser's review stages important elements of her thinking about film as a medium for developing new modalities of poetry. One of the first visual records of the communist Eighth Route Army, *China Strikes Back* was compiled from film shot by Harry Dunham, a ballet dancer turned cameraman. Dunham reportedly smuggled several hundred feet of film in ginger jars back to the United States, where it was compiled by Frontier Films editors and writers including Maddow.[91] The focus on the "picture of the Chinese people's defense, centered around the Eighth Route Army," struck Rukeyser as one of the film's particular achievements. She praised the way *China Strikes Back* rejected the genres of the "newsreel" and "travelogue" through an artful exposition of scenes that depict a range of people's lives "in their full activity" and a deft juxtaposition of image and text that resists mere captioning. According to her, Maddow's film script functioned "to heighten and approximate the images, rather than in any sense to be notes to the film."[92]

For Rukeyser, *China Strikes Back* reached its climax "in the poem read as a young Chinese boy sings—a poem which belongs with the pictures it illustrates so closely." She judged that the poem, "Song of the Chinese Soldier," had "its own worth," and she reprinted it in her review as both a summary of *China Strikes Back* and as an example of "the first film-poem used in this country," comparable to Auden's poems for the British General Post Office (GPO) film unit.[93] In her review, Rukeyser foregrounds the function of poetic language as it works in concert with images to heighten their effect. "Song of the Chinese Soldier," on its own, is filmic because it is structured as a montage of images. It becomes a "film-poem" in Rukeyser's sense because in addition to working as part of the film's voice-over narration, it contributes to the filmmakers' creation of a dialectical synthesis as *China Strikes Back* moves toward a depiction of political unity.[94]

In Maddow's and Rukeyser's distinct yet related ruminations on combining the techniques of poetry and film, Maddow tended to suggest that film could learn from poetry, whereas Rukeyser argued for a fusing of the two that would create a third meaning that is irreducible to its constituent parts.[95] In the 1936 essay "Film into Poem," Maddow cites passages from Archibald MacLeish's *Conquistador* (1932) to argue that poets can provide "scenarios" for filmmakers endeavoring to create "cine-poems." Based on Maddow's own speculative definition, the climactic moment in *China Strikes Back*, when "Song of the Chinese Soldier" plays alongside a montage of scenes of the Eighth Route Army, might be considered a "cine-poem" contained within the film. Maddow's notion of the "cine-poem" illuminates ideas about the poetic circulating during the Depression. Maddow wanted film to borrow from poetry so as to give it "the close emotion, the extreme passionate lucidity, that we find in certain forms of the other major arts." He proposes a new "form" of cinema that "would correspond to the scope and concentration of poetry" through techniques such as intensely focusing on a single idea or metaphor, centering human beings but "avoiding personalities," and incorporating a "continuous voice" that is distinct from the documentary voice-over.[96] As in his review of *U.S. 1*, Maddow conflates poetic forms and tropes with emotional intensity.

Even if Rukeyser did not idealize poetry as a space for intense concentration, as Maddow did, "Gauley Bridge" reflects much of what she found compelling about his work in *China Strikes Back*. Indeed, the preposition "into" in "Film into Poem" suggests a conceptual and physical fusion of two media in order to create a new practice for representing the totality of "modern events."[97] The polished sketches of scenes that Rukeyser published in *Film* demonstrate her continued thinking about the relation between poem and film. Her script is often lineated and uses a montage style reminiscent of her poetry, especially the cinematic style of later volumes such as *The Speed of Darkness* (1968). Rukeyser also deployed film techniques to heighten the stakes of her documentary poems. In her unpublished story outline for "Gauley Bridge," she suggested that "a new technique" for combining the "acted story-picture" and "the documentary picture" "may well be worked out" in "Gauley Bridge." The film realizes the alternate set of representational coordinates for *The Book of the Dead* that are embedded in the original poem sequence. In the section "The Dam," the power of the "diverted water" rushing through the tunnel is described in terms of film technology: "printed in silver, images of stone / walk on a screen of falling water / in film-silver in continual change."[98] Here, the film reel becomes a way to imagine the industrial landscape. We must also remember, however, that film reels required silver crystals in order to be processed, and so the very media of perception is implicated in the industrial scene.

The film adaptation "Gauley Bridge," like *The Book of the Dead*, uses the tunnel mouth as a primary trope for reorienting the relationships among the natural landscape, the industrial development of the gorge, and the human agents working within the tunnel. From the start, the film emphasizes how the workers' bodies are subsumed by the valley's natural resources. The opening scenes show the men drilling, with close-up shots that focus on the musculature of their backs and chests. The camera then pans out to a "long shot of the group of men outside the tunnel mouth" with the pine-forested gorge behind them. Then it moves to a "distant shot" that reinforces how "small" the tunnel opening is in relation to the gorge and how "unimportant" the men are in relation to both.[99]

Structurally, "Gauley Bridge" also approximates the poem sequence by using a focus on specific figures to tell the story. Rukeyser writes in her draft that, while the film tells "of shifting groups and movements of men and women, . . . certain figures leap out against this background."[100] On the basis of the archival materials, the main characters in the film were to be Mearl Blankenship, George Robinson, Juanita Tinsley, and Arthur Peyton and his lover, Frances Jones. Through these figures, Rukeyser would depict the violent realization of the illness and its effects, as well as the local effort to form a committee that would seek justice for the dying. The film, more than the poem, also seeks to highlight the formation of cross-racial alliances by foregrounding the importance of Robinson's testimony and activism.

In the extant materials, the most developed story line is Blankenship's, and his scenes exemplify how Rukeyser also challenged documentary tropes related to political representation and agency. Rukeyser employs sound techniques, especially voice-over, in ways that highlight how she figures voice in *The Book of the Dead* and that further illustrate the importance of the transposition of the body onto the landscape in the sequence's persona poems. For example, in an expanded "Mearl Blankenship" scene published in *Film*, Rukeyser refigures the poetic and documentary trope of the "authentic" voice. One of the first scenes featuring Blankenship, who is described in the draft story outline as a "tall, inarticulate man, who had been without a job for a long time," shows him and his wife eating dinner in silence: the sounds of "eating, of the fork falling against the plate, of the salt being moved, or the coffee-pot set down, is all that is heard." These diegetic sounds are interrupted by Blankenship's wife:

> The wife looks up at Blankenship; an earnest, long-suffering look of question, a look of habit.
> The wife: "Don't you want it, Mearl?"
> Blankenship, seen in close-up, opens his mouth for an answer. Flash to the table with the letter on it, and during the time taken by his answer, which is not heard, his voice reads:

> *Dear Sir, My name is Mearl Blankenship.*
> *I have worked for the Rinehart & Dennis Co.*
> *Many days and many nights.*
> *And it was so dusty you couldn't hardly see the lights.*[101]

The scene begins as a face-to-face encounter between husband and wife, but neither her "long-suffering" gaze nor her question is met with an answer, even though we see Blankenship's mouth open. As the camera cuts away from Blankenship's face, Rukeyser breaks the connection between voice and body and instead links his enunciation to his letter. The voice-over suggests a form of spoken testimony that is at once detached from the worker and fused with the documentary material. Rukeyser employs the same technique in two subsequent scenes: in one, the camera pans to the same letter, now sealed and stamped, while Blankenship is heard in a voice-over; in another, Robinson's description of the white dust is heard in his voice, although he "does not speak."[102]

Even though Blankenship is one of the major figures in the film, his voice is rarely heard in dialogue. Rukeyser's unpublished story outline suggests that this decision is in part to tell a story of moving from silence to speech. In a scene depicting a town meeting about the silicosis deaths, in which Peyton, Robinson, and Tinsley all speak, Rukeyser describes Blankenship's admiration of Tinsley, and she penciled in a note: "he has been inarticulate, & this speaks for him, too."[103] The first time Blankenship speaks in the film is after Robinson's presumable death, when he calls Tinsley's house to suggest holding a town meeting in Robinson's honor. While this development in Blankenship's character might seem like an entrance into political agency through "speaking up," a key scene describing one of Blankenship's dreams lays bare the desire to witness in ways that question such forms of recognition. Indeed, the displacement of Blankenship's voice onto documentary materials via voice-over mirrors metonymically the transposition of individuated faces and lungs onto the surface of rock faces in *The Book of the Dead*.

The material of Blankenship's dream sequence is only briefly alluded to in *The Book of the Dead*, when Blankenship recollects, "in the dream I always see: / the tunnel choked / the dark wall coughing dust."[104] Rukeyser planned for the film to show the dream "in negative" with "three notes of dropping water, in different order and different rhythms," providing the soundtrack. Blankenship's figure first appears in the distance, and then "the tunnel contracts violently." The contraction is accompanied by musical notes meant to make it seem "as if the tunnel were choking." The viewer then sees Blankenship in close-up:

> His face is very sorrowful, but remote, as in sympathy for someone; suddenly his face is covered with tears. He looks down at his drill, and the tears run down his face. The camera moves down as he looks. It is plain

now what he is drilling into. On the ground, under his drill, is seen in negative the chest of a man, his chest, as shot in close-up in Sequence 1. The drill is planted in the chest. There is no blood, and the wound is not visible. There is only the chest with its fine skin, its hair, the nipples, and the drill moving in it. As we watch the chest, Blankenship's tears fall on it, and roll gleaming down the side.[105]

The image of the chest on the tunnel floor resembles the image of the "X-ray plate enlarged" on the river rock in the "Mearl Blankenship" poem as well as other images in the poem sequence in which workers' bodies are projected onto the landscape of the valley. In the proposed film scene, however, techniques such as the tilt shot and the combination of image and soundtrack allow for a depiction of a self in the process of encountering its own material limits that is seemingly impossible to focalize in a persona poem or first-person lyric. In the dream, Blankenship at once witnesses and takes part in the "death work" of drilling into silica-rich rock.

The inability of the drill to ever force a wound in the ground-turned-body is also a significant contrast to Shirley Jones's request to be opened up, which is depicted in the proposed film much differently than it is in the poem sequence. Jones's character is relatively undeveloped in Rukeyser's story outlines for "Gauley Bridge": he is depicted as gravely ill, and his request to have his body examined is delivered rather matter-of-factly to a group of men who have met to discuss what is transpiring at the work site.[106] Whether in the simple film dialogue or in the more complex terms of the poem "Absalom," Jones's request is predicated on an individual passage from life to death, where death promises material knowledge of his condition and thus testimony to the industrial disaster. Blankenship's dream enacts a move past such individuation, signified by the fact that the sentimentalized image of the tear-soaked face is redoubled in the image of the impenetrable chest. The dream thus recounts the horror of Blankenship's illness at the same time that it glimpses his desire to exit the limited scale for witnessing the events of the valley. Put another way, Blankenship's experience is irreducible to his singular body and his capacity to speak from it; as such, his testimony cannot be conveyed simply through telling his story.

As demonstrated through the Blankenship story line, Rukeyser combined image, voice, and sound in an effort to bear witness to the Gauley Bridge tragedy and, at the same time, theorize acts of bearing witness that seemed impossible in poems alone. Her planned final sequence for "Gauley Bridge" carries through the work of the Blankenship scenes by eschewing the tropes of, for example, the first-person poem or the portrait photograph and by pointing to the ineffectivity of such forms to convey the totality of the events in the valley. The scene, based on the "Power" section of *The Book of the Dead*, shows the "Chief Engineer" leading his lover, "city-bred" and a "stranger" in Gauley Bridge, on a tour of the power plant. As the couple walks down the plant's spiral staircase, they pass masked workers and industrial machinery. The scene is visually and aurally dizzying: "They go down iron spirals. They are seen from every angle as they descend; watched through the steps, from below and above.... He snaps his light on again as they go down, across patterns of mesh flooring, their voices grow hollow as they talk snatches of comment on the instruments, going through empty galleries and down the volute stairs."[107] At first, the new construction, gleaming bright white, strikes the woman with its beauty. As they continue to descend, however, she becomes increasingly aware of the true horror of the place. When they reach the last floor, a welder pushes up his mask to reveal the face of a young boy. He tells her, "If you want to see a place, lady, five men were killed a hundred yards down. When the tunnel was widened."[108]

The moment in which the young boy tells the woman what she does not yet see precipitates a shift in her consciousness, though her ability to react is delayed momentarily by the engineer. The engineer asks his companion to sing to test the echo. Then, overtaken by the beauty of his own construction, he begins to sing a hymn. His pride is articulated suddenly as a desire to possess his lover, and, energized by the knowledge that the river rushes behind the wall of the plant, he "starts kissing her, possessively, in conquest." The woman breaks from him, suddenly consumed by her knowledge of the tunnel's horror:

> She recoils at the place, feeling horror at so much suffering; she runs up the dizzy ladders, finds the quickest way into the sunlight, past the blueprints in his brain, the X-rays, the long sicknesses, the many voices of suffering people; emerges breathless, with him a step behind her in the sunlight, to face ...
>
> The committee standing quietly before them, not speaking, but with their mouths shut, the fragments of speech and action come pack, pile up, to make them a voice for their country and for all people. They have suffered; they have died; but many still fight, in the work and their words and their children, for an America of more meaning, more fairness, more love.[109]

The way the woman is bombarded with documentary materials such as blueprints, x-rays, and "the many voices of suffering people" connects this scene to the scene of Blankenship's dream. In both, a piling up of evidence that seems to be moving toward a totality disrupts existing coordinates of knowledge and experience. The woman ceases to stand outside the scene and, instead, becomes a part of it: her lover's mouth suffocates her as if it is the contracting tunnel mouth, and the spiral staircase closes in on her as her new knowledge of the landscape's reality creates a sense of existential panic. It is this panic that propels her up the stairs, where the members of the committee face her.

The piling up of fragments of "speech and action" evokes the investigative work performed by the members of the committee as well as the documentarian. But the way it heaps behind the members of the committee also recalls Benjamin's angel of history who, face turned toward the past, "sees one single catastrophe, which keeps piling wreckage upon wreckage and hurls it in front of his feet. The angel would like to stay and awaken the dead and make whole what has been smashed. But a storm is blowing from Paradise; it has caught itself up in his wings and is so strong that the Angel can no longer close them. The storm drives him irresistibly into the future, to which his back is turned, while the rubble-heap before him grows sky-high."[110] Yet, unlike the angel's vision, historical experience is not a diachronic pile of various catastrophes from different historical moments. Running up the staircase, the Chief Engineer's lover outmaneuvers such a diachronic view of history, which Rukeyser further evokes by eschewing the forward momentum of story-driven film. In the power plant's underground, the woman senses the specific catastrophe of the events at Gauley Bridge. The beginning of the scene is described as "lyrical," a description rendered in the scene through the lyric trope of singing a song and listening for its echo. In the end, the coordinates of the lyrical are interfered with by broader relationships that include the industrial machinery as well as the persons that compose the committee. The truth of the events are not reduced to singular, or lyric, expression: unlike the singer, and unlike the angel whose "mouth stands open," the committee members' mouths are closed as the truth of the events become manifest in the entire scene.

Rukeyser's adaptation of *The Book of the Dead* does not simply dramatize the formal innovations of the poem sequence. Her deep engagements with the shifting ontology of "poetry" as it encounters and melds with other media reveal a complex negotiation of the relationship between historical materials and representations of them. Rukeyser's interest in film grew from her work in film cutting rooms, but her desire to combine multiple media in order to explore alternate forms of representation also dates back to her time working in the Office of War Information (OWI) Graphics Workshop. In *The Life of Poetry*, she discusses how her time with the Graphics Workshop taught her that words and images could make an impact when used in combination.[111] As evidence, she describes one of the projects resulting from the workshop that combined poems and prose with visual wall displays: "Any single contribution might have stood alone. In juxtaposition, they were all set in motion toward each other."[112] In this recollection, Rukeyser shifts our thinking about poetic practice to the world of images. Visual objects and textual objects do not merely "reinforce" a message through some sort of shared communicative work. Their copresence also calls attention to their respective failures to fully convey the message at hand.

The "setting in motion" to which Rukeyser refers sets up aspects of the potentiality of film that she expands in *The Life of Poetry*, especially in her discussions of cutting and sequencing films. She writes, "The cutting of films is a parable in the motion of any art that lives in time, as well as a parable in the ethics of communication." Rukeyser suggests that cutting has its own kind of rhythm, one that makes editing a film the most like writing a poem. She describes the process in detail:

> The cutting room is a different landscape. There you sit, in a bright cubicle, with a stack of shallow cans of film at your elbow, a red china-pencil in your hand, your face bent to the viewer of the Movieola, where the film is passing, enlarged to the plainness of a snapshot. You stop the machine, run it backwards for a moment or two, send the sequence through again, and mark a suggested ending with your red pencil. You copy the number of feet counted by the meter. That is the end of a crucial sequence in a film. What has been done?[113]

The hope that Rukeyser has for film—for film as the new "life" of poetry—is deeply rooted in producing a new experience of reality that opens up a space, or gap, within the reader. To illustrate this, and by way of conclusion, I want to consider the resonances between the opening sequence of "Gauley Bridge" and the "Ajanta" section of *The Life of Poetry*. Rukeyser was drawn to the art of the Buddhist painter-monks at the Ajanta caves because of their contrast with traditions of "representational painting." She writes that in Western painting, "the beholder knows he is meant to look *through* the canvas at the painted scene. Cezanne paints solids, but we reach them beyond the canvas." By contrast, the painters at Ajanta "felt that the sensation of space within ourselves is the analogy by which the world is known." Knowing that "the rocks of the cave walls were real," the monks emphasized the constituent parts of the cave so that viewers would not be led "away from reality." The paintings, Rukeyser writes, are "said to have the energy of a locomotive."[114]

Creating a sensation of space within the self that leads to a reality that is "beyond" the representation of an image is something like what Rukeyser depicts in Blankenship's dream or in the lover's mad dash up the spiral stairs of the power plant. It is also the experience that Rukeyser sought to create for her film's potential audience. Tellingly, Rukeyser planned for a locomotive to open "Gauley Bridge." The first frame of the film would be a screen "clouded over, filled with a fog, the eye does not understand. The fog is salty somehow, sharper than is natural, more granular."[115]

This planned opening sequence for "Gauley Bridge" recalls the techniques of Frontier Films group productions such as the 1937 film *People of the Cumberland*, which opens by foregrounding textile materials in order to highlight relationships between product and production as well as to hint at the allegorical nature of the film itself.[116] While an audience with background knowledge of the Gauley tunnel tragedy might assume that the grainier fog indicates the presence of poisonous silica dust, this atmosphere is suggested rather than given as information. What strikes the senses are loud sounds. As Rukeyser writes in the plans for "Gauley Bridge":

> The sound of many planes, motors cut open, very close.
> A shout, muffled and in the far distance.
> The sound of planes again.
> The fog swirls, there are currents of it, thicker near the ground.
> The nearest plane-sound stops. The rest continue. The change is
>   barely audible.[117]

Once "the full sound goes on," the image of the train rushes at the viewer: "From far to the right a light advances, feeble against this cloud. It reaches the camera, and its background is visible. It is the headlight of a gasoline locomotive, coming down the tracks, which are the first visible details of the scene."[118]

Given that *The Book of the Dead* begins with the "roads to take," one might wonder why the first image of "Gauley Bridge" is a train. Read in the context of *The Life of Poetry*, the locomotive is not simply a representation of industry, of the movement of goods across the country. The "energy of a locomotive" is equal to the Ajanta paintings. Thus, Rukeyser perhaps intended the image of the locomotive in "Gauley Bridge" to effect an experiential change in the film's viewers that paralleled her shifts in thinking about subjective and historical experience in *The Book of the Dead*. Rukeyser assaults her reader with sound, light, dust—always reaching toward a mode of representation that might open up gaps in symbolic and imaginary coordinates rather than conceal them. In China Miéville's retelling of the Russian Revolution, the unfinished story of revolution is imagined as a train: "Onto such tracks the revolutionaries divert their train, with its contraband cargo, unregisterable, supernumerary, powering for a horizon, an edge as far away as ever and yet careening closer. Or so it looks from the liberated train."[119] The locomotive, a stand-in for history itself, is always moving, and the viewer is always in and of the scene.

Part II
Lyric

CHAPTER THREE

Lyric Effects
Singing the Futures of Poetry with Genevieve Taggard and Edwin Rolfe

I don't think in abstract principles but I believe in the abstract and ideal attitudes to the specific end.
—Genevieve Taggard, undated personal journal entry

Lyric Effects

"There's nothing more up that street." So said Philip Rahv about lyric poetry in a 1932 "Open Letter to Young Writers" published in Jack Conroy's *Rebel Poet*.[1] The same year, in the more mainstream magazine the *New Republic*, Malcolm Cowley declared that a growing concern with "more public issues" was causing a decline of interest in the lyric.[2] The proletarian poet Isidor Schneider argued in a 1935 address to the American Writers' Congress that the lyric was a debased type of poetry that emerged only after the establishment of a free market system in which "the liberation of the individual and his consecration became the principal content of bourgeois thinking." "It was only under capitalism," Schneider continued, "that poetry, attempting to adapt itself, began to attempt individualistic forms, especially the lyric."[3] Ruth Lechlitner upped the ante on Schneider's claims about lyric individualism in her 1937 poem "This Body Politic," which equated the pronoun "I" with a fascist dictator and his misguided "servants":

> Heil, I! Heil, Comrade Love-rage-fear!
> While the clock strikes and maggots feed
> O weep for I the regimented tear![4]

The litany of statements by Rahv, Cowley, Schneider, and Lechlitner evinces a set of shared assumptions about lyric poetry prevalent across diverse sectors of the left during the 1930s. In Rahv's and Cowley's accounts, "lyric" functions as an adjective that is synonymous with "private" and "unsocial."[5] In Schneider's and Lechlitner's accounts, "lyric" acts as a noun that denotes, respectively, the formulation of liberal selfhood that is the product of capitalism or a figure of a fascist body politic. Appearing in forums as unalike as *Rebel Poet* and *New Republic*, and straddling the shift from the Third Period to the Popular Front, each speaks to a prevailing definition of lyric as the solitary expression of an "I" unmoored from social and historical contingency. "Lyric," according to these definitions, is the product, expression, and representation of the bourgeois capitalist subject and, as such, is antithetical to the aims of communism.

In the field of North American poetry, the critique of the lyric subject as continuous with the liberal social imaginary of Western capitalism is familiar—even if names such as Isidor Schneider and Ruth Lechlitner are not. The discourses about lyric that took place within Depression communist culture reorient contemporary ascriptions of anticapitalist politics to "anti-" or "nonlyric" forms.[6] Lechlitner, for example, rejected the pronoun "I" as a synecdoche for a fascist dictatorship; but she also argued that revolutionary poetry should be rooted in the same brand of Hegelian universalism that has given way to contemporary ideals of lyric. In a *Partisan Review* forum on poetry, she wrote, "the revolutionary poet who fails to keep in mind the force that transcends . . . is as rudderless as the nature poet who attempts to describe a tree or a flower, per se, without recognizing and placing it in relation to his object the fact of physical evolution."[7] The writing considered in this part of the book negotiates lyric modes in order to reimagine the parameters of lyric subjectivity and lyric address in relation to Marxian concepts of history and attendant ideals of revolutionary praxis. I historicize and theorize an alternative record of lyric practice situated at the nexus of class, gender, and race politics that emerged in the thirties and forties left but that has since been obscured. Here I will track this alternative mode of lyric practice in the work of Edwin Rolfe and Genevieve Taggard, where lyric becomes a means to reinvent structural aspects of self in relation to the dialectics of historical change.

The interwar period is a critical turning point in the history, criticism, and theory of the lyric. In a way, such an argument is a new spin on old news. The emergence of American New Criticism in the 1930s has marked the Depression decade as a crucial moment in the history of defining lyric and learning how to read it. The version of lyric codified during the Cold War, based on the New Critical model of a lyric speaker who was "overheard," has, as Gillian White argues, continued to inflect discourses opposing "traditional" or "conventional" lyricism and avant-garde antilyricism. Both discourses assume as "natural" a New Critical definition of lyric and attendant interpretive practices that "only awkwardly" fit writers "conventionally thought to be 'lyric.'"[8] The emergence of Language writing in the 1970s and its academic institutionalization in the decades following effectively soldered experimental formalisms and anticapitalist politics. In consequence, diverse poetries grappling with complex issues of social identity related to feminist and antiracist politics were reduced to the narrow terms of the expressivist "lyric" associated with the "confessional" or "workshop" poem.[9]

This part aims to get outside the impasses of lyric reading predicated on the dominance of New Criticism and the subsequent opposition of "lyric" and "Language" by returning to the 1930s and 1940s moment when New Critical discourses were emergent but not fully established. Scholars of left poetry have taken as a given that the postwar influence of New Criticism distorted views of thirties poetic culture. And yet reevaluations of thirties poetry tend to perpetuate New Critical values and models even as they attempt to recuperate and theorize Old Left variants of anticapitalist poetics. In one version of this story, the ostensibly private lyric is conflated with poetry and then contrasted with popular verse genres meant to reach mass audiences. For instance, Cary Nelson distinguishes between poetry "as literary studies has often held it to be, the sign of an isolated and self-contained subjectivity" (that is, lyric) and poetry as "an occasion for working-class oral community" that opens "a space for sharing experiences and developing collective agency" (that is, not lyric).[10] Here, Nelson perpetuates the New Critical fiction that "lyric" and "poetry" are the same thing and, consequently, forecloses other possibilities for the political lyric. In another version, also a legacy of New Criticism, the binary between the personally expressive lyric subject and the radically decentered subject of experimental poetics is used to judge a poem's political efficacy. This view of the thirties is a product of the Language-school critique of traditional lyricism that produced the assumption that the lyric tradition is a liberal tradition.[11] Within this paradigm, communist-affiliated poets such as Louis Zukofsky emerge as exemplary because they used nonnarrative or paratactic forms to register capitalist crises.

What remains to be fully realized are the ways that left poets innovated and theorized lyric to imagine an anticapitalist poetics. The writings of the communist poets Genevieve Taggard and Edwin Rolfe allow for an exploration of alternate historical and political conceptions of the lyric. After demonstrating how Rolfe's engagements with the Romantic lyric reasserted the terms of lyrical agency on the historical ground of capitalist crisis, I mobilize Taggard's notion of a "lyric effect" to show how she conceptualizes the lyric as both an effect of history and a way to produce an effect. Rather than fracturing the lyric subject (as in an experimental form) or dissolving it into anonymity (as in a folk form), Taggard attempted to recalibrate the subject, the "I," whose experiences and emotions lyric purported to express. Ultimately, Taggard's notion of a "lyric effect" provides different parameters for understanding the ideological contours of the lyric subject as well as the links between experiments with lyric and the imagination of new forms of subjectivity and collectivity.

I am interested in the formal and rhetorical strategies that Rolfe and Taggard used to reconstitute the lyric—to provide a competing "lyric ideal" that attached alternate ideological fantasies to the concept "lyric." Taggard imagined the lyric as an effect of history, a mode of expression beholden to Marxian ideas about historical progress. The notion of a "lyric effect" resonates with Antonio Negri's statement, "To be a communist today means to live as a communist."[12] The lesson that Negri takes from Marx is the way the "subject" of the proletariat as a revolutionary class is created under the conditions of capital. Although this reality stems from within the dominant coordinates of bourgeois subjectivity, it also challenges its assumptions. In the case of the left lyric, the lyric mode becomes a means to rethink the structural aspects of the self, especially the way this self is oriented toward both the historical structures of capitalist antagonisms and the future potentials of communism. Taggard's intervention in poetic traditions and discourses pushes both literary-historical narratives and traditional Marxian ones: opening up nuances that left discourses might miss on their own.

I chart these meditations and experiments in distinct yet interrelated contexts that relate to broader Depression discourses and debates: the reception of Rolfe's Depression poetry in the left press; Taggard's and Rolfe's engagements with Romanticism, especially in relation to the legacy of Walt Whitman; Taggard's interest in the relationships between poetry and music; and Taggard's investment in radio technology. Across these topics, I demonstrate how abstracted versions of the meditative Romantic lyric, choral music, and oral recitation become "lyric," and I argue that Taggard views this new ideal of "lyric" as the establishment of a politics. In the chapter's final section, I turn to the contemporary reception of Rolfe's poetry, using my readings' momentum to forward a methodological polemic about the relationship of lyric reading to historical practice.

I trace a different mode of lyric's formal logic that depends on retracing and re-creating elements of lyric's history. Through Rolfe and Taggard, I grapple with two aspects of Depression lyric poetry: the presumed shift from the singular "I" to the collective "we" and the constellation of lyric with song. By showing how readers have focused on the syntactical elements of Depression poems apart from their semantic content, I seek to move around entrenched biases about what constitutes formal experiment. Contemplating the relationships among subjective expression, musical composition, and folk forms, Taggard expressed a desire for what lyric could be by constructing an ideal lyric that never was: an ancient mode of public singing to the accompaniment of a lyre. By returning to what she called the "arts of the past," Taggard crafted a redemptive historiography, an archive for a future utopia, out of the remains of poetic history. Taggard's work is thus akin to what José Esteban Muñoz describes as a "not-yet-conscious" representational practice that "is knowable, to some extent, as a utopian feeling" and a "critical investment" that is "profoundly resistant to the stultifying logic of a broken-down present."[13] Lyric—as impulse, as effect, even as affect—is like a reverberation, an imagination of future historical and political conditions that could change the social parameters for the production of lyric subjectivity.

"The Mind behind the Hand That Holds the Gun": Reforming Lyric in Crisis

Decades after the publication of Edwin Rolfe's first poetry volume, *To My Contemporaries* (1936), the communist poet was remembered by a friend as a "Jewish replica of Keats."[14] The comparison is befitting: over the course of a career that spanned the Wall Street crash, the fight for Republican Spain, and the political repression of the Cold War, Rolfe composed poems expressing Marxian ideals in a style traceable to Keats and T. S. Eliot. In content, Rolfe's early Depression poems were shaped by the Communists' Third Period ideology, and they shared with popular workers' poems of the time images of red banners, homages to revolutionary heroes, and other "blazing signals of a world in birth."[15] In form, however, Rolfe's poems were more influenced by strains of twenties modernism, especially as it had developed from the Romantic conviction that the poetic imagination could be a means to comprehend the self caught in the sweep of history. In separate reviews of Rolfe's work, Mike Gold and Joseph Freeman noticed, as Gold put it, how Rolfe's poetry demonstrated a "conflict" between "the influences of modern bourgeois poetry" and "the crude primitive material of revolution."[16]

Rolfe's early-thirties poems were significant for his contemporaries because they presented possibilities for reforming the modern lyric in relation to the historical horizon of capitalist crisis; and his oeuvre has remained important for modern American poetry scholars for much the same reason.[17] From a historical standpoint, volumes such as Rolfe's *To My Contemporaries* as well as Sol Funaroff's *The Spider and the Clock* (1938), Horace Gregory's *Chorus for Survival* (1935), and Kenneth Patchen's *Before the Brave* (1936) marked for reviewers across the left-liberal spectrum the emergence of a socially conscious poetry that refused prescriptions for simplicity in Communist Party–sponsored publications such as *Poems for Workers* (1927) and little magazines such as Jack Conroy's *Rebel Poet*. Within this milieu, the awarding of the 1935 Yale Younger Poets Prize to Muriel Rukeyser's *Theory of Flight*—with its opening lyric's admonition, "Not Sappho, Sacco"—may have marked a shift away from high-modernist lyricism, but it also reiterated that communist content could be successfully integrated with established modes of writing. The shadow that Rolfe's poems cast on the present unsettles what Anne Janowitz describes as the "lyric hegemony," codified by Mill in the 1840s and reiterated by modern and contemporary critics, which determined the Romantic lyric "as a secure poetic infrastructure for the transcendent self of lyric solitude." For more contemporary critics, Rolfe's poems have come to represent possibilities for lyric as, to borrow Janowitz's formulation, "a theatre of engagement for competing and alternate versions of personal, political, and cultural identity."[18] As Walter Kalaidjian writes, "Rolfe's repression haunts the political unconscious of American poetics as a specter of revolutionary social forces that are no longer culturally permitted within the public sphere."[19] But just what is "no longer permitted" in the contemporary conjuncture? Is it revolutionary content per se? Or revolutionary content tuned to the lyric mode? The condition and horizon of possibility for Rolfe's lyrics is the inevitable end of capitalism. Caught in the tumultuous present of the Depression years, his poems present a subject suspended in a moment of crisis; but, in their very assuredness of an imminent revolution, they ultimately reassert the terms of Romantic lyrical agency against the new totality of the coming communism.

The publication and reception of Rolfe's *To My Contemporaries* highlights a fraught moment in the history of the lyric's relation to leftist politics. Rolfe's readers in the left press attempted to maintain the category of lyric, even when the poems in *To My Contemporaries* pressed against its bounds. Mike Gold, for example, defended the importance of Rolfe's lyric poems by arguing that they were weapons useful for inviting reflection and keeping alive "a spirit of faith and wonder."[20] Gold, like fellow *New Masses* editor Joseph Freeman, based his understanding of lyric in a revolutionary Romantic tradition that was skeptical of the "doggerel" promoted in certain sectors of the cultural left.

Gold's comments are part of a wider debate about the place and function of lyric in relation to anticapitalist struggle that includes the foregoing commentaries by Rahv and Schneider as well as ongoing dialogues in magazines such as *New Masses*, *Partisan Review*, and *Dynamo*. For example, a short satirical piece called "The Love Campaign," adapted by Stephen Foster from the Soviet journal the *Crocodile* and published in the May–June 1935 issue of

Dynamo, aimed to extend "the horizon of revolutionary poetry beyond the sectarian limitation of journalese verse" in advance of discussions about poetic form planned for the upcoming American Writers' Congress. The story's protagonist, Kenneth Edwin Haze (surely a conglomerate of Kenneth Fearing, Edwin Rolfe, and Alfred Hayes), is asked by the editor of the fictional magazine *Left Pass* to write "something lyrical. About the Spring . . . magnolias . . . love" because, after all, "Communists are not machines but men who live full lives." Haze's first draft of his "lyric poem about love"—about two people sitting on a bench together and gazing at the moon—is met with skepticism by his "Responsible Editor," who has no "ideological objections" to park benches but insists on knowing just who is sitting on the bench because "the important thing is their social origin." What is more, he asks, "Why should they waste their time gazing at the moon? . . . Let's say they were on their way to a meeting. Suddenly there was a terrific cloudburst and they seated themselves on the bench." With that advice, the Responsible Editor sends Haze off to finish the poem, which is to be no longer than sixteen lines.[21]

Adapting the *Crocodile* piece for the U.S. context, Foster and the *Dynamo* editors disclose their own narrow definition of lyric—that is, that "lyric" denotes a short first-person poem (no longer than sixteen lines!) that eschews realist description in order to express timeless universals of human experience such as love. At one point in the story, we learn that Haze "had been secretly writing lyrical odes." He concealed them out of fear "that his endeavours were ideologically criminal" because "the poems contained no timely date." The moral of the story, it would seem, is that the modality of the lyric cannot be made political by cramming it with social content. Indeed, the dejected Haze ultimately composes a lyric that negates each movement of his first draft. It is this poem that is printed on the front page of *Left Pass*:

> More Power to Love
>
> A Note on a Note on a Note
> There was no bench, there was no moon,
> There were no birds, no flowers,
> They did not kiss, they did not spoon,
> They utilized the hours.
> She said, "I finished my report."
> And he replied, "I'm glad."
> They rose . . . and turned to go away,
> For everything was . . . said.[22]

The apparent point of "The Love Campaign" it to expose the limits of proletarian verse. We are left with nothing because "everything was . . . said," and this state of affairs is, as the final off-rhyme hints, a sad one. What this satire of left poetic culture ends up exposing is how the hegemony of the Romantic lyric imposed an interpretive limit for readers who insisted on the potential political efficacy (or, at least, acceptability) of lyric. The joke misses the more complex zone of possibilities that thirties communist poets such as Rolfe, Fearing, and Hayes negotiated through their play within a lyric frame. This point is borne out in the pages of the very same issue of *Dynamo*, which included lyric poems such as Rolfe's "To My Contemporaries," Fearing's "Denoument," and Rukeyser's "Poem out of Childhood."

By focusing on the manifest content of lyric poems, the fictional editors of *Left Pass* and the real editors of *Dynamo* misconceive the horizon toward which the moon-loving couple and, through them, the poet gazes. "The Love Campaign," like the reception of Rolfe's *To My Contemporaries*, evinces confusion about the historical and political logics possible for the lyric mode within the Depression-era communist left. This is perhaps no more apparent than in readings of Rolfe's poem "Credo," which opens the volume by renouncing "the fiction of the self":

> To welcome multitudes—the miracle of deeds
> performed in unison—the mind
> must first renounce the fiction of the self
> and its vainglory. It must pierce
> the dreamplate of its solitude, the fallacy
> of its omnipotence, the fairytale
> aprilfools recurring every day
> in speeches of professors and politicians.[23]

"Credo" is continually read as a lyrical poem that repudiates the bourgeois foundations of the lyric. In a review of *To My Contemporaries* for *New Masses*, Freeman praised the manner in which "Credo" renounced the fiction of bourgeois selfhood underwriting lyric expression while describing the poem as a "serene lyric animated by faith in the workers' struggle for a socialist society." Freeman wrote that "Credo" gave "poetic reality" to "the central idea of the revolutionary movement" with a "freshness of phrase, melody, and irresistible feeling"; the poem indicated "a sense of solidarity with his [Rolfe's] contemporaries in revolutionary literature . . . as distinguished from the lone singing of the isolated poet."[24] In this reading, the content of Rolfe's poem exemplifies the emergent historical need to represent and understand processes of revolutionary subject formation. "Poetic reality" is distinguished from "reality" per se as a "truth" of revolutionary feeling that is relational rather than purely subjective. By introducing communist content, "Credo" extracts qualities typically associated with lyric (serenity, melody, the expression of feeling) and reactivates them to rouse a new political collective.

The assuredness with which "Credo" announces that one must "renounce the fiction of the self" in order to imagine its replacement by a formation of selves unified in "a common cause" is something of a red herring that distracts from the more complex negotiations at work in the poem and in *To My Contemporaries*. "Credo" does not reject the lyric so much as it lyricizes the creed, a formal statement of beliefs or aims. Nonetheless, Freeman praised Rolfe's poems as "revealing a gift for expressing abstract ideas lyrically."[25] Freeman's formulation suggests the hermeneutic impasse that Virginia Jackson describes as the closed circle of lyric reading, whereby "the reading of the lyric produces a theory of the lyric that then produces a reading of the lyric, and that hermeneutic circle rarely opens to dialectical interruption."[26] Freeman, we might say, redraws the hermeneutic circle of lyric reading with a red pen: so that even if a given poem's political content effects a dialectical interruption of the lyric mode, this possibility is ultimately foreclosed because the poem is recognized as lyric and then interpreted as such.

Freeman's reading does not address the potentials opened by the content of *To My Contemporaries*. One way out of this lyric tautology is developing an account of how lyric, as an object produced by the practice of lyric reading, was irreparably shaped by the historical horizons of the Depression. In the early thirties, communist poets such as Rolfe wrote from a militant belief that they were entering the final stages of history—socialism and communism—as Marx had outlined in *The Communist Manifesto*. As such, Rolfe's poems fill the open antagonisms of his moment with fantasies of their inevitable resolution in the future. "We toiled for ourselves and all our other selves," he writes in "Testament to a Flowering Race," "transmuting stone to gold / transcribing fantasy to actuality."[27] Poems such as "Testament to a Flowering Race" seem suspended in the processes of toiling, transmuting, and transcribing. At the same time, they assert that the totality of the historical dialectic can be grasped in the present. What results is a reassertion of lyrical agency on a changed historical and political ground.

In this way, Rolfe's poetry might be even more like Eliot's than Gold or Freeman thought: both poets prompt questions about the place of lyric in history as well as about where and how history might take place within the structure of the lyric. C. D. Blanton uses the phrase "Eliotic Marxism" to describe Eliot's engagements with Marxist dialectical thought in the late 1920s and early 1930s.[28] Holding onto the suspicion that Marxism can be Eliotic, what we might discern instead is a small army of Marxist Eliots. A number of communist writers riffed on Eliot's poems, including Sol Funaroff, who wrote a version of "What the Thunder Said" that replaced *The Waste Land*'s "Datta . . . Dayadvham . . . Damyata" (the principal values of giving, compassion, and control outlined in the Upanishads) with the exclamatory "Thalatta! Thalatta!" (the shout of "The Sea! The Sea!" let out by ten thousand Greeks marching away from battle against the Persian empire). The fragments shored against the ruins of capitalist culture are constantly moving, awaiting future synthesis. Thus, Funaroff's "What the Thunder Said: A Fire Sermon" opens with scattered papers, a stammering and stuttering that is

> awaiting what code,
> what code to translate
> Capital, Famine, Predatory War,
> into what dialectic odyssey
> the machine gun's riveting shall inscribe—
> the Leatherjacket fatally indite?[29]

Like Rolfe's poems, Funaroff's evoke an atmosphere of assured waiting, in which the "code" to translate the problems of the present capitalist crisis will arrive and the "dialectic odyssey" toward pure communism will begin. In Funaroff's "Fire Sermon," the syllables "Da Da Da" are the sounds of machine guns, and the thunder's rumbling anticipates a burning world.

In Rolfe's poetry, the focal point for the charged ground of the present is the mind, which he figures as a space that holds revolutionary potentials. To return to "Credo," the lyric "I" is not replaced by the plural "we" signifying the masses but by the "It" that signifies the mind. Throughout *To My Contemporaries*, the poet's mind mediates the dialectical replacement of "self" with "multitude" and "lone singing" with "solidarity." In "Homage to Karl Marx," the sweep of revolutionary history is imaged in "the huge sweeping movement" of Marx's "brain." The poem's first section expresses the certainty of "victory" for the "accumulate power" of the "mass" and then turns, in the second section, to a more direct homage:

> In his great rooms, the countries of the world—his
> cumulative fatherland—how many candles guttered
> unnoticed? the huge sweeping movement of his brain
> (rooted in poverty, love as great as deep

as he was poor) unhindered? How many hands,
dripping with blood, the torment of numberless men,
crept across boundaries at night, the fingers feeling their way
into his moments of peace? (the prophet grappling with worlds,
suspended between
  yet rooted in both
    the old and the new)
left him at last, broken in strength, to die—[30]

Envisioning "numberless men" creeping "across boundaries at night" while Marx toils at his philosophies, the poet uses the singular figure of Marx as a means to imagine a revolutionary possibility, the borderless world ruled by the masses, that exists adjacent to the present.

Like "Credo" and "Homage to Karl Marx," the eponymous closing poem locates revolutionary agency in the space of the mind. At the time of publication, Rolfe's readers viewed "To My Contemporaries" as distinct from other poems in the volume. Freeman faulted the final poem for limiting the opening vision of "Credo" to a series of communications between the few revolutionary poets named in the poem. Freeman may be right that "the fiction of the self and its vainglory and the fallacy of its omnipotence are too old to be abrogated in a day by lyrical fiat"; but what he ultimately gets wrong is that there is not much of an ideological difference between "Credo" and "To My Contemporaries."[31] In both poems, constructs and metaphors related to "mind" and "brain" demonstrate how Rolfe used the lyric mode to mediate an individual subject's relationship to an imminent communist future.

The first of the three sections that compose "To My Contemporaries" describes a connection between political despair and the poet's doubts about his writing practice. Reminiscent of Eliot's "fragments shored against ruins," he has ceased to be "master" of his poem and feels doubtful that he can "synthesize" his "fragmentary feelings." Such doubt is extrapolated in the poem's second section, as the fragments that the poet is attempting to synthesize are events announced by *Daily Worker* headlines. Imagining that he is speaking to Funaroff, he asks,

But where's the victory?
I read in the Daily Worker the other day:
the Chinese peasants seizing arms and bread,
in Mexico they fashion dolls of clay,
chimneys spout red leaflets in Berlin,
Italian flyers bomb the land with calls

116 Chapter Three

> Of *Avanti poplo!* and in England a poet quits ancestral halls
> to call for the knife, *the major operation.*
>
> The Indians are dying on their reservations,
> black men are lynched, the jobless legions creep
> from day to hungry day, driven from railway stations.
> We have no place to sleep.[32]

The antidote to the weariness of the *Daily Worker* headlines is the imagination of a face-to-face encounter between a poet and a woman in a New York City subway. The encounter produces a fantasy of understanding in which the poet "could say everything" to the woman "without a word," but nonetheless "she would understand." Similar fantasies of identification are prevalent throughout *To My Contemporaries*, such as in the antilynching poem "Georgia Nightmare," in which the spectacle of the lynched body prompts the poet's revelation, "The black man looks like me."[33] "To My Contemporaries" suggests that "the fugitive fragments of an earlier self" must be surrendered to the memories of these faces and the communities they portend. This involves overcoming the alienation that would

> create a village-suburb in the brain;
> partition the skull, decree which part
> shall live, observe, feel joy and pain,
> and which vast area grow dulled,
> the senses, all awareness, killed.

The partitioned brain is replaced in the poem by the community of revolutionary poets who enter together "the farthest regions / of space and time," imagined as

> the brain surveying
> the contours of the land, destroying
> the cancerous trees and men, restoring
> the spark to bodies overwhelmed
> by drudgery and dross and dust.[34]

The end of "To My Contemporaries" reinforces the centrality of the mind and returns the reader to the opening vision of a mind "renouncing the fiction of the self" in order to clear the way for future synthesis. In the final stanza, the disparate parts of the poem are synthesized within a "single self" who is attendant to the masses. The resulting formation "blazes the way" for a new world that the poets' "*minds* foresee" and their "poems celebrate."[35]

The move from the image of a partitioned brain (an alienated self) to the brain surveying the land (an actualized self) represents the development of revolutionary agency. This brain is supplanted by a reassertion of the Romantic mind that foresees the coming "new world." The minds in mutual understanding—be they a community of revolutionary poets or strangers on a subway—are joined together by a transmission of knowledge that is presumed to be unmediated. In the opening sequence of *Before the Brave*, Kenneth Patchen writes, "Chains and sickles have equal base / The mind behind the hand holds the gun."[36] If the poem is a weapon, we might read Patchen's statement as an assertion about the relationship between form and content, or even form and intent. All guns take the same form—what matters is whom the gun is pointed at. By this logic, Rolfe's poems can be "lyrical" without being "lyrics." The mind behind the hand that holds the pen imagines the poem as a synapse, where the changed content of the poem travels along the unchanged syntax of lyric.

Was Gold right to say that in certain hands the lyric solidified into a cold, metal weapon? As my reading of Rolfe demonstrates, writers have attended to the semantic content of left lyrics at the expense of their syntactical innovations. The etymological relationship between "synapse" and "syntax" provides a means to understand the possibilities for lyric that Rolfe's poems open as well as foreclose. Both words share the prefix *syn-* from the Greek *sun*, or "together." "Synapse" is from *haptein*, or "join," while "syntax" is from *tassein*, or "arrange." The logic of the synapse, of joining, conceptualizes the melding of the collective against a temporal space that encompasses present and future, filling the gap created by the scission of historical antagonisms with fantasies about the future. By contrast, the logic of syntax, of arrangement, resists such prescriptions and focuses instead on the multiple horizons of possibility opening in the conflicts of the present. Communist writers such as Taggard and Rolfe both worked to reform a predominant tradition of lyric, but, as we will see, they used varying formal approaches. Schematizing their strategies as synaptic versus syntactic demonstrates how different formal approaches to the same historical antagonisms change how we think about the development of lyric in the thirties.

Communists among the Romantics: How to Read Walt Whitman

Rolfe's use of the lyric mode to express a utopian vision of a communist future branded him a "revolutionary Romantic." Taggard, by contrast, rejected the notion that the Romantic tradition offered anything for the present revolutionary movement. In her 1934 *New Masses* essay "Romanticism and Communism," Taggard argued that the "proper function of poetry" might only be comprehended "after the false principle of the individual, a little universe sealed away from all the rest of life, has been ridiculed to death." She asked, "Should the poetry about to be born belong to the Romantic Family?"—and then decidedly answers, *no*. The "Romantic Family," she asserts, is surely a "bourgeois" one; the future communist poetry must reject a Romantic inheritance that she traces from Rousseau to Shelley, Whitman, and T. S. Eliot because to believe that the Romantic thinker or artist "expresses our revolutionary meaning today is nonsense."[37] *The New Masses* editors, in an uncharacteristic move, appended a note to Taggard's essay faulting her for contrasting Romanticism with communism without defining clearly the former term. "Obviously she means bourgeois Romanticism," they aver, suggesting the possibilities of a "'revolutionary romanticism'—a poem, story, or play projecting a vision of a socialist society: an outgrowth of the dialectical forces perceived in the present breakdown of capitalism." Thus, while the editors agreed with Taggard that forms of modernist literature such as Dadaism, Objectivism, and Futurism are the present-day inheritors of bourgeois Romanticism, they contest her blanket dismissal of the tradition.[38]

At stake in defining and promoting any one version of Romanticism was not the historical or literary record of the period but rather the political and aesthetic ideologies for which it stood. Renouncing Romanticism as bourgeois or claiming it as revolutionary was part of a complex process whereby period descriptions could be translated into, and then promoted as, a political aesthetic. More specifically, Taggard's rejection of the Romantic inheritance—her own or anyone's—in "Romanticism and Communism" was an important strategy for theorizing lyric self-expression as well as ideas about personhood that were attached to it. Building on Janowitz's contention that "the literary and analytical bridge between the social historian's and the moral philosopher's version of [the Romantic period] is built from the stuff of lyric poetry," we might say that Taggard's polemics against Romanticism are integral to understanding the formation of the poetic lyric in relation to the global economic depression of the 1930s.[39] If it is true that the concept of "lyric" predominant in modern criticism has been projected onto Romanticism and mobilized as a way of understanding lyric poetry, then Taggard's theorization of a political lyric in opposition to Romanticism provides an important alternative discourse that potentially reframes the relationship posited between lyric expression and the Romantic imagination.[40]

Taggard's description of Romanticism in "Romanticism and Communism," if not consistent with how the left cultural leaders at *New Masses* would have described it, was in line with other accounts circulating at the time. Her sense that modernist poetry was an outgrowth of Romanticism mirrors Edmund Wilson's point in *Axel's Castle* (1931) that early-twentieth-century poetic movements were a "counterpart" to Romanticism, "a second flood of the same tide." Wilson, like Taggard, opposed a Romanticism that celebrated individual subjectivity to a prior classicism that was more interested in producing objective portraits of society as a whole.[41] Wilson's denouncement shares with Carl Schmitt's arguments in *Political Romanticism* (1919) that "political romanticism" is a form of "occasionalism"—that is, the use of historical and political events as "the occasion for subjective creativity." Romanticism thus has no relation to left politics or to revolution because "the isolated and absolute ego is elevated above both and uses both as an occasion."[42] Taggard echoed such sentiments in "Romanticism and Communism," arguing that Romantic poetry was nothing but a celebration of individual creativity that was divorced from the political realm. For her, the notion that "man is essentially good and potentially perfectible has been fully exploited by capitalism."[43] Not unlike Schmitt, Taggard posits that Romanticism bears no revolutionary potential and "prepares the way for the triumph of liberalism."[44]

Taggard's rejection of the Romantic-modernist tradition does not amount to a wholesale rejection of the lyric mode. Like Rolfe, Taggard reconfigured lyric according to her communist politics. At the same time, Taggard rebuked the notion that a lyric tradition based in Whitman could be the basis for communist poetry. As left culture gained influence during the Depression, it was Whitman who provided a usable model for how to say "I" in a poem. In a 1946 Communist Party edition of Whitman's poetry, Langston Hughes insisted that Whitman's "I" was not "introspective" but "the cosmic 'I' of all peoples who seek freedom, decency, and dignity, friendship and equality between individuals and races all over the world."[45] While communist poets faulted Whitman for his belief in political democracy, they salvaged the forms he innovated as a means to represent a range of persons and positions. Gold named the gray bard a "spiritual forefather" of the proletarian movement and argued that Whitman's poetry intuited a socialist democratic vision that was more radical than his actual politics.[46] Rolfe's poem "Catalogue of I" (1955) employs a Whitmanesque catalogue of places and persons in an effort to synthesize multiple subject positions. Rolfe's poem is not as pluralist as Whitman's catalogues because it gestures toward a hard choice: "Who fears inclusion in this catalogue of I," Rolfe writes, "Is useless, valueless, deserves to die." Yet, the poem ends democratically, asserting that the speaker's "doomed and unloved brother, / Is also I, is also I."[47]

Even though Rolfe's poem was written during the fifties, it suggests how Whitman's influence permeated thirties revolutionary poems. In Lechlitner's response to Rolfe's assessment of political poetry, published as part of a forum in a 1935 issue of *Partisan Review*, she compared Whitman and John Greenleaf Whittier to explain the available options for writing revolutionary poetry. For her, Whitman "understood the immediate problems of his day; but he saw also above and beyond them." By contrast, most revolutionary poets took a position "similar to that of Whittier who, as compared to Whitman's larger view, found a subject in his concern for the abolition of slavery. The Whittiers, of course, play a necessary part. . . . But if a poet is to leave more than a 'fragmentary mark' on his time, he must have a more embracing conception that may act as a standard or guide by which to measure his themes."[48] Reading Rolfe's poem along Lechlitner's lines, we might say that Rolfe is a better version of Whitman because the transcendent vision of Rolfe's poems is shaped by the utopian horizon of communism rather than the cosmos. But if we turn more concertedly to the form of the catalogue, we might discern how the commitment to Whitman's forms translates to a commitment to political democracy. As Wai-Chee Dimock makes clear, the syntax of Whitman's poem—that is, its grammar, its use of catalogues with substitutable parts—is the foundation of Whitman's view and expression of the subject. Whitman's "Song of Myself," Dimock demonstrates, works through a process of "accumulation and divestment" in which the self is removed from all contingencies so that it can be defined against them "until it is purified into no more than an idea, an empty form, but, for that very reason, a form of transcendent dignity."[49]

In "Night Letter to Walt Whitman," the poem that opens Taggard's 1936 *Calling Western Union*, Taggard offers a critique of Whitman's "noncontingent poetics," which also creates a "noncontingent" form of selfhood, through the syntactical arrangements of her own poem. In it, she fuses the printed page and the radio wave to criticize Whitman's fantasy of commerce between poet and reader. "Night Letter" questions the proletarian championing of the nineteenth-century bard as the poet of the masses by formulating Whitman's "I" as an effect of democratic-capitalist expansion. The poem trades celebratory images of the proletariat for an urban cityscape where earth's horizon line idiotically smiles on "radio-infested rooms," "deranged cities," and "deadlocked farms." The industrial landscape rendered in the poem is characteristic of the *Dynamo* group, and it resists unifying the natural and mechanized, the cityscape and the landscape. For Taggard, Romantic tropes of nature are no longer sufficient for synthesizing disparate parts within a vanishing, but always present, transcendent center; and she replaces the fusion of city/land with a different desire:

> They are brother and sister City and land   They are sick   I think
> They are going to die   I swear I want another pair
> A swarthy sister with strawberry mouth   I say
> Another smelling of new-mown hay and the fur of cattle[50]

The "I" emerges in this passage, which occurs about halfway through the poem, to arrange the coordinates of the poem's political vision in a different manner than a Whitman-like "I" that would fix various diverse parts in the creation of a structured network of meaning. Taggard's "I" is pushed to the end of each line and so is folded into the breaks between each. By presenting the "I" as both an afterthought and a hinge from one thought to the next, the poem leaves possibilities for thinking, swearing, wanting, and saying open-ended. The "I" is not a stabilized signifier; rather, it exists in a zone of interference between the actualities of the "sick" pair of city and land and the possibilities for that other pair—the strawberry-mouthed sister and her twin smelling of new-mown hay. The formal enfolding of the "I" in the enjambment represents lyric expression as an effect of an outside historical reality that also incorporates a speculative thought.

Representing the "I" in this way, Taggard also rethinks the relationship between poet, poem, and reader that Whitman dubs "commerce." "Night Letter" reinforces the ways that *Calling* draws on tropes and technologies of communication, both because it is a letter and because of its references to radio signals. But these technologies scramble the coordinates of reality rather than present them as a possible or coherent whole. Near the end of "Night Letter," Taggard expresses her desire for "images of order," but they are scattershot transmissions, enacted in the poem through irregular spacing:

> I want the well-curried coat of the meadow again
>
> And images of order   plenty   equal work with ease
> The combine harvester   clever gigantic   slim elms
> Lilacs manifold   orchards pruned   fences gone trespass antique
> The sister's arm around the city the   athlete boy
> Clean able quick   Both lavish with good and peace

While the coordinates for a changed social reality exist in the fragmented messages coming through the radio at night, they are still in the process of being reformulated. And so "Night Letter" does not end with clear singing or saying but with the production of senseless babble:

> Bla Bla
> The radio coos   lies   blather dope
> On the   bad land
> The thistle
> Scatters
> Wrong[51]

Taggard reduces the communiqués between the poet and Whitman to "blas," "coos," and "lies." The final lines—"The thistle / Scatters / Wrong"—are broken so as to produce ambiguous meanings. The thistle is scattered and not collected and, therefore, is arranged wrongly. When it does scatter, presumably to sow seeds, it sows "wrong" rather than "right." "Wrong" is placed in its own line; the word draws attention to itself in a way that foregrounds error—the error of scattering perhaps—over hope and the possibility of democratic unity. In this situation, the early-twentieth-century appropriation of Whitman's address, invoked in such texts as William Carlos Williams's *Spring and All* (1923), is untenable.[52] Taggard's "Night Letter" is ultimately a document of interrupted or failed communication. Contemplating how attempts at communication devolve into "blas" and "coos," Taggard breaks up the lyric's privileging of the represented voice, and through the image of scattering wrongs, she questions the presumption that the "I" can become one with the reader to whom it speaks.

Taggard's critique of Whitman is emphasized later in *Calling Western Union* in "Adding Up America—*You Try*," a parody of the catalogue. The trick of "Adding Up America" is that nothing quite adds up; the poem resists Whitman's logic of the multitude and suggests instead different possible arrangements based in antagonism. While the poem is presented in the title as a provocation, it is Taggard's own attempt to make a list of "America." She tries to do it quickly from memory: "Take time to think of fifty; then you must stop and add . . . Get it all down in a jiffy. If you wait it is gone," she writes in the poem's first lines, "Here is my list. I remember too many to write."[53] The poem continues by playing on these opening gestures: adding up elements of America (from a "Vermont farmer named Stark" to "Coolies with the Black Plague" to "cranky" women in hot kitchens) with a mocking tone. Taggard's self-conscious adding in "Adding Up America," reinforced by the presence of an "adding machine" that "clicks," follows the critique of the expansive Whitmanian self in "Night Letter." As Dimock explains, the effect of Whitman's catalogues is the creation of a self that is "endlessly renewed by its procedures, a self whose perennial innocence translates into democratic largesse, a self always open to new experience but always unencumbered by that experience."⁵⁴ Taggard uses Whitman's syntax—the list—to introduce different semantic content. Whitman's syntactic subject contrasts with the semantic subject that, "clogged with connotations of the past, . . . is made unwieldy by the weight of memory, antecedence, and context."⁵⁵ Taggard, in contrast, opens with the weight of memory: "Your memory different from mine: but they make the same total."⁵⁶

But if the poem opens with the notion that whoever tries to "add up America" will end up with "the same total," it ends with reorienting the very attempt:

> Will you add up America for all of us, pretty girl? Can you add quickly?
> Up to a million? Who cares? Would you jump if I scribbled
> *Comrade*, potential, in the margin?⁵⁷

In these final lines, Taggard moves from the logic of accumulation ("adding up") to the logic of antagonism. The simple question "Who cares?" bucks the ideal of disparate parts coming together evoked in the task of making a list. This task is presented as mechanical and laborious "play[ing] on an adding machine." What emerges at the end of the poem is the comrade who does not appear in the margin but who exists as a potential that might be scribbled in by the poet. Introducing the figure of the marginal comrade, Taggard introduces a different system that does not "add up" but that suggests the potential for a new arrangement of the list's disparate parts. Rethinking Whitman, Taggard complicates attempts to represent poetically individual subjects as well as potentials for "group life" or "the common good."

Lyric Transgressions

Taggard's rereading of Whitman is part of her broader attempt to reconceive formally the relationship of the individual to the group in relation to specific historical and material antagonisms. The extensive framing materials that Taggard incorporated into *Calling Western Union*, including an autobiographical preface meant to serve as "a frame for the verse" and a series of prose "Note Books" that explicated her views of the poetic tradition and her prescriptions for political poetry, further illuminate the ways in which the individual poems demonstrate social relations and antagonisms. Through autobiographical explication, Taggard positions her individual development within a framework of capitalist social relations, most evident in her descriptions of the damages wrought by the individualistic, "pioneer" spirit of her family in western Washington State as opposed to the communities she found as a child in Hawaii and as an adult activist in Vermont.

The way Taggard imagines these new relations is evident in the prose and poetry that open the second portion of *Calling Western Union*. In "Note Book I," the volume's first short prose passage, and in "Funeral in May," the poem immediately following it, Taggard further theorizes new modes of expression and address through an imagination of a poet's death. In both pieces, the death of a poet becomes symbolic for the figurative death of a condition for poetry as well as the social order that had sustained it. "Note Book I" continues the arguments that Taggard began in "Romanticism and Communism," identifying one of the main assumptions hindering the development of revolutionary poetry: "the romantic notion that the individual is capable of godlike perfection." "This is poison food," she writes, "and those who eat it die a lingering and pallid death. But before he dies the poet repeats the doctrine that poisoned him. He feeds his audience on the gigantic fiction of a Free Personality."[58] "Funeral in May" plays out this idea by describing the death of a poet and an elaborate funeral dance carried out by a group of "infidels." The poem deserves to be read allegorically as the death of Romantic and modern artistic practices and their replacement by new modes of song and singing. But the death in the poem seems less the death of poetry itself than a reference to the finitude of capitalist modes of relation.

"Funeral in May" begins at the deathbed of a worn-out poet. This poet imagines himself as Christ-like—a self-declared "mouthpiece of the divine" whose "voice starts from the throat in gold song / in the breathing peace of the lord." But, try as he might, God has eluded him. He has been "forsaken by metaphor" and damned to the worst of fates: "to be literal literal." In his dying gasp, he begs, "Lovely metaphor, redeem me from sin / and deliver us from meaning." "Then he died," the poem succinctly declares, "snap like any business man / worry overstrain / burst a blood vessel."[59] The imagined death of a poet in "Funeral in May" is but one of many examples of how radical Depression-era poets mobilized the trope of death in order to figure how poetry might be reformed to serve new political functions. At the close of *Exile's Return*, for instance, Malcolm Cowley posits that the decadent modernist poet Harry Crosby's 1929 suicide became an emblem for the defunct notion that art "was purposeless, useless, wholly individual and forever opposed to the stupid world."[60] The figure of the dead poet might be seen to serve multiple functions in Taggard's poem. Perhaps he is a model of an authoritarian modernist figure (a representative of what Taggard referred to in another poem as the "Sick Generation") whose death signifies a break with coteries and aesthetics that she associates with 1920s high modernism. Or he might be seen as representative of a dying Romantic tradition, in which "individual grandeur" trumps the "common good."

The figuration of the poet's death in "Funeral in May" marks a shift in configurations of lyric expression and address. The poem opens by putting to rest the straw man for the Romantic conception of lyric, in which lyric is rooted in the individual ego (whether that be the Romantic or the modernist genius). In "Funeral in May," the figure of the solitary poet is literally written over, when the infidels use the dead poet's mirror to mark his grave, scrawling his epitaph in the space where his image would have appeared:

> Set here for his grave-stone
> His perfect companion the mirror. Put it here out of doors,
> In its blank write his epitaph out. Newsreel our day.
> Let windy leaves toss in its flash.
> When we gather fresh laurel
> Blow blasts on the factory whistle. Ring loud early bells.
> Dance in the meadows
> young and old
> stalwart and swarthy.[61]

Using the mirror for a gravestone is, at first, a bit of a joke. Calling the mirror the poet's "perfect companion," the poem pokes fun at his narcissism and solipsism. But this gesture takes a more serious turn when the "voice of the infidel" gives the command to write out "Newsreel our day" in the mirror blank. The act of filling in the blank space where the dead poet's image would have appeared effectively replaces the individual poet with the very historical realities he tried to avoid and transcend.

The funeral that Taggard stages takes place in a metaphoric meadow that, while overshadowed by the space of the factory, also does not heed its bells. In the last section of "Funeral in May," "the voice of the infidel" commands,

> Turn funeral to fete.
> Here we inter folly
> Gluttonous villainy stupidity the vanity of man.
> Again and again we must dance on the grave of this death
> Beating down with determined feet what is already dead;

> Weeds growing here will wear to rags where we step.
> Dance
>   it is May
>   of all Mays the gayest with promise.
> You who are skilled with the songs lead the way with your singing.[62]

These last lines suggest how the imagined death of a poet, and thus a paradigm for a particular poetics, provides a productive space for crafting a new radical poetics. This is apparent in the double meanings of "Here we inter folly." The poem reiterates the literal act of interring (of placing in a grave) the dead poet and thus the follies of an irrelevant poetic culture. But "inter" also suggests a state of transition between the death of one paradigm and the birth of another. "Folly" here might not just refer to the senseless practices represented by the dead poet but also to an ornate structure serving no practical purpose. This meaning of "folly" emphasizes how the "infidels" are burying the notion that poetry does not have a practical political function. It is especially significant, then, that the funeral-turned-fete takes place in May, considering the month's association with the May Day parades that celebrated working-class solidarity.

Most significantly, the poem ends with a command that allows us to understand a key formal innovation of Depression-era radical poetics: "You who are skilled with the songs lead the way with your singing." In this line, Taggard's poem begins to chart a shift from an individuated lyric "I," modeled on bourgeois forms of subjectivity, to an emerging address to a collective "you" in the process of formation. "Funeral in May" contains a lyric mode of address, as it addresses a group "you." At stake is not just how the "you" is invoked but who is speaking to that "you." At the moment of the "poor poet's" death, the "voice of the infidel," not unlike the comrade scribbled in the margin of "Adding up America," enters and issues the command to "Bury the poet deep in his words." This infidel speaks to the others in the poem; but this "voice" also calls out to, and therefore implicates, the reader. While it might seem counterintuitive to read a poem such as "Funeral in May" in relation to lyric, the poem works out a critique of lyric through the death of the bourgeois poet and the address to a plural "you" that emerges in his wake, suggesting the reemergence, or reinvention, of lyric on changed ground rather than its complete eradication.

What Taggard begins to accomplish in "Funeral in May" is in the spirit of how she described her lyric poems in 1938, but there are some fundamental differences. On the back flap of her 1938 *Collected Poems*, Taggard stressed a different form of identification between poet and reader. She explains that she "tried to use the 'I' in a poem only as a means of transferring feeling to identification with anyone who takes the poem, momentarily, for his own. 'I' is then adjusted to the voice of the reader."[63] In this way, Taggard claims that her poems can have "effects": the adjustments in the poem work to create an affective community.[64] Rather than merely interrupting lyric's solipsism by positing an "adjusted" identification between poet and reader, "Funeral in May" foregrounds a second-person "you" that is, in effect, a political community in the process of formation. In Taggard's logic, the "you" is not merely a fictive placeholder—an imagined audience that is, in the end, the poet's own voice echoing back to her. Rather, the "you" is a modification of the speaking "I": a material body that is called on to replace the "I" with a collective singing that eschews the "individualistic absolutism" that Taggard associates with the Romantic tradition.

The rhetoric of "the people" that was ubiquitous in midthirties artistic and popular culture prompts us to read Taggard's revision of the lyric's "I/you" relationship at the close of "Funeral in May" as a reversal of the dominant form of modern lyric, which supposes that the "I" speaking to "you" is primarily a conduit for the poet's emotions and meditations.[65] At the same time, "Funeral in May" complicates readings of Depression-era poems that assume a relatively uncomplicated shift from "I" to "we" and thus from personal to collective expression. In such readings, "we" either marks a "communal 'we'" that extrapolates the intimacies of the "I/you" dyad to a social scene or functions as a transcendent vantage point from which the writer can chart the political and historical terrain.[66] A good deal of Taggard's poems from the 1930s and 1940s take this tack: such as "Mass Song," which uses the third-person plural to express a common ground and to demarcate the boundaries between revolutionary hope and "delusive hope," and "Feeding the Children," which speaks for a community of women concerned with child welfare and ends with the refrain, "We must feed the children."

"Funeral in May" does not simply posit a communitarian shift from "I" to "we." The voice that speaks in "Funeral in May" does not just come from outside the poem—it is named an "infidel" voice that smuggles dissent into the scene. As in "Night Letter to Walt Whitman," this outside voice is disembodied: assuming an exterior position while ordering the poem's interiority. The infidel's voice in "Funeral in May" stages a struggle in the present, as the voice directs various movements of class antagonism. Taggard again restages Whitman's "I" by using a voice that is at once interior and exterior to the poem in order to portray a series of possible movements and conflicts that are ultimately the means through which new modes of subjectivity, collectivity, and class consciousness are formulated. In "Funeral in May," as the collective dances and sings in the ambiguous shadow of the factory, ignoring but also acknowledging the factory bells, Taggard positions collective expression within embodied historical realities. By creating a situated scene, in which the group represented by "we" gathers "fresh laurels" and dances "in the meadows" to the sounds of the factory's "whistle" and "early bells," Taggard frames the forming of the collective in relation to existing capitalist forces. The funeral-cum-fete takes place in a metaphoric meadow that is simultaneously penetrated by the space of the factory, even as the dancers do not heed its ways of marking time.

Rather than read *Calling Western Union* as an expansion of the "personal," "feminine" lyric of the twenties to more public writing that transmutes the "poetic line" to the "picket line" or "breadline," we might instead read it in terms of antagonism. Taggard may have been alone in her assessment that Whitman was not the harbinger of revolutionary poetics, but she was even more exceptional in her use of Emily Dickinson as a model for generating effective political lyrics. The development of Taggard's career from the twenties to the thirties coincides with the publication of her biographical study *The Life and Mind of Emily Dickinson*, a book so popular that it went into a second printing. Taggard found in Dickinson's poems a "double reality" that allowed her to reimagine the relationship between inner and outer existence.[67] In handwritten annotations for a second study of Dickinson, never published and tentatively titled "Emily Dickinson and Other Poets," Taggard wrote that Dickinson's "The wind begun to rock the grass" produced the "strange effect" of feeling "as if one were the whole universe and were in everybody."[68] The opening poem from Taggard's 1942 *Long View*, "To Arm You for This Time" (dated 1936–41), also uses the scattered seed as a metaphor for building collectives. "Hurry. / We are in / Battle," she writes. "Drop / The life personal, dry pod / Colored once, now drab, ready to split / To scatter seed."[69] Indeed, *Long View* begins with an epigraph from Dickinson—"My business is circumference"—that suggests a rejection of the line and of the modalities of transcendence that Whitman's long line suggests.

Importantly, Taggard continued to refer to herself as "primarily a lyric poet" at the heightened political moment of the early forties. During the twenties, she staunchly defended women's lyric poetry in a response to Amy Lowell's critiques of the "feminine movement," and she challenged the equation of "lyric" with "personal." In a 1925 essay published in the feminist magazine *Equal Rights*, Taggard dismissed distinctions between so-called objective and subjective poetry, arguing that modernist critics misconstrue "the driving force behind the whole lyric impulse." She writes, "An eternal feud between centripetal and centrifugal forces sunders and reunites all magical expression. There is one impulse for control and its antagonistic impulse for abandon, one pressing inward, the other exploding at the center. This battle holds the little atom of creative intensity almost quiet because of its balance. If either gains the upper hand entirely, the moment of creation is destroyed. To despise lyric poetry or call it personal—and this, I think, is what many people are doing when they say subjective—is to miss the point of its being uttered at all."[70] As Melissa Girard points out, Taggard's *Equal Rights* rejoinder appropriated "the 'masculine' discourse of science" to forge "yet another metaphor for this new lyric tradition" that is "held in the balance between a nineteenth-century subjective tradition" and "the objective poetics of Imagism and impersonality."[71] "Exploding" bears a relationship to the word "effects" that Taggard used in the 1940s: both terms suggest potentially antagonistic encounters between two forces that have ramifications for historical material realities.[72] By calling attention to how "subjective" was employed to describe lyrics written by women, Taggard's twenties essays also pointed to the conventional gendering of personal lyrics as feminine, an assumption that she and other women radicals would both mobilize and rebuke in their politically committed poems.[73]

To further exemplify this point, we might turn to Taggard's "At Last the Women Are Moving," oft cited as an example of Taggard's shift from the privacy of lyric to the more public form of the protest poem. Eschewing white male modernist traditions, Taggard, Nancy Berke writes, "literally takes her writing *out on the line*."[74] Such a movement is evinced in Taggard's depiction of female laborers leaving their homes for "the militant march." She asks, "How did these timid, the slaves of breakfast and supper / Get out in the line, drop for once dish-rag and broom?" While the poem never answers the question directly, it suggests that these women's intensive knowledge of the effects of labor on the body have pushed them to strike:

> Oh, but these who know in their growing sons and their husbands
> How the exhausted body needs sleep, how often needs food,
> These, whose business is keeping the body alive,
> These are ready, if you talk their language, to strike.[75]

Following Berke's and Bonnie Costello's logic, "At Last the Women Are Moving" can be understood in terms of simple dichotomies: as the women move from the private to the public sphere, they transmute the traditional poetic line to the reality of the breadline. The move from individual to collective is suggested in the final lines: "*Not for me and mine only. For my class I have come /*

To walk city miles with many, my will in our work."[76] Poems such as "At Last the Women Are Moving," however, cannot be so easily sorted according to the binaries of private/public or poetic line/breadline. One of Taggard's main concerns in "At Last the Woman Are Moving" is to problematize her subject position as a middle-class woman; but that intellectual work happens in a poem that considers the arrangement of bodies in a specific space and time. The poetic lines in "At Last the Women Are Moving" are not the lines of a chant to be repeated, nor are they just "metaphors" for other types of "lines" that represent social engagement.[77] Taggard alters the parameters of lyric expression in order to represent historical embodied relationships, opening the terms of lyric expression to a scene of historical antagonism.

Redefining Song

In a letter to the Marxist literary critic Granville Hicks, Taggard identified "Funeral in May" along with her poems "Definition of Song," "Image," "Remembering Vaughan," and "Lark" as her "legacy to the Left."[78] Taken together, these poems dramatize the importance of Taggard's metaphoric killing off of a forlorn poet cloaked in symbol and metaphor, and they suggest her new attention to representing the collective voice of the "infidels" who dance and sing "on the grave" of bourgeois poetic traditions.[79] Reviewing *Calling Western Union* in *New Masses*, the poet Rebecca Pitts described the range of genres Taggard employed to respond to the realities of thirties America: "The poems range from little satirical portraits of decay, through simple and moving records of poverty and sorrow, and militant chants of the masses, brave and unbeaten, to songs of the future which somehow clothe with emotional reality our dreams of collective living."[80] Within this range, perhaps the most prominent genre Taggard reworks is song. In "Funeral in May," the infidels' power and potential comes from the effect of their songs, as the poem ends with the command, "You who are skilled with the songs lead the way with your singing." Taggard's fete places us at an intermediate juncture where the meaning of lyric was being reconfigured through the concept of song.

Just as the "voice of the infidel" enters the scene in "Funeral in May" to coordinate the singers' movements, Taggard uses framing devices throughout *Calling Western Union* to conduct the volume's "revolutionary movements."[81] "Definition of Song," for example, frames the poem as a pedagogical act. The way the poem defines song for its audience in many ways outlines the argument that I present in its section. The poem begins with the importance of song as form:

Singing is best, it gives right joy to speech
Six years I squandered, studying to teach,
Expounding language. Singing it is better,
Teaching the joy of song, not teaching the letter.

Taggard's definition counterposes song with language. Language can communicate concepts such as "joy," but song affectively charges speech with "right joy." The syntactical construction of the second line suggests that when singing, the "I" assumes a less authoritative position. The "I" is placed in the middle of the line and is modified by "squandered" as if to intimate that the pronoun itself is wasted. The possibilities for community formation through collective participation in song are further elaborated when the poem argues that "of all forms of song surely the least / Is solo." It is here that, in defining (or redefining) song, Taggard explores the possibility of collective expression:

Singing is the work of many voices.
Only so when choral mass rejoices.
Is the lock sprung on human isolation
And all the many welded into one.[82]

The use of the choral to imagine collective voice was ubiquitous in Depression radical culture, especially in the shift from the Third Period to the Popular Front. Just as Taggard's use of the "I/you" dyad challenges readings of the Depression "we," her experimentation with song and choral demonstrates another permutation of the Depression lyric.

From the beginnings of the communist movement in 1919, "the form of poetry favored by U.S. Left activists and political leaders was very much in the tradition of workers' songs, ballads, and folk culture."[83] The ubiquity of popular song was part of the new historical dynamics of the Popular Front and the antifascist crusade. As pressure mounted for writers to create works that could quickly reach mass audiences, musicians felt the imperative to compose "accessible" songs for "unskilled singers." During the era of the Popular Front, left-wing musicians simplified their compositional styles and tried out more basic choral forms. This often meant that songs that were favored musically were not those best suited to a composer's political ends. Charles Seeger recalled that, in a 1934 competition for the best May Day song, sponsored by the radical Composers Collective, everyone in the collective "preferred Aaron Copland's setting of Alfred Hayes's 'Into the Streets May 1st.'" On the other hand, Seeger's own entry was deemed "much more singable": "This was, after all, a marching song, and what worker could carry a piano with him on a march?"[84]

In addition to "singability," which resembles "transparency," composers also focused on choral forms that invited mass participation. Choral and dance ensembles were prominent in Popular Front culture: the performance of choral music was both an occasional event and an experiment with new forms of group expression. To give one example, *No for an Answer* (Marc Blitzstein's follow-up to his wildly successful opera *The Cradle Will Rock*) made the "working-class chorus the narrative and musical center" of the production.[85]

Taggard's poems developed in relation to the circulation of these songs as part of radical Popular Front culture, and she was influenced by artists such as Blitzstein, Woody Guthrie, Paul Robeson, Earl Robinson, and Huddie William Ledbetter (Lead Belly). But rather than follow this line of association, we might take our cues from the former *Masses* editor Floyd Dell, who scolded Taggard for writing didactic verse. "Tut! Tut!" he reprimanded. "Edwin Markham can do it so much better—why show how badly you do it?"[86] Speaking to a New York student chorus in 1942, Taggard addressed the notion of artistic complexity in relation to the geopolitical realities of World War II. "How can I make sense of such complexities—for myself or for you? And in a few minutes when it takes years & years?" she asked, adding. those who study art seek to give people "pleasure, happiness, new energy, a sense of form."[87] The "sense of form" that Taggard explores vis-à-vis her choral pieces is obscured by arguments about accessibility, which elide the more nuanced questions of representation that these compositions raise. Taggard's thinking about song and musical composition suggests an inherent tension between the desire to write music for unskilled singers and the closing gesture of "Funeral in May," that those who are skilled in song lead the way. Taggard increasingly used the practice of musical composition to think through possibilities for lyric expression. The pleasure, happiness, and new energy that Taggard described in 1942 as "a sense of form" might thus be seen as the realization of the "right joy" of song that she gestures to in "Definition of Song."

Taggard's poem "Lark," which closes *Calling Western Union*, is one basis for her experiments with musical composition. The poem evokes "singing" as the act that will call forth "the great day-rise" of revolution, and the lark in the poem is a figure for a revolutionary singer. The poem's refrain "O Lark" recalls the fantasy of the lyric's origins in the orality of the "O" as well as the trope of the songbird. As text, "Lark" evokes a song without ever becoming one. Taggard wrote in *The Life and Mind of Emily Dickinson*, "The lark argues with God and we call it song. Emily wished to argue ... but she did not call it song. ... Even while she hummed, Emily did not call it a poem."[88] In this way, "Lark" suggests what Robert Kaufman identifies as the lyric's mode of "semblance."

Kaufman argues that the "unique character" of lyric is to "subjectivize" language, "affectively to stretch conceptuality's bounds in order to make something that seems formally like a concept but that does something that ordinary, 'objective' concepts generally do not do: sing." He goes on to suggest, "In lyric, semblance primarily involves making speech acts appear, feel, as if their very logic has compelled them somehow to burst—naturally, justifiably, as it were—into song." This effect of "bursting" "allows for a renewed sense of capacity or agency vis-à-vis materials that can eventually be grasped as reconceived or newly conceived sociopolitical, historical, or ethical content in the newly stretched form or formal capacity."[89]

"Bursting" is how one might describe Aaron Copland's setting of "Lark." Even though Taggard did not compose the poem to be set to music, it was set three times during the 1930s by three different composers. "Lark" has been called one of Copland's most exceptional compositions. Nick Strimple describes how the piece masterfully combines "typically open sonorities, the swaggering confidence of bright parallel triads, and jazzy rhythms, which at one point become so exuberantly complicated that the piece threatens to explode."[90] We might see Copland's choral setting as manifesting a fantasy that was already embedded in the poem, as creates the effect of bursting from the inside. As Taggard reflected, she did not write the poem "with the idea that it would be set to music or sung": "There was a primitive music in my own head when I wrote it, but when I finished the poem I closed that off as if to cut connections with chaos."[91] The "primitive music" that occasioned the poem is rendered as an actual musical composition; but the music is, itself, an abstraction for the work that the poem already presumed to accomplish.[92]

In "Notes on Writing Words for Music," Taggard drew on V. C. Clinton-Baddeley's book *Words for Music* in order to stress how, to quote Baddeley, song and music would allow the poet to "speak again with a public voice" and, in so doing, aid in "the birth of a new conscience in musicians and the discovery of a new lyric voice among the poets."[93] Taggard tellingly departs from Baddeley, suggesting that he "is not able to help us about the best problem of all, and brightest possibility: our American speech, its music, its ring. Our free verse poems contain a new quality and it is musical." Taggard provides scansion for lines from E. E. Cummings's "Buffalo Bill," Carl Sandburg's "Cool Tombs," and Kenneth Fearing's "Lullaby" (see figure 9), writing that she would not want to see any of these poems set to music, for "the cadences they contain are the new music of our poetry."[94] Taggard's composition notebooks are full of scansion marks with no accompanying words, allowing her (or us) to imagine the poem composed only of metrical marks. Taggard's adherence to

134 Chapter Three

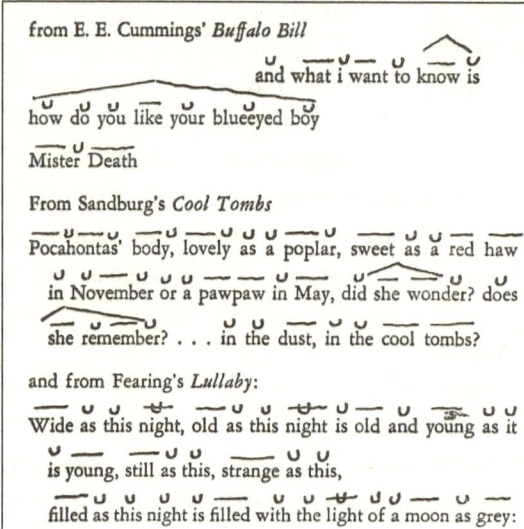

FIGURE 9 Genevieve Taggard, scansion marks on poems by E. E. Cummings, Carl Sandburg, and Kenneth Fearing in "Notes on Writing Words for Music," in *Long View*, 1942. Used by permission of Judith Benet Richardson.

strict metrical formulas was part of a verse culture that Edmund Wilson posited was dying. In his 1938 essay "Is Verse a Dying Technique?," he wondered if "verse was a dying technique" because so many poets had abandoned its musical qualities. He points out that the Greek name for prose was "bare words," meaning "words divorced from music."[95] Taggard's notes give us bare music, what she imagines as an expressive conduit for the "right" feelings that structure the "joy" of being in a socialist collective.

In the late 1930s and early 1940s, Taggard wrote and, with her Sarah Lawrence colleague William Schuman, composed and staged choral works that sought to actualize her poems' ideals of song and music. Unlike the settings for "Lark," Taggard had an active role in revising her poems for Schuman's musical settings. The fact of the musical performance reveals how "lyric" and "song" become figures for "body" and "speech." Taggard's choral pieces make literal and material the forms of embodiment and position-taking imagined in her earlier poems at the same time that they reveal left fantasies about the poem as a perfect representation of and conduit for people's speech.

In 1939, a student group from the New York City High School of Music and Art performed *Prologue*, with music by Schuman and lyrics by Taggard, at Carnegie Hall. Like many other classical composers of the era, Schuman composed more accessible works during the interwar period, and in the late 1930s and early 1940s, his choral works shifted from difficult arrangements intended for skilled singers to more simplistic ones that could be sung by youth choirs.[96]

Prologue, his first collaboration with Taggard, began as a draft that Taggard had set aside as a "useful failure":

> (Knocking)
>   On this rock, change
>   From this insolence, rage.
>   In this chaos, plan.
>   Here, here, here.
>   Open tomorrow's door.
>   (Knocking)[97]

Upon reading the poem, Schuman believed it had potential for a work "suitable for an audience of young artists and musicians about to face the responsibilities, the pleasures, and possibly the disappointments of life." Schuman's eventual arrangement, however, emphasizes not the personal but the political urgencies of Taggard's lyrics. As Steve Swayne describes, the first four lines "are set against a militaristic and insistent march, ending with the chorus emphatically shouting 'Here!' followed by a lumbering passacaglia whose materials are extracted from ideas that appeared in the first section." The last three words of the poem—"Open tomorrow's door"—are sung over the passacaglia, "with the lugubrious tempo providing a sense of both the effort and the seriousness involved in opening tomorrow's door." The piece ends "with a major triad that signals affirmation and hope."[98]

Following the success of *Prologue*, Taggard and Schuman worked together on his cantata *This Is Our Time* (1941), and Taggard reprinted the lyrics to both pieces, along with other songs she wrote to be set for choruses and ballets, in a section titled "Texts for Music" in *Long View*. Following Carrie Noland, we might read Taggard's experiments with choral forms as an example of performative genres becoming models for verse writing.[99] Thinking about the choral as a formal strategy related to lyric, we can see Taggard's choral pieces as a template for a new logic of the "lyric effect" as it emphasizes embodiment and position-taking within a specific historical moment. Taggard's 1941 piece *This Is Our Time* is a subsequent choral work that suggests how she troubles, rather than reifies, the cohesiveness of a group "we." The piece opens by celebrating collective song, but the "we" that celebrates shared time and space is described as an individual body, broken down into various parts. In a section titled "Work," the chorus sings,

> The idle are sad.
> Our day has work to do.

> Our day's necessity
> Our will
> Is work.
> Lung and throat of the people
> Body and breath,
> Palate and tongue,
> Heart and will,
> We in necessity one,
> One in our will,
> We rivet hand to hand.[100]

"Work" posits terms of solidarity that are not reducible to the conventional Depression "we" that speaks with a voice so unified that it is merely another version of the lyric "I." Historically speaking, the mode of political subjectivity explored in Taggard's chorals is the product of major shifts occurring between the publications of *Calling Western Union* and *Long View*. *Long View* appeared in the wake of the escalating violence of World War II and the aftermath of the Hitler-Stalin pact. Taggard's chorals seem to stage the new formation of "the people" engendered by late 1930s Popular Front discourse and, therefore, her use of "we" is tantamount to the invocation of "the people" in Ma Joad's famous speech at the end of the film version of *The Grapes of Wrath*. We might, however, read Taggard's evocation of "the one" in terms of Jacques Rancière's description of the "people" as "a polemical form of subjectification that is drawn along particular lines of fracture, where the distribution of leaders and led, learned and ignorant, possessors and dispossessed, is decided."[101]

In this reading, Taggard moves through a "we" to arrive at an "I" that represents an assemblage of social groups and identities. In this way, Taggard's chorals are at odds with later idealizations of the choral lyric by scholars such as W. R. Johnson. Arguing that the history of lyric should account for the choral, Johnson wagers that just as "solo lyric can be forced to promote varieties of solipsism, so choral lyric can be forced to promote varieties of evil nationality and of totalitarianism." He ultimately determines that "in either case, the possibilities for good are in exact proportion to the possibilities for evil," and he goes on to describe a "modern choral" that "has been on the side of angels."[102] Taggard, by contrast, uses the scene of the choral performance, and of multiple bodies singing with "one voice," as a means to imagine the expression of a "one" that, while not solipsistic, is singular.

Such a modality of expression is apparent in the last section of the cantata, which begins in a third-person voice and ends with a first-person plural voice.

The third-person voice describes how "in the old days" participants in barn raisings "worked together" and then "danced together"; this exterior voice instructs "Americans" to do the work of building and then, once the work is done, to celebrate it. At the end of the poem, the first-person plural voice returns to the opening refrain: "This is our time, our own, our only time. / Together we make / Today."[103] The different parts of the choral create the occasion for Taggard to imagine a new type of collective or multitude that she described in "Definition of Song" as a "many welded into one" and, in her choral lyrics for "In Our Time," as a "We in necessity one." The sheer physicality of these images, coupled with the physical act of performing the choral, raise difficult questions about how forms of poetic representation relate to embodiment. The liberalism on which the traditional lyric rests also, as Elizabeth Anker explains, "scripts the human": "the dignified individual in possession of rights is imagined to inhabit an always already fully integrated and inviolable body: a body that is whole, autonomous, and self-enclosed." This liberal discourse around the body, Anker argues, translates to discourses around a "liberal body politics" that is "imagined as comparatively impermeable, nuclear, and cleansed of alien or subversive elements."[104] We could read Taggard's choral pieces according to this logic that moves from the body to the body politic. (Indeed, this is probably the move that a critic such as Johnson would want to imagine—so as, of course, to keep everything on the side of those liberal tolerant angels.) But in so doing, we would miss the ways in which the singing bodies carry the news of history.

Lyric Frequencies and the Future of Poetry

Taggard's poems from the 1930s and 1940s suggest that she viewed music as one way of training listeners to hear poems so that they would not need to see those poems in print. It is not surprising, then, that in a radio broadcast that was probably aired from New York City in the late 1930s, Taggard told her listeners that she would read poems "that appeal directly to the ear, poems that make a material music while the words are still on their way through the microphone," suggesting that the present materiality of the poem could modulate the voice and thus train the ear for the future.[105] In the broadcast, Taggard fused the "poetry of the future," as she titled her broadcast, to the modern technology of the radio with reference to a traditional verse genre—song.[106] Near the end of the broadcast, Taggard read aloud her "Definition of Song." Despite the poem's engagement with the ostensibly "old" genre of song, Taggard explained to her listeners why "Definition of Song" "belongs to our modern world": "This is a poem against individualism in the arts, against the outworn idea of the lonely genius, the prima donna, the hero of literature; a poem that talks about the art of doing things together. And so this is poetry inspired by the city, and by modern ways of doing things. *Participation for all.* After I read this poem you will see why I think the person who listens is important to the poet. A good poet tries to say what his listener needs to hear."[107] Here we see Taggard's desire to reproduce an imagined (and idealized) oral and collective context for song: what she describes in the poem as publishing "good news" on the "public street" and expressing a "common good" that states "the massive power of our love."[108] For Taggard, this fantasy was enacted through the medium of the modern radio, through which she enjoyed an instantaneous mass audience for sharing what the "listener needs to hear." A poem reverberating through the airwaves might reach the "ears of millions," and the poet, not unlike labor union leaders who used radio to communicate with their constituents, could promote political solidarity.[109] Even so, the radio does not necessarily shift the terms, or fantasies, conditioning the poem's circulation in print. The notion that a poem could create conditions for communitarian expression and the binding of a political community was, especially for politically committed poets, already inscribed in folkloric genres such as song; and these ideals were magnified, rather than produced, by the radio. As Taggard put it to her own listeners, the "medium" of the radio "returns to us, marvelously amplified, the old art of the ballad makers and the troubadours."[110]

But Taggard also imagined this return to the past as a means to a possible future. Later in the broadcast, she predicted that eventually one would "never see a poem in print," and the listener would become "such a good judge of the poetry you hear, that you will know right away, whether you like it or not."[111] Radio, in this context, becomes a way to train listeners for a future in which the art of poetry would "escape from the prison of the printed page."[112] In the broadcast, we encounter an idealization of poems as lyrical melodies made to be heard rather than seen. It would seem that Taggard's "Poetry of the Future" broadcast, punctuated by her reading of "Definition of Song," tells us everything we already know about Depression-era radical poetry: left poets favored traditional verse genres because they were presumably widely accessible and promoted communitarian ideals. In this context, Taggard's poetic practice amounts to simply brushing the dust off verse genres such as the chant, ballad, and song. But what might be missed in such a reading? A closer listen reveals Taggard's deep and ongoing engagement with imagining a new mode of political subjectivity by reinventing the terms of lyric subjectivity. Taggard's fantasy that wireless radio transmission could disperse her singular speaking voice into "a million vibrating lines" is an important iteration of Taggard's poetic impulses during the 1930s and 1940s, indicating her desire to eradicate the "futile," "false," and "manufactured" opposition between the "Individual" and "Society" that characterized the art of "the liberal and the Romanticist."[113] The poetics that Taggard describes in her radio broadcast is her penultimate fantasy about the way historical conditions will change—and relations between people will change—through shifts in form and media. Poetry must pass through the physicality of the voice, and Taggard seeks out multiple ways for the materiality of voice to pass over into the realm of form in ways that push past binaries of seeing and hearing.

When Schuman teamed up with Taggard, he made something of her "useful failure." So I want to close my reading of her by digging around in her old drafts. In *Down in the Dumps*, Jani Scandura salvages the trash of the Depression in places such as Florida's Key West. Scandura reads Key West as "an outlaw site that embraces the in-between spaces of racial heterogeneity, androgyny, and labor rebellion," and she compares it to Cesare Casarino's reading of nineteenth-century ship space as "the inside of an unrepresentable outside, as the fold-effect through which the immanent cause of the outside comes into being as form in the world and comes to disrupt the history of forms."[114] Taggard attempts to represent historical antagonisms being worked out alongside political communities forming within the realm of poetic expression. By the late 1930s and early 1940s, Taggard is attempting a lyric that is an expression of some outside historical reality, its fold-effect. With this in mind, I want to read Taggard's short, unpublished draft titled "In the Plural." It is a funny poem because, despite its title, it is spoken by a single "I":

> It was sung into me
> It was sung out of me
> And into me
> And out of me
> What became part of me
> And did I make
> A single song[115]

The poem fragment implies that the "I" of a poem is not a self-expressive speaker but rather a conduit for the message or song referred to by the pronoun "it." This is the ultimate version, perhaps, of the lyric effect. It is the lyric-as-effect: the outside, historical embodied reality smuggled into the lyric. Rather than a form expressing a subjective interior, the lyric becomes the embodiment of the historico-political outside—a lyric turned inside out.

We might find for Taggard, then, a rather unexpected comrade in Louis Zukofsky. During the Depression years, the Objectivist poetics associated with the practice of avowed communists such as Zukofsky were situated uneasily within a cultural front represented by Communist Party–affiliated institutions such as *New Masses*. Indeed, when *Poetry* magazine published the Objectivists issue in 1931, the *New Masses* stalwart Stanley Burnshaw wrote to Harriet Monroe asking if she was playing a prank.[116] Nonetheless, the Objectivist thinking through the relationship of subject and object on Marxist terms, which Zukofsky figures through his early-thirties poems in terms of "song," provides a means to resituate Taggard's practice in relation to experimental syntactical forms developing in the early twentieth century. Taggard posited musical composition as a way to experiment with poetic sounds and lines, producing "right" (read: communist) "joy." One of Zukofsky's most well-known political poems, "To My Wash-Stand," is also, in the context of Taggard's writings, another lyric turned inside out. Rather than writing "to his contemporaries," Zukofsky writes to his marble sink, and from the sink comes a song:

> Comes a song of
> water from the right faucet and the left
>   my left and my
> right hand mixing hot and cold
>
>   Comes a flow which
> if I have called a song
>   is a song
> entirely in my head
>   a song out of imagining
> modillions descried above
>   my head   a frieze
> of stone completing what no longer
>
> is my wash-stand[117]

Ruth Jennison remarks that the speaker of "To My Wash-Stand" "emerges only after a double reconciliation: first with a collective accessed by his newly solidaristic imagination, and second, with his own status as a prismatic mediation of that larger totality."[118] In this comparison, perhaps we can see that Taggard was not thoroughly unmodern, so overly eager and old hat. In one of my favorite portraits of her, from the Sarah Lawrence archives, she is leaning back in a desk chair, holding a cigarette in one hand. Of course, in her other hand, she must have had a match.

Then, Love

So why read songs and chorals as lyrics? Why, to employ Virginia Jackson's terminology, lyricize the diverse genres circulating on the left? My lyrical reading of Taggard considers lyric history, or lyricization, not from the perspective of poetics but from the perspective of some inevitable history. Lyric, in this instance, is an insurrection. Returning to Rolfe's poetry and its reception, I want to close by suggesting that the modes of lyric reading produced by Cold War consensus and the eventual reaction to it have made it difficult to discern the more radical representational strategies at work in 1930s lyric practice. Rolfe is key to making such an argument because interpretations of his poetry so often circle around questions of lyric. Reading Rolfe's lyric poems in relation to influential interpretations of them, I argue that critical attempts to reconcile lyric reading with radical history have limited the view of history expressed in the poems at hand.

In what is perhaps the most foundational reading of Rolfe, Cary Nelson suggestively titles his long introduction to Rolfe's *Collected Poems* "Lyric Politics." Nelson's introduction begins with an assumption based on a particular contemporary version of lyric: suggesting that Rolfe's poems about the Spanish Civil War, collected primarily in the volume *First Love and Other Poems* (1951), are the best point of entry for the uninitiated reader in part because "*First Love* is Rolfe's most overtly lyrical book." "It is there, then," Nelson continues, "that readers who feel hailed by Rolfe's language and his passion can discover part of what is most distinctive about his subject."[119] While Nelson assumes that Rolfe's lyricism makes his poems accessible, his introduction also continually qualifies Rolfe's tendency to use the lyric. Such readings might be seen to evince what Gillian White has dubbed "lyric shame," especially as that shame revolves around the abstraction of lyric as the private expression of a coherent subject.[120] Nelson's shame at Rolfe's lyrics is perhaps most notable in his reading of "First Love" (1943), Rolfe's "lyrical tribute" to the battlefields of Spain. Central to Nelson's reading of the poem is the image of the "lyric lake" that appears in the final couplet: "and always I think of my friend who amid the apparition of bombs / saw on the lyric lake the single perfect swan."[121] The reference to lyricism, and thus to a moment that transcends time, is, according to Nelson, "historically warranted."[122]

I do not disagree with Nelson that Rolfe's "poetic lyricism is historically warranted." But why would a critic feel compelled to make this statement? Nelson's need to situate historically Rolfe's "first love" and his vision of a "lyric lake" seems part of a need to demarcate Rolfe's lyric as separate from the lyric's claims to transcendentalism that are part of a twentieth-century version of the Romantic lyric that we have come to associate with lyric itself. This is further evinced in Nelson's reading of "Madrid": "Rolfe, we realize, was not interested in indulging himself in a transcendentalizing lyricism but rather in displaying a lyrical impulse that is itself historically occasioned and necessarily in dialogue with other kinds of language. We have become accustomed to thinking of poetry as a space where lyricism can be entertained for its own sake, but Rolfe was not willing to pursue lyricism as an independent cultural value."[123] The notion that Rolfe would pursue lyricism as a cultural value rests on the assumption that the cultural value of lyric means the same thing across disparate times and places. What is more, the need to pursue a claim for Rolfe's lyrics that is grounded firmly in the historical record so as to avoid a supposedly apolitical transcendentalism might miss the revolutionary representational potential of Rolfe's and others' poetic practice.

The eschewal of the transcendental discloses an anxiety about lyric that comes from outside the historical situation in which Rolfe wrote his poems on Spain. While the essay on Rolfe's "Lyric Politics" is ostensibly about Rolfe's lyrics, it ends up being about the art of a lyric genealogy—a fact betrayed by the essay's end, where Nelson writes that Rolfe felt the need to make the moment of the Spanish Civil War part of "the lyrical historical record."[124] This phrase suggests any number of permutations: Is the historical record lyrical? Does writing a lyric poem about Spain inscribe the moment in a different historical arc? Do Rolfe's formal choices in his lyrics on Spain revise the historical record of the poetic lyric?

Of all of these questions, I am most interested in the last one. The anxiety about—the shame of—lyric causes a distortion of the historical relations at work in the poem that distorts the potentialities encoded in the poem itself. This is, in part, the problem of eschewing the transcendental altogether in the effort to distance the abstraction *political historical lyric* from the abstraction *transcendent Romantic lyric*. What is ultimately at stake is not the poet's attempt to ground the poem in history but the role of poetry to conceptualize a new claim for lyric, a new subject represented by that old pronoun "I." Here, we might turn to Rolfe's poem for Charlie Chaplin, "The Melancholy Comus." In it, Rolfe asks "what kind of world is this" where one who "speaks of love / is laughed at, reviled, showered with steel and filth?"[125] Rolfe's Chaplin-as-Comus, silently performing acts of love, might be the rebel signifier for a new mode of lyric subjectivity.

CHAPTER FOUR

Lyric Internationalism
Jacques Roumain and His Committee

And in brief, the destiny of our culture does not depend upon ideal creations of the intellect but on the effect of immediate historical conditions on the economic and political structure of our countries.
—Jacques Roumain, speech delivered at the Harlem YMCA, November 15, 1939

At This Very Moment

On August 15, 1936, the Haitian communist poet Jacques Roumain left Haiti on a cargo ship for Europe. The previous year, Roumain was twice arrested for communist activity under Sténio Vincent's presidency. Following his early release from prison in June, illness and continued government surveillance forced him into exile. "This paralyzing vigilance in a milieu as limited as ours and where I am only too well known means being reduced to powerlessness," he wrote from aboard the ship. "I felt that I was under the constant threat of new machinations by the government."[1] Roumain spent one year in Brussels and two in Paris. By 1939, he no longer felt safe in Paris, both because he had been convicted by a French court for publicly offending a chief of state and because of impending war between France and Germany. In November, Roumain left Paris for New York City, where he would stay for roughly three years, enrolling in anthropology courses at Columbia and collaborating with U.S.-based leftist writers.[2] While in exile in the United States, Roumain composed several speeches and essays describing the changed role of poets and their poems in relation to the rising threat of fascism in Europe, which, he wrote, "made as one the destiny of all mankind" and created the need to make "our history at this very moment."[3]

At the same time that Roumain abandoned questions of the literary in order to focus attention on historical necessities and to forward a concept of the poem as a utilitarian "weapon" in the international class war, he wrote lyric poems addressed to the contemporary political climate. Because in Anglophone literary criticism lyric poetry is often viewed in terms of an "aesthetic impulse" through which the "poetic imagination" can transcend, or exist outside of, historical reality, these two aspects of Roumain's late-1930s and early-1940s work might at first be understood as at odds.[4] This chapter seeks to defamiliarize such narratives by examining how Roumain theorizes processes of historical transformation in relation to immediate threats of fascism and, along with it, the possibilities of global antifascist solidarity. Such a consideration generates an alternate means to understand the lyric as a mode for representing and processing history at the same time that it puts pressure on the very idea of history itself. In what follows, I analyze the production, circulation, and reception of Roumain's writings and his authorial persona. In so doing, I explore several connected variants of a communist internationalism that is imagined through the idea of "lyric" or "lyricism," and I demonstrate how these international imaginaries are tied to developing conceptions of history. For Popular Front leftists, Roumain became a figure for resistance to U.S. imperial agendas in the Caribbean as well as for the multinational antifascist resistance, in part because his position as a Haitian writer linked him to the historical promise of the Haitian Revolution. At the same time, Roumain's own lyric practice engaged with discourses about art and history on the international black left, such as those articulated in C. L. R. James's defining 1938 historiography of the Haitian revolution, *The Black Jacobins*.

Behind my arguments is a provisional sketch of a "poets' international" to complement Michael Denning's conception of a "novelists' international." Denning traces the history of "a novelists' international" whose "aspirations and aesthetics ... remain the forgotten, repressed history behind the contemporary globalization of the novel"; and he describes "this emerging novelists' international and its proletarian novel" not "as a fully-formed genre, but a continuing dialectic between a self-conscious literary movement and the literary forms it developed."[5] Contrasting contemporary formations of globalization under advanced capitalism with internationalist politics of class struggle, Denning submits Roumain as an influential proletarian novelist in the Americas.[6] I am interested in how Roumain's work as a poet provides another means to understand these contrasts and contexts. Roumain's writings allow us to trace what Nahum Dimitri Chandler calls the "historicity of another transcendental" that might map another possibility for black radical aesthetics in relation to a developing international communist movement that posits new conceptions of the world.[7]

Like each preceding chapter, this chapter considers how Depression-era left writers waged struggles over the function of poetry as an object and an ideal of political efficacy. While I have addressed, in various ways, how issues of race and imperialism influenced communist and Popular Front poetics, this chapter confronts such questions more directly: setting readings of Roumain against the backdrop of international antifascist solidarity campaigns, especially as they were imagined as a struggle against colonial powers in the global South.[8] As Benjamin Balthaser points out, Haitian history, politics, and culture were "at the center of a story of antifascism," and "Haiti" became "a kind of code word, a trope, to signify not only the potentialities of the antifascist coalition, but also the dangers should fighting fascism leave the colonial order in place."[9] A key figure in the Haitian nationalist movement and founder of the *Parti Communiste Haïtien* (the Haitian Communist Party), Roumain was also an important figure in networks of black internationalist and communist activists, participating in writers' conferences in France and Spain and collaborating on journals such as *Commune, Regards*, and *Les Volontaires*.[10] For U.S. radicals, Roumain became an emblem of Haiti's anti-imperialist and anticapitalist resistance to foreign occupation and an example of how revolutionary writers and writing might intervene in political processes.

Examining how Roumain interacted with U.S. left cultural workers evinces complex intersections between national and international literary traditions during the era of the Popular Front, and the ways his work circulated in the United States before his 1939 arrival give different insights into the development of Popular Front poetics. Roumain's late-thirties and early-forties writings, composed and distributed from his experience of exile, articulate the role of the poet and poetry in relation to routes of black radicalism that cross, or cross-pollinate, with those of socialist internationalism.[11] The questions Roumain poses to his U.S. audiences—about the changing definitions and roles of the poet and of poetry in relation to realities of international struggles against fascism—thus emerge at the crossroads of sometimes united, sometimes vexed political formations. Roumain remains concerned across these commitments with how alternative conceptions of poetry might arise from different understandings of historical necessities and effects.

One of the broadest aims of this chapter, then, is to analyze historically competing versions of the abstract idea of "poetry" at a particular moment of crisis. In Roumain's 1941 American Writers' Congress speech turned *New Masses* essay "Is Poetry Dead?," he describes a "historical cross-roads" in which "the forces of socialism and of capitalism are facing each other in a decisive struggle"; at this crossroads, the bourgeois capitalist social order invests in an "idealistic construction" of poetry as an "ideological weapon of counter-revolution." The "idealistic construction" of poetry, which Roumain explains using Stéphane Mallarmé as an example, signals the complete exhaustion of bourgeois society and art at the presumptive end of capitalism. He writes, "Mallarmé is the product of an epoch when the progressive curve of capitalism has already reached its dead climax, when bourgeois society has entered its declining stage, at which, to the destruction of the productive forces, it adds the negation of cultural values." The other side of this ideal is, of course, the understanding of poetry as a type of revolutionary praxis, built on the notion that radical poems are weapons for the worldwide socialist front. If poetry is "dead," then it might also be reborn as something akin to "a leaflet, a pamphlet, a poster" that speaks to and for the "common people" rather than the ruling classes.[12]

From the perspective of Popular Front poetic culture as we think we know it, the lyric poems that Roumain wrote stand in contrast to the varieties of didactic verse often associated with the poetry-as-weapon dictates that he too espoused. In the "Introductory Note" to the 1944 antifascist anthology *Seven Poets in Search of an Answer*, for instance, Shaemas O'Sheel suggested a return to the "older days" when "people were often fired and welded by ballads sung on the streets and sold on penny broadsides," and he called for poets to come together to "survey the needs of this tremendous hour, map deliberate campaigns: books of high poetry; ballads celebrating our heroes and our cause; doggerel to take the hide off Hitlerites; lyrics for rousing popular songs."[13] Nostalgia for the "older days" when poems did political work was in many ways the "social disease" of Old Left poetic culture.[14] At what point does the desire to resuscitate the genres of the past foreclose the possibilities for new experiences and communities in the present? And how do those desires resonate with views of genre and expression circulating on the international black left? The archive of Roumain's time in exile, which includes his writings as well as the impressions of his writings on left cultural workers, has historical and critical purchases for thinking about how the formation of left lyric intersects with developing internationalist formations.

This chapter proposes to cut out those other genres and to pursue an idea of lyric as cut. In the context of the black radical tradition, especially in the writings of Afro-Caribbean Marxists such as Roumain and C. L. R. James, the lyric, or the lyrical, is an irruption in the apparently smooth surface of Euro-American historiography as well as the interiority of the Euro-American lyric. Considering transnational modernist poetics from the perspective of Afro-Caribbean Marxists such as James, as well as theorizations of that work by contemporary black studies theorists such as Fred Moten, provides another means to reorient an emerging antagonism in poetry studies between the historicist critique of lyric and the defense of a capacious view of lyric.[15] If "lyricization" denotes the consolidation of specific genres under the sign of "poetry," then the critic's task is to detect the differentiated operations of poems as they circulate in different times and different places and for different reading communities. Within this framework, one might point to my preceding assumption about Roumain—that imagining poetry as a weapon (in theory) and writing lyrics (in practice) is paradoxical—as symptomatic of "lyric reading" paradigms. Indeed, if we could discern an alternate historical construction of "lyric" as a mode of expression, and of "lyric reading" as a mode of interpretation, then could we also come to understand lyrics as historical weapons too?

The moment that I discuss here, although brief, provides a fuller understanding of the histories of lyric as well as the lyric's claim to the historical, one that dilates the concerns of the book to a transnational register. As I will demonstrate, Roumain's writings illuminate a moment just before—or, perhaps more accurately, just *as*—predominant New Critical definitions of lyric qua "poetry" were codified in the U.S. academy. The consolidation of an international antifascist front was, I speculate, accompanied by an attempt to consolidate poetic genres into a different order of "lyricized" ideal.[16] Roumain's writings suggest an alternate path of lyricization that, based in black radical and communist traditions, interrogates the often unspoken assumption that the core concepts of modern poetic interpretation are products of a conservative, white, Euro-American elite.

While I will delve into this idea more fully in the next section, I want to illustrate my point by way of a brief example from another national context. The May 1935 issue of *International Literature* published an essay titled, "On Soviet Poetry: A Soviet Poet Writes on the Function of Lyric Verse," by the Russian poet Ilya Selvinski. Reflecting on the second Five-Year Plan for the Soviet Union, Selvinski calls for a "revival of the poetic" in the form of a renewed "lyricism." According to him, the forms of "propaganda verse" (he lists fables, slogans, satires, oratory, and songs for the masses) that "replaced" lyric poetry during the first Five-Year Plan must now give way to a "socialist lyricism" that will "deepen and emotionally enrich the personality of the worker for socialism in a collective which has already been brought into being."[17] While the timeline and context of Selvinski's essay does not align perfectly with the creation of the Fourth International or the U.S. Popular Front, his sentiments nonetheless ring true in that context.[18] As I argued in chapter 3, during the mid- to latethirties, the lyric seems increasingly to denote, or represent, the emotions and interests of the collective through the individual ("the 'I'"). At the same time, as I examine in this chapter and chapter 5, during the late-thirties and earlyforties, specific folk forms seem to be understood increasingly in terms of the parameters of lyric expression and address. Selvinski's essay betrays how ideals about poetic expression on the international communist left were often circumscribed by a hermeneutics of lyric that was structurally similar to Anglophone New Critical models. That is, Selvinski's essay replaces the abstract, universalized speaker of the New Critical lyric with the abstract, universalized worker of the communist lyric.

Roumain's writings provide new interpretive contexts that help us to see anew the relationships among lyric poetry, communist politics, and anti-imperialist futures. In many ways, Roumain's poems exemplify a mode of communist lyric described by theorists such as Stathis Gourgouris and Alain Badiou, in which the poet envisions "the ethical demand of communism's historical intervention as a poetic task and, conversely, their poetic project as a chance to hone history's materiality into a language that metabolizes itself in turn to an actual historical praxis."[19] Roumain's writings, however, demonstrate a relationship between communist historical practice and lyric practice that is shaped by black radical traditions and that reminds us, to use Jeremy Matthew Glick's phrase, that "black radicalism is always already radical internationalism."[20] With regard to the black radical tradition, we might turn to Fred Moten's observation that "lyric materiality" is necessary to disrupt the narrative of "European domination and accumulative apotheosis" so that "the line of that dialectic has got to be broken by another dialect." I lean on Moten's readings of James's *The Black Jacobins* to understand how Roumain's lyrics represent historical processes as well as theorize ways of doing history. Especially useful is Moten's account of how "the form and content of the cut" in James's retelling of the Haitian Revolution "is tied to another opposition—that between lyric and narrative—that in turn shapes yet another fundamental disjunction between the science and the art of history."[21]

This chapter begins by sketching the historical and political import of Roumain as a figure for U.S. radicals. I then turn to Roumain's friendship with Langston Hughes, showing how the exchange of poems between the two artists allows us to move beyond straightforward historical accounts that show how radical African American artists and intellectuals referred to Haiti's revolutionary past in their protests against Jim Crow policies, colonial occupations, and the rise of fascism in Europe. I argue that Roumain and Hughes harness and experiment with the unique temporality of the poetic lyric in order to present black radicalism as a rhizomatic formation unbounded not only by spatial and temporal borders but also by the borders of subject. The final sections turn to the prose and poetry Roumain composed during his exile in the United States, using them to rearticulate ideas about the relationship of the poetic lyric to historical praxis.

Free Jacques Roumain!

Roumain's connections to African American intellectual communities and to the CPUSA date back to the late 1920s and early 1930s. In 1932, Roumain traveled to the United States to visit Alain Locke in Washington, D.C., and to ask CPUSA leaders in New York City for assistance creating a Haitian Communist Party. While Roumain's writing was reviewed and translated in U.S.-based publications earlier in the decade, attention to his writing and his politics increased in the United States after he was arrested for "communist conspiracy" in October 1934 and sentenced to three years in prison.[22] Shortly after the 1934 arrest, the Committee for the Release of Jacques Roumain was formed in New York City. Chaired by the radical Latin America journalist Carleton Beals, the committee was organized by prominent artists and public intellectuals on the liberal and communist left, such as Sherwood Anderson, Langston Hughes, George B. Murphy Jr., Jean Toomer, Thomas Benton, Alain Locke, and Broadus Mitchell. The leftist activists Conrad Komorowski (also the secretary of the Committee for Cuba) and Martha Gruening (former NAACP assistant secretary and labor activist) also served on the committee.

Roumain's political imprisonment united many ideological segments of the Popular Front left, and his imprisonment was framed in military as well as economic terms.[23] Beals opened a May 1936 meeting of the committee by determining that "such unjust and unpopular acts as the imprisonment of Jacques Roumain, Haiti's leading writer, would be impossible for President Vincent to enforce without his National Guard. By deliberately building up this Guard, the American Marine occupation has given a weapon to anyone placed in power, and enabled such a person to assume dictatorial power against the wishes of the people. This situation may be seen not only in Haiti, but in other Caribbean countries that have known American occupation."[24] Beals framed Roumain's arrest in terms of the effects of the U.S. military occupation; but the cause of his imprisonment was also linked to economic concerns. At the same meeting, committee members adopted a resolution to "carefully and convincingly" present the "matter of the economic vassalage of Haiti" as a prelude to picketing the National City Bank and other organizations "involved in the economic control of Haiti."[25] As Balthaser points out, "radical energies focused around the case of Roumain not only because of his status as a writer, but also because the fight for his release intersected with so many segments of the Popular Front Left, redirecting antifascist solidarity campaigns to the global South." Such campaigns linked Haiti's history of revolt, embodied in figures such as Toussaint Louverture, as well as the recent history of the U.S. military occupation, to antifascist struggles. Left cultural workers placed "Haiti at the center of a story of antifascism" in a way that "serves to remind us that in the same way the death of the French Revolution lay in its colonial policy and its colonial ambitions, so too would antifascism not succeed unless the global colonial system was abolished."[26]

It is equally significant that the interest in Roumain's case also coalesced around his status as one of Haiti's most well-known writers. One of the other major resolutions adopted by the Committee for the Release of Jacques Roumain at its May 1935 meeting was to spread Roumain's writings in the United States through publications and cultural events. As Balthaser argues, "What makes Haiti thus a symbol for the Popular Front period is precisely this nexus between the literary and the political, the symbolic and the real."[27] Indeed, Roumain's creative work would continue to be a focal point for U.S. activist artists well into the twentieth century. In the 1980s, during the era of Jean-Claude Duvalier's regime, the Haitian poet Boadiba and the San Francisco poet Jack Hirschman founded a Haitian cultural support group in the United States called the Jacques Roumain Cultural Brigade. The group produced *Boumba (Canoe)*, a newsletter featuring translations of Haitian poets from French and Creole, and members generated a number of new English translations, including Ronald F. Sauer's translations of Roumain's selected prose and poetry.[28]

The Popular Front blending of the political and the literary is evinced by one of the most public appeals to "free Jacques Roumain"—an open letter penned by Langston Hughes and published on the cover of the May–June 1935 issue of *Dynamo: A Journal of Revolutionary Poetry* (see figure 10):

> Jacques Roumain, poet and novelist of color, and the finest living Haitian writer, has been sentenced at Port-au-Prince, Haiti, to two years in jail for circulating there a French magazine of Negro liberation called the *Cri des Negres*. Jacques Roumain is a young man of excellent European education, formerly occupying a high post in the Haitian government, and greatly respected by intellectuals as an outstanding man of letters. He is one of the very few upper class Haitians who understands and sympathizes with the plight of the oppressed peasants of his island home, and who has attempted to write about and to remedy the pitiful conditions of ninety percent of the Haitian people exploited by the big coffee monopolies and the manipulations of foreign finance.
>
> As a fellow writer of color, I call upon all writers and artists of whatever race who believe in the freedom of words and of the human spirit, to

immediately protest to the President of Haiti and to the nearest Haitian Consulate the uncalled for and unmerited sentence to prison of Jacques Roumain, one of the few, and by far the most talented of the literary men of Haiti.[29]

The *Dynamo* cover allows us to understand empirically the shifting place of Haiti in the U.S. imagination during the mid-1930s and to read symptomatically a range of left artistic productions that drew on Haitian history, politics, and culture. These particular imaginations of Haiti demonstrate how "the blackness of the island is a symbol of global and interracial anti-imperialist antifascist struggle," an idea proven by the fact that Hughes's letter appeared on the front page of *Dynamo*, a radical poetry journal with socialist and communist sympathies, rather than an African American newspaper such as the *Chicago Defender*.[30] The proximity of the letter's title ("Free Jacques Roumain") and its byline ("A Letter from Langston Hughes") seems almost as significant as the forum itself. Hughes, like Roumain, was an important literary figure in the international black diaspora as well as a representative of cross-racial alliances on the Popular Front. A few months prior to the publication of the *Dynamo* petition, the secretary of the Committee for the Release of Jacques Roumain, Francine Bradley, sent Hughes a letter thanking him for his work on behalf of Roumain, which she deemed "of great value to [the committee] as it helps to gain the interest of a certain group of people."[31]

But I want to turn the page—to where the *Dynamo* editors reprinted Hughes's English translation of Roumain's 1931 poem "Quand bat le tam-tam" ("When the Tom-Tom Beats"). If Hughes's front-page petition provides insight into how Haiti functioned as an imaginative construct that could unite multiple segments of the Popular Front, then the appearance of Hughes's translation demonstrates how such constructs were structured by poetic figures and by translation. The appearance of the English translation of "Quand bat le tam-tam" in *Dynamo* was in fact a reappearance: Hughes first published his translation of Roumain's poem in the December 1931 issue of *Crisis*, and Nancy Cunard reprinted it with Hughes's framing note in her 1934 anthology *Negro*. It also reappeared in Dudley Fitts's 1942 *Anthology of Contemporary Latin American Poetry*. As the poem moves—from French to English, from the pages of one publication to another—its meanings and significance also shift, so that by the time the English translation of "Quand bat le tam-tam" arrived in *Dynamo* in 1935 as part of an appeal to "free Roumain," it circulated as the ideally lyric figure of the black revolutionary and the embodiment of "the freedom of words and of the human spirit."[32]

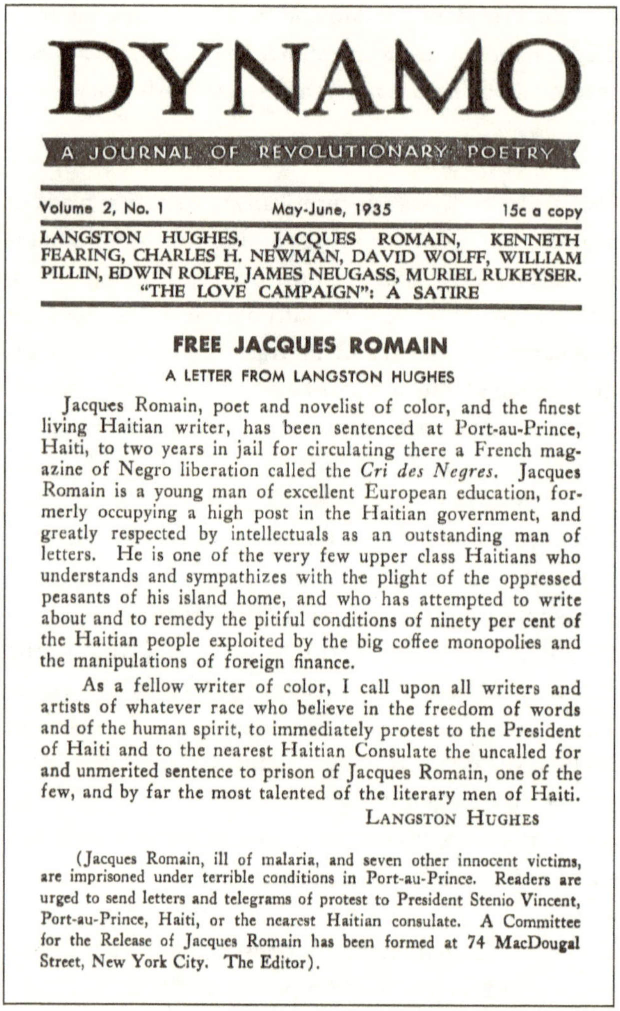

FIGURE 10 Langston Hughes, "Free Jacques Roumain," on the cover of *Dynamo*, May–June 1935.

DYNAMO

A JOURNAL OF REVOLUTIONARY POETRY

Volume 2, No. 1   May-June, 1935   15c a copy

LANGSTON HUGHES, JACQUES ROMAIN, KENNETH FEARING, CHARLES H. NEWMAN, DAVID WOLFF, WILLIAM PILLIN, EDWIN ROLFE, JAMES NEUGASS, MURIEL RUKEYSER. "THE LOVE CAMPAIGN": A SATIRE

FREE JACQUES ROMAIN
A LETTER FROM LANGSTON HUGHES

Jacques Romain, poet and novelist of color, and the finest living Haitian writer, has been sentenced at Port-au-Prince, Haiti, to two years in jail for circulating there a French magazine of Negro liberation called the *Cri des Negres*. Jacques Romain is a young man of excellent European education, formerly occupying a high post in the Haitian government, and greatly respected by intellectuals as an outstanding man of letters. He is one of the very few upper class Haitians who understands and sympathizes with the plight of the oppressed peasants of his island home, and who has attempted to write about and to remedy the pitiful conditions of ninety per cent of the Haitian people exploited by the big coffee monopolies and the manipulations of foreign finance.

As a fellow writer of color, I call upon all writers and artists of whatever race who believe in the freedom of words and of the human spirit, to immediately protest to the President of Haiti and to the nearest Haitian Consulate the uncalled for and unmerited sentence to prison of Jacques Romain, one of the few, and by far the most talented of the literary men of Haiti.
                                        LANGSTON HUGHES

(Jacques Romain, ill of malaria, and seven other innocent victims, are imprisoned under terrible conditions in Port-au-Prince. Readers are urged to send letters and telegrams of protest to President Stenio Vincent, Port-au-Prince, Haiti, or the nearest Haitian consulate. A Committee for the Release of Jacques Romain has been formed at 74 MacDougal Street, New York City. The Editor).

"Quand bat le tam-tam" describes a process of self-transformation that takes place through a journey to an ancestral home. The sound of the drumbeat evoked in the poem's title raises an "old mirage from the pit of the night" (L'ancien mireage se lève au creus de la nuit), and it initiates a journey toward an ancestral landscape. As the addressee is carried on a river far from shore, he is compelled to listen to and incorporate the sounds he hears around him as he prepares to encounter his forebears. The original appearance of "Quand bat le tam-tam" in *Haiti-Journal* signaled a shift in Roumain's poetry from the "tropicalism" of 1920s poems such as "Midi," "Aprés-Midi," and "Miragône." Carolyn Fowler points out that Roumain's poems from the early thirties, as opposed to those from the twenties, used images of the Haitian countryside as a means to link a local experience to "universal blackness."[33] As Anita Haya Patterson notes, "Quand bat le tam-tam" is also marked clearly by Hughes's influence, conjoining elements of Hughes's 1920s poems "The Negro Speaks of Rivers" and "Danse Africaine."[34]

What, then, do we make of the republication of "Quand bat le tam-tam," in English translation, in *Dynamo*? The appearance of the translation is informed by two separate, but related, contexts: the Popular Front interest in black folk forms and the cultures of translation on the international black left. The appeal of black folk forms on the U.S. Popular Front is, even if subtly, underwritten by concepts of translation. Russ Castronovo argues that "collective formations emerge when American literature is understood as a site of translation," and he asks, "what new constellations come to light when literature is recognized not simply as international but also as Internationale in the sense of a revolutionary project that employs a language inflected with accents of mass subjectivity?" Drawing from the arguments of Walter Benjamin's "The Task of the Translator," Castronovo points out that translation does not "pin down meaning" but rather opens up "as-yet unopened possibilities," and he suggests that American literature should be understood as *translational* rather than transnational, as the latter focus would only fix expression in place.[35]

Such a notion of translation is framed, at least figuratively, in U.S. Popular Front culture as an issue of accessibility, or mass appeal, that negotiates both national-popular and internationalist imaginaries. The task of many Popular Front artists was, indeed, seen as the "task of the translator." As Kenneth Burke wrote to Malcolm Cowley in 1932, "I am, in the deepest sense a translator. I go on translating, even if I must but translate English into English."[36] It is within this culture of translation that Hughes's version of Roumain's poem is presented to an English-speaking readership. Returning to the *Dynamo* issue, we might notice how the recirculation of Roumain's poem blends fantasies of translation-as-connection with fantasies of commonality undergirding Popular Front poetics. Mediated by Hughes's letter, which calls for the unification of "all writers and artists of whatever race who believe in the freedom of words and of the human spirit," the call to solidarity is also announced as a call to find languages in common.

In this context, the act of translation also combines powerfully with ideas about genre. Roumain is transported not only through or by translation but through the mode of the lyrical itself.[37] The "authenticity" that was so often linked to lyric expression also bears on the tendency among Popular Front writers and critics to link ideas about form and genre to ideas about race. This might be read as a thirties left version of what Anthony Reed has called "racialized reading," a "prescriptive account of the project of black aesthetics as one of rejoinder, protest, or commentary, figuring black writing as reactive rather than productive."[38] James Smethurst has helpfully traced the relationship between the "Black Belt Thesis" proposed by the 1928 Comintern and communist writers' interest in an "authentic" African American folk culture. Smethurst explains, "notions of an ur–African American culture in the South were quite questionable and were, in fact, derived largely from European national romances of the folk." This "romance," however, was one "that the Communists substantially shared with non-Communist black intellectuals and writers—many writing in advance of the 1928 Comintern congress."[39] The content of race relations and race struggle was abstracted into folk forms, especially musical forms such as spirituals, blues, and jazz as well as what Smethurst describes as the "folk voice" of African American Depression left poetry.[40] Arguably, Hughes, one of the most prominent black left poets of the period, makes Roumain readable in the U.S. national context both by registering his situation with *Dynamo* readers and by translating his poetry for a predominantly English-speaking audience.

The ideological fantasies about race inherent in the decision to reprint "Quand bat le tam-tam" were reinforced by cultural activities sponsored by the Committee for the Release of Jacques Roumain. At one point in 1936, for example, the committee hosted an event at the Harlem YMCA that featured Hughes reading translations of Roumain's poems, Miriam Blecher performing dance interpretations of Hughes's poems, and Horace Gregory and Babette Deutsch speaking on Roumain's work and on the present situation in Haiti. In a letter to Jean Toomer, Bradley emphasized that the event was meant to be a celebration of black culture, telling Toomer that the program was to include "Negro folk songs . . . presented by a Negro choir."[41] In the context of the committee's political goals, these performances can be seen to infuse "old" folk forms with a new form of class consciousness that was developing in relation to anti-imperialist struggles.[42] At the same time, however, the poems circulate the figure of Roumain as *the* authentic black revolutionary in ways that rely on Popular Front idealizations of black expression.

These celebrations of Roumain bear a relation to other appropriations of black expressive traditions by white poets, such as Muriel Rukeyser's and Kenneth Fearing's use of blues forms and Sol Funaroff's and V. J. Jerome's use of dialect poems, as models of political expression. To give one particular example, at a talk for a union membership meeting, Genevieve Taggard told her audience that the "greatest" revelation of "genius" in American culture was the "spirituals" and "work songs" of the "negro people." While there, she read her poem "To Paul Robeson," which uses the figure of the black communist artist to imagine cross-racial solidarity and universal humanity:

> White men who are slaves, dark men who are slaves,
> Look at this man called Paul
> In the speech of many countries
> He sings the whole range of man from darkness to light.
> Hear the unspoiled heart; feel the unthwarted will
> More human than Prometheus, gentle as a teller of tales.
> He came from the loins of our country
> And wherever he goes men get back their lost pride
> In being human[43]

Robeson, Jeremy Matthew Glick points out, was an "embodied synecdoche of Black revolutionary aspiration. In the larger-than-life figure of Robeson, a whole philosophical and aesthetic register of Black radicalism is compressed."[44] Equal to Robeson's stature was his voice, idealized in Taggard's poem as singing "the whole range of man" as well as across the late-thirties cultural left through, for example, his popular recording of the "unofficial" Popular Front anthem "Ballad for Americans."[45] "To Paul Robeson" is similar to Taggard's early-forties sequence "To the Negro People," which invokes the genre of the spiritual to imagine the future leader of the proletariat as a black American. The final poem of the sequence, "Chant for the Great Negro Poet of America Not Yet Born," ends with a black poet "of all rising people" arriving "with the authority of those who cried" and "singing with the universal singing of his people."[46]

Through the example of Taggard's poems, we might return to the different ways that Hughes evokes freedom, or some notion of being "free," in his *Dynamo* piece. This idea about the circulation of "Quand bat le tam-tam" takes us outside of fantasies about authentic "folk" expression, demonstrating an interest in how a poem might provide a figuration of an *identity* of a person. In the end, the consolidation of a multifarious political front into an appeal to "freedom" takes the logic of a complex collective and distills it into the logic of personhood. That is, the focus on freeing Roumain consolidates an antagonism into the importance of a singular person while also raising the question: What is the situation whereby a person can be free?

The concern with Roumain's work on the Popular Front ultimately does not rest on the "authenticity" or "mass appeal" of the folk form but rather on the politics of liberalism that presumably underwrite modern lyric expression. Reading Hughes's Spanish Civil War poems, Brent Hayes Edwards has demonstrated the influence of writers such as Federico García Lorca on Hughes's epistolary poems and ballads, analyzing how in these works a "breaking or doubleness is pursued through a writing that attempts to meld the transport of lyric into the traditional narrative of the folk form."[47] I tend to read the recirculation of "Quand bat le tam-tam" in *Dynamo* the other way: as the incorporation of the ideal of the folk into the ideal of lyric expression.

Importantly, the appearances of Hughes's translations of "Quand bat le tam-tam" in other forums points to another significant dynamic culture of translation, one that united black leftists in the Americas. Such structuring of black internationalism is evinced by the publication of Hughes's translations of the poem in *Crisis* and in Cunard's *Negro*. These circulation contexts for "Quand bat le tam-tam" demonstrate Edwards's influential argument that "translation practices" and "transnational coverage more generally" are "crucial to the fabric of transatlantic print culture." According to Edwards, the bilingualism of black periodicals was a "practice of linguistic connection" and "one of the ways the 'turbine' of the cultures of black internationalism is lubricated."[48] Translation, as Steven Lee has more recently argued, simultaneously "highlights the gaps between languages and cultures" and "the desire to overcome them," acting as "a tool for binding together the internationalist, interwar ethnic avant-garde."[49] As I demonstrate in the next section, the collectivities imagined and produced in these sites of translation remain distinct from Popular Front attempts to find "languages in common" because they remain relational. That is, even as they take place within a seemingly "totalizing" Marxist vision of history and international solidarity, they acknowledge differences that exist across national cultures and contexts.[50]

A Lyrical Leap

In the previous section, I argued that, in a Popular Front milieu in which Haiti functioned as a master signifier for revolutionary revolt, the figure of Roumain became a synecdoche both for resistance to the U.S. imperial agenda in the Caribbean and for the broader antifascist resistance that culminated in the International Brigades of the Spanish Civil War. Appeals to "free" Roumain, however, distilled the logic of a complex collective into the logic of liberal personhood, a process underwritten by the circulation of "Quand bat le tam-tam" in English translation. In this section, I reread "Quand bat le tam-tam" in relation to Roumain's 1931 tribute poem "Langston Hughes" in an effort to discern different political stakes for Roumain's lyrics. Doing so, I do not abandon the proper (or properly lyrical) names "Jacques Roumain" and "Langston

Hughes." Rather, I ask if the emergence of these figures might provide an alternate path for thinking about the relationship between personification and lyricization in the context of black radicalism.

C. L. R. James asserts in his preface to the first edition of *The Black Jacobins* that the true business of the historian is to portray the limits of what was possible at a given place and time: "Today by a natural reaction we tend to a personification of the social forces, great men being merely or nearly instruments in the hand of economic destiny," he writes. "As so often the truth does not lie in between. Great men make history, but only such history as it is possible for them to make. Their freedom of achievement is limited by the necessities of their environment."[51] Glick finds in this line "the crystallization of James's entire critical method," which involves a "balancing act between an individual protagonist and his or her accompanying social base" that is "the heart of history's dialectical motion."[52] Riffing on James, Moten also takes up how the "theory and practice of revolution is bound to the way the individual emerges as a theoretical possibility and phenomenological actuality in and out of the revolutionary ensemble." For Moten, James's evocation of a "truth that does not lie in between" is an opportunity to lay open the theoretical and political stakes of James's history writing through an attention to aesthetics. The "truth" that is "not in-between" is "nothing less than a complex recasting of the dialectic" enacted in part through a "lyrical interruption of narrative" that "marks a different mode, within the same mode, of literary production."[53] Turning and returning to Roumain, I seek an irruption of the historical in the lyric that allows us to rethink the politics of Roumain's poetry-in-translation. Such a reading then provides a ground for interpreting his later antifascist writings.

Fowler points out that Roumain's poetry and prose from the late twenties and early thirties reflects on "the hero in various settings." His 1930 short-story volume *La proie et l'ombre* (*The Prey and the Shadow*), especially, depicts young urban intellectuals who, "unable to find fulfillment in the old values and unable to find any new ones," exist in a void.[54] However, the first story of *La proie et l'ombre*, "Propos sans suite" ("Talk and Nothing More"), suggests a way to understand the void between past and future that, forgoing narratives about the "aimlessness of bourgeois existence," glimpses aspects of Roumain's black radical thought that underwrite his poetic practice.[55] "Propos san suite" opens in the middle of a conversation between two friends, Jean and Daniel. As the two walk the streets of Port-au-Prince at night, they hear "the sinister and joyous voice of a drum." In the first line of dialogue, Jean asks, "What made you say, Daniel, that they all look pathetic?" Jean then turns "toward the darkness that his question addressed," and Daniel's voice floats into the story: "Because it is all moving towards pleasure. Gaiety doesn't attract happiness," Daniel responds. "I would show you these men and women, show you their faces, and then you would realize that a happy crowd is composed of sad people. You'd see the hopelessness of their pleasure." At the moment Daniel falls silent, a song pierces the air, and he implores Jean, "Listen. The voice of our race. All the sad pain of plantation-slaves living under the whip." Daniel then interrupts the song, and his own speech, with an enraged laugh that he describes as "white."[56]

For Daniel, the song he imagines coming from "a beautiful, strong negress" is "the most awful of all possible songs, the obscene song, the mad call for oblivion, for total annihilation."[57] The attraction of Daniel, a character that speaks out of the darkness of the city streets, to song that calls for "total annihilation" resonates with the Afropessimist thought of scholars such as Jared Sexton, Frank B. Wilderson III, Achille Mbembe, and others. And yet in a similar way that Moten, describing a moment of Wilderson's biography, wants to "assert the presence of something between the subjectivity that is refused and which one refuses and the nothing, whatever that is," Roumain's story uses the connection between Daniel and the distant singer to consider other possibilities for relation.[58] The song that materializes in the flesh of one person enters the body of another: as a sound in the ear and later in Daniel's monologue as an "aching kiss." The materialization of the song is emphasized in an image of red flowers and their shadows, which loom on the wall behind Jean. The flowers, native to Haiti, "diffused an acrid odor, fleshy and delicious; bleeding like a voluptuous wound, and their shadow, in splashes on the wall, seemed like a second bouquet, but of black roses, stained with the blood of others, in clots."[59]

As Jean and Daniel continue walking through the Port-au-Prince night, they see the poet Emilio. Even from a distance, the sound of Emilio's voice engages them, "full, as it was, of commotion and leaps of brilliance." After a few moments of joking conversation, Daniel asks pointedly, "Tell me, Emilio, ... Why are you no longer writing?" Smiling wryly, and with a despairing tone, Emilio answers, "One doesn't live by poetry; at least, not here, in Haiti. Yet the work is there, ripened, grown large—but then it shrivels up." As the sun begins to rise, a sense of futility sets in. After Jean sets off, Daniel, riffing on the Italian poet Giacamo Leopardi, tells Emilio, "This is without a doubt our very problem: our despair in the face of the poverty of our lives is now but a mere bad habit; it doesn't motivate us, it doesn't force our minds to leap: on the contrary, it's a heavy burden that weighs us down, bending us more and more towards the ground." The story ends with the sound of the waves, materialized as "rustling silk" that laps "against the pilings" of the wharf.[60]

Whatever atmosphere of aimlessness and despair clings to "Propos sans suite," Daniel's closing provocation to leap points to another possible way. In Moten's analysis of *The Black Jacobins*, he reads in James's prose a leaping forward akin to Jean-Jacques Dessalines's jumping into the ditch: "Dessalines leaps forward; he jumps into the ditch, sounding, descending. That jumping descent is coded as a jumping forward. Another dialectic. It's what James's phrasing does to the sentence. Oscillation, bridging over to leaping forward, jumping into. This is a question of music."[61] Indeed, as Daniel falls further into despair with the music, he mocks Jean's attempts to cheer him, admonishing, "Besides, you're forgetting that I'm black!" And yet Daniel's closing wish to leap out of despair, read in relation to the "leaps" that fill Daniel's voice the way the sounds of drum and song fill the night air, suggests the instantiation of a new dialectic out of the void.[62] Daniel's declaration "I'm black" is followed by a quick analysis of his environment. The environment "has its reasons," Daniel tells Jean, and "in Haiti this is the way things are: as soon as a man tries to find his own way and leave the herd, he gets treated like a black sheep; as soon as a head rises above the level of the crowd, it is crushed. The *environment* fights back."[63] Here, we glimpse again James's account of Haitian revolutionary figures: "Their freedom of achievement is limited by the necessities of their environment."[64]

It is from this vantage that I propose to return to Hughes's translation of "Quand bat le tam-tam" and to turn to Roumain's tribute poem "Langston Hughes": discerning alternate political formations in translation. "Quand bat le tam-tam" describes a process of self-transformation that takes place through a journey to an ancestral home. The sound of the drumbeat evoked in the poem's title raises an "old mirage from the pit of the night," and it initiates a journey "toward the ancestral landscape." As the addressee is carried on a river "far away from the banks," he is compelled to listen to and incorporate the sounds he hears around him. Hughes chooses to translate the question "Do you hear those voices?" (Entends-tu ces voix) to the imperative, "Listen to those voices":

> Listen to those voices.
> They sing the sadness of love.
> In the mountain, hear that tom-tom
> Panting like the breast of a young black girl.
> Your soul is a reflection in the whispering waters
> Where your forefathers bent obscure faces.[65]

> Entends-tu ces voix: ells chantent l'amoureuse douleur
> Et dans le morne, écoute ce tam-tam haleter telle

la gorge de'une noire jeune fille.
Ton âme, c'est le reflet dans le'eau murmurante
où tes pères ont penché leurs obscurs visages.⁶⁶

Through the act of listening, the journeyer reconstitutes himself, and he is able to see his soul's reflection in a different context. This movement is doubled in the poem by the figure of the "tom-tom panting like the breast of a young black girl," with the incorporation of the exterior sound of the drumbeat into the interior of a woman's body. Moving toward the "ancestral landscape," the subject of the poem alters his vision of himself. His reflection changes as he moves further into the darkness and sees that "the white that made you mulatto / is only a bit of foam thrown away, / like spit, on the face of the river." (Et le blanc qui te fit mulâtre, c'est ce peu / d'écume rejeté, comme un crachat, sur le ravage.)⁶⁷ The reflection of the soul on the water is mediated by sound: the whispering of the water modifies the image, therefore allowing the subject to negate or overcome the whiteness that is marked visually in the poem as a "bit of foam."

Issuing "listening" as a command, Hughes emphasizes how the incorporation of an exterior voice into the subjectivity of the speaker is essential to the process of negating whiteness, and it suggests parallels between "Quand bat le tam-tam" and "Propos sans suite." Certainly, in "Propos sans suite," talk is not nothing, for it is through talk that Daniel begins to arrive at a theory of black music. Talk, in other words, contains within it the (lyrical) leap of and into song. The beat of a drum is not a universally translatable sound; rather, it is a condition of black music in excess of the task of translation itself.

Indeed, the importance of "Quand bat le tam-tam" inheres in translation. Here, we might turn to another moment of exchange between Roumain and Hughes, Roumain's 1931 poem "Langston Hughes." The poem describes a subject who is constituted through connections to multiple places and times, as it narrates Hughes's travels to ports in Nigeria, France, and Italy. At times, attempts at connection are narrated through meetings with women. The poem begins at Lagos, where Hughes "knew those melancholy girls" who "adorn their ankles with silver bracelets and offer / themselves naked / As the night ringed by the moon" (Tu connus à Lagod ces filles mélancoliques / Elles portent aux chevilles des colliers d'argent et s'offrent nues / Comme le nuit encerclée). In the third stanza, Hughes seeks "the shade of Desdemona" in Venice but finds instead a woman named Paola. "You said to her: Amorissima / And sometimes / Babe, Baby / Then she wept and claimed her twenty lira from you" (A Venise, tu cherchas l'ombre de Desdémones / Elle s'appelait Paola /

Tu lui disais: Amorossissima / Et parfois / Babe, Baby / Alors elle pleurait et te réclamait vingt lires).[68] The reference to Shakespeare's *Othello* mediates Hughes's encounter in Venice: pronouncing Hughes (like Othello, like L'Ouverture and Dessalines) a tragic figure but also, potentially, calling on the tragic form to, as Glick writes with reference to restagings of the Haitian Revolution, balance "the imperative to theorize individual political leadership's interdependence on collective mobilization and collective knowledge."[69]

It is from this vantage that we might consider the previous stanza's narration of Hughes's arrival in France, which is marked by a refusal to speak that then becomes a refusal of the country's scenic beauty:

You saw France without pronouncing historic words:
-Lafayette, we are here-
The Seine appeared less beautiful than the Congo[70]

Tu vis la France sans prononcer de paroles historiques
-Lafayette nous voici-
La Seine te parut moins belle que le Congo.[71]

A reference to aid that France gave the U.S. army during the American War for Independence, the phrase "Lafayette, we are here" is commonly uttered by Americans upon arrival to France. Refusing to say "Lafayette, we are here" (Lafayette nous voici), Roumain's Hughes refuses to give credence to U.S. legend as he breaks from a model of selfhood based in national belonging. The description of these words as "historic" (paroles historiques) also suggests a refusal of Eurocentric narratives of history and historical experience; and it is through such a rejection that new formations of black radical thought are potentially instantiated.

Hughes's arrival in France, marked by the realization that "La Seine parut moins belle que le Congo," compares to the imagined return to an ancestral landscape figured in "Quand bat le tam-tam." Both arrivals open up into an untimely network of black experiences that is something like the "not in-between" that Moten discerns in *The Black Jacobins*. It is "the ongoing presence and the irrecoverable possibility of what gets coded as conditions and foundations. There and not there, not hybrid, not in between marks the presence and loss of Africa. Blackness and black radicalism are not in between but neither one nor the other." The return to Africa, Moten explains, is not a return to authenticity.[72] In this way, when the end of the poem places Hughes in the circuits connecting "Harlem and Dakar," Roumain does not depict Hughes as a wandering subject so much as he suggests that, by existing between these sites, the figure "Langston Hughes" emerges as "not in-between."[73] What is more, he does not ask Hughes to speak but implores him to sing:

> Your nomad heart wandered
> like a Baedecker from Harlem to Dakar
> The sea bestowed a sweet, rasping rhythm to your songs, and
> its biting flowers opened in the salt spray.
> Now in this cabaret at sunrise you murmur:
> Play the blues for me
> O play the blues for me
> Do you dream of palm trees and negro paddlers singing down the dusk?[74]

> Tu as promené ton cœur nomade, comme un Baedecker, de Harlem à Dakar
> La mer a prêté à tes chants un rythme doux et rauque et
> Ses fleurs d'amertume écloses de l'écume.
> Maintenant dans ce cabaret où á l'aube tu murmures:
> O jouez ce blues pou'moa
> Rêves-tu de palmes et de chants de pagayeurs au crépuscule?[75]

The sea gives shape to Hughes's person and his poetry; it "bestows a sweet rasping rhythm" to his songs. The cabaret where the poem ends exists in two places at once: at dawn and at dusk, in the desire to hear the "blues" and in the "dream of palm trees and negro paddlers singing down the dusk." Ultimately, the figure "Langston Hughes" is constituted by overlapping spaces and times, and he becomes unbounded by European historical narratives as he navigates alternate modalities of being that refuse national belonging. This release from historical narrative is not nonideological in the same way that the conventional Anglophone lyric pretends to exist outside the bounds of history and ideology. This lyric disrupts history. The rhythmic accompaniment of the sea, which also evokes the transoceanic passage of black slaves, interrupts the lyric. The murmur in a cabaret is a leap forward. And this, as Moten writes, "is a question of music."[76]

Haiti to the Universe

Let us jump to another arrival that is also another refusal. On November 15, 1939, roughly three years after the Committee for the Release of Jacques Roumain paid tribute to the Haitian radical through a "celebration of black culture" at the 135th Street YMCA, Roumain delivered a lecture at that very spot. That day, Roumain bypassed the proposed topic for his talk—the culture and history of Haiti—and asserted that an analysis of the impending war was the more "urgent task."

The war, he tells his audience, "which threatens to crush us all in its murderous machinery, and its effect upon the present day history of the American people seems to me a more urgent task than to stir the dust of archives in a professorial manner or to orate upon the future of literature." Roumain argues that the war "internationalizes" local spaces and histories. "At this very moment," he says, "the entire world, because of the war, is facing problems which affect our fate in a most fundamental manner: politically the facts can not remain localized and isolated any longer in time and space. They are immediately internationalized by the very substance of war for a new re-division of the world."[77] Leaving the dust on the archive, and therefore forgoing whatever research might lead to an oration "upon the future of literature," Roumain rejects historical narrative emplotment: refusing both past and future in the service of the immediate present.

Given the extent of the cultural left's interest in Haiti, as well as the extent of popular interest in Haiti during the early twentieth century, Roumain denies his U.S. audience just what it wants by refraining from speaking about Haiti. His speeches (the one he decides *not* to give and the one that takes its place) resist the fetishization of Haiti as a specific local carrying the promise of a future new world. Roumain instead posits a dialectical relationship between varied and diversified "local spaces and histories" and the new "immediately internationalized" present. His November 1939 speech communicates his broader conception of global political realities and the relation between political communities in the modern world. He asserts, "The war fronts, bristling with arms, where the enemy troops face each other, constitute a geographic reality, a strategic factor; but in view of the actual historic process: there exists in this war—which already embraces two continents and threatens to engulf *our* America—only one front: that of *all* peoples, fighting on the *entire* surface of the earth for liberty, peace and a better life in which man will cease to be a wolf for man."[78] Roumain's articulation of "one front" battling for "liberty, peace, and a better life" should not be mistaken for a hegemonic political community—even if that community is antiwar, antifascist, and anti-imperialist. Indeed, even though he points to a common "destiny of all mankind" that seems to transcend "country or race," Roumain does not suggest that left revolutionaries form a community in which local particulars are sacrificed to a universal vision, as in Guy Endore's proclamation at the end of his Haiti novel *Babouk*, "This is the world of men and women and of children. This is THE world. The ONLY world. The WORLD of ALL."[79] Roumain offers a model for understanding the relationships of parts to wholes that, in the context of his poetry, might be seen to mediate the localized particular of "Quand bat le tamtam" and the geographic plurality of "Langston Hughes."

Roumain's 1939 speech provides an important context for understanding his developing ideas about the role of poetry within an "immediately internationalized" reality. At around the same time that Roumain spoke at the Harlem YMCA, he gave a talk at the symposium "The Frustrated Poetry Renaissance," sponsored by the League of American Writers, a version of which was published in *New Masses* about two years later as "Is Poetry Dead?" For Roumain, the act of imagining poetry's death creates the conceptual space to imagine a new type of revolutionary community via a new poetry. While this fantasy of poetry's death and rebirth might express his desire for a new world to come, by 1939 there is already a new world afoot—a "re-division of the world" and an "immediately internationalized" reality caused by global warfare. It is within this present reality that a different conceptualization of poetry's form and political function might be realized. As Roumain puts it, "it is a question of *making our history at this very moment*," not "of raising memorial stones to the glory of the past."[80] Roumain rearticulates the meanings of poetry in relation to a volatile terrain in which history must be made in the immediate conjecture.

It is worth noting briefly how Roumain's conception of poetry's death and rebirth differed from conceptions of poetry's death put forward by African American cultural leaders such as Alain Locke. Roumain and Locke both were variously involved in the communist movement (even if only, in Locke's case, as a supportive literary critic and fellow traveler), and both shared an interest in how to craft a black proletarian aesthetic that resisted imitating European models. They were also correspondents, and Locke positively reviewed and promoted Roumain's work in U.S. magazines.

The two did, however, maintain different views of the poetic.[81] In an *Opportunity* review of "the literature of the Negro for 1934," Locke noticed the flowering of left culture and the increased predominance of proletarian aesthetics. He suggests that African American artists are creating in response to major historical transitions and declares, "It is the eleventh hour of capitalism and the eleventh hour of Nordicism, and all our literature and art are reflecting that."[82] Locke, however, thought that the suffusion of the "social question" within the realm of art caused a decline in the production of poetry. After dedicating a considerable portion of his retrospective to the year's fiction, Locke notes "the almost complete cessation of poetry" and laments that "the poetic strain has dwindled in quantity." He determines, "Evidently it is not the hour for poetry; nor should it be,—this near-noon of a prosaic, trying day. Poets, like birds, sing at dawn and dusk, they are hushed by the heat of propaganda and the din of work and battle, and become vocal only before and after as the heralds or the carolling serenaders."[83] While Locke thought poetry should rise above the fray of historical disruption, Roumain insisted poetry must be dialectically reconfigured in relation to critical historical moments. Locke drew a sharp line between "poetry" and "propaganda." Roumain, however, saw a use for poetry that was potentially propagandistic—"as effective as a leaflet, a pamphlet, a poster."[84]

At a moment of intense revolutionary pressure, "poetry" signifies a space outside of history and, perhaps, a space in excess of predominant historical narratives. Here, we might turn again to James, who, thinking the Haitian Revolution against the backdrop of the events of midcentury, wrote, "The violent conflicts of our age enable our practiced vision to see into the very bones of previous revolutions more easily than heretofore. Yet for that very reason it is impossible to recollect historical emotions in that tranquility which a great English writer, too narrowly, associated with poetry alone."[85] For James, neither poetry nor history alone allows for the recollection of historical emotion. Rather, the dialectical synthesis of the historical and the poetic, marked by an excess of tranquility, anticipates new modalities of political thought.[86]

The dialectical transformation of poetry into history for James is similar to Roumain's conception of poetry's dialectical transformation via its imagined death. Roumain opens "Is Poetry Dead?" by claiming, "Poetry is not a pure idealistic distillation. . . . It reflects that which in common language one calls epoch: that is to say, the dialectical complexity of social relations, of contradictions and antagonisms of the political and economic structure of a society at a definite historical period. Hence, poetry is a testimony and one of the elements of analysis of this society."[87] Roumain insists that revolutionary poetry must testify to material realities. But by imagining that poetry might die and be reborn, Roumain is striving for a poetry that can conceive of another realm, and this realm is a realm of otherness that is shaped by what is on the ground.[88]

One can see, then, that Roumain "inquires into the fate of poetry" in order to imagine a new order of poetry that is based on the political landscape from which it springs. Roumain does not ask if poetry is dead in order to comment on a perceived decline in the quality or quantity of poetic productions; rather, he intends to expose the ideological landscape that shapes the championing of poetry as an art that transcends the din of politics and history. Roumain argues that, at a time when "the forces of socialism and capitalism are locked in a decisive struggle," the "old society" holds up an ideal of "pure poetry." It is from this position that Roumain protests what he views as the current idealization of poetry, calling it one of the "ideological weapons of counter-revolution." He writes,

> On the eve of a fundamental historical transformation, the crumbling old society finds in idealistic construction, in the submission to the metaphysical idols, in recourse to the dark forces of mysticism, the ideological weapons of counter-revolution.... One must examine with the scientific care of an entomologist these specimens that invent moral pretexts in order to pass over, through the service entrance, to the camp of the people's enemy. Thus one discovers the pitiful petty bourgeois overwhelmed by an abject anguish, seeking refuge in the cocoon of pure poetry or of what *they* call "the freedom of the spirit," because the inexorable march of history threatens the class interests of their employers who have debased intellectual production to the level of merchandise, a grocery article.[89]

At this climactic point in the essay, Roumain suggests that an ideal of poetry, one that elevates the art to the status of religion (as "metaphysical idol") or relegates it to the realm of pleasure (as "pure poetry"), is a screen for conservative—and, at its worst, fascist—politics.

Contrasting Mallarmé with the revolutionary Russian poet Vladimir Mayakovsky, Roumain insists that, when the old social order is crumbling, writers must "grasp in the death of an obsolete social organism its replacement by another of a higher quality."[90] If they fail to do so, their poetry will be like Mallarmé's—an "evasion of reality" written in language that is "aloof from the class struggle."[91] Roumain imagines a new order of poetry (that is, poetry that is "of a higher quality") that does more than testify to colonialism, the rise of fascism, and the encroaching war. Roumain's vision for a reborn poetry contains within it the utopian hope that a different existence for poetry might help to imagine a different political existence as well.

Roumain dialectically reworks the question of poetry's death, and his essay poses the additional question: If, at a moment of historical crisis, the banner of poetry is being held aloft by counterrevolutionary forces, then can the art of poetry effectively serve the purposes of revolutionary struggle? At this historical moment, would the true revolutionary act be to let poetry die? Taking Roumain's suggestions about poetry to their endpoint opens up new ways for thinking about poetry's perceived social and political function in the years leading up to the Second World War. On one hand, it seems that Roumain desires a death of poetry that is related to a moment of historical crisis or rupture. In other words, at a time of historical crisis, poetry must die so that it can be reborn as something else. Through this teleological fantasy of poetry's death, Roumain imagines the coming of a new political community via a new poetry. This is something like poetry's abolition or self-abolition, a revolutionary model suggested in contemporary discussions about the relationship of poetry to revolution (and, conversely, its relationship to capitalism) that sees poetry as the last bastion of conservative (and, in our contemporary conjecture, liberal-democratic) magical thinking about art.[92] Indeed, this is something Roumain approaches in his essay when he reduces poetry to a weapon: to a material instrument meant to be fired in the class struggle. In other words, when poetry becomes a weapon, poetry as such is abolished.

But this seemingly idealistic fantasy—this replacement of an ideal with another ideal—is complicated by the contexts out of which Roumain constructs a notion of poetry "reborn." Death, in this case, is not a terminus but rather the opening of a new conceptual space for considering the relationship of art to communism and, more specifically, the construction of art related to developing forms of black radicalism. Nahum Dimitri Chandler writes of how we might "speak of something that has too long gone by the name of death," and he evokes the "generosity of death" and the "excessive giving that arises in the space of absence."[93] The conceptualization of death depends on a trembling in the present and opens a way "to begin otherwise." The act of "beginning otherwise," for Roumain the different potential for poetry promised by the schematic of death and rebirth, takes place within the fold of the present. In this sense, a political ideal of poetry is mobilized through a new modality of materialism. So while Roumain's "Is Poetry Dead?" essay is traditionally dialectical-materialist, his ideas about poetry, as well as his own poems, also point toward an interruption that might establish a new dialectic in Moten's and Chandler's sense.

Poetry Does Not X-ist

"We're all going to die."[94] These words, the first in Hughes's English translation of Roumain's landmark peasant novel *Gouverneurs de la rosée* (*Masters of the Dew*; 1944), are uttered by Délira Délivrance as she surveys the decaying landscape of her drought-stricken village, Fonds Rouge. The plot of *Gouverneurs de la rosée* is centered on the return home of Délira's son, Manuel, who spent fifteen years working on a sugarcane plantation in Cuba. Set in the 1920s and 1930s, during or just after the U.S. occupation of Haiti and when the United States was attempting to build a sugarcane industry in Cuba, *Gouverneurs de la rosée* transfigures the nostalgia of Délira and Manuel's father, Bienamé, for an ideal past into a future vision that is at once rooted in the Caribbean locale and informed by international communist politics. Manuel, drawing on the lessons he learned in Cuba, organizes the collective labor of the villagers to find water and transport it to the fields. Through the novel, Roumain "connects the local space of the Haitian peasantry to the global context of labor revolt and decolonization," thus creating "a figure for an alternative modernity that is both rural and cosmopolitan, traditional and future oriented."[95]

Gouverneurs de la rosée, translated by Langston Hughes and Mercer Cook and published in English in 1947, demonstrates how, during the immediate World War II period, Caribbean intellectuals were influenced by an international communist movement that foregrounded black liberation struggles and linked those struggles to the liberation of the global working classes.[96] More specific to the arguments of this chapter, the novel provides historical and ideological contexts for the poems Roumain produced from the mid-1930s to the mid-1940s. These contexts also allow for a conceptualization of the relationship of communist historical praxis to lyric practice from the perspective of black radicalism.

As Michelle Clayton has demonstrated in her book-length study of César Vallejo, modernist models of lyricism and avant-gardism are inadequate for understanding how poets such as Vallejo negotiated nationalist and Marxist commitments. Clayton argues that Vallejo's poetry "takes conversation as its covert model, ushering in a new conception of the lyric: no longer the self-contained statement of an individual speaker, but an opening up to the world's voices, which implode into the poetry's fragmented utterances."[97] Such a view of lyric coincides with Anthony Reed's argument that black experimental writing seeks to "break the common sense link between poetry as personal and group expression without claiming some reified notion of the 'universal,'" effecting a "dialectical interruption of the lyric mode" that presents a voice suspended between 'I' and 'we,' centered and diffuse at once."[98] Focusing on the textual aspects of Negritude poetry, Carrie Noland also troubles accounts of lyric subjectivity that connect lyric expression with a unified speaker. Noland discerns what she calls a "lyric regime," "a historical epoch dating from the Romantic period onward during which printed poems with first-person speakers generate peculiar problems for reception and interpretation." Through an exploration of "the impact of racial identification on lyric production and the impact of modernist textuality on the representation of race," she argues, "Negritude authors demand that we attend to many contexts at once (colonialism *and* modernism; the Black Atlantic *and* the Parisian avant-garde; racial identity *and* the lyric construction of the self) while never letting our eyes stray from page."[99]

Roumain takes us off the page of the history of lyricization. The poems he composed from the mid-1930s until his untimely death in 1944 develop ideas established in earlier poems such as "Quand bat le tam-tam" and "Langston Hughes," but they also more explicitly figure black radical subjectivity in terms of a communist internationalism that, like his 1944 Harlem YMCA speech, links the specific struggles of Haiti to the global antifascist front. For philosophers of communism such as Alain Badiou, the "historical praxis" that might be ascribed to lyric is a speculation about a world after the triumph of communism. In "Poetry and Communism," Badiou describes a lyric poem by Nazim Himket in such terms: "It is also lyric poetry of what communism, as the figure of humanity reconciled with its own grandeur, *will have been* after victory, which for the poet is already regret and melancholy as well as 'nostalgic hope' of his soul, past as well as future, nostalgia as well as hope."[100]

Lyric poems emerging from the black radical tradition are tuned to different figurations of humanity and of history and thus a different relation to the before and after of the coming communism. Roumain's political activities during the last ten years of his life, especially his work as part of the antifascist front in Spain, evince his connection to global struggles. At the same time, he remained deeply invested in ethnographic work and in theoretical analyses of racial capitalism, such as his 1939 study of racism in the U.S. South, *Griefs de l'homme noir* (*Grievances of the Black Man*) and, upon his return to Haiti, his establishment of the Bureau d'Ethnologie. The poems he produced around this time, while written in what would be typically considered "lyric" (that is, expressed from a singular subject, traditionally lineated and compressed, conveying meaning through imagistic impressions), use lyricism to destabilize the fiction of the modern subject as well as the modernist project of globalization. In Roumain's lyrics, the language of transnational solidarity is formulated in terms of blackness in order to envision the space of shared freedom that Cedric Robinson calls "the ontological totality."[101] In this sense, Roumain's lyrics do not serve a historicizing function so much as they subject historical narrative to theorization vis-à-vis the lyric.

Here we might turn to Roumain's poem "Bois d'ébène" ("Ebony Wood"), composed in Brussels in 1939 and dedicated to Francine Bradley, who served as secretary for the Committee for the Release of Jacques Roumain. The dedication opens the poem with a gesture of cross-cultural solidarity that acknowledges shared participation in freedom struggles; and this gesture anticipates the poem's closing imagination of "one race" that includes "workers peasants of all countries." The ultimate internationalist vision of the poem is, however, mediated by histories of colonialism and enslavement. The first half of "Bois d'ébène," titled "Prelude," uses a series of suggestive images—what another critic, in reference to *Gouverneurs de la rosée*, has described as an "all encompassing system of imagery"—to evoke the spatial and historical routes of the transatlantic slave trade as well as histories of black rebellion.[102] The poem begins in the conditional: "If the summer is rainy and dreary..." (Si l'été est pluvieux et morne...), and it tells the addressee, "If a sail of ruthless wings carries the island toward shipwrecks... you will leave / abandoning your village" (si une voliure d'ailes sauvages emporte l'ile vers les naufrages... tu partiras / abandonnant ton village). The poem documents racial and colonial exploitation, starting with the slave trade and also citing the conscripted labor that built the Congo-Ocean railway line, lynchings in the U.S. South, and the Italian invasion of Abyssinia. Underscoring these descriptions of racial and colonial violence is the question, "O my people / winter's winds in flames spreading a storm of flying ashes / will I recognize the rebellion of your hands?" (ô mon peuple / les hivées en flamme dispersant un orage / d'oiseaux de cendre / reconnaitrai-je la révolte de tes mains?).[103]

Through the mention of black rebellion, which elsewhere in the "Prelude" section of the poem is imagined as "un vin de haine" (a wine of hatred) flowing from factories and fermenting in "dans les taudis cuves d'émeute" (slum cauldrons of riots), Roumain underscores how any internationalist vision must acknowledge and incorporate the histories of slavery and of black revolt. This idea culminates in the closing stanzas of the "Prelude":

> Africa I kept your memory Africa
> you are in me
>
> Like a splinter in a wound
> Like a guardian fetish in the village center
> make of me your catapult stone
> of my mouth the lips of your wound
> of my knees the broken columns of your abasement... [104]
>
> Afrique j'ai gardé ta mémoire Afrique
> tu es en moi
> Comme l'écharde dans la blessure
> Comme un fétiche tutélaire au centre du village
> fais de moi la pierre de ta fronde
> de ma bouche les lèvres de ta plaie
> de mes genoux les colonnes brisées de ton abaissement... [105]

The second part of "Bois d'ébène" begins just after the ellipsis and is demarcated by the conjunction "but" or "yet" (pourtant) that signals a desire to be one with "workers peasants of all countries" (ouvriers paysans de tous leys pays). The second part of the poem emphasizes a shared space superseding national and cultural boundaries, where persons are joined by their "common indignity" (commune indignité) and "servitude under every unchanging sky" (servage sous tous les cieux invariable).

Roumain begins to articulate this possibility by listing persons and populations united in the fight against oppressive regimes. Coming together allows these persons to "trample down the ruins of our solitude," and so the poem also breaks the bounds of lyric solitude:

> Red Guard of China Soviet citizen German worker
> of Moabite prison Indian of the Americas
> we will rebuild
> Copan
> Palenque
> and, socialists of Tiahuanaco,
> white worker of Detroit black sharecropper of Alabama
> countless multitudes of capitalist galleys
> destiny unites us shoulder to shoulder
> and repudiating the ancient malefice of blood taboos
> we trample down the ruins of our solitude[106]

> garde rouge de la Chine soviétique ouvrier allemand de la
> prison de Moabit indio des Amériques
> Nous rebâtirons
> Copen
> Palenque
> et les Tiahuanacos socialistes
> Ouvrier blanc de Détroit péon noir d'Alabama
> peuple innombrable des galères capitalistes
> le destin nous dresses épaule contre épaule
> et reniant l'antique maléfice des tabous du sang
> nous foulons les décombres de nos solitudes[107]

Similar to Hughes's poem "Wait," discussed in chapter 1, "Bois d'ébène" uses the format of the list to destabilize the modern lyric subject: positing a subject that encompasses the universality of working-class struggle while acknowledging historical, social, and geographic difference. In Roumain's poem, the multitude is reassembled and harmonized in the closing image of a single face:

> As the contradiction of features
> is resolved in the harmony of the face
> so we proclaim the unity of suffering
> and of revolt
> of all the peoples on the surface of the earth[108]

> Comme la contradiction des traits
> se résout en l'harmonie du visage
> nous proclamons l'unité de la souffrance
> et de la révolte
> de tous les peuples sur toute la surface de la terre[109]

This image resembles a significant moment in *Gouverneurs de la rosée* when Manuel explains to Anna the *huelga* he was part of in Cuba. Manuel first shows his open hand, describing how "small" and "weak" a "single finger" is on its own. He then clenches his fist and says, "But now is it solid enough, firm enough, united enough? You'd say yes, wouldn't you? Well, that's what a strike is: A NO uttered by a thousand voices speaking as one and falling on the desk of the boss with the force of a boulder."[110]

Important to understanding the unification of multiple persons and struggles into "the harmony of the face," or the clenched fist that is a "NO uttered by a thousand voices," from the perspective of lyricism is the way in which the speaker's mouth is formed from the "memory of Africa" that acts as a "splinter in the wound." The poet does not attempt to suture this wound. Instead, by leaving the wound open and turning it into the mouth of the poet, Roumain suggests a different, and ultimately more radical, possibility. Leaving the crisis or interruption caused by historical violence open, he posits a model of history that, similar to his fantasy of poetry's death, is based on discontinuity and disruption. This moment of crisis or disruption creates a space where a new mode of revolutionary being is glimpsed as possible. Through this image, we might reread other moments in the first half of the poem when the violence wrought on the black body is figured as a materialization of the sonic. For example, the voice of the "black messenger of hope" (noir messager d'espoir) who knows all the songs of the world is supplanted by "an echo of flesh and blood," and the "wailing song" of the slave is choked by an iron collar. The resulting silence is "known" by the poet and imaged as the "twenty-five thousand railroad ties of Ebony Wood" (de vingt-cinq mille traverses de Bois-d'Ebèbe) and "petals of black bloodclots" (des pétaless de noirs caillots) on trees where black persons were lynched in Georgia.[111]

Ultimately, the figure for communist lyric, or for the possibility of communist lyric, in "Bois d'ébène" is not the singular harmony of a face but "the oppressed breath of the sea in a conch shell" (la conque le soufflé oppressé de mers).[112] When one holds a shell to the ear, one hears not the ocean roaring in the shell but the noise of the surrounding environment. In Roumain's poem, the shell reverberates with sounds of the environment that are immediately present as well as historical: African "wailing songs" and the "song of boundless affliction" that the poet heard sung by an Antillean woman. The song echoing in the shell is the lyrical irruption of interiority (the sound does not come from the shell but from the environment, which includes history) as well as of the historical realization of communism. This is echoed in a literal interruption—a parenthetical phrase—that appears in the second half of "Bois d'ébène": "(I cross your threshold—and outcast / I take your hand in mine—an untouchable)" (je franchis ton seuil—réprouvé / je prends ta main dan ma main—intouchable).[113]

Describing the process of "reassembling" those "forces" that have been "divided" by economic and imperial violence, Roumain forms a figure for poetic expression created from the wounds of history. One of Roumain's midthirties poems, "Sales nègres" ("Filthy Negroes"), also uses black revolt as a means to develop multiracial class consciousness. The poem, which appears in a posthumous volume of Roumain's work in English translation, was previously translated by Hughes in the mid-1940s. Though never published, Hughes read the poem at events, including a lecture on Latin American writers that he delivered at the Schomburg Center in New York. In the final lines, Roumain again employs the list form to imagine an assembly of proletarian forces that takes the black radical tradition as its origin. At the same time, the poem strategically uses line breaks to highlight singularities and thus call into question the relations among the individual constituencies that compose such forces:

> For even the tom-toms will have learned
> The language of the Internationale
> and we shall have chosen our day
> the day of the damned niggers
> of the damned Indians

>   of the damned Hindus
>   of the damned Indo-Chinese
>   of the damned Malays
>   of the damned Jews
>   of the damned proletarians
>   and here we are rising
>   all the wretched of the earth[114]
>
>   car jusqu'aux tam-tams auront appris le langage
>   de l'Internationale
>   car nous auron choisi notre jour
>   le jour des sales nègres
>   des sales indiens
>   des sales hindous
>   des sales indo-chinois
>   des sales arabes
>   des sales malais
>   des sales juifs
>   des sales prolétaires
>   Et nous voici debout
>   Tous les damnés de la terre[115]

"Sales nègres" composes a common language based in the tom-toms' mediation of the "Internationale," often comparing the sound of the tom-tom and its transportability to the typewriter or the telegraph. The language of "Sales nègres" also mediates, as Glick points out, the English translation of Frantz Fanon's *The Wretched of the Earth*. Glick cites Miguel Mellino's essay "The *Langue* of the Damned: Fanon and the Remnants of Europe," in which Mellino writes, "The obvious allusion to the '*Internationale*' ('*Debout le damnes de la terre*' / 'Arise, ye wretched of the earth') is mediated through an allusion to something less obvious," Roumain's "Sales nègres," which was "first cited by Fanon in 1958."[116] Roumain's poem thus allows us to understand forties communist internationalism as a vital historical site that creates linkages between historical moments. In the essay "Mikey the Rebelator," Stefano Harney and Fred Moten imagine Roumain's contemporary C. L. R. James giving Mikey some "uncoordinates."[117] Roumain's poems, even as they sketch a provisional geography of the communist international imaginary, also potentially map its uncoordinates: prompting us to consider the assembled and disassembled international as uncooperative with the panoply of liberal capitalist globalisms operative today.

For Roumain

Almost one year after Roumain died in his home city of Port-au-Prince, Langston Hughes published "A Poem for Jacques Roumain (Late Poet of Haiti)," an elegy for his comrade and fellow artist, in *New Masses*. A few months prior to its publication, Canada Lee read Hughes's poem at a memorial service for Roumain organized by the Association Democratique Haïtienne, where CPUSA leader Earl Browder also spoke.[118] These circulations of Hughes's elegy are significant in that they demonstrate Roumain's importance to both African American leftists (Party affiliated or not) and to white rank-and-file members such as Browder. At the same time, the text of the poem suggests the ways in which, as the forties wore on, the possible worlds imagined by communism seemed out of reach. Hughes's poem opens by posing two questions to Roumain: "When did you / Find out about the world, / Jacques?" and "When did you learn to say / Without fear or shame / *Je suis communiste*?"[119] Hughes's opening questions are laudatory, honoring the legacy of Roumain's activism, at the same time that they are, as Arnold Rampersad has observed, "fraught with self-reference."[120] Indeed, Hughes's opening stanzas resist the conventional function of many elegies, which use apostrophe to reanimate the dead. Hughes finds himself unable to "answer for" the dead Roumain, a point painstakingly emphasized in the multiple variations on the phrase "And you are gone."

In contrast to other tributes in circulation—such as Countee Cullen's "Elegy (In Memoriam: Jacques Roumain)," which declares that he will "never speak of him as dead, / Nor speak of him as one who *was*"—Hughes's poem begins on a definitive note of irrevocable loss.[121] But what has been lost? What is symbolic about Roumain's death? As has been well documented, black communists in the United States became disillusioned with the Party when it abandoned domestic race struggles to focus efforts on the antifascist fight abroad, and the Party, on the whole, struck a blow when Stalin signed a nonaggression pact with Hitler in August 1939.[122] As the Second World War ended, Henry Luce's vision of globality in "The American Century" (1941) trumped both the imagination of a "People's Century," as articulated by Henry Wallace in 1942, and the communist promise to unite "scattered but kindred peoples into a whole," expressed by Richard Wright.[123] Indeed, Wright's retrospective account of his entrance into the Communist Party, framed by his public renunciation of his Party membership, suggests in microcosm the weariness that characterized Party politics during the mid-1940s, especially for black communists in the United States and elsewhere.

In this context, we might read Hughes's elegy for Roumain as a meditation on the difficulty of realizing his vision of global race and class solidarity as the possibilities for that vision were in the process of being foreclosed. But as with so many of the materials examined over the course of this book, the possible lessons and meanings of Hughes's poem have been erased. The significance of the opening questions for the dead Roumain in Hughes's poem might be further understood in light of a line that was to be added to an earlier draft of the elegy but that was left out of the final version: "When did you learn / That nobody is anywhere / When the least is left behind?"[124] The phrase "nobody is anywhere" could be read to mean that "nobody exists" or "nobody has the grounds for personhood" when others are left behind. In this reading, Hughes's poem might be seen to attempt to establish a new ground for political existence and belonging by forging, with those who are "left behind" by the existing social order, a revolutionary community on the margins. But "nobody is anywhere" could also be read to mean that "no one progresses" or "no one goes anywhere" when "the least is left behind." In this reading, the poem seems to slip into liberal pluralism, where those who are "left behind" seek recognition and inclusion within the democratic capitalist system.

As I have demonstrated, Roumain theorized the relationship of poetry to politics and history while in exile in the United States and at a moment of crisis, when the organized left was entrenched in the antifascist struggle and reeling from the effects of the nationalist victory in Spain and the Hitler-Stalin pact. The possibilities for lyric inherent in Roumain's writings have been obscured by the realities of Cold War geopolitics, especially because the realization of the magnitude of fascist violence restored a moral ground to lyricism that Roumain eschews. Such tensions and foreclosures are evident in the second half of "A Poem for Jacques Roumain," when Hughes, after again emphasizing that Roumain is "gone," declares,

> But you are still here
> From the point of my pen in New York
> To the toes of the blackest peasant
> In the *morne*,
> Because you found out
> What it is all about.

With these lines, Hughes resurrects the dead poet by declaring that he is "still here." But while Roumain's connection to "the point" of Hughes's "pen in New York" and "the toes of the blackest peasant" suggest the sweep of his influence and his vision, there is a way in which Hughes's ultimate portrayal of Roumain is in tension with Roumain's own vision of the coming revolutionary community. The poem ends,

> Always
> You will be
> Man
> Finding out about
> The ever bigger world
> Before him.
> Always you will be
> Frontiersman,
> Pathfinder
> Breaker down of
> Barriers,
> Hand that links
> Erzulie to the Pope,
> Damballa to Lenin,
> Haiti to the universe,
> Bread and fish
> To fisherman
> To man
> To me.
>
> Strange
> About eternity
> Eternal
> To the free.[125]

By portraying Roumain as a "Hand that links" disparate times, people, and places, Hughes's elegy shares Roumain's vision of a revolutionary community that is constituted by global networks and that, to use Hughes's language, "breaks down barriers." However, the elegy's act of labeling Roumain a "Frontiersman" undercuts this vision. While "Frontiersman" connotes the act of exploring uncharted territory, it also, especially in the U.S. context, employs the rhetoric of U.S. democracy and manifest destiny. Even the final lines are somewhat at odds with Roumain's notion of what a radical poet might be or do: intimating that a poet who insisted that "a rather good definition of 'writer' should be that essentially he is *not* free, that thoughts are so deeply determined by history, that they have no real value if they do not reflect and express the dialectic pulsation of life," is, above all else, "free."[126]

Robin D. G. Kelley suggests that recovering the emancipatory vision of black activists can help in the urgent task of imagining, in Jayne Cortez's phrase, "somewhere in advance of nowhere."[127] One wonders what claims we should make for the status of poetry at a time when the violences of globalization eviscerate individual lives from within neoliberal fantasies about "creative expression" and "human dignity." The undersides of the poets' international are the early-twentieth-century juggernauts of U.S. imperialism, forms of racial violence, and totalitarian terror. If the wounds of the past are also always bound to tear open, the task is to find a new poetics for imagining global solidarity and, to paraphrase Harney and Moten, imagining what exists.[128]

Part III
Rhythm

CHAPTER FIVE

The Left Needs Rhythm
Popular Front Poetry, Antifascism, and the Counterarchives of Modernism

In the general sense, the dilemma of modern poetry will be resolved as the people resolve the dilemma of the split atom: shall it be for Life or Death?
—Martha Millet, "Modern Poetry: For or Against?"

Ransacked Libraries

Have we really given up the ghost of a modernism written in Ezra Pound's name? This chapter asks what is at stake in the critical erasure of writers such as Martha Millet, a communist poet and labor journalist who, from the late 1950s through the early 1970s, worked on a book-length examination of Ezra Pound tentatively titled "The Ezra Pound Myth." Millet's study was born from a lifetime commitment to the principles of international Marxism that manifested itself as a deeply felt need to address the political and intellectual climate of the Cold War. Encouraged in part by her father, Joseph, a garment-industry unionist and founding member of the CPUSA, Millet had been active in Party organizations since she was a teenager in the first years of the Depression. She attended her first May Day parade in 1929, when she was just eleven, and she joined the Young Communist League about five years later (see figure 11). In the immediate post–World War II period, Millet faced precarious employment because of her communist affiliations, and around 1948, she lost her job as a writer for the National Maritime Union newsletter in the first round of interunion McCarthyite witch hunts.[1] Meanwhile, Pound's literary prominence was secured despite his far-right politics. In 1949, three years after the dismissal of Pound's indictment for treason, his *Pisan Cantos*, a poem sequence that included profascist content, was awarded the inaugural Bollingen Prize for Poetry. Millet does not remark on this particular confluence of late-forties events in her manuscript for "The Ezra Pound Myth," but her arguments reproach both Pound and the surrounding conservative intellectual conglomerate that promoted "poetic achievement" as a transcendent cultural value. At roughly the same time that this self-described "working woman, mother and activist" summoned a lifetime of political commitment for a critical project that condemned the U.S. institutionalization of fascism under the

FIGURE 11 Teenage Martha Millet featured on the cover of *Labor Defender*, January 1936. Used by permission of Alex Garlin.

guise of modernist aesthetics, a Yale Ph.D. and beginning assistant professor at the University of California, Santa Barbara, staked his claim with a hagiography of Pound that, at least for a time, became synonymous with modernism itself.[2]

To the contemporary reader, Millet's assessments of Pound are not be so surprising. In 2017, a National Public Radio report on antifascist activism cited Pound as a "fascist propagandist" and did not mention his legacy as a poet. A host of scholars have addressed problems of racism, anti-Semitism, and profascism as they relate to Pound's writings, and recent surveys of modernism have evinced "a sharp decline in market value" for the once-hero of the modernist avant-garde.[3] For decades, scholarship in the field of modernist studies has worked outside a monolithic concept of Pound-era modernism to establish "alternative and different modernities" that account for geographic differences as well as sociopolitical issues of race, class, gender, and sexuality.[4] Such work, summed up by Douglas Mao and Rebecca Walkowitz under the rubric of "new modernist studies," significantly expands the purview of the "old" modernist studies by further blurring the boundaries between high art and popular cultural forms, reconfiguring literary canons, and centering works by members of marginalized social groups. As I mention in this book's introduction, however, the liberal logic of an "expansionist" or pluralist modernism also covers over deep historical antagonisms and thus has the potential to foreclose alternate ideological and aesthetic configurations.[5]

We might take a cue from V. F. Calverton, who, in the 1931 inaugural issue of *The Left: A Quarterly Review of Radical and Experimental Art* (Spring 1931), put it this way: "*Industry respects no traditions; bows to no customs; slowly but steadily it destroys differences and establishes resemblances.* The similar becomes dominant, and diverse traditions very soon become one tradition."[6] Millet began composing "The Ezra Pound Myth" during a Cold War moment when the history and meaning of modernism was "up for grabs."[7] The purpose of Millet's study of Pound, however, was not to redefine modernism from the perspective of the left but to abolish it as a category of literary and intellectual significance. As she wrote in another unpublished essay, "Footnote on Modern Poetry," "To write in one's time is not necessarily to write as a *modern*."[8] For Millet, "Modernism" and "New Criticism" were fascist and racist ideologies that registered "contempt" for humanity and, therefore, did not serve the antiracist, feminist, and anti-imperialist Marxist literary traditions of which she was a part.[9] Millet, therefore, does not fit properly within modernist studies even at its most expansive. And she should not. Her work suggests that the multiplication of modernisms is always already part of literary studies institutions' complicity in liberal capitalist formations.[10]

Tariq Ali writes in his contemporary meditation *On Lenin*, "Today's dominant ideology and the power structures it defends are so hostile to the social and liberation struggles of the last century that a recovery of as much historical and political memory as is feasible becomes an act of resistance. In these bad times, even the anti-capitalism on offer is limited. It is apolitical and ahistorical."[11] Opening Millet's archive, I rethink narratives about modernism from the perspective of the Jewish American communist left. The period from the publication of Millet's first poems in the early thirties to the composition of "The Ezra Pound Myth" in the sixties encompasses significant changes in modern American poetics. If, for most of the 1930s, there was little regard for the New Critical pronouncement that poetry and politics do not mix, by the end of the decade the spoils had fallen to those who were on "the side of the eternal verity of purportedly apolitical art."[12] Following the disillusionments of the 1939 Nazi-Soviet Pact, certain strains of leftist writing and criticism began to echo the New Critics' dismissals of "propaganda" as well as their emphases on form and freedom of expression. The stylistic techniques and attitudes that had defined modernism earlier in the century (such as allusiveness, abstraction, fragmentation, and the impersonality of the artist) were emptied of their political content and replaced with a celebration of individual freedom of expression.[13]

Through a study of Millet, I excavate discourses about poetics that expand the scope of contemporary reading practices and theories. More specifically, I trace an alternative history and theory of modernist rhythm that, I argue, also provides a new sense of the relationship between modernist forms and left politics. The concept of "rhythm" in poetry was a nodal point for shifting ideas about aesthetic and political value from the thirties to the fifties. It was, of course, in *The Pisan Cantos* (specifically, Canto 81) that Pound penned the line—"To break the pentameter, that was the first heave"—that would become a slogan for modernist poetic achievement.[14] Accepted stories about Anglophone poetics have turned on Pound's fiction of modernism as a historical rupture. As Meredith Martin and Erin Kappeler demonstrate, the notion that modernist prosodic experiments freed writers from the shackles of nineteenth-century genteel forms presents a homogeneous view of turn-of-the-century verse culture.[15] In the anticommunist postwar milieu, the rejection of traditional forms was a rejection not necessarily of the genteel Victorians but, rather, of the communist dupes: the break from the regular stanza, rhyme, and meter patterns of workers' songs and people's ballads was tantamount to a break from Party control over artistic expression. Indeed, by 1939, the same Philip Rahv who damned lyric poetry in Jack Conroy's worker-writers rag *Rebel Poet* would argue in Robert Penn Warren's New Critical *Southern Review* that the writing formulas promoted by the Communist Party during the thirties were "empty of aesthetic principle" and served as a "complex political mechanism" whereby writers were made to believe that they were allying themselves with the working class when, in effect, they were surrendering their "independence to the Communist Party."[16]

This chapter suggests an alternate tagline for understanding the development of modern American poetry in terms of rhythm. As Martin argues, in discourses about modernism, rhythm is often posited as a rejection of "meter," which stands in for "convention and tradition in verse." Within historical modernist discourses, as Kappeler points out, the abstraction of meter into rhythm often turned on ideologies about race and nation.[17] In 1938, Millet submitted an editorial to the *New Masses* arguing, "The Left needs rhythm, in all its implications, in order to combat the profit system in its latest manifestation, the totalitarian state."[18] On first read, Millet's statement seems to be evidence of a commonly held thirties belief that the only poems suitable for combat—the only poems that could act as weapons in the class struggle—were those the rhythm and rhyme patterns of which provided a beat for a May Day march.

Millet's editorial, however, also reveals that communist poets used rhythm as a signifier for embodied collective experience: prosodic rhythms literally marked the time of protest poems, but rhythm was also used in a figurative sense to evoke the joy of existing in the out-of-time of revolutionary futurity. Rhythm, in this latter sense, was an abstract way to describe a poem's political usefulness as well as a way to name, even if imprecisely, a poem's political effects.

Across the sections that follow, I retrieve Millet's poetic and scholarly contributions in order to map an alternate set of critical coordinates that does not rely on the putative modernist/antimodernist split. Millet, a devoted communist and active writer throughout her life, thought about rhythm in ways that give insight into the cultural and political changes from the revolutionary third period of the early 1930s to the Popular Front "people's poetry" of the late 1930s to the "wartime progressive poetry" of the 1940s.[19] In the chapter's second section, I use Millet's early involvement with the communist children's magazine the *New Pioneer* to unpack the complex relationship between traditional forms and political community formation during the thirties. The generic histories enacted by communist children's poems provide a foundation for considering how rhythm was evoked in late-thirties Popular Front poetic discourses as well as early-forties antifascist discourses. As I show in the third section, during the Popular Front, diverse traditional genres were collapsed into an ideal poem that had rhythm, where rhythm described both form (that is, a regular stanza, rhyme, and/or metrical pattern) and function (that is, a poem that is accessible to the masses, easy to circulate, and/or representative of common people). In the fourth section, which focuses on Millet's contributions to the World War II–era volume *Seven Poets in Search of an Answer* (1944), I demonstrate how in antifascist discourses and activism, rhythm was defined in ways that elide conventional high/low divides. The chapter closes by returning to Millet's Cold War criticism in order to revisit what is at stake in her critical erasure as well as her critical recovery. I examine these moments in Millet's career both in their institutional contexts and in relation to the works of poets including Carl Sandburg, Lorine Niedecker, and Kenneth Fearing.

Communism for Kids

One of Millet's first published poems appeared in the May 1933 issue of the communist children's magazine the *New Pioneer*. The poem, which occupied a full two-page spread, explains how the peaceful community of Children's Town was taken over by a band of gluttonous Boy Scouts (see figure 12). The

Scouts forced the town's children to labor in mills and on farms with barely enough food to fill their stomachs, while the newly inducted Boy Scout mayor and his council grew fat on oysters and butter—until, that is, the arrival of the "Pioneer Pied Piper," a young man clad in a blue uniform with a hammer and sickle sewn in red on his shirt pocket and a bugle hanging by his side. The Piper appears at a Town Hall organized by the Children's Town workers, who are protesting their poor working conditions:

> The mayor was not a little amazed,
> And the council were sitting slightly dazed.
> "Mr. Mayor," said he, that was all he uttered,
> The mayor moistened his lips and stuttered:
> "A Savior! A Savior!—See here, my good fellow,
> I'll fill both your pockets with gold fine and yellow,
> If only you'll rid us of troubles and worry."
> The council all stood and they bowed in a flurry.
> "I do not want gold, I have come as you'll see
> To set these wretched children free."

Upon the Piper's announcement to the mayor of Children's Town that he has come "To set these wretched children free," the Piper uses his trumpet to bring the toiling workers into formation. In a reversal of the "Pied Piper of Hamelin" fairy tale, Millet's "Pioneer Pied Piper" uses the music of his bugle to organize, and ultimately liberate, the youthful working-class masses. His trumpet blast sets the children on a march that forces the ruling-class Scouts out of town and to their deaths. (As the Scouts flee, the bridge they are crossing collapses, and they all drown in a river.) Finally free, the citizens of Children's Town stay to rebuild their community as a "Pioneer Commune," the home to a "happy race" of "folks" bursting with "carefreeness and mirth."[20]

Some twenty years after "Pioneer Pied Piper" appeared in *New Pioneer*, Earl Robinson responded to Millet's long poem *Thine Alabaster Cities: A Poem for Our Times* (1952) by welcoming her to "the good fight." While his letter is full of praise for Millet's efforts, the famed composer expressed frustration with her tendency to abandon rhyme and rhythmic patterns just as they were starting to intrigue the reader. "I would love to see you do something for singing. It seems to me that you could," he encouraged her before offering a last bit of advice: "One method would be to go to the opposite extreme and write something for children. Think of the kind of language and image a kid would understand and enjoy singing or listening to."[21] In short, Robinson suggested that Millet do something she had started to do in the thirties and had continued to do since. Millet had multiform experiences writing and publishing children's verse. In addition to publishing poems such as "Pioneer Pied Piper," she joined the editorial board of the *New Pioneer* in 1934 and contributed poems and commentaries for the magazine throughout the thirties. Millet also went on to compose a large body of unpublished work for children in the years after the publication of *Thine Alabaster Cities*, including two story collections and two poetry collections as well as the book-length poems *Kid with Kazoo* (1957) and *Last of the Lemmings: An Allegory* (1967). Her return to writing avidly for children in the 1950s and 1960s cannot be attributed to Robinson's suggestion. A mother of two, Millet often crafted handmade books of verse for her own children, and during the mid-1950s, the family lived near their friends the communist children's writers Mary Folsom and Franklin ("Dank") Folsom, in a leftist artist community in Roosevelt, New Jersey.

Writings for children are logical counterparts to popular thirties compositions such as Robinson's collaborations with the poet Alfred Hayes on the folk song "Joe Hill" (1936) and with John LaTouche on "Ballad for Americans" (1939). Like "Joe Hill," which elevated the storied wobbly to an archetype, children's tales spin fundamental truths in ways that seem widely accessible. Writing in the *Daily Worker*, Mike Gold pointed to the significance of children's stories for left literary culture: "Even today I find time to read fairy tales, folk stories, legends," he wrote. "They reveal, better than any other literature, the permanent soul of mankind."[22] And yet the point of Robinson's advice is not what truths to tell but how to tell them; and, according to him, they are best told in rhyme. Robinson's wish for a poem a kid would understand *and* love to sing is continuous with the demand—prevalent in nineteenth- and twentieth-century labor poetry traditions but increasingly salient during the era of the Popular Front—for sonically and rhythmically regular compositions written in traditional verse genres. Looking back at Millet's "Pioneer Pied Piper" suggests more complicated logics of form and genre than what is immediately apparent in Robinson's desire for a political poem a kid would like. Like much of the work published in *New Pioneer*, Millet's poem is deceptively complex: it acts out aesthetic and political agendas that, in turn, offer much to unpack about the variegated relationships between form and political community formation during the thirties.

"Pioneer Pied Piper" is an allegory about the political function of rhythm that appears in the recognizable generic frame of the ballad. While a reader adhering to stable definitions of the ballad stanza (a quatrain rhyming *abcb* or *abab* with alternating iambic tetrameter and trimeter lines) might hesitate to give Millet's poem the label, my point is not that "Pioneer Pied

FIGURE 12 Martha Millet, with illustrations by Mayra Morrow, pages from "Pioneer Pied Piper," *New Pioneer*, May 1931. Used by permission of Alex Garlin.

Piper" is a textbook ballad but that it approximates one through its folkloric content, its use of alliteration and rhyme, and its formatting on the magazine page. Scholars of nineteenth-century poetics have demonstrated the instability of the ballad as a prescriptive genre, arguing instead that it is a labile poetic category that has come to stand in for "communal ideals."[23] The early-twentieth-century folklorist and literary critic Francis Barton Gummere, a student of the famed Anglo-Saxon ballad anthologist Francis Child, linked the rhythms of the ballad to national community formation in his influential study of popular ballads. Before Benedict Anderson used "imagined community" to theorize how national belonging is imagined in relationship to print media, Gummere identified "the cadent feet" of "the imagined community" of the nation in the ballad form.[24]

For left poets and critics, the "imagined community" of the ballad was not the nation as Gummere understood it but a broad working-class alliance that was simultaneously rooted in national traditions (a version of Antonio Gramsci's "national-popular") and imagined as part of an international community of workers.[25] Nonetheless, a similar relationship between ballad rhythms and political community formation appears in poems such as "Pioneer Pied Piper," when the successful organization of the Children's Town working class is inaugurated by the Piper's bugle blast:

> Then silently into the street he stept
> With bugle to lips, like an adept.
> Knowing well what powers slept
> Within his trumpet—there he blew
> A blast upon it, and e'er one knew
>   What was happing
>   There came a tapping
>   Of torn shoes flapping
>   And loose heels rapping,
> And down the street, the people's feet
> Leaped with an unceasing beat.
> Little children, big children, small and tall
> To the sound of the bugle they raced all.[26]

The Piper's bugle is a figure for a ballad form that "Pioneer Pied Piper" imperfectly imitates. When the Piper starts to play, the beat of the poem picks up. The introduction of the shorter lines, rhyming "happing," "tapping," "flapping," and "rapping," suggest that a new rhythm might be enough to propel a nascent political community to action. The bugle song's "unceasing beat" gets the "people's feet" moving "down the street," a movement emphasized by the trochaic feet that also move the middle rhymes along. The poem's formatting, which recalls the conventions of ballad broadsides, reinforces the form through what might be called a visual rhythm that capitalizes on the supposed cultural work of the ballad rhythm. Through strategic use of print conventions, the page creates, as if by the magic available only in fairy tales, the kind of oral event described and inscribed in the poem itself.[27]

Poems such as "Pioneer Pied Piper" evince ideas about poetic form and function operative on the communist left. At the same time, because they are meant to provide an alternative political education for Young Pioneers, they are marked by the very schoolroom cultures they aimed to subvert. Mainstream critics such as Gummere viewed ballad reading as an essential part of human development that was linked to national development. Scott Newman sums up Gummere's position in his explanation of the early-twentieth-century appeal of the ballad: "Helping the student to pass from 'the world's childhood' into 'the epic phase' of adolescence, the ballad becomes part of a curriculum that is American by virtue of the agency it democratically attributes to the individual imagination, honoring the child's 'experience' and expanding his or her imaginative repertoire."²⁸ In the communist milieu, the ballad form had a special relationship to representations of working-class experience and community formation that ran counter to Gummere's idealistic assertions. For Gummere, ballads honor the "experience" of childhood by expanding a youth's "imaginative repertoire." Pseudoballads for communist kids cut through received notions about childhood and poetry alike. The children in "Pioneer Pied Piper" are not pure vassals moving from innocence to experience. They are ideological subjects who have been interpellated by a socioeconomic system, whether they are the rulers of that system (Boy Scouts) or oppressed by it (Children's Town's workers). When, at the end of the poem, the child workers become revolutionary subjects, it is not because their youth makes them capable of expressing or living out a utopian vision; rather, it is because they develop an awareness of their material conditions.

When "Pioneer Pied Piper" was published in *New Pioneer*, communist activists and political leaders favored poems written in the tradition of workers' songs, ballads, and folk culture.²⁹ Compared to the surge of interest in the ballad during the Popular Front era of the late thirties, it seemed that communist cultural workers paid scant, even skeptical, attention to ballad and folklore traditions in the early part of the decade. Even so, ballads mediated local field organizers' encounters with working-class and rural agrarian communities, and they used transcriptions of ballads and work songs to communicate information about the conditions they encountered.³⁰ By the late thirties, Woody Guthrie famously remarked that his experiences traveling the country led him to "major" in the "art and science of Migratin' . . . at a school so big you can't get out of it."³¹

The ballad was thus a means to learn and teach outside of the assembly line of the modern school system, which promoted bourgeois cultural values and encouraged learning by rote. Despite Guthrie's distaste for corporate radio, he himself participated in programs such as the *American School of the Air*, which aimed to provide a progressive education to school-age children through folksong programs that offered counternarratives to the versions of American history learned in schools.³² John Lomax framed the beginning of his ballad-collecting career as a rejection of the university system. In his autobiography, he recalls a turning-point moment, when he handed his college professor, an Anglo-Saxon specialist, the packet of Texas cowboy songs he had been collecting. The next day, the professor told him that the samples were "tawdry, cheap, and unworthy" and then encouraged Lomax to give his attention "to the great movements of writing that had come sounding down the ages" because "there was no possible connection ... between the tall tales of Texas and the tall tales of Beowulf."³³

Ballad singers such as Guthrie and collectors such as Lomax might have rejected the schoolroom altogether, but the *New Pioneer* editors often recontextualized and reinterpreted aspects of schoolroom culture for their readers. Julia L. Mickenberg explains that, in general, "the *New Pioneer*'s stories and articles tended to be more factual than fanciful, with a heavy emphasis on historical and scientific themes." Every issue of the magazine featured historical fiction, biographical essays on revolutionary figures, and series such as "American History Told in Pictures," which retold major events in U.S. history from a left perspective.³⁴ The history of U.S. poetry was also recast from the standpoint of left politics and aesthetics, as the magazine's editors and contributors ransacked the nineteenth century for a "usable past" for poetry, one that would illuminate a long tradition of "popular" poems written for the "common people." For instance, Millet contributed a short piece on the revolutionary poet Philip Freneau, aptly subtitled "An American Poet of All the Peoples." In it, she suggests that Freneau's poetry reached a large number of citizens because it addressed important political issues of the time. According to the article, Freneau wrote about slavery and oppression "almost a hundred years before the slave issue grew into Civil War" and penned "fierce poetry with which he lashed out against the oppressive rule of the British king." He became a national figure through the writing of "fiery songs," giving "new power to popular issues."³⁵

Millet's little sketch of Freneau says a lot about how 1930s left prescriptions for poetry, especially those that emerged in the Communist Party's shift to its Popular Front policy, were read back into early American poetic cultures. Left interpretations of nineteenth-century verse cultures assume that, if a poem is written in the voice of the "common people," its content is self-evident. A *Daily Worker* reviewer for Jean Thomas's collection *Ballad Makin' in the Mountains of Kentucky* (1939), for example, observed that Appalachian balladeers "probably never heard of Marx or Lenin, but there can be no doubt where his roots lay as he sings 'Union men have a say in what they receive each hour / Factories cannot operate without labor power.'"³⁶ The reviewer thus suggests that knowledge of anticapitalist ideology can be transmitted through rhyme and that working-class identification also takes place in communal recitation. The circulation of the rhymed and rhythmic ballad in these contexts contrasts the schoolroom scene, where recitation was part of a child's interpellation into the national-capitalist order.

Children's poems—deliberately constructed but in forms so familiar that they seem natural—illuminate the slippage between the left ideal of the accessible poem and the historical reading practices on which this ideal relies. This slippage is perhaps nowhere more apparent than in the biographical sketch of Henry Wadsworth Longfellow that Millet penned for the October 1938 *New Pioneer*. Millet casts Longfellow as, above all, a social poet who was enraptured by "the love of literature and writing" and the uses to which such writing could be put. Over the course of the essay, she highlights his interest in the "impoverishment and oppression" of the people of Spain, his "deeper awareness" of Native American culture, and his condemnation of the "criminal institution" of slavery.[37] Millet's narrative of Longfellow's political activism is overly forgiving, if not downright wrong. But it is also canny. In mentioning Spain, the colonization of the American West, and the antislavery movement, Millet alludes to the U.S. left's solidarity with the international antifascist front in Spain as well as the anti-imperialist and antiracist discourses characterizing Popular Front politics. In so doing, she also extracts Longfellow from the conservative schoolroom, where, as Angela Sorby explains, his poems served a "fantasy of universal humanity" that is rooted in nationalist discourses.[38] Millet repurposes Longfellow for the *New Pioneer* schoolroom, where the ideal of a united "common people" is meant to enact an international, multiracial, and potentially revolutionary political community.

Millet revises Longfellow's politics not only so that they adhere to her own but also so that Longfellow's use of traditional forms and genres might be redeemed. She highlights the fact that his poems' political messages are conveyed through simple and musical verse that can be enjoyed by all. She praises Longfellow as a writer who "wrote simply and understandably. He will be remembered as the ever-musical poet of simplicity who could make people see the traditions and folklore of the much-abused Indian through his poetry, and who dealt with life and people in a manner that *all* could enjoy."[39] Millet does not mention Longfellow's use of classical meter (such as the distinctive trochaic tetrameter lines of "Song of Hiawatha," which she eventually quotes); she instead describes him as an "ever-musical poet" whose work reached the "people." In Millet's estimation, Longfellow, in a strange way, becomes the ideal radical poet. And as she suggests through strategic excerpting from "Song of Hiawatha," he advocates peace and solidarity by speaking to children:

O children; my poor children!
Listen to the words of wisdom,
Listen to the words of warning,

>From the lips of the Great Spirit,
>From the Master of Life, who made you.
>...............................
>I am weary of your quarrels,
>Weary of your wars and bloodshed,
>Weary of your prayers for vengeance,
>Of your wranglings and dissensions;
>All your strength is in your union,
>All your danger is in discord;
>Therefore be at peace henceforward,
>And as brothers live together.[40]

Capitalizing on the poem's apparent popularity while eliding its nationalist and imperialist discourses, Millet's short article makes "Song of Hiawatha" read like a Popular Front political vision of "strength in union." Her appropriation of this widely circulating nineteenth-century poem stands as yet another example of Longfellow's continued popularity, but it also provides insight into the significance of children's poetry for understanding Old Left poetic culture. Millet's own children's poems, as well as her rereadings of popular poems such as "Song of Hiawatha," illustrate the complex ways in which poets associated with the communist and Popular Front left attempted to make poetry "popular" in more specialized forums such as *New Pioneer* as well as in more widely circulating publications such as *New Masses*. Read in this context, the radical children's poetry in *New Pioneer* also archives significant dimensions of left poetic output during the 1930s. Even if these poems remain obscure, and howsoever they represent political appropriations of popular texts, they index the history of a poetic left involved in the radical reappropriation of popular poems, generic conventions, and traditional forms.

As I outline in the next section, from the late 1930s through the 1950s, cultural front commentators consolidated the diverse functions of genres such as the rhyme and the ballad into an ideal poem that had "rhythm." Within this milieu, Longfellow's trochaic tetrameter was conflated with Walt Whitman's free-verse lines underneath a broad banner of political effectiveness. Before turning to how these debates played out during the Popular Front, I want to consider one more child rhymester: Jules Golden, the child Whitman at the center of the 1955 novel *The Changelings*, by Jo Sinclair (Ruth Seid). While Sinclair's novel, written in the Cold War period, is a retrospective on the Popular Front and the antifascist crusade, the novel's representations of poetry and its uses are very much of that era.[41] Indeed, Jules's poems are near-perfect representations of what Popular

Front poets imagined poetry could do: they simultaneously explore the complexities of racial and ethnic prejudice, offer hope for an ideal world, and provide Judy and the other "changelings" (Jules's word for young radicals) with comfort, support, and guidance. Sinclair, through the character of Jules, imagines poems whose messages can be immediately transmitted to readers. In contrast to Millet, however, Sinclair's example is not the generic verses of the fireside poets but Whitman's long line.

Dying of a weak heart, the young poet Jules writes poems about the prejudices and injustices that he witnesses in his home and in his neighborhood, referred to in the novel as "the street." The prejudices of "the street" are complex: Jules's mother fears that the *Schwartze* (an epithet for African Americans) will begin moving to the neighborhood; a young Italian woman is sent to a convent because of her supposed relationship with an African American man; and the sister of Jules's best friend, Judy Vincent, has been alienated from her Jewish family for marrying an Irish Catholic. Throughout the novel, Judy evokes Jules's poems as she attempts to make sense of these social complexities and her place in them. Judy looks to Jules's poetry to reveal her world to her, to expose the invisible structures that engender physically and emotionally violent behavior. To Judy, Jules *is* his red notebook of poems, and its contents are "a kind of oracle advice."[42] Jules's poems begin to resonate even more deeply with Judy as her friendship with Clara Jackson, the young African American girl she meets after being attacked, further develops her antiracist consciousness. Judy hears Jules's poem "Die Schwartze" (Yiddish for "the black ones") after her first encounter with Clara, and she seems deeply affected by the poem's message about the psychology of racism. After returning home that night, Judy realizes that "it was that brown-skinned girl who lingered in her mind, *along with Jules' new poem*, not the knowledge that she had lost her position in the gang."[43]

The influence of Whitman is readily apparent in Jules's most important poem, "The Changelings." The poem describes the concept of "changelings"—children who do not belong to their parents in their "heart" and who act against the discrimination pervading "the street." Judy considers the poem "her most precious possession," and it is the gift handed from Jules to Judy binding them together as child radicals. At the end of *The Changelings*, Judy inherits Jules's notebook of poems, and as she pages through the notebook, Judy, along with the reader, is able to study "The Changelings" in its entirety. The poem opens with the invitation, "Come, Changeling, let us look into our hearts for identity!" and then moves into a description of the conditions, emotions, and energies that constitute a "changeling identity." These themes are reinforced by the last stanzas of "The Changelings," which Judy discovers at the end of Jules's manuscript after his death:

> But a street marches upon the rest of the world.
> The rope knotted by shivering people chains all of us, enmeshes our minds.
>
> And who will untie the knots of rope?
> The Changeling!—coming upon her parents' wailing wall, hearing the chant of all her grandfathers and all their fathers in her parents' lamenting prayer.
>
> And who will pause to sing at that wall?
> The Changeling!—meeting all the world there, taking her place, lifting her voice, so that the prayer will be anyone's now—love without fear—music so strong as to soar over the wall.[44]

Read as an addendum to the poem's previous iteration, the version familiar to Judy, this last fragment seems to condense the broader idea of identifying as a "changeling" into the microcosms of "the street" and Judy's family. Jules's poem, at its finish, becomes a personal call to Judy to "come upon her parents' wailing wall" and move forward as a political actor who sings and prays her way over the wall and, therefore, out of the knots and chains that "enmesh our minds." Through Jules's words, Judy is able to forge a personal identity in opposition to the logic of her family and the street. "The Changelings" can be read as an ideal Popular Front poem because it moves Judy both emotionally and politically. Reading it, she is brought to tears, but she also feels it "moving with her into the street, like a singing." The poem also can be read as a map of how diverse genres circulating on the left collapsed into an idea of poetry as a transcendent political action. In "The Changelings," disparate forms of expression—chant, prayer, song—are collapsed into an ideal of poetry that can float over the adults' wailing wall.

This Poem Kills Fascists!

Left poets and readers of left poetry did more than simply draw on the poetry of the past; they actively reimagined the history of poetic forms and the discourses about the social uses that those forms might have. In the Depression years, even Mother Goose joined the picket line, as evinced by Harry Alan

Potamkin's "Mother Goose on the Breadline," featured in the May 1931 *New Pioneer*:

> Little Miss Muffett
> Ate such vile stuff, it
> Made her feel rotten inside
> Black coffee, stale bread—
> Miss Muffett saw Red!
> She joined with the workers and cried:
>   "Don't Starve, Fight!
>   Don't Starve, Fight!"[45]

Rhymes such as Potamkin's exemplify the ideal of an accessible political poem chock-full of what Granville Hick's called communism's "good news."[46] After all, what could be easier to read than a rhyming poem written for a child? What kind of poem is more widely understood than a simple nursery rhyme, even if that rhyme puts a starving Little Miss Muffett on the picket line?

The formal traits associated with children's verse (rhyme, metrical regularity, refrain, the use of mnemonic devices) were valued by a large sector of left poets who identified those traits as central to the formation of political communities. In this section, I concentrate more fully on the Popular Front discourses of the late 1930s in order to demonstrate how "rhythm" was used to describe and evaluate political verse. Within cultural front discourses, diverse genres—songs, ballads, nursery rhymes, and abecedarians—were collapsed into an ideal poem that has "rhythm." Popular Front cultural workers' use of rhythm as a prosodic-cum-political descriptor ran counter to how the term was mobilized by "high" modernists such as Pound. ("As regarding rhythm," Pound famously wrote in "A Retrospect," one should "compose in the sequence of the musical phrase, not in sequence of a metronome.")[47] However, the ways that left poets conceptualized rhythm in order to mediate ideas about social life and belonging are applicable to a wide range of poems produced within and outside the Popular Front milieu.

In 1938, when Millet wrote a letter to the *New Masses* editors asserting that "the Left needs rhythm in all its implications," she was responding to an ongoing debate in the magazine. Written on behalf of her New York City poetry group, her letter was one response among many to an editorial on the topic "Poetry: Dead or Alive?" that summarized a debate in Toledo, Ohio, between the English professor George Gulette and the CIO field representative Albert Shepard. Gulette pronounced poetry dead: "It has no mourners," he posited, "because nine out of ten persons never knew it was alive, and the other one refuses to recognize its demise. . . . American civilization is active, virile, and extravert; poetry has no place in it." Shepard countered that Gulette's "premature obituary" was based on a narrow view of American poetry. As the *New Masses* summarized Shepard's arguments, "the only dead poets were those who were obsessed with images of death and decay because they had lost all touch with the vigor of the American people." For Shepard, American poets such as Genevieve Taggard, Langston Hughes, and Carl Sandburg vitalized poetry because they captured the "rhythm" and "vivid imagery" of workers' everyday lives: "The workers, who made America so 'virile' and 'active' a country, feel that poetry does have a place in their civilization. But it must come out of its wastelands and its tired intellectual towers; it must wander into the factories and the movies and the hamburger joints; it must know the sorrows and joys of the picket lines; it must learn the rhythm and vivid imagery of everyday conversation."[48] Shepard's editorial is reflective of predominant discourses of the time as well as a strain of anti-intellectualism in left cultural circles.[49] In the pages of Communist Party–affiliated magazines such as *New Masses* as well as more mainstream publications such as the *New Republic*, critics and everyday readers alike demanded poems that were accessible to wide audiences: simple, direct, easy to memorize, and immediately useful for political activities such as union meetings, picket lines, and May Day parades. Over and over again, they denigrated the poems being produced in "wastelands" (a jab at T. S. Eliot, of course) and "tired intellectual towers," and they pitted a "difficult" or "cerebral" or "despairing" modernist aesthetic against a more "straightforward" or "populist" or "optimistic" one. In a letter to the editor, one *New Masses* subscriber wrote that he liked "simple, direct little verses" and disliked "the amorphous type" by writers such as Muriel Rukeyser.[50] Readers of more mainstream progressive magazines such as the *New Republic* also demanded clarity at a time when, to quote one letter to the editor, so many people "are seeking truth, inspiration, courage, to live and carry on in the midst of our present world insanity."[51] Clarity was associated not only with simplicity or directness in content but also with particular type of verse that was "little" or, as another *New Republic* reader put it, composed of "neat lines."[52]

In the context of the *New Masses* heavy-handed dismissals of syntactic experimentation and modernist "free" verse, especially during the Popular Front period, Millet's injunction seems at first glance like simply another call for poems suitable for the picket line. (Recall, for example, my chapter three's discussion of how left-wing musicians shifted to more simplistic compositional styles in the late thirties.) Somewhat typical of Shepard's brand of antimodernism, Millet suggests that for poetry to stay relevant, it has to "mean more to more Americans," and therefore, it "should, even when representative of the Left, not be confusedly ornate, pretentiously intellectual, and cerebrally dull." These opinions of course reentrench easy divides—between the difficult and accessible, obtuse and direct, despairing and hopeful, modernist and not—that account little for complexities of form-content relations.[53] When Millet herself rewrote T. S. Eliot's "The Love Song of J. Alfred Prufrock" as "The Love Song of J. Anonymous Proletariat," she replicated the form of the refrain of Eliot's poem in a way that emphasizes the importance of content:

> About us people come and go
> Talking of the C.I.O.[54]

Even though Millet's play with Eliot's couplet is not a perfect prosodic match, it opens up alternate ways of thinking about how communist writers imagined form-content relations. The content itself bears directly on the supposed political effectiveness of a given poem's rhythm; even though "In the room the women come and go / Talking of Michelangelo" *sounds* the same as Millet's lines about people "talking of the C.I.O.," they do not have the same ideological and/or historical effects. Put differently, the demand for "neat little lines" helps to delineate how rhythmic consistency was idealized as a unique means to access social content.

Millet asserts in her *New Masses* letter that rhythm enables people to assimilate powerful ideas because an idea presented rhythmically "permeates the reader and becomes part of himself and his actions." Her evidence, however, is not merely formal. To make her point, Millet asks her audience to consider the rhythm of phrases such as "Workers of the world, unite" and May Day parade refrains such as "Wages up and hours down / Make New York a union town." While both are presumably catchy, they do not share significant formal commonalities. Indeed, when Millet references these phrases' powerful rhythms, she is not necessarily asking her reader to scan them. What the phrases do share, however, are rhythms that, in contrast to what Millet calls "fascist prose," help to convey progressive political ideas and empower the people who read or say them. It is in this way that rhythm, according to her, "meets a basic human need." Finishing her reading of the power of May Day parade refrains, she deliberately equates "rhythm" and "poetry," writing, "One of the important reasons that these eleven words ... hit joyfully and strongly the ears and minds of some hundreds of thousands of persons on the streets of Manhattan was the rhythm, or, put otherwise, its poetry."[55] "Rhythm" no longer describes a given poem's formal patterning but instead becomes shorthand for a poem's potential mass appeal.

Millet's editorial is not merely about form but about a specific closing of form and content. Simple rhythms such as those demanded by antimodernists such as Shepard could perhaps serve a purpose on the left, but they could also potentially serve the historical imaginary of fascism. In the late 1930s, the image of thousands marching to the same rhythm could have just as easily signified a picket line as a line of soldiers in a fascist army.[56] As Michael Golston explains, in Hitler's Germany, rhythm was lauded as a means to "integrate" young people into the nationalist social body. Rhythmic language helped to make "propaganda more distinct and clear," especially when it was coupled with marching exercises that "orient[ed] the young person rhythmically" so that one's human body seemed to naturally fall in step with the body politic.[57]

For Millet, however, a rhythmic poem is only realized as "poetry" when it expresses the exigencies of communism, or what Millet refers to as "a basic human need." For her, "real poetry" is opposed to "fascist prose," which she also refers to as "bad formal prose." She writes, "We think that real poetry is an opponent of that bad formal prose at its worst, which in politics, is fascism. Fascism is against the life of man. Poetry has always been for it. And it can be today, more than ever." The choice of "formal" as a descriptor for bad fascist prose further suggests that Millet is not merely pitting poems with regular sound patterns against those that engage other types of experiment. Millet's redefinition of rhythm as poetry (and vice versa) proffers both terms as political ideals that are sutured to her specific communist milieu.[58] Millet's use of rhythm in her editorial is related to, but also distinct from, the abstract definition of rhythm as an adjective for a poem that is easily reproduced and circulated. In Edmund Wilson's 1938 essay "Is Verse a Dying Technique?," he observed a decline in the use of metrical verse forms during the decade, and he argued that "poetry" had become a more capacious term that describes an intensity of feeling or experience that could be expressed in prose or verse.[59] By producing affective responses such as excitement and joy, rhythm operates not as a beat to march to but as a desire to cling to—what we might call, after Fredric Jameson's phrase "a desire called utopia," a "desire called rhythm" that signifies a collective yearning for that which does not yet exist.[60]

The increasing generalization of rhythm *as* poetry in the midthirties appears to be deeply entangled in emergent Popular Front structures of feeling. The era of the Popular Front, as Michael Denning has described it, was marked by "insurgency, upheaval, and hope"; but it was also underwritten by deep anxieties about racial violence in the United States and the rise of fascist dictatorships in Europe.[61] Rhythm, in this context, might be seen as a means to cling to revolutionary hope while simultaneously managing deep unease about the world's future. While traditional verse genres appeared useful for immediate political struggles, there was also marked anxiety about how such genres could mediate new imaginations of political reality, especially as nostalgia is constellated with fascist imaginaries.

To better understand this dynamic, we might turn briefly to two radically different Popular Front experiments with traditional genres: Carl Sandburg's book-length poem *The People, Yes* (1936) and selections from Lorine Niedecker's *New Goose*, a portion of which was printed in a 1937 issue of James Laughlin's *New Directions* under the title "Mother Geese." At the time, Sandburg's poem was considered a quintessential poetic document of the Popular Front. Though critics were puzzled by its form, they were convinced that it was required reading for the movement.[62] Not surprisingly, Wilson spends time puzzling over Sandburg's book in "Is Verse a Dying Technique?," describing it as "a queer kind of literature which oscillates between something like verse and something like the paragraphs of a newspaper column."[63] Writing *The People, Yes* was an urgent task for Sandburg: the dramas of the Depression years pulled him out of the past in which he had been dwelling by writing folk songs and toiling away at his biography of Abraham Lincoln.[64] *The People, Yes* was Sandburg's attempt to represent the lives of the "common people" by catching their manners and speech through the use of multiple genres and registers of diction. Throughout, he uses anaphora, lists, and catalogues to describe landscapes and to weave together dialogues, anecdotes, aphorisms, and proverbs.

What interests me, however, is how Sandburg's attempts to describe *The People, Yes* to others suggest that the book's composition was marked by a very real anxiety. Early on, Sandburg confessed to Archibald MacLeish, "[The poem] has such length and windings . . . that I would have doubts about it had I not lived so long with the authorities inside me who say I will not handle this particular theme any better until I hit hither and yon in reincarnated flesh and feathers."[65] Writing to Malcolm Cowley in 1935, he attempted to communicate the always shifting, perhaps uncertain, form of the poem by rattling off a long list of categories, describing it to Cowley as "a ballad pamphlet harangue sonata and fugue titled 'The People, Yes,' standing now somewhat over 100 typed sheets, an almanac, a scroll, a palimpsest, the last will and testament of Mr. John Public, John Doe, Richard Roe, and the autobiography of whoever it was the alfalfaland governor meant in saying, 'The common people will do anything you say except stay hitched.'"[66] In a subsequent letter to his close friend Brenda Ueland, he wrote that the book was "quite something else again, a saga sonata fugue with deliberate haywire interludes and jigtime babblings."[67] Sandburg's need to express the various levels and categories at play in *The People, Yes* are finally evident in the book's preface, which attempts to lay bare its contents through a litany of terms and descriptive phrases:

> Being several stories and psalms nobody
> would want to laugh at
>
> interspersed with memoranda variations
> worth a second look
>
> along with sayings and yarns traveling on
> grief and laughter
>
> running sometimes as a fugitive air in the
> classic manner
>
> breaking into jig time and tap dancing
> nohow classical
>
> and further broken by plain and irregular
> sounds and echoes from
>
> the roar and whirl of street crowds, work
> gangs, sidewalk clamor[68]

The People, Yes contains contradictions: telling stories "nobody would want to laugh at" while composing itself of "sayings and yarns" that travel on laughter. Its music is "classic" and "nohow classical" at once. This series of contradictions is inherent to the life of the poem, as evinced by the fact that these myriad descriptors hinge on one word, "Being," which suggests that the poem's state is continually open and shifting. Because of the many and competing ways the poem can "be," it remains, in the end, indefinable.

Sandburg's grappling with the form of *The People, Yes* displays a significant tension on the left between a desire to mobilize preestablished forms, genres, and traditions and the desire to chart the undefined revolutionary space where the utopian potentials promised by communism's "good news" will come to be. Ultimately, what Popular Front poets and critics most hoped for was a pure expression of the tradition of the common people; and they imagined that such an expression would find real and immediate use in those very people's lives. But as Sandburg's book reveals, this imagined use for poetry also raises questions about what poetry is and does in the first place. If poetry is defined by its rhythm, and if this rhythm only indicates poetry's potential usefulness, then why does one need the borders of genre and form?

Whereas Sandburg's *The People, Yes* is a sprawling, untidy mishmash of genres, the poems that Niedecker composed as part of her book *New Goose* are compact syntactic experiments with the structures of Mother Goose rhymes. Niedecker's experiments with nursery rhymes, not unlike Potamkin's in *New Pioneer*, point to the social origins of Mother Goose as they had been described in a 1930 book by Katherine Elwes Thomas titled *The Real Personages of Mother Goose*. Elwes's book, which also influenced Millet, located the historical events and personalities described in the rhymes, emphasizing how their political content eventually led to their suppression. Rather than update the content of the popular nursery rhymes to encourage children (and perhaps adults) to join a community of social protest, Niedecker breaks the metrical and syntactical arrangements of the originals in order to make the world new.

Michael Davidson has noted that Niedecker's left political commitments have not been as well regarded as those of George Oppen and Louis Zukofsky, the Objectivist poets with whom Niedecker is often associated, and Davidson usefully places Niedecker's work in an expanded Popular Front context by foregrounding her interest in Popular Front forms such as the folk ballad and travel guide and in mass technologies such as film and radio. *New Goose* particularly, Davidson points out, demonstrates Niedecker's relationship to the Popular Front through the self-conscious deployment of folk idioms and ballad meters.[69] Conversely, the confluences between Niedecker's poetic practices and Popular Front forms also point to the ways in which other Popular Front artists self-consciously experimented with folk genres and idioms. Niedecker's "Mother Geese" poems play with rhythmic structures at the same time that they treat rhythm allegorically. For example, in one section, she references a pendulum to play with notions of marking time:

> There's a better shine
> on the pendulum
> than is on my hair
> and many's the time
> . . . .
> I've seen it there.[70]

The dullness of the speaker's hair coupled with the monotony of the "many times" she has seen the shine elsewhere is underwritten by the evocation of the pendulum, which the reader cannot help but imagine swinging back and forth as if on a metronome. The predictable rhythms of the everyday lives of the poor and the possibility of bursting out of them (as in a shine) continue in a later stanza, which employs a familiar nursery-rhyme rhythm:

> My coat threadbare
> over and down capital hill,
> fashions mornings after.
>
> In this Eternal Category's
> land of rigamarole
> see thru the laughter.[71]

Several narratives happen here at once. The speaker, wearing a threadbare coat, is being laughed at as she sets out because she is unfashionable. But the logic of fashion, as well as the logic that would make her poor, is mere rigamarole. The nonsense implied in the evocation of both rigamarole and laughter exists in a different timescape than the regular rhythms of the everyday, such as walking up and down a hill (a daily chore) or "fashioning" a "morning after" (the monotony of waking up in the morning).

When Laughlin introduced the poems in the 1937 *New Directions* volume, including Niedecker's "Mother Geese," he forwarded an idea about linguistic experimentalism that still conditions evaluations of poems: "I believe then, that experimental writing has a real social value, apart from any other." The "social value" of experimental writing is, for Laughlin, related to the ways in which linguistically experimental writing can provide a means to think through social and economic reality against what he called "standardization." By the 1940s, such arguments would be leveraged in dismissals of thirties protest verse as (Soviet) propaganda. But in 1937, Laughlin saw his contributors "as agents of social reform as well as artists" whose "*propaganda* is implicit in their style."[72] Placing Niedecker's experiments next to mainstreamed Popular Front discourses about rhythm suggests that, during the late thirties, definitions of "experimental writing" were more in flux than they were in the decades immediately following.

In the next section, I turn to Millet's contributions to the 1944 antifascist anthology *Seven Poets in Search of an Answer*, arguing that, in her antifascist poems, Millet breaks with generic convention not to adhere to a modernist aesthetic but in order to imagine alternate possibilities for embodied experiences in time. Such prosodic experiments are, I hope to suggest, a direct result of Popular Front experiments and anxieties. By way of transition, we might look at a section of Niedecker's "Mother Geese" rhymes subtitled "Fascist Festival." In that section, temporal juxtapositions or confusions are applied to—and take a different resonance because of—the threat of war. "Fascist Festival" begins,

> The music, lady,
> you demand—
> the brass
> breaks my hand.
>
> ***
>
> To war they kept
>   us going
> but when the garden
>   bloomed
> I let them know
>   my death.
> With time war
>   is splendid
> and the rainbow
>   sword
> they do not break
>   my rest,[73]

One cannot help but notice the abundance of formal punning in the use of "break" and "rest" throughout the poem. Niedecker syntactically disturbs the rhyme and rhythm of Mother Goose in ways that suggest how a line must break before a joyous celebration can truly begin. Whereas Sandburg's casting about for a means to describe *The People, Yes* indicates an unproductive nostalgia, Niedecker's attempts to re-create nursery rhymes from within their own formal systems posit something of a break. Such a break, for Niedecker as for Millet, takes place as part of a feminist and anticapitalist ethics that is not a modernist aesthetic rupture, conflated with a historical rupture, but rather an opening to alternate historical modalities.[74]

Poets in Search of an Answer

Almost ten years after Millet urged *New Masses* readers that "the left needs rhythm" to counter the totalitarian state, she contributed a set of poems to the antifascist anthology *Seven Poets in Search of an Answer* (1944). Edited by the Jewish American book publisher Thomas Yoseloff and featuring an introductory note by the Irish American communist poet Shaemas O'Sheel, the volume is situated in a transitional moment, when definitions of modernist and political poetry were sharply contested. Alan Filreis characterizes *Seven Poets* as a "liberal-left anthology" produced during an "ideological warp," when the promises of the united fronts were just beginning to be "excoriated" by "a few pioneers in red baiting."[75] Contextualizing the volume more precisely within Popular Front debates about form, Alan Wald describes *Seven Poets* as a "cultural bridge" between the "people's poetry" of the 1930s and "emergent wartime progressive literature."[76] The volume's attention to fascist regimes abroad as well as to racist violence in the United States also demonstrates what Chris Vials had identified as the "intersectional nature" of U.S. antifascism.[77] While Yoseloff's volume may have quickly become fodder for vehement anticommunists, it was also highly popular, going through three large printings in a short time.

Millet's inclusion as one of the eponymous seven poets marked a breakthrough in her poetic career. The poems she contributed to the volume are markedly different from her thirties poems, such as the ballad "Silicosis in Our Town," in their employment of techniques such as enjambment and slant rhyme. Such changes from the thirties to the forties could be used to demonstrate Millet's evolution from child rhymester to a full-fledged modernist poet.[78] Besides obscuring Millet's later experiments with traditional genres, such as her verse drama *Dangerous Jack: A Fantasy in Verse* (1953), this narrative would map the predominant idea that American poetry is a "drive toward modernism" onto Millet's poetic development.[79] Rather than consider Millet's forties verse solely in terms of a modernist trajectory, I propose to read her poems in *Seven Poets in Search of an Answer* as a continuation and evolution of her ideas about poetry and antifascism. Millet's poems in *Seven Poets* experiment with concepts of rhythm and rhyme not merely to adhere to a midcentury modernist aesthetic but to imagine alternate possibilities for embodied experiences in time.

Considering Millet's poems on these terms opens another perspective on "people's poetry." Rhythm, which I have posited as a poetic function idealized to political effect, acts as a historical and conceptual flashpoint for such inquiry. O'Sheel's introduction, which announces the necessity "to postpone the threnody and sound the clarion-call," fantasizes that traditional verse genres are most effective in the antifascist struggle: "In older days the people were often fired and welded by ballads sung on the streets and sold on penny broadsides. Perhaps we need that sort of poetry again, to seize the popular imagination and stir the people's emotions; that will set more feet marching against fascism, upset the plots of traitors and force the timid hands of statesmen."[80] Wald notes that O'Sheel was firmly in the camp of those leftist poets and critics who believed that rhymed and metrical verse was the most effective, or only, means to stir the masses. "Only rhymed verse in metrical rhythm can reach the minds and emotions of masses of people, and can take hold and be remembered and repeated," O'Sheel wrote in a 1945 letter to Aaron Kramer, echoing his sentiments in *Seven Poets* and encouraging Kramer to stick to rhyming verse.[81] We should read the poems collected in *Seven Poets in Search of an Answer* both along and against the grain of O'Sheel's introductory pronouncements. Reading beyond the introductory note, one encounters rhythm as a poetic problem that is directly related to antifascist discourse and that, therefore, destabilizes the category of rhythm as wedge in the modernist/antimodernist split. The types of rhymes that O'Sheel promotes in his introductory note do not necessarily characterize the poems collected in the anthology. Of all the poems selected, Langston Hughes's and Kramer's are the most formally regular. Maxell Bodenheim, known as a Greenwich Village bohemian, and Norman Rosten, whose career was later derailed by conservative Cold War critics, provide more formally experimental contributions. Strikingly, however, despite these aesthetic differences, all of the poets in the volume use various generic signifiers—ballad, elegy, dirge, lullaby—that conjure an affective sense of rhythm, one that is often, but not always, indicative of the poems' formal traits.

What seems to unite the selections across formal differences are the ways the poems employ various techniques to think through the temporal dislocations of fascism, both when referencing white nationalism in the United States and in relation to fascist dictatorships in Europe. Before exploring this aspect of the volume in more depth vis-à-vis Millet, I would like to illustrate this point through two brief examples from Hughes and Rosten. Hughes's poem "The Bitter River," dedicated to the fourteen-year-old lynching victims Charlie Lang and Ernest Green, employs regular end rhymes and uses the repetition of "steel bars" at the end of several lines.[82] One of Rosten's contributions, "Prelude," is less sonically regular than Hughes's, but it also explores notions of time in relation to present fascist threats. Rosten's poem draws connections between fascism at home and abroad, ending,

> The clock ticks, the hand moves.
> Eight o'clock in Boston, noon in Madrid,
> one o'clock Berlin, four towards the Volga,
> evening over endless Asia, the long Pacific,
> dawn glides coastward, leaps the Rockies,
> eight o'clock Boston ... The clock ticks,
> the time-bomb in our own heart.[83]

In both of these poems, rhythm is used on various planes to reinforce and make sense of political extremity. These evocations of rhythm are, importantly, different from the "rhythm" and "vivid imagery" of everyday life that Shepard insisted poetry must capture in order to reach the lives of men and women.

Millet's contributions to *Seven Poets* use references to sound and to natural cycles in order to register resistances to fascism. The first poem in her selection, "Unforgotten Village," enacts a touching tribute to the Czech village Lidice, which was destroyed by Hitler's army in 1942. The poem opens by describing a valley where "spring came every year" and children and birds sang "sweet words." The "life" of the village in spring is expressed in multiple references to sound:

> Spring came every year
> to Kladno valley, blossoming with sheer
> birth-joy. How all the children laughed to hear
> the upstart songs of perky little birds!
> There were sweet words
> and sighing looks of lovers
> slow-stepping over their earth's grain-cover;
> and dishes clattered with a merry young sound
> between the dreamy housewife's hands—
> as if they too were leaping from the ground.
> And men were deep at work within the land.

The first stanza of the poem is filled with sound: laughter, birdsongs, sighs, and clatters. While these lines certainly rhyme, the poem also uses enjambment to convey a sense of spilling over, so that the joys implied by the singing and clattering seem to exceed the bounds of the rhyme scheme. By contrast, the stanza narrating the arrival of Hitler's army uses couplets composed of end-stopped lines:

> Spring came every year . . . until one year
> the fascists came
> shutting the valley's throat with noose of shame,
> frightening the flowers with their boots,
> wresting children from their mother-roots.[84]

The constraining effect of the couplets underscores the image of the "valley's throat" being choked by a "noose of shame." What is more, the rhyme of "boots" and "roots" emphasizes the stamping of the army into the town. Such images recur in a later line describing the hearts of Lidice's women, upon seeing how "the men they had warmed in their beds and kissed" are strewn dead on the ground. The women turn "paler than the mist," and the view of dead bodies wraps "tight on their hearts the barbed wire wounds." "Unforgotten Village" resists the violence of fascism by imagining alternate modalities of time. The poem rewrites total destruction as a deep sleep:

> The helpless homes were toppled when
> deep in the valley lay the silent men.
> The colors of the Kladno valley wept.
> The fascists sent reports. *Lidice slept,*
> expunged from time and memory of men—
>
> Then did they see rise terribly again
> that *Lidice*—an angry flower-flame
> bursting its seed over the earth's great ground.
> Lidice a thousand cradles found.
>
> No rest for fascists, no peace by night or day.
> Wherever fascists turn . . . stands *Lidice*.[85]

One cannot help but see in "Unforgotten Village" the traces of Children's Town, both in the narrative and in the rhyming couplets. In the last stanzas of "Unforgotten Village," Millet also invokes rhythm in a figurative manner through the cycles of the seasons (spring coming and going) as well as the circadian rhythms of sleeping and waking. Lidice, in its slumber, exists out of time, but sleep also rewrites the permanence of death. Thus, the memory of Lidice returns to "stand" and bear witness "wherever fascists turn."

In "Unforgotten Village," Millet links the natural "rhythms" of days and seasons to fascist resistance. The linking of poetic rhythm to human biological functions stretches over centuries, but it has a particular resonance in the context of the forties. In *The Dialectic of Enlightenment*, Theodor Adorno and Max Horkheimer use the term "rhythm" to describe the alienation of individuals within capitalist systems. They relate rhythm to assembly-line production as well as to the popular cultural amusements that serve as an escape. They write,

> The regression of the masses today lies in their inability to hear with their own ears what has not already been heard, to touch with their hand what has not previously been grasped. . . . Through the mediation of the total society, which encompasses all relationships and impulses, human beings are being turned back into precisely what the developmental laws of soci-

ety, the principle of the self, had opposed: mere examples of the species, identical to one another through isolation within the compulsively controlled collectivity. The rowers, unable to speak to one another, are all harnessed to the same rhythms, like modern workers in factories, cinema, and the collective.[86]

The conception of rhythm as the repetition of motions and behaviors welding persons to capital (both through work and through popular cultural amusements) indicts Shepard's aforementioned view of progressive poetry as a product and representation of "everyday conversations" that take place in factories, at movie theaters, and in "hamburger joints."

In Millet's poem "Historian," also collected in *Seven Poets in Search of an Answer*, her formulation of rhythm moves away from Shepard's and closer to Adorno and Horkheimer's. The opening lines of "Historian" are,

> They will say of this age:
> It set a blight
> On every living impulse

These lines evoke the idea in *The Dialectic of Enlightenment* that the masses have been reduced to mere compulsiveness. Alongside the violent effects of capitalism, the age also displays for historians the "chopping block," the "entombed bodies," and "the blood on the rock"; this image of dead bodies locates the transcendent ideal of rhythm-as-life in the material historical realities of fascist violence. Millet, however, ends "Historian" with a hopeful vision, writing,

> they will see
> Rising over these
> Whose beat was stilled that morning might be won.
> A green increase
> Of love's enduring pillars, filling sky
> With blossoms sprung from peril's mastery,
> Fed by a ceaseless stream of countless hearts
> Whose beat was stilled that morning might be won.[87]

In this poem, those who lost their lives in the wreckages of poverty, Jim Crow, and fascist violence are represented by silence. But the fact of the poem itself is underscored by Millet's persistent faith in its rhythms. The pulse of the poem resists the "blight" on "every living impulse," asking the reader to know it by heart and beat.

210 Chapter Five

The End of an Era

Arguing that Millet and the other contributors to *Seven Poets* resisted mechanizations of rhythm, I do not mean to suggest that the volume moves toward later critiques of Popular Front poetry as propagandistic. Indeed, the ascendancy of New Criticism in the immediate postwar period obscured the diverse ways in which critics theorized artistic autonomy in relation to social and political life. As a result, subsequent literary critics and historians have, often unwittingly, conflated a variety of interpretive practices with New Critical formalism. Perhaps, then, we might return to an origin myth and find another way. Following the publication in 1971 of Hugh Kenner's *The Pound Era*, it became a modernist tome, establishing Ezra Pound as a synecdoche for the aesthetic category "Modernism" and setting in motion a narrative about modernist genius that arguably persists today, even if weakly. Millet's unfinished "The Ezra Pound Myth" was never published and, until recently, was not even available to researchers. As this chapter moves toward its close, I ask, what happens when we let Millet's voice intervene in our own narratives about the shape of U.S. poetry in the so-called American Century? In addition to echoing Millet's disgust at Pound's fascist alliances, his anti-Semitism, and his racism, we must also reject the Cold War legacies that stand in his place, even if we no longer call them by his name.

During the 1940s and 1950s, Millet continued to contribute poems and essays to magazines, including *Masses and Mainstream, Contemporary Issues, New World Review*, and *Jewish Currents*. In addition to her volumes *Thine Alabaster Cities* and *Dangerous Jack*, she coedited the anthology *Rosenbergs: Poems of the United States* (1957), which included contributions from left intellectuals such as W. E. B. DuBois, and in 1955, she attended the Helsinki Peace Conference. Outside of these published writings, Millet wrote an abundance of poetry and criticism that was never published, ranging from book-length children's poems and school "samplers" to long poem cycles, plans for anthologies, and extensive essays on figures such as Allen Tate, John Crowe Ransom, T. S. Eliot, Walt Whitman, and, of course, Pound. A volume of her work never appeared in English, but there was a volume of her selected poems in Chinese translation.

Through the Cold War years, Millet was firmly outside the literary establishment and was even sometimes ostracized by left editors over her political writings.[88] Nonetheless, her manuscript continued predominant leftist critiques of Pound's politics from the thirties and forties. In an open letter published in the September 1931 *New Masses*, for example, Mike Gold chided Pound for requesting that the Communist Party state its platform when literature on the subject was so widely available, and he signed off, "hoping to see you in hell first."[89] In 1936, "Ezra Pound, Silvershirt" graced the cover of a *New Masses* ("Noo Masses" in Pound's idiom) issue in which the editors reprinted correspondence between Pound and R. C. Somerville of the Silver Shirt Legion of America, an underground American fascist organization.[90] In 1945, while Pound was facing trial for treason, the editors bluntly asked, "Should Ezra Pound Be Shot?" A forum on the question featured replies from prominent left-leaning writers, including Arthur Miller and F. O. Matthiessen, next to reproductions of previous *New Masses* features on Pound's fascism. Rosten wrote, in his own contribution to the 1945 forum, that Pound's crimes were "millionfold" precisely because of his status as a poet. Somewhat paradoxically, however, it was Pound's achievements as a craftsman that saved him during his trial and for posterity.[91]

When Millet began writing "The Ezra Pound Myth," the prestige of the poet-critic archetype had reached its apogee, and conservative formalist modernism was firmly entrenched in the academy.[92] Millet aligned the apologetic stance toward Pound's fascism with the conservative stance of the southern agrarians, a group that she saw as an anachronistic vestige of the old, proslavery South that was disguising itself as "modern" under the aegis of university classrooms, literary prizes, and magazines. Her criticism of Pound thus extended to what she dubbed the "holy trinity" of Pound, T. S. Eliot, and Allen Tate as well as other devotees of what she described in her unpublished essay "Poets and Poverty" as the "malevolent rule" of New Criticism.[93] There, she linked the ascendancy of New Criticism to developments in modern capitalism, outlining how the poet becomes separate from the "people" as poetry itself is increasingly commodified: "Capitalist values applied all along the line," she wrote, "from the commodity market to the market of ideas which could be handled like commodities. Sycophants were wanted. No others need apply."[94]

In "The Ezra Pound Myth," Millet points specifically to Charles Norman's *The Case of Ezra Pound* (1968) and Cornell's aforementioned *The Trial of Ezra Pound*, writing of the latter, "Cornell had earlier told 'his' story in the mistitled *The Trial of Ezra Pound*. He took the occasion not only to report Pound's version of matters, but to provide a forum for the continued attack on 'the Rooseveltian dung-hill' and the super-McCarthyite propaganda that never stopped. Cornell took the approach that Pound had indeed been merely carrying out his constitutional right of free speech—regardless of the known nature of his broadcasts."[95] In the early 2000s, when the question of Nazi punching is up for ethical debate and contemporary academics defend avant-garde racial appropriation, the invocation of "free speech" to justify racist discourse under the banner of poetic innovation is all too familiar and sadly prescient.[96] As Maxwell Bodenheim warns in his *Seven Poets in Search of an Answer* contribution, "The Game," "In war the inside devils love free speech— / . . . the right to preach / Contention, skepticism, minor hate."[97]

Millet's indictment of Pound thus brings up questions about how political content becomes aligned with poetic forms. Her Cold War criticism advances an argument about the shifting political content of traditional and experimental forms. As Greg Barnhisel demonstrates, during the Cold War period, the stylistic techniques and attitudes that had defined modernism earlier in the century (he identifies several aspects of modernism, including allusiveness, abstraction, fragmentation, and the impersonality of the artist) were emptied of their revolutionary and reactionary content and replaced with "a celebration of the virtues of freedom and the assertion that the individual is sovereign."[98] Literary genres associated with socialist realism became modernism's presumed opposite: "Socialist realism was everything modernism was not," Barnhisel explains, "opposing experimentation and formalism and downplaying the individual artist, stressing instead art's role in helping the state and party achieve political and social goals."[99] Millet's Cold War criticism suggests how the multiple definitions and implications of "rhythm" for left artists scramble the presumptive alignment of rhythmic experiment with individual free expression against the specter of Party control.

Millet composed "The Ezra Pound Myth" as well as several essays on modernist poetry criticism at a flashpoint moment when conservative anti-Marxist intellectuals as well as Marxist anticommunists privileged form over content. Despite the disparate political predilections of the New Critics and the New York Intellectuals, both groups shared an interest in promoting cultural high modernism and in pursuing formalist modes of reading that dovetailed with ideals of aesthetic autonomy.[100] In the early 1940s especially, such practices were formulated as a reaction to proletarian and social-realist styles predominant on the literary scene during the thirties. The New Critics had long disparaged vehemently what they called "propaganda art" in their promotion of formalist reading practices and traditional poetries, a position encapsulated in essays such as Cleanth Brooks's "Metaphysical Poets and Propaganda Art" from his *Modern Poetry and the Tradition* (1939). For Brooks, communist critics valued poetry only as a vehicle for propaganda, and politically committed poetry is itself "incapable of enduring ironical contemplation."[101] Following the disillusionments of the 1939 Nazi-Soviet Pact, certain strains of leftist writing and criticism began to echo the New Critics' dismissals of "propaganda," as well as their emphases on form and freedom of expression. Two essays that usher in the 1940s helpfully illustrate this shift: Philip Rahv's "Proletarian Literature: A Political Autopsy" (1939) and Clement Greenberg's "Avant-Garde and Kitsch" (1939). Rahv's and Greenberg's essays demonstrate attempts to craft Marxist reading practices outside what they perceive to be the stringent ideologies of the Communist Party; in so doing, both emphasize the relative autonomy of aesthetics and politics.

Rahv published "Proletarian Literature: A Political Autopsy" in *Southern Review*, a literary magazine established by Robert Penn Warren at Louisiana State University. The forum for Rahv's essay alone gives some indication of the similarities between the New Critics' and New York Intellectuals' interpretive methods at the start of the 1940s. As Wald notes, by the time Rahv published the essay, his own left-leaning magazine, *Partisan Review*, had been reinvented as "an organ of modernist high culture," to the detriment of literary modes associated with the proletarian literatures of the Depression decade.[102] In "Proletarian Literature," Rahv writes against the imposition of political doctrine on literary works. He suggests that the writing formulas promoted by the Communist Party during the thirties were "empty of aesthetic principle" and served as a "complex political mechanism" whereby writers were made to believe that they were allying themselves with the working class when, in effect, they were surrendering their "independence to the Communist Party." Thirties proletarian literature thus, according to Rahv, mistakes the "literature of a party," which only reproduces party ideology, for the "literature of a class," which allows for "conflict" and "free exchange" and which "constantly strives and partially succeeds in overcoming its social limitations."[103]

Rahv's closing emphasis on the superiority of the "media of art" over the "media of politics" not only replicates the art-propaganda distinction outlined by Brooks but also instructively sets up the principles of formalist analysis put forward in Greenberg's influential essays on abstract art.[104] Greenberg's "Avant-Garde and Kitsch," published in Rahv and William Phillips's *Partisan Review*, is the first of a series of essays Greenberg penned during the 1940s and 1950s that, in outlining the principles of abstract art, promoted cultural high modernism.[105] Like Rahv, Greenberg argued for the distinctiveness of artistic and political realms, but he also emphasized the separation of high art from mass culture. The avant-garde, as both an aesthetic descriptor and value, favors the abstract, or nonrepresentational, over the direct representation of everyday experience. Such art emphasizes compositional processes over subject matter—or, as Greenberg puts it, "cause" over "effect." As his title suggests, the opposite of avant-garde art is kitsch: "Where there is an avant-garde, generally we also find a rear-guard," he writes, labeling this rear guard the "popular and commercial art and literature" associated with kitsch.[106] In Greenberg's theory of avant-garde art, realism qua propaganda is related to the category of kitsch, and he uses the constellation of realism with propaganda and kitsch to advance his arguments for the irreconcilability of political art and avant-garde practice.

By focusing on form over content, Brooks, Rahv, and Greenberg all indicated that art in which the work's formal conditions were its primary concern—whether that be Jackson Pollock's drip technique or William Faulkner's fragmented, stream-of-consciousness narration—was also art that was intrinsically valuable. Their shared interest in formalist critique and in a version of modernism that would later be described as "high" suggests similarities among the New Criticism, the *Partisan Review* circle, and avant-garde art critics and visual artists.[107] Indeed, all three groups contributed to the institutionalization of high modernism during the 1940s, helping canonize writers such as T. S. Eliot, Henry James, and William Faulkner by making them objects of critical reflection and attention.[108] The canonization of this version of modernism by academics and professional critics also extended to larger institutional scenes during the decade, as evinced by the 1949 awarding of the Nobel Prize to Faulkner, the first exhibition of Pollock's abstract expressionist paintings at the Museum of Modern Art in 1943, and the museum's subsequent acquisition of his free-form painting *The She-Wolf*.

When we understand modernist form qua modernist ideology, we edit out the perspectives of left writers such as Martha Millet, who argues for a social-realist approach to reality, rooted in a Marxist viewpoint, that can be expressed through a diversity of techniques. To illustrate this other story, we might return to another pedagogical scene: Millet's poetry workshop at the New York Jefferson School, which she used as a basis for her 1957 *Masses and Mainstream* essay "Modern Poetry: For or Against?" To open the essay, Millet summarized a debate she facilitated with her workshop students on the question of whether modernist "techniques" could convey a progressive political message. She questions if it is "proper to make traditional, accustomed poetry techniques synonymous with progressive poetry" and, on the other side, "to make 'modern' poetry in the lump synonymous with all that is reactionary or nihilist." It is tempting to read Millet's suppositions as another piece of evidence that her poetic career developed toward an acceptance of modernist poetic technique. But Millet finds both experimental and traditional forms to be "dead" when they are based in a conservative view of reality. She concludes her essay, "What is easy to understand may be gripping. What is less easy to grasp on the spot, in all its implications, may have an equal strength by gradual 'absorption' by the reader or hearer. Either or both may have the same ultimate effect."[109]

What ultimately matters to Millet is the political position from which the poet approaches reality, not necessarily the form chosen to represent it. Millet often chose to use traditional forms to challenge Cold War culture, most notably in *Dangerous Jack*. She also continued to be interested in folk forms, especially as they were rooted in Jewish culture. At the same time, she lambasted poets such as John Crowe Ransom for their formal regularities. In "Modern Poetry: For or Against?" as well as in several unpublished prose pieces she penned during the fifties, Millet relates the southern slave economy that bred the New Critics to the development of postwar American capitalism and the crude technologies that created the atom bomb. Ransom's rhymes, she argued, were merely the vestiges of southern slave society redressed as New Criticism. She writes, "The Southerner John Crowe Ransom writes elegantly and in rhyme, of charming, and (I get the impression) freshly-dead women, with a light smile on his lips. His form could not be considered anything but traditional. Yet the total ring is completely different. . . . In a poet like Ransom one seems to feel the breath of a fantastically outmoded South, that never existed in the way portrayed or recollected except in the bored leisure-time imaginings of the underdone sons of slaveowners, who knew how to turn a phrase and how to handle a whip or a gun."[110] The southern folk poet Don West proves Millet's point: a working-class poet who worked in traditional forms, West despised the conservative, backward vision of the Southern Agrarians, and he wrote a rhyming poem, "They Take Their Stand (For Some Professional Agrarians)," that said so, dividing the "professional" southern critics from the present realities of the South.[111]

Millet's formulation of ideas about poetry and, more specifically, poetic rhythm intervened in historical discourses about modernist aesthetics at the time of their formation. Her writings from the 1950s and 1960s also demonstrate a figure reflecting on the disappointments of the decades following the 1930s. Millet's sense that someone such as Kenner would win the day is palpable in her manuscript for "The Ezra Pound Myth," and her assessment of the state of literary studies is so prescient that it is worth quoting in full:

> In the Hungry Thirties the unprecedented took place. Intellectuals were lining up with exploited workers in militancy, in acts on the level of

livelihood and of art separately, or together. In the crisis time many reached a sense of community and of *fighting together* for a human society that would never be *handed* to the multitude. Some intellectuals reached their highest point then, and sank back, forever after, into mundane professional absorption or later defense of a hostile Establishment. Few if any could have been found to head up an ideological crusade for the System that ate its nurturers. Among those who could—but who were not called on then—were the Southern Agrarians—who, by the time they got a publisher for *I'll Take My Stand*—that passionate manifesto of a vanished Southern slave system (with the deserving aristocrat in firm charge), with a cry for a reversal of the social trend to that same kind of culture-bearing order—it was too late, or not yet time, for that kind of ideological leadership. The years had been borne forward on a torrent of rising energy out of despair.... People in controlled motion, learning what their lives and grievances meant, and about this society that had them in its grip, were not likely customers for a new reaction; that was to be clamped on in after years. The Southern Agrarians bided their time.[112]

And what about us? Is it too late—or just not yet time? In an interview that then–presidential candidate Donald Trump did with the NBC political analyst Chuck Todd regarding his infamous retweeting of a quote by Mussolini, Trump assured his public that he was not a fan of Mussolini but a fan of "good quotes."[113] What struck me about the answer was how it resonated with the excuses made for Pound's fascist politics. (Not a fan of fascism—just good art!) We can continue to skate on the surface or plunge the depths of the archive for a new story. Maybe, then, it will be time for Millet yet.

Coda: Not Yet!

In 1950, when Kenneth Fearing was subpoenaed by the U.S. Attorney in Washington, D.C., he responded to the inevitable question—"Are you a member of the Communist Party?"—with, "Not yet." The story about Fearing and the FBI is a well-known one. As McKenzie Wark points out, what makes it good is "the enigma of the answer. Is he saying that the FBI's harassment is, ironically enough, the very thing that will drive him into the arms of the Party? Or is he saying that he is not worthy of the Party? Not ready? Or, more interestingly, that the Party itself is not ready for him?" Later in Wark's essay, he translates the effect of Fearing's quip to the affective world of his writings, a world in which "a woman in heels passes a man in a trench coat. The sun gleams off a polished office window, and each just misses stepping in a pile of dog shit. They meet later over cocktails."[114]

Jacques Rancière writes that Greenberg's "Avant-Garde and Kitsch" effectively destroyed historical modernism in the name of what might be called a theoretical modernism or a 1940s high modernism that could only be hyperformalist. How else, of course, to proffer apologies for the likes of Ezra Pound? Fearing, like Millet, was a communist and avowed antifascist. But while Millet was dismayed by the idea that the "unacknowledged legislators" of her day were "steel, chrome, supercolossals of every kind, umptydimensional movie screens, girders, plastics, the swank bank," Fearing trafficked in the slick silver surfaces Daniel Tiffany associates with kitsch.[115] (And given Millet's and others' defense of the Rosenbergs, one cannot help but think of another kitschy art piece: Andy Warhol's 1964 *Electric Chair*, screen printed with silver acrylic paint.) The third poem in Fearing's "American Rhapsody" sequence, for example, anticipates how "bona-fide life will arrive at last, stepping from a non-stop monoplane with chromium doors and a silver wing and straight white staring lights." The sleekness of the industrial machinery glares. It is a diaphanous cover over great horror that emerges in the second verse as sound:

> There will be the sound of silvery thunder again to stifle the insane silence;
> A new, tremendous sound will shatter the final unspoken question and drown the last, mute, terrible reply;
> Rockets, rockets, Roman candles, flares, will burst in every corner of the night, to veil with snakes of silvery fire the nothingness that waits and waits;
> There will be a bright shimmering, silver veil stretched everywhere, tight, to hide the deep, black, empty, terrible, bottom of the world where people fall who are alone, or dead,[116]

The rhythm of "American Rhapsody (III)" comes from laughter, from the "solid silver laughter" that ends the poem but that also seems to float over it. Another of Fearing's antifascist poems, "Bulletin," enacts a similar movement in its evocation of a staccato news bulletin that eventually ends with the question of life or death:

> Filled with life where there was no life before,
> Death where there had been so much life;
> Still reliving yesterday's coup and obeying, still, decrees long revoked;

> How many times, hearing the heart beat, again aware that the heart beats just so many times,
> (How many times?)

It is strange for a heart to be actually beating in a Fearing poem. But the heart, like in Millet's poem, marks a time that becomes an imperative for only a singular possible action: "Time after time, / This, / This and no other unforeseen way."[117]

Epilogue

and this our region
desire, field, beginning. Name and road,
communication to these many men,
as epilogue. Seeds of unending love.
—Muriel Rukeyser, *The Book of the Dead*

When the washed-up vaudeville ventriloquist Tommy Crickshaw (Bill Murray) starts naming the names of his Federal Theatre Project (FTP) comrades in Tim Robbins's 1999 film *The Cradle Will Rock*, his dummy grows agitated. Then one evening, as Tommy prepares for a show, the puppet suggests that the two do "the old act one more time, for old time's sake." And so they do. But, after warming up with a few well-rehearsed red-tinted jokes, the puppet revolts. "Dummies, rise up!" he exclaims and bursts into a solo rendition of "The Internationale." On the last note, the dummy drops dead. Mourners place his small wooden body in a modest coffin marked, "Federal Theatre Project / Born 1934 / Died 1937 / Killed by an Act of Congress," and carry him off in a dizzying, carnivalesque funeral march. Meanwhile, Marc Blitzstein (Hank Azaria) pounds out his prounion opera *The Cradle Will Rock* for a packed house at New York City's Venice Theatre, Hallie Flanagan (Cherry Jones) testifies before the Dies Committee, and the construction crew of Nelson Rockefeller (Ed Norton) destroys the mural *Man at the Crossroads* by Diego Rivera (Ruben Blades). In the film's final scenes, the ventriloquist dummy's funeral procession marches straight out of late-1930s New York City and into turn-of-the-century Times Square.[1]

What do you do when the corpse of past left-wing art appears in the present? Robbins's dead dummy represents the FTP's abolishment as well as art's misuse; it is the corpse of political art carried into the colorful contemporary capitalist haze of Times Square. But, when paired with Diego Rivera's image of a syphilis cell, which in *The Cradle Will Rock* remains stuck to Rockefeller's wall, the dummy signals possible critiques of capitalist reality. The presence of the cell allows the viewer to narrate the dummy's death in terms of potential change: the cell that sticks reminds us of the potentials residing in even the biggest of failures.

Part of the appeal of Robbins's ending might be the way it evokes (certainly unwittingly) Theodor Adorno and Max Horkheimer's description of their task in *The Dialectic of Enlightenment*: "The task to be accomplished," they wrote, "is not the conservation of the past, but the redemption of the hopes of the past."[2] The problem with the dummy, however, is that it does not do anything but arrive in the present. Times Square is still lit. (For all we know, our thirties vaudevillians would find themselves waiting in line for tickets to *Hamilton*.) Consequently, the dead puppet's linear historical march from 1937 to 1999 ignores the ways in which the desire to redeem the past must be coupled with a desire to irrevocably change the present. Perpetuating a stock image of thirties cultural production as wedded, for better or worse, to the welfare state, the film simply assumes that art dies when it is choked off from federal funding and handed over to the corporate elite. (In the closing montage, Rockefeller and his cronies declare that they will "control the future of art" because they will "pay for the future of art.") Such a portrait reduces the vitality of art to its relation to democratic forms of public support: obscuring the multiple, complex relations between the aesthetic and political planes that I have examined in this book and forgoing variegated narratives that have been offered by scholars of the Depression decade.

An epilogue, when adhering to generic convention, looks backward and forward simultaneously: summarizing a book's major conclusions in order to double down on its potential interventions. It may seem like a cheap shot to pin the latter aim on an admonition against Hollywood mainstreaming of art's radical past. But is it also somehow appropriate? In our current era, when the languages of global capitalism pervade scholarly discourse in obvious as well as unacknowledged ways, the distance between the film lot and the ivory tower does not seem very far. In the early 1990s, Alan Wald argued that one of the main "constraints" on earlier scholarship of U.S. communist writers had been "the limitations of liberal thought as it has manifest in politics and literary criticism."[3] As I hope to have shown, Wald's statement continues to ring particularly true in influential areas of modernist literary studies and poetry studies. In both fields, calls to expand scholarly work to new sites of inquiry have largely reinforced neoliberal paradigms of connection and compromise.

In my own examination of how a moment of economic crisis and communist insurgence affected the literary scene, I have not set out to offer new historical data to be added to an ever-growing file, nor have I sought to promote a set of aesthetic criteria for proper anticapitalist art. By imposing thirties communist poetics on current discussions of political poetry, historical poetic practice, and modernist literary studies, I do hope to have qualitatively altered their logics and assumptions. This book's epigraph quotes a 1932 essay by Edmund

Wilson. In it, Wilson writes, "It has now become plain that the economic crisis is to be accompanied by a literary one."[4] Throughout this book, I have argued that the shared ground of economic and literary crises in the thirties do not merely accompany each other, like two separate travelers on a road, but rather that they interfere with each other in complex ways. In my chapters, I have been concerned primarily with how the revolutionary historical imagination and the revolutionary poetic imagination are mutually constituted. I hope that other scholars take up further questions prompted by this inquiry: about the more explicitly economic- and policy-based coordinates of the period and the international scale of the communist presence, as well as the specific interventions offered by interwar poets and literary genres not covered here.

As we collectively move forward, we must resist the temptation to consecrate the objects of the past. When this book had its first life at the University of Michigan, the 2008 economic collapse, the ensuing "Great Recession," and the emergence of the Occupy movement created a new desire to look back at a previous era of economic crisis and its attendant mass political mobilizations. I finished this book in Houston, Texas, in the months just after Hurricane Harvey hit the Gulf Coast. Witnessing a city's reckoning with the devastating effects of reckless economic development and sweeping deregulation of environmental protections—a catastrophe further compounded by histories of racial inequality and new waves of brutal immigration policy—I have increasingly questioned the usefulness of these old stories. At the same time, resistance to the mainstream erasure and defanging of past radicalisms remains an urgent task.

To give another example, in September 2017, days after Keith Lamont Scott was shot and killed by police, sparking uprisings in Charlotte, North Carolina, the *New York Times* dedicated an entire page of the newspaper's print edition to Langston Hughes's 1926 poem "I, Too." The poem begins with the famous line, "I, too, sing America," and then moves from descriptions of present inequalities to visions of a different future. "Tomorrow," the poem asserts, "I'll be at the table / When company comes," and "they'll see how beautiful I am / And be ashamed."[5] The projection of a better tomorrow in "I, Too" is fundamentally different from Hughes's imperative: *Wait!* Indeed, what if the *New York Times* would have, instead, reminded its readers of the Hughes who wrote,

> I shall raise my hand
> And smash the spines of you
> Who shoot me.

> I shall take your guns
> And turn them on you.

That Hughes did not "sing America" but rather declared that he would make the world his own.[6]

As I have hoped to show, "poetry" in the 1930s was a speculative attempt to, as Hughes says, make the world. Indeed, in Muriel Rukeyser's 1968 "Poem (I lived in the first century of world wars)," she muses that poetry is something of a smoke signal sent up amid "vast distances" toward and for "others unseen and unborn." Rukeyser continues,

> As the lights darkened, as the lights of night brightened,
> We would try to imagine them, try to find each other,
> To construct peace, to make love, to reconcile
> Waking with sleeping, ourselves with each other,
> Ourselves with ourselves. We would try by any means
> To reach the limits of ourselves, to reach beyond ourselves,
> To let go the means, to wake.[7]

The poem, unlike the puppet, is not interred in a vault that we might dig up. Rather, it opens a matrix of possibilities in its purported leap into the future. From our present vantage, it is necessary that we meet the challenges signaled in Rukeyser's poem. Perhaps this means turning toward the past, or, perhaps, it means turning away. Either way and in the end, Rukeyser's late poem seems to suggest that it is high time we used poetry to get over poetry.

Notes

Introduction

1. Buuck and Spahr, *Army of Lovers*, 80–81.
2. Hays, "Wants a Communist Poetry," 21.
3. Williams, "Muriel Rukeyser's *U.S. 1*," 141.
4. Calverton, "Leftward Ho!," 26.
5. Wald, *Writing from the Left*, 71.
6. In *DuBois's Telegram: Literary Resistance and State Containment*, Juliana Spahr writes that, "No one is more convinced than writers of literature that literature can provoke and resist. They assert it all the time. While often theoretically sophisticated, much of this assertion is fairly ahistorically optimistic." While many of the authors and works I study in this book fit what Spahr describes as "optimistic narratives about the resistance of literature," I do not seek to reproduce such narratives here. Rather, I am interested in the particular ways communist-affiliated writers constructed fantasies about literary resistance and how those fantasies consequently generated histories and theories of poetry and poetic genres. Spahr, *DuBois's Telegram*, 4–5.
7. The publication of Alan Wald's *The Revolutionary Imagination* and Cary Nelson's *Repression and Recovery* restored to critical view previously overlooked left-wing poets. Both studies use a sustained focus on left writers to reveal the forces shaping critical views of literary periods and aesthetic movements as well as to establish new paradigms for understanding them. Wald's and Nelson's monographs inspired a number of studies that critically reconsidered the relationships between left poetics and predominant literary movements. See especially Coiner, *Better Red*; Kalaidjian, *American Culture between the Wars*; Berke, *Women Poets on the Left*; Filreis, *Modernism from Right to Left* and *Counter-revolution of the Word*; Green, *Social Life of Poetry*; Lowney, *History, Memory, and the Literary Left*; Smethurst, *New Red Negro*; C. Spahr, *Poetics of Global Solidarity*; and Thurston, *Making Something Happen*. On the culture of the literary left, also see Barnard, *Great Depression and the Culture of Abundance*; Rabinowitz, *Labor and Desire*; and Szalay, *New Deal Modernism*.
8. See, for example, Balthaser, *Anti-Imperialist Modernism*; Gore, *Radicalism at the Crossroads*; Higashida, *Black Internationalist Feminism*; Mills, *Ragged Revolutionaries*; Vials, *Haunted by Hitler*; and Higashida, Holcomb, and Lecklider, "Sexing the Left," a special issue of *English Language Notes*.
9. I thus concur with Ruth Jennison's argument that "examin[ing] the texts of crisis in a comparative hermeneutic ... opens up the retroactive illuminations afforded by textual artifacts of more aged crises, lays bare prehistories, and inoculates against habitual, myopic pronouncements regarding the 'newness' of our own moment." Jennison, "29 / 73 / 08," 37–39.
10. See, "Gambling with Debt," 497.

11. Major features of these two fields of inquiry are outlined in respective anthologies: for the historical poetics approach, see Jackson and Prins, *Lyric Theory Reader*. For the poetry and cultural studies approach, Damon and Livingston, *Poetry and Cultural Studies*. Also see Chasar, *Everyday Reading*; and Damon, *Postliterary America*.

12. Dean, *Crowds and Party*, 5.

13. Fearing, *Collected Poems*, 68.

14. Rabinowitz, *Labor and Desire*, 17.

15. Countering the reduction of the thirties to a mere "icon," Michael Denning makes the case that "the communisms of the depression triggered a deep and lasting transformation of American modernism and mass culture." Denning, *Cultural Front*, xvi.

16. White, *Lyric Shame*, 2.

17. See White, *Lyric Shame*. Mary Helen Washington offers a personal take on New Critical influences in *The Other Black List*, acknowledging how New Critical biases shaped a generation of scholars and, in turn, the construction of cultural histories and literature anthologies. Washington's subsequent readings of Gwendolyn Brooks's radical poems tend to employ assumptions about the poetic speaker that are rooted in New Critical reading practices. Clemens Spahr, in his rich account of engaged poetry across the twentieth and twenty-first centuries, relies on accepted models of lyric interpretation in his account of thirties radical poems by Arturo Giovannitti, Edwin Rolfe, and Muriel Rukeyser. See Spahr, *Poetics of Global Solidarity*, chap. 1.

18. Chen and Kreiner, "The Politics of Form," 28.

19. Lessing, *Golden Notebook*, 16.

20. Cowley, *Exiles Return*, 287.

21. Hughes, *Collected Poems*, 43.

22. Michael Cohen, *Social Lives of Poems*, 13. Cohen describes how the "bifurcation of poetry and prose" in the late nineteenth and early twentieth centuries "has worked in tandem with two related processes: the abstraction of 'poetry' into a synonym for pure expressiveness . . . and a concomitant elevation of 'poetry' into a standard for absolute literariness. This tripartite process of abstraction, isolation, and elevation has meant that 'poetry' is something few poems, and certainly few early American poems, can easily be." Cohen traces how the idea that an individual "poem" can be judged according to its ability to realize itself as "poetry" was formed at the turn of the twentieth century.

23. Wilson, "Literary Class War," 539.

24. Kazin, *On Native Grounds*, 363.

25. Here I am referring to what Gilles Deleuze and Félix Guattari define as "that which cannot be thought and yet must be thought." Deleuze and Guattari, *What Is Philosophy?*, 60.

26. Freeman, introduction to *Proletarian Literature*, 24; O'Sheel, "Introductory Note," 8.

27. Burnshaw, "Notes on Revolutionary Poetry," 22.

28. Wald notes in *The Revolutionary Imagination* that the Soviet Communists' slogan "Art is a Class Weapon" had a negative impact on left-wing poetry because it "encouraged the use of political criteria to judge the quality of literature" and "created a hostile and disparaging attitude toward the poetic achievements of the 1920s." As Wald demonstrates, however, seemingly antimodernist poems published in the communist milieu, such as Hughes's deployment of nursery-rhyme meters in "Share-croppers," are more complexly rendered than they seem once submitted to formal as well as political analysis. Wald, *Revolutionary Imagination*, 3, 8.

29. Brian Reed suggests that readers of left poems have been caught in the binds of their own "two-pronged strategy" for convincing "skeptical modern poetry specialists that the Old Left produced more than . . . verse rightfully consigned to oblivion." Reed, *Phenomenal Reading*, 5. See also Harvey Teres's critique of Nelson's and Kalaidjian's monographs in *Renewing the Left*. For an example of scholarship that foregrounds communism as a theoretical or formal principle in modernism relatively untethered from historical and political formations, see Steven, *Red Modernism*. Steven's book concentrates on a limited selection of canonical white, male poets (Ezra Pound, William Carlos Williams, and Louis Zukofsky) and ignores a rich tradition of left literary production and scholarship that illuminates the complex relationships among the Third International, traditions of Marxist theory, and formations of modernist literature. Steven's elision of this tradition and of writers associated with early-twentieth-century communism potentially reentrenches established aesthetic values and, at the same time, elides the significant feminist, antiracist, and anticolonialist dimensions of communist literatures as well as the very diversity of the movement itself.

30. This line of argument shares in some ways with recent scholarship on nineteenth-century cultures of reading, especially Cohen's *The Social Lives of Poems*.

31. See, for example, Balthaser's arguments in *Anti-Imperialist Modernism* about how writers used genres associated with proletarianism, such as the social realist novel, to question the limits of national identity formation.

32. Rahv, "Open Letter to Young Writers," 3.

33. Gold, "Go Left, Young Writers," 3.

34. Fearing, *Collected Poems*, 33–34.

35. Prins, "What Is Historical Poetics?," 37.

36. Culler, "Lyric, History, and Genre," 883. In *Theory of the Lyric*, Culler argues for the necessity of retaining lyric as a transhistorical category.

37. Izenberg, *Being Numerous*, 31. Many critics treat historical poetics as the second coming of New Historicism, where, as Izenberg writes, "what counts as responsible historicist reading requires the elaboration of ever-more-finely differentiated micro-histories of literary genres and functions; it involves situating literary work within richly articulated networks of symbolic and discursive practices; it demands close-up description of the material form of the literary artifact and an aerial charting of the channels of production, circulation, and reception." Izenberg's use of the term "micro-history" elides Marxist theorizations of a microhistorical approach as a means to understand broader networks of relation through emphases on the particular. See Howard, *Publishing the Family*, 2.

38. Jackson, "Please Don't Call It History."

39. Ibid.

40. Prins, "'What Is Historical Poetics?,'" 13.

41. Posmentier, *Cultivation and Catastrophe*, 4.

42. Here I am referring to the examinations of poetry's role in national identity construction in books such as Cohen's *The Social Lives of Poems* and Meredith Martin's *The Rise and Fall of Meter*. While these and other studies effectively critique nationalist and imperialist positions, they seem to do so from within liberal historical models as well as liberal notions of the public. Continuous with, though slightly different from, such studies is modernist poetry scholarship focused on popular cultural forms and "everyday" readers. Together, this body of work provides necessary critiques of the myopia of current interpretive practices.

Nonetheless, their horizons tend to be diachronic and pluralist in ways that rub against the left perspectives on offer in thirties communist culture.

43. Kelley, *Freedom Dreams*, 9. Kelley draws his ideas about poetry from Aimé Césaire's 1945 essay "Poetry and Knowledge."

44. Wang, *Thinking Its Presence*, 2.

45. As Dorothy Wang points out, "Form, whether that of traditional lyric or avant-garde poems, is assumed to be the provenance of a literary acumen and culture that is unmarked but assumed to be white." Wang, *Thinking Its Presence*, 22

46. Terada, "After the Critique of Lyric," 195.

47. Rolfe, *Collected Poems*, 59.

48. Gourgouris, "Communism and Poetry," 43.

49. Ronda, "Not Much Left." Jennifer Ashton has argued that lyric and antilyric poetries are "united in their commitment to liberal (and now neoliberal) value of self-expression." Ashton, "Labor and the Lyric," 219.

50. See Chen and Kreiner, "The Politics of Form," for an indispensible account of how writers associated with the Language movement asserted a politics of form in which poetic experimentation was deemed tantamount to social struggle, and in which poetries associated with New Left liberation movements were reduced to unmediated expressions of racial, gender, and/or sexual identities.

51. I draw the phrase "innovation paradigm" from Ronda, *Remainders*, 15. Writers such as Juliana Spahr have attempted to craft a more expansive definition of lyric that makes room for "language writing's more politicized claims" and acknowledges the lyric as by definition innovative. See Spahr and Rankine, introduction to *American Women Poets*, 2, 13. In the early 2000s, a good deal of scholarship rearticulated the presumed opposition between the lyric tradition and the forms of linguistic experimentation associated with the Language movement. See Kinnahan, *Lyric Interventions*; Frost, *Feminist Avant-Garde*; Keller, *Thinking Poetry*; Yu, *Race and the Avant-Garde*; and Jeon, *Racial Things*. Recent anthologies such as Cole Swensen and David St. John's *American Hybrid* and Reginald Shepherd's *Lyric Postmodernisms* have attempted to demonstrate a synthesis of, rather than an opposition between, the lyric and the experimental.

52. Chen and Kreiner, "Free Speech."

53. See especially Jeon, *Racial Things*; Kinnahan, *Lyric Interventions*; Nielsen, *Black Chant*; A. Reed, *Freedom Time*; Shockley, *Renegade Poetics*; and Wang, *Thinking Its Presence*.

54. For example, see Bernes, *Work of Art*; Chen and Kreiner, "Free Speech"; Clover, "Autumn of the System"; Jennison, *The Zukofsky Era*; Jennison, "29/73/08"; Kreiner, "Long Downturn"; Nealon, *Matter of Capital*; Nealon, "Reading on the Left"; Ronda, "Not Much Left"; Ronda, "Not One." In an *American Quarterly* review essay, Tiana Reid uses Marx's *Capital* to introduce her useful assessment of the shaping role of poetics in present and future American studies scholarship. See Reid, "Shape of Poetics to Come."

55. Nealon, *Matter of Capital*, 4. For Nealon, the major breakthroughs in poetry criticism during the 1970s and 1980s were conditioned by "the crises and triumphs of global capitalism from about 1973 on." The critics responsible for this turn in poetry studies, however, leave out "the history of the century" that produced their ideas about poetry.

56. Jennison, "29 / 73 / 08," 39. See also Clover, "Autumn of the System," 29. Clover concludes with the presumption that the "non-narrative—that 'poetics' including poetry"—

might be "better situated to grasp the transformations of the era: a more adequate cognitive mode for our present situation."

57. Jennison, *Zukofsky Era*, 10. In an overview of thirties poetry for the *Cambridge Companion to American Literature of the 1930s*, Jennison repeats the narrative that radical U.S. poets "sought to suture" art and revolutionary politics through experimental forms that marked "signature breaks with the lyric and with poetic conventions of the nineteenth century." Jennison, "Radical Politics and Experimental Poetics in the 1930s," 72.

58. Nealon, *Matter of Capital*, 9. Following his description of how contemporary poets negotiate the supposed "flaws of leftist critique," including the notion of "a ritualized empty leftism—or, worse, a preening, damaging leftism"—Nealon writes, "it is hard to imagine a more durable twentieth-century victory for the right than the persistence of this structure of feeling, which dates at least to the 1930s, and the international left's horrified disavowal of Stalinism."

59. I am not, however, necessarily advocating for reading these genres as kitsch. See Tiffany, *My Silver Planet*; and Tiffany, "Cheap Signaling"; as well as Fred Moten's thinking about kitsch in *Black and Blur*, 207–10.

60. While this narrative was challenged by scholars such as Nelson and Wald and increasingly explored and complicated in studies by Berke, Filreis, Kalaidjian, Lowney, and Thurston, among others, pat narratives about radical Depression poetry endure. To give just three examples, Charles Altieri's *The Art of Twentieth-Century American Poetry* characterizes the 1930s as a decade of "disappointment" after the 1920s "liberation" of writers by formal experiment; Milton Cohen's *Beleaguered Poets and Leftist Critics* proceeds comfortably from the assumption that during the 1930s "modernism is out; proletarian literature is in"; and Bonnie Costello's recent essays on "the third person plural" readily assume that the 1930s was simply the decade of the "communal we" ("Lyric Poetry").

61. Nealon, *Matter of Capital*, 3.

62. Lowenfels, *Some Deaths*, 21.

63. Hayes, "Untitled response to Edwin Rolfe," 47.

64. Wald, *American Night*, xii.

65. Zaturenska, letter to Harriet Monroe, 13 August 1935.

66. Jennison, "29 / 73 / 08," 40. T. J. Clark writes, "Modernism was regularly outspoken about the barrenness of the working-class movement—its politics of pity, its dreary materialism, the taste of the masses, the Idea of Progress, etc. But this may have been because it sensed socialism was its shadow—that it too was engaged in a desperate, and probably futile, struggle to imagine modernity otherwise. And maybe it is true that there could and can be no modernism without the practical possibility of an end to capitalism existing, in whatever monstrous or pitiful form." Clark, *Farewell to an Idea*, 9.

67. Nelson, *Revolutionary Memory*, 65.

68. The relationships between competing ideologies and the aesthetics attached to them were complicated. Left writers and New Critics alike gleaned ideas about form and function from similar (often diffuse) sources, and left critics sometimes pulled on New Critical discourses as they crafted theses about political art. For instance, Stanley Burnshaw, in his 1934 *New Masses* polemic "Notes on Revolutionary Poetry," cited I. A. Richards and T. S. Eliot in support of his points about the inseparability of form and content. Burnshaw's essay is but one example of the various ways that, as Benjamin Kohlmann has demonstrated,

New Critical ideas shaped, even if often in negative ways, discussions about 1930s radical poetics. On the relationship between leftist and New Critical reading practices, see Kohlmann, *Committed Styles*.

69. For overviews of the expansion of modernist studies, see, for example, Friedman, "Definitional Excursions"; and Mao and Walkowitz, "New Modernist Studies." Paul K. Saint-Amour posits a "weak modernism" that, in his assessment, has produced a "weak theory" of modernism that has consequently strengthened the field of modernist studies. See Saint-Amour, *Tense Future*, 41. Jessica Berman's *Modernist Commitments* is an important expansion of the definitional concerns of modernism to include issues of social justice.

70. See, for example, R. Smith, "Six Propositions."

71. Calverton, "Need for Revolutionary Criticism," 5.

72. Marx, "For a Ruthless Criticism of Everything Existing," in Marx and Engels, *Marx-Engels Reader*, 8.

73. Perloff, "Janus-Faced Blockbuster," 210–11. *Symploke* 9 featured a forum on Perloff's review, which included rejoinders by Marsha Bryant, Edward Brunner, Michael Thurston, Robert Dale Parker, and Carter Revard and a response by Perloff.

74. Perloff, 205. Perloff's critique of Nelson's anthology is just one part of her career-long defenses of the white avant-garde, including her more recent condoning of the conceptual poets Kenneth Goldsmith's and Vanessa Place's appropriation of racialized bodies in their process-based poetics. See Hofer, "If You Hear Something Say Something"; Moten, "On Marjorie Perloff"; Chen, "Authenticity Obsession"; and Hong, "Delusions of Whiteness in the Avant-Garde."

75. Rancière, *Aesthesis*, 253, 257.

76. Jackson and Prins, "General Introduction," 1.

77. Taggard, *Long View*, 110.

78. Millet, "Is Poetry Dead," 21.

79. Halberstam, "Wild Beyond," 5.

80. Agee and Evans, *Let Us Now Praise Famous Men*, 7.

Chapter One

1. Hughes, *I Wonder as I Wander*, 3.

2. Smethurst, *New Red Negro*, 92. Though Hughes was probably never a card-carrying member of the Communist Party, in 1934 he served as president of the Communist-affiliated League of Struggle for Negro Rights. Starting in the early 1930s, he was associated with the John Reed Club in New York, and he regularly published in left magazines such as *New Masses* and *Dynamo*.

3. Mullen, *Langston Hughes*, 3.

4. Hughes, *Collected Poems*, 165–66. See Balthaser, *Anti-Imperialist Modernism*, for a discussion of how Hughes's travels in the Caribbean engendered new thinking about forms of racialization and U.S. imperialism.

5. On the establishment of countervisuality, see Mirzoeff, *Right to Look*.

6. See Blair's reading of Wright's photo-textual projects in *Harlem Crossroads*.

7. Cartier-Bresson, Letter to Langston Hughes, 7 August 1935.

8. Hughes, *I Wonder as I Wander*, 58.

9. See especially Smethurst, *New Red Negro*; Maxwell, *New Negro*; Thurston, *Making Something Happen*; Dawahare, *Nationalism*; and Lowney, *History*.

10. Neigh, "Transnational Frequency," 268.

11. A. Reed, *Freedom Time*, 7.

12. Blair, *Harlem Crossroads*, 11.

13. According to James Smethurst, critics who "compare unfavorably his [Hughes's] writings of the 1930s to his work in other decades" view his thirties efforts as "largely sound[ing] over the same ham-fisted didactic note." Smethurst, *New Red Negro*, 93. An example is Helen Vendler's review of Arnold Rampersad's *The Collected Poems of Langston Hughes* in the 6 March 1995 issue of *New Republic*.

14. Rancière, *Aesthesis*, 250.

15. Hughes and Ingram, "Official Daily Log Book," n.p.

16. Guridy, *Forging Diaspora*, 151.

17. Hughes, *Essays*, 51–52.

18. Hughes and Ingram, "Log Book," n.p.

19. These photographs evince Hughes's attempt to immerse himself in "the folk life of the Haitian people," described in *I Wonder as I Wander*. In Haiti, Hughes refused to use letters of introduction from prominent African American intellectuals such as Walter White and James Weldon Johnson, preferring instead to spend his days in nontourist hotels.

20. Batchen, *Each Wild Idea*, 57.

21. S. Smith, *Photography on the Color Line*, 10.

22. Thompson, *Eye for the Tropics*, 17.

23. Waligora-Davis, *Sanctuary*, 14.

24. Thompson's analysis of early postcards in *An Eye for the Tropics* establishes a frame of reference for reading Hughes's snapshots as a counterpoint to souvenir items in his archive.

25. Rosenberg, "Watch How Dem Touris' Like Fe Look," 42.

26. Hughes, *Essays*, 47.

27. Hughes, *Collected Poems*, 138.

28. Hughes, *Essays*, 141.

29. Benjamin Balthaser argues that Hughes's experiences in Cuba and Haiti marked "the beginning of an exploration of the diasporic meanings of race" that complicated "easy binaries between black and white." Balthaser, *Anti-Imperialist Modernism*, 50.

30. Hughes, *Essays*, 141. Hughes develops the notion that a photographic shadow "holds" something "more" in the same 1935 review of Cartier-Bresson and Álvarez-Bravo's photographs in which he defines "pictures more than pictures."

31. Beals, *Crime of Cuba*, 17.

32. Gronbeck-Tedesco, *Cuba*, 75.

33. Hughes, *Essays*, 141.

34. Rampersad, *Life of Langston Hughes*, 206.

35. Ibid., 202.

36. Ibid., 206–7.

37. Hughes, *Essays*, 52.

38. Barthes, *Camera Lucida*, 92–93. For Barthes, the photograph replaces the monument as the "somehow natural witness of 'what-has-been,'" so that "mythic time" has been

abolished and "everything, today, prepares our race ... to be no longer able to conceive duration."

39. Waligora-Davis, *Sanctuary*, 121.

40. Tejada, *National Camera*, 8. According to Mirzoeff, "the Haitian Revolution, the first successful act of decolonial liberation," was also a "key transformation in producing modern visuality," in which the "countervisuality of antislavery produced the revolutionary hero as the embodied counter to the sovereign authority represented by the overseer." Mirzoeff later argues that, "It is precisely ... with 'blackness' and slavery that a counterhistory of visuality must be concerned." Mirzoeff, *The Right to Look*, 11–12, 13.

41. On U.S. paternalism toward Haiti, see Renda, *Taking Haiti*. I borrow the phrase "visual laboratory" from Tejada's reading of Mexico City as the metropolitan space that Manuel Álvarez-Bravo used "as historic backdrop and as a photographable field for representing material and social markers in relation to time and power at various points of vulnerability." Tejada, *National Camera*, 95.

42. Feder, "Experimental Dorothy Wordsworth," 541.

43. Brinkman, "Modern American Archives," 23.

44. Ellen Gruber Garvey outlines how after the Civil War African Americans used scrapbooking as a means to construct histories that were otherwise unavailable. See chap. 4 of Garvey, *Writing with Scissors*.

45. Stewart, *On Longing*, 138.

46. Blair, "About Time," 162.

47. Goble, *Beautiful Circuits*, 231–32. Mark Goble reads Susan Stewart's theorization of the miniature and the souvenir as a precursor to theories of modernist materiality. Goble's shift from thinking about objects' "intrinsic qualities as things" to "their capacities as mediums" is useful for considering the role of Hughes's scrapbooks in his thinking about representational practices during the 1930s.

48. Caws, *Art of Interference*, 4. W. J. T. Mitchell frames the concept of interference in terms of ekphrasis in *Picture Theory*, 159.

49. In *The Real Thing*, Miles Orvell argues that early-twentieth-century realist writers were anxious that their prose was unable to equal the accuracy of the camera.

50. Chasar, *Everyday Reading*, 42.

51. See Brinkman, "Modern American Archives"; Brinkman, *Poetic Modernism*, chap. 3; and Nealon, *Matter of Capital*, chap. 4.

52. Socarides, *Dickinson Unbound*, 3.

53. Jacobs, "Files in Amber," 55.

54. For Alberto Toscano and Jeff Kinkle's definition of representation in relation to their interpretation of Fredric Jameson's concept of cognitive mapping, see *Cartographies of the Absolute*, 8.

55. Hughes, *Collected Poems*, 174.

56. Ibid.

57. Neigh, "Transnational Frequency," 268.

58. Allred, *American Modernism*, 134.

59. Toscano and Kinkle, *Cartographies of the Absolute*, 7.

60. Jameson, "Cognitive Mapping," 349.

61. Ibid.

62. Ibid. Jameson outlines an "aesthetic of cognitive mapping" in his preface to *The Geopolitical Aesthetic*.
63. Quoted in Toscano and Kinkle, *Cartographies of the Absolute*, 159.
64. Ibid., 36.
65. For example, see Nelson's contextual interpretation of "Goodbye Christ" in *Repression and Recovery*, 200.
66. Toscano and Kinkle, *Cartographies of the Absolute*, 38.
67. Sekula, "Traffic in Photographs," 22.
68. This phrase is from the title of Mackenzie, *An Engine, Not a Camera: How Financial Models Shape Markets*.
69. Hughes, *Collected Poems*, 174.
70. Ibid., 160.
71. Ibid.
72. Stott, *Documentary Expression*, 36.
73. Goble, *Beautiful Circuits*, 231, 260. Manovich, *Language of New Media*, 218.
74. Tejada, "Vanishing Acts," 5.
75. Hughes, *Collected Poems*, 165.
76. Ibid., 165–66.
77. Tejada, "Vanishing Acts," 5.
78. Hughes, *Essays*, 199.
79. Hughes, *Collected Poems*, 166–67.
80. Hughes, *I Wonder as I Wander*, 41.
81. Hughes, typescript of "Kilby Prison: Scottsboro Boys."
82. Extant archival evidence does not indicate whether Hughes took the photograph of the Scottsboro defendants, but it is highly likely.
83. Hughes, *Plays to 1942*, 126–27.
84. Ibid., 128–29.
85. Ibid., 117.
86. Maxwell, *New Negro*, 135.
87. Smethurst, *New Red Negro*, 105.
88. Thurston, *Making Something Happen*, 110.
89. Michael Cohen, "Paul Laurence Dunbar," 248.
90. Moten, *In the Break*, 202.
91. Allred, *American Modernism*, 7.
92. North argues that modernist writers negotiated photography by seeking out new methods of representation in the utopian space between the linguistic and the pictorial. He suggests that "mechanized sense impressions could hardly have presented the challenge they did if they had not conflicted so obviously with what had come to be accepted as unmediated experience." North, *Camera Works*, 4, vii.
93. Cassarino, *Modernity at Sea*, xix.
94. Moten, *In the Break*, 201.
95. Hughes, *Essays*, 141.
96. Tejada, *National Camera*, 110–11.
97. Blair, *Harlem Crossroads*, 52. Hughes, *Simple*, 1.
98. Hughes, *Collected Poems*, 137.

99. Agee and Evans, *Let Us Now Praise Famous Men*, 10.

100. Rabinowitz, *They Must Be Represented*, 46.

101. Agee and Evans, *Let Us Now Praise Famous Men*, 210. Agee's sentiments are akin to Susan Stewart's assumption that poetry "is a force against effacement" for individuals and communities through time because it gives form to the "oblivion of darkness." The photograph literally makes subjects visible by writing with light, hence the etymology of the word photograph as "light writing." Stewart, *Poetry and the Fate of the Senses*, 2.

102. Agee and Evans, *Let Us Now Praise Famous Men*, 172.

103. Ibid., 252.

104. Moten, *In the Break*, 253.

Chapter Two

1. The most thorough account of the Gauley Tunnel disaster remains Cherniack, *Hawk's Nest Incident*.

2. See Rosler, "In, Around, and Afterthoughts."

3. Rabinowitz, *They Must Be Represented*, 3–4.

4. Rukeyser, *Book of the Dead*, 80.

5. Kadlec, "X-ray Testimonials," 27.

6. Rukeyser, *Book of the Dead*, 82.

7. Rukeyser, *Collected Poems*, 604.

8. Nealon, *Matter of Capital*, 19.

9. Ronda, *Remainders*, 6. See also Posmentier, *Cultivation and Catastrophe*.

10. Rukeyser, *Book of the Dead*, 122–23.

11. On Thoreau's vitalism, see Arsić, *Bird Relics*.

12. Agee and Evans, *Let Us Now Praise Famous Men*, 200. Agee's attempts to decenter human subjects through a refusal of anthropocentric narrative structures has been underexplored, and I am thankful to Alexandra Naumann for illuminating this aspect of his work. In this chapter, I am interested in how Rukeyser, like Agee, dissolves the human into the matter of industry. As I suggest, however, she does not go so far as to establish what Jane Bennett terms a "political ecology of things." Bennett seeks "to articulate a vibrant materiality that runs alongside and inside humans to see how analyses of political events might change if we gave the force of things more due." Bennett, *Vibrant Matter*, 14. Certainly Rukeyser gives the force of industrial and natural objects their "due," but she ultimately returns to the question of how persons are constituted by such things, not the question of how they exist in a horizontal relation to such things.

13. Nowak, "Documentary Poetics."

14. Harrington, "Docupoetry and Archive Desire."

15. Ibid.

16. Sanders, *Investigative Poetry*, 10.

17. Magi, "Poetry in Light of Documentary," 247.

18. Stott, *Documentary Expression*, 291.

19. Olsen, *Yonnondio*, 196.

20. Denning, *Cultural Front*, 119. For an account of the relationships among 1930s, 1960s, and 1980s documentary practice, see Rabinowtiz, *They Must Be Represented*.

21. Magi, "Poetry in Light of Documentary," 247.

22. Rukeyser's work is conspicuously absent from two of the major accounts of documentary as it reemerged in the 1970s: Sanders's "Investigative Poetics," which turns to Pound, Olson, and Ginsberg, and Stott's *Documentary Expression and Thirties America*, which centers Agee and Evans. Feminist scholars and poets have offered correctives, most recently Susan Briante, in "Defacing the Monument"; Mark Nowak, in "Documentary Poetics"; and Juliana Spahr, in *Well Then There Now*.

23. In "Projective Verse" (1950) Olson lamented "the removal of verse from its producer and its reproducer, the voice" and encouraged writers to invent ways to score the breath, or voice, on the page. Olson, *Selected Writings*, 22.

24. Benjamin, "Author as Producer," 82.

25. Kalaidjian, *American Culture*, 170.

26. Maddow, "Document and Poetry," 23.

27. Ibid., 24.

28. Quoted in Ellis, *John Grierson*, 28.

29. Maas, "Lost between Wars," 102.

30. Williams, "Muriel Rukeyser's *U.S. 1*," 141.

31. Quoted in Stott, *Documentary Expression*, 13.

32. Davidson, *Ghostlier Demarcations*, 143.

33. Rukeyser, *Book of the Dead*, 62.

34. Kalaidjian, *American Culture*, 167.

35. MacLeish, *Land of the Free*, 89.

36. Kaplan, *American Exposures*, 29.

37. Rukeyser, "We Aren't Sure," 26–28.

38. Benjamin makes a similar suggestion about how successive images caption one another in *The Work of Art in the Age of Mechanical Reproduction*.

39. Lange and Taylor, *American Exodus*, 6.

40. Caldwell and Bourke-White, *You Have Seen Their Faces*, 51.

41. Rukeyser, *Book of the Dead*, 70.

42. Benjamin, *Berlin Childhood*, 65.

43. Rukeyser, *Book of the Dead*, 70.

44. Rukeyser, foreword to Berenice Abbott, *Photographs*, 9.

45. Rukeyser, "Adventures of Children," 27.

46. On the relation between gendered depictions and New Deal liberal reform, see Kozol, "Madonnas of the Fields."

47. Tim Dayton labels these sections "lyrical monologues" in order to stress the "lyrical nature" of these sections and emphasize how they form the "subjective pole" of *The Book of the Dead* by expressing "subjective experiences" and "statements of feeling" as they "render the internal world of the private self." In Dayton's formulation, "lyrical" modifies "monologue" much in the way "inwardness" was used to describe documentary photographs. Dayton, *Muriel Rukeyser's "The Book of the Dead,"* 42–44. Dayton's classification illuminates the messy coexistence of "lyric" and "dramatic monologue" in twentieth-century poetry reading, in which lyrics are increasingly read as dramatic monologues. See, for example, Tucker, "Dramatic Monologue."

48. Such a focus on the landscape might also serve as a counter to New Deal photography that, by focusing on the body, "deemphasized" social and environmental contexts and thus "appeared to universalize, perhaps inadvertently, the nature of alienation by embodying it in rather general terms." Stein, "Peculiar Grace," 63.

49. Rukeyser, *Book of the Dead*, 70.

50. Ibid., 71.

51. Rukeyser's approach in *The Book of the Dead* thus resonates with contemporary ecological theory that seeks to reveal and move past Romantic modalities of experience and representation. See especially Timothy Morton's arguments in *Ecology without Nature* and *Dark Ecology*.

52. Rukeyser, *Book of the Dead*, 77–78.

53. Thurston, *Making Something Happen*, 181.

54. Wheelwright, "Muriel Rukeyser—U.S. 1," 142.

55. The shifting conception of the personal is reminiscent of Morton's supposition that, in our moment of climate catastrophe, the intimate impressions are no longer "personal" or "subjective only." Morton, *Hyperobjects*, 5.

56. Rukeyser, *Book of the Dead*, 87.

57. Kadlec, "X-Ray Testimonials," 26.

58. John Lowney notes that, while the "virtual erasure of blackness in the deadly silica dust" points to "the racial coding of Gauley Bridge," the "commonality compelled by shared adversity also suggests a potential for interracial alliances to contest the white supremacist thinking that Robinson so bitterly mocks." See Lowney, *History*, 61–62.

59. Rukeyser, *Book of the Dead*, 85.

60. Sonya Posmentier demonstrates the importance of blues in African American and diasporic representations of environmental catastrophe, arguing that blues forms capture the unrepresentability of what Rob Nixon terms "slow violence." Posmentier, *Cultivation and Catastrophe*, 148. For a thorough investigation of the concept of slow violence, see Nixon, *Slow Violence*.

61. For a reading of African American poetic experiments with blues that resist expressivist traditions, see A. Reed, *Freedom Time*, chap. 4. In *The Life of Poetry*, Rukeyser acknowledges the blues as an important African American mode of collective expression (110).

62. This argument bears a relation to Monique Allewaert's theorization of new forms of "ecological personhood" in early Atlantic plantation zones. See Allewaert, *Ariel's Ecology*.

63. Rukeyser, *Book of the Dead*, 100.

64. Ibid.

65. Jonathan Kahana argues that "the figure of the photographer who appears throughout Rukeyser's poem to thread together its views was a foil for the poem's politics. . . . This character experienced technological vision as objective truth, an ideological error that the poem, with its panorama of voices and perspectives, seeks to correct." Kahana, *Intelligence Work*, 63.

66. Izenberg, *Being Numerous*, 6; Metres and Nowak, "Poetry as Social Practice," 11.

67. Fredric Jameson writes, "History is what hurts, it is what refuses desire and sets inexorable limits to individual as well as collective praxis." Jameson, *Political Unconscious*, 102.

68. Lesley Wheeler argues in *Voicing American Poetry* that the ambiguity of the term "voice" has made it a contested site for waging debates about experiment and tradition, private and public, and notions of the political.

69. See especially Wechsler, "Mat(t)er of Fact and Vision"; and Rowe, *New American Studies*.

70. Prins, "Historical Poetics," 230.

71. Staub, *Voices of Persuasion*, ix.

72. Dos Passos, *42nd Parallel*, xiv.

73. Couch, *These Are Our Lives*, xiv. The end of Rabinowitz, *The Must Be Represented*, also turns to the importance of speech and voice in documentary. She writes: "Who is speaking? To whom? About what? Those who cannot represent themselves and so must be represented have been historically dispossessed. One can read this admonition—they must—as a declaration of failure: because *they* cannot speak for themselves; *we* must do it for them. Or perhaps it is a plea for recognition: because *they* have not been heard; *we* must listen." In raising these questions, Rabinowitz self-consciously shifts "from a language of images to a rhetoric of speech," observing that: "After having explored the various forms of visualization that have been the core of the documentary project for at least one hundred years, the question of voice now appears central to me." Rabinowitz, *They Must Be Represented*, 218–219.

74. Rabinowitz, "Class Ventriloquism," 202; Stewart, *Poetry and the Fate of the Senses*, 116. My formulation about Rukeyser's resistance to neoliberal logics of self-presence is derived from Athanasiou and Butler, *Dispossession*, 13, 17.

75. Denning, *Cultural Front*, 123. For a poetic perspective on refusal as a political act, see Boyer, "No."

76. Gold, *Jews without Money*, 55.

77. Agee and Evans, *Let Us Now Praise Famous Men*, 367.

78. Rukeyser, *Book of the Dead*, 82.

79. Dimock, *Through Other Continents*, 61.

80. Rukeyser, *Book of the Dead*, 96.

81. Rukeyser, *Life of Poetry*, 92.

82. Rukeyser, *Book of the Dead*, 111–12.

83. Boggs, *Animalia Americana*, 76.

84. Rukeyser, *Book of the Dead*, 112.

85. Ibid., 120.

86. Rukeyser, *Life of Poetry*, 98.

87. Rukeyser, *Book of the Dead*, 110.

88. Perhaps the best reading of this moment in *The Book of the Dead* is Juliana Spahr's poetic appropriation in "The Incinerator." See Spahr, *Well Then There Now*.

89. Lobo, "From 'The Book of the Dead' to 'Gauley Bridge,'" 78. Lobo reads Rukeyser's interest in making the documentary film as evidence of her desire to engage the national-popular aesthetics of the cultural front. His essay offers an important interpretation and contextualization of "Gauley Bridge"; but I tend to disagree with Lobo's arguments that "Gauley Bridge" was intended to be more "commercial" than *The Book of the Dead*, and I find in the film sketches a rich continuation of Rukeyser's experiments with genre and media. One of Rukeyser's notes on *The Book of the Dead* indicates that she was also developing a radio script based on the poem, which she described as a "documentary radio oratorio" that would be played as a "Living Newspaper." Quoted in Rukeyser, *Collected Poems*, 605. Rukeyser traveled to Killorglin, Ireland, in 1958 to scout the annual Puck Fair festival for a

documentary film Paul Rotha was planning. Her correspondence with Rotha also indicates that she was planning a film version of her resulting 1965 travelogue *The Orgy*. Rotha, letter to Muriel Rukeyser, 22 March 1965.

90. Rukeyser, *Life of Poetry*, 153.

91. *China Strikes Back* depicted Mao Tse-tung and his associates' stronghold in Northwest China during the 1931 Japanese invasion of Manchuria. The twenty-three-minute film followed the tactics and programs of young Mao, notably his orthodox Marxist belief in the capacity of the Chinese peasantry as the foundation for a new China.

92. Rukeyser, "Sights and Sounds," 27.

93. Ibid.

94. On *China Strikes Back* as a dialectical film aiming to depict the unity of the Chinese people, see Campbell, *Cinema Strikes Back*.

95. See especially Rukeyser, "Words and Images."

96. Maddow, "Film into Poem," 23.

97. Ibid.

98. Rukeyser, *Book of the Dead*, 106.

99. Rukeyser, "Gauley Bridge," 63.

100. Rukeyser, "Story Outline for Gauley Bridge," 2.

101. Rukeyser, "Gauley Bridge," 56–57.

102. Ibid., 58–59, 55. Rukeyser perhaps learned this strategy from Alfred Hitchcock. Discussing Hitchcock's film *The Thirty-Nine Steps* in *The Life of Poetry*, she writes of how, when the landlady finds a corpse, the sound of her horror-filled scream was not identified until later, "when you saw the train . . . as it hurled out of a black tunnel, still screaming, and you know that the blast of its whistle served for both voices." Rukeyser, *Life of Poetry*, 143. The image of the locomotive also has resonances with the imagery of "Gauley Bridge."

103. Rukeyser, "Story Outline for Gauley Bridge," 6.

104. Rukeyser, *Book of the Dead*, 77.

105. Rukeyser, "Gauley Bridge," 58.

106. Rukeyser, "Story Outline for Gauley Bridge," 3.

107. Ibid., 63.

108. Ibid.

109. Rukeyser, "Story Outline for Gauley Bridge," 6.

110. Benjamin, *Illuminations*, 257–58.

111. Rukeyser, *Life of Poetry*, 137.

112. Ibid., 138.

113. Ibid., 142.

114. Ibid., 154.

115. Rukeyser, "Gauley Bridge," 51.

116. Ibid., 51; Kahana, *Intelligence Work*, 77–78.

117. Rukeyser, "Gauley Bridge," 51.

118. Ibid.

119. Miéville, *October*, 320. The locomotive also recalls the advent of the steam engine as the beginning of the anthropocene era.

Chapter Three

1. Rahv, "Open Letter to Young Writers," 3.
2. Cowley, "Last of the Lyric Poets," 300.
3. Schneider, "Proletarian Poetry," 116–17.
4. Lechlitner, *Tomorrow's Phoenix*, 25.
5. In Rahv's "Open Letter," "lyric" is used as an adjective to describe any writing attempting to transcend class interests. In "The Last of the Lyric Poets," Cowley also defines the lyric in relation to subject matter.
6. Jackson and Prins point out, for example, that Christopher Nealon's arguments in *The Matter of Capital* are predicated on both a narrow definition of lyric and a reductive assessment of arguments about lyricization. See Jackson and Prins, introduction to section 8, "Avant-Garde Anti-lyricism," in *Lyric Theory Reader*, 456.
7. Lechlitner, "Poetry," 50.
8. White, *Lyric Shame*, 6. As Jackson and Prins outline, the New Critical version of "lyric" established in American universities starting in the 1930s used John Stuart Mill's famous definition of poetry as "overheard" as a pedagogical and interpretive strategy. "Students were addressed by poems precisely because they were taught that they could all 'overhear' the poet speaking to herself." In the New Critical classroom, the "lyric I" was understood as "a speaker" who "could speak to no one in particular and thus to all of us." Jackson and Prins, introduction to *Lyric Theory Reader*, 5.
9. The most cogent explication of this phenomenon is proffered in Chen and Kreiner, "The Politics of Form and Poetics of Identity." Also see Kinnahan, *Lyric Interventions* and A. Reed, *Freedom Time*.
10. Nelson, *Revolutionary Memory*, 197.
11. Margaret Ronda, drawing on Gayatri Spivak, suggests that contemporary experimental poetry poses "counter-questions" to the "liberal/lyric concept of the person as locus of potentiality and possessor of value." Ronda, "Not Much Left." Joshua Clover worries that the poem's claim to political recognition acts as "a sort of convenient reinterpretation" of the "once necessary and provocative claim, that the personal is political." Clover, Nealon, and Spahr, "Poetry and Politics Roundtable." Also see Ashton, "Labor and the Lyric"; and R. Smith, "Six Propositions on Compromise Aesthetics."
12. Negri, *Marx beyond Marx*, xvi.
13. Muñoz, *Cruising Utopia*, 3, 12.
14. Wald, *Exiles*, 12.
15. Rolfe, *Collected Poems*, 71.
16. Gold, introduction to *We Gather Strength*, 8. Freeman noted the influence of T. S. Eliot in "They Find Strength," 23. On the influence of twenties modernist techniques for Marxist writers, see Wald, *Revolutionary Imagination*.
17. See especially Kalaidjian, *Edge of Modernism*; Nelson, *Revolutionary Memory*; Nelson, "Lyric Politics"; C. Spahr, *Poetics of Global Solidarity*; and Thurston, *Making Something Happen*.
18. Janowitz, *Lyric and Labour*, 7.
19. Kalaidjian, *Edge of Modernism*, 136.
20. Gold, introduction to *We Gather Strength*, 8.

21. Foster, "Love Campaign," 24–27.
22. Ibid., 29.
23. Rolfe, *Collected Poems*, 50.
24. Freeman, "They Find Strength," 23.
25. Ibid.
26. Jackson, *Dickinson's Misery*, 10.
27. Rolfe, *Collected Poems*, 61.
28. See Blanton, *Epic Negations*, chap. 4.
29. Funaroff, *Spider and the Clock*, 31.
30. Rolfe, *Collected Poems*, 70.
31. Freeman, "They Find Strength," 24.
32. Rolfe, *Collected Poems*, 98–99.
33. Ibid., 68.
34. Ibid., 100–101.
35. Ibid., 101 (emphasis mine).
36. Patchen, *Before the Brave*, 18.
37. Taggard, "Romanticism and Communism," 18–19.
38. "Editors' Note on 'Romanticism and Communism,'" 20.
39. Janowitz, *Lyric and Labour*, 7.
40. Taggard and the *New Masses* editors were negotiating tensions between individual and communitarian ideals and between the aesthetic and political imagination central to understanding Romanticism. Following Michael Löwy and Robert Sayre's arguments in *Romanticism against the Tide of Modernity*, Alan Wald explains that, while left writers might have dismissed aspects of Romanticism, they embraced many of its strains. Wald, *Exiles*, 11–15.
41. Wilson, *Axel's Castle*, 6.
42. Schmitt, *Political Romanticism*, 160.
43. Taggard, "Romanticism and Communism," 19.
44. Kuiken, *Imagined Sovereignties*, 12.
45. Quoted in Wald, *Exiles*, 36.
46. Gold, "Towards Proletarian Art," in *Mike Gold: A Literary Anthology*, 68. In the introduction to his anthology of Gold's writings, Michael Folsom notes that Gold's assessments seemed to rest primarily on what Whitman *said* more than on what he *did*. Folsom, "Introduction," 9.
47. Rolfe, *Collected Poems*, 212.
48. Lechlitner, "Poetry," 51.
49. Dimock, *Residues of Justice*, 113–14.
50. Taggard, *Calling Western Union*, 2.
51. Ibid.
52. Williams, *Spring and All*, 3–4.
53. Taggard, *Calling Western Union*, 15.
54. Dimock, *Residues of Justice*, 119.
55. Castronovo, *Necrocitizenship*, 128.
56. Taggard, *Calling Western Union*, 15.
57. Ibid., 17.

58. Ibid., 31.
59. Ibid., 34–36.
60. Cowley, *Exile's Return*, 287–88.
61. Taggard, *Calling Western Union*, 36.
62. Ibid., 37.
63. Taggard, *Collected Poems*, back flap.
64. On the creation of affective communities through genre, see Berlant, *Cruel Optimism*.
65. In historical terms, one might read this as an unlinking of lyric from Romantic discourses. Jackson explains that the logic of address that dominates post-Romantic theories of lyric reading "converts the isolated 'I' into the universal 'we' by bypassing the mediation of any particular 'you.'" Within this framework, "the poet's solitude stands in for the solitude of the individual reader—a self-address so absolute that every self can identify it as its own." Jackson, *Dickinson's Misery*, 128. Taggard reasserts the presence of another in order to disturb such claims to pure self-expression.
66. See Costello, "Lyric Poetry"; and Allred, *American Modernism*, chap. 4. Michael Szalay observes that "the thirties and forties upped the ante considerably on T. S. Eliot's famous dictum in 'Tradition and the Individual Talent' (1919) that 'the progress of the artist is . . . a continual extinction of the personality.'" Szalay, *New Deal Modernism*, 128–29.
67. Taggard, *Life and Mind*, xv.
68. Taggard, annotated typed copies of *The Poems of Emily Dickinson*, n.p.
69. Taggard, *Long View*, 3.
70. Quoted in Girard, "Jeweled Bindings," 107.
71. Ibid.
72. Following Gillian White, Taggard's establishment of a "new lyric tradition" might be seen as a way to understand lyric outside the assumption that "the best interpretations of poems cohere around an identification with the image of a person divined through analytic interpretation." White, *Lyric Shame*, 15.
73. On the gendering of lyric as feminine, see Prins, *Victorian Sappho*.
74. Berke, *Women Poets on the Left*, 90.
75. Taggard, *Calling Western Union*, 8.
76. Ibid.
77. Berke, *Women Poets on the Left*, 88–89.
78. Quoted in Wald, *Exiles*, 233.
79. The way Taggard imagines her "legacy to the Left" might, in other contexts, be viewed as an unselfconscious embrace of mass action. For an approach that understands the left's legacy as more strongly related to individual creativity and intellectual freedom, see Teres, *Renewing the Left*.
80. Pitts, "Tough, Reasonable, Witty," 22.
81. Van Nyhuis, "Revolution," 32.
82. Taggard, *Calling Western Union*, 7.
83. Wald, *Exiles*, 18.
84. Lieberman, *"My Song Is My Weapon,"* 30–32.
85. Denning, *Cultural Front*, 295.
86. Floyd Dell, undated letter to Genevieve Taggard.

87. Quoted in Swayne, *Orpheus in Manhattan*, 123.
88. Taggard, *Life and Mind*, 5.
89. R. Kaufman, "Lyric Commodity Critique," 211.
90. Strimple, *Choral Music*, 224.
91. Taggard, *Long View*, 102.
92. Prins explains, "the identification of lyric with song is figurative; through a metaphorical transposition of musical 'notes' with verbal 'tones' readers [are] asked to imagine each word of a poem as if it were a sound to be heard, ... as if it were a song to be sung." Prins, "Break, Break, Break into Song," 106.
93. Quoted in *Long View*, 108.
94. Ibid., 108–10.
95. Wilson, "Is Verse a Dying Technique?," 28.
96. Swayne, *Orpheus in Manhattan*, 123–30.
97. Taggard, *Long View*, 83.
98. Swayne, *Orpheus in Manhattan*, 125.
99. Noland, *Voices of Negritude*, 4.
100. Taggard, *Long View*, 85.
101. Rancière, *Staging the People*, 15.
102. W. Johnson, *Idea of Lyric*, 177. Taggard's conception of the choral departs from Sharon Cameron's idea that the choral nature of lyric is an effect of the "radical inequality" between "lyric speech and the voice or voices it represents." For Cameron, "the lyric's choral voice" rises from the center of a "contradiction" between "lyric speech" and "the reality from which it diverges." This choral voice, "however disguised under the cloak of a customary first-person speaker," is emphasized in Emily Dickinson's poetry "by the hymn meters that structure her poems (meters that imply a union of many voices), and by the frequent existence of multiple pronouns within a given poem." Cameron, *Lyric Time*, 207. A Dickinson scholar, Taggard would have been familiar with Dickinson's meters. In her own notes on poetics, she scribbled the word "hymn" next to the phrase "collective nature of song." Taggard, drafts in preparation for *Long View*.
103. Taggard, *Long View*, 86. Taggard's interest in poetry as part of a scene of communal work, such as the barn raising, is probably derived from her reading of Christopher Caudwell's 1937 book *Illusion and Reality*. Taggard's extensive notes on Caudwell's book are preserved in her archive at the New York Public Library. Taggard, notes on Christopher Caudwell's *Illusion and Reality*.
104. Anker, *Fictions of Dignity*, 4.
105. Taggard, "Poetry of the Future," 4.
106. The transcript for Taggard's radio broadcast is undated in her archive. Its frequent references to New York City indicate that it was recorded there; in the transcript, she references her "new book," *Collected Poems, 1918–1938*, probably placing the broadcast in the late 1930s or early 1940s.
107. Taggard, "Poetry of the Future," 18–21.
108. Taggard, *Calling Western Union*, 7–8. This is the logic of Susan Stewart's notion of a "distressed genre" or "new antique" in *Crimes of Writing*, 90–92.
109. For the role of national radio in efforts to promote working-class solidarity, see L. Cohen, *Making a New Deal*, 134–43, 341–57.

110. Taggard, "Poetry of the Future," 22.
111. Ibid., 2.
112. Ibid., 15.
113. Ibid., 6; Taggard, "Romanticism and Communism," 20.
114. Casarino, *Modernity at Sea*, 13-4. See Scandura, *Down in the Dumps*, chap. 4.
115. Taggard, draft of "In the Plural."
116. Burnshaw and Monroe feuded about the political role of poetry in public forums and in their private correspondence. Just after the "Objectivists issue" of *Poetry* appeared in February 1931, Burnshaw wrote to Monroe asking if it was a hoax. Burnshaw, 6 February 1931 letter to Harriet Monroe.
117. Zukofsky, *Anew*, 52.
118. Jennison, *Zukofsky Era*, 188.
119. Nelson, "Lyric Politics," 2.
120. White, *Lyric Shame*, 2–4.
121. Rolfe, *Collected Poems*, 190.
122. Nelson, "Lyric Politics," 37.
123. Ibid., 42
124. Nelson, "Lyric Politics," 51.
125. Rolfe, *Collected Poems*, 175.

Chapter Four

1. Quoted in Fowler, *Knot in the Thread*, 317.
2. Ibid., 205–10. The exact date of Roumain's departure is unclear. Carolyn Fowler notes that he left for Cuba at some point between November 1940 and March 1941.
3. Roumain, untitled speech given at Harlem YMCA, 7, 11.
4. Gourgouris, "Communism and Poetry," 43. Michelle Clayton writes, "In Anglophone criticism, poetry has had its strongest defenders among New Criticism–trained critics, who have tended to present it as an utterance set outside history, insulated from real-world reference. Politically inflected Anglophone literary criticism has been disinclined to press poetry for its connection to history but for a different reason: a sense that the lyric fails to render a significant image of the individual's relation to a multidimensional sociopolitical environment." Clayton, *Poetry in Pieces*, 26.
5. Denning, *Culture in the Age*, 53, 59. Denning's formulation runs counter to scholarship in modernist poetry studies particularly that analyzes internationalism as a theme or trope, often in ways that treat internationalism as primarily, sometimes almost purely, literary without accounting for the specificities of political formations. See for example Ramazani, *Transnational Poetics*; and Maxwell's critique, "Global Poetic." Aarthi Vadde's conceptualization of a "chimera" as a figure for modernist internationalism also risks thematizing historical-political formations. In addition to Benjamin Balthaser, *Anti-Imperialist Modernism*, Harris Feinsod provides a significant account of how "the poetry of the Americas coevolved with the modern inter-American political system, driven in many instances by networks and institutions of hemispheric exchange, and in others by structural forces that link isolated poetic activities through the retrospective gaze of transnational literary history." Feinsod, *Poetry of the Americas*, 2. For a reading of how

contemporary poetry responds to histories of globalization, see Hunter, *Forms of a World*.

6. Denning, *Culture in the Age*, 72.

7. Chandler, *X*, 87. Chandler's formulation is a contrast to Vadde's account of how modernist internationalism is imagined formally. Vadde's book considers "how idealized dreams of internationalism are staged and situated, restrained or wholeheartedly pursued, such that modernisms' chimeras of form reveal the analytical power embedded in aspirations—even, and perhaps especially, when those aspirations face accusations of fantasy, triviality, or misguided illusion." Vadde, *Chimeras of Form*, 7.

8. See Von Eschen, *Race against Empire*.

9. Balthaser, *Anti-Imperialist Modernism*, 129. Jeremy Glick compellingly theorizes the Haitian Revolution as "a grand refusal to forget," and he studies its literary afterlives as rich sites for "speculative thinking on the interrelationship between Black radical pasts, presents, and futures." Glick, *Black Radical Tragic*, 3. Also see Buck-Morss, *Hegel, Haiti, and Universal History*, for a theorization of the importance of the Haitian Revolution in Hegelian conceptions of universal history.

10. Fowler, *Knot in the Thread*, 178.

11. Baldwin, *Beyond the Color Line*, 11. In 2001, Brent Edwards noted a turn away from scholarship focused on the participation of African Americans in the CPUSA, such as Mark Naison's *Communists in Harlem during the Depression*, and to "what we might term the *autonomy* of black radical groups and to their theoretical grappling ... toward a position and a praxis that would attend to both class *and* race in promoting social transformation." Edwards suggested that such a "historiographic shift" is "not only a departure from party-centered considerations of radicalism; it is also a return: it indicates a renewed attention to the methodologies and strategies embedded within key works within the African diasporic intellectual tradition itself." Edwards, "Dossier on Black Radicalism," 2.

12. Roumain, "Is Poetry Dead?," 22–23.

13. O'Sheel, "Introductory Note," 11.

14. Stewart, *On Longing*, ix.

15. As I have suggested in chapter 3 and in this book's introduction, one way to understand the history of Depression-era poetics is vis-à-vis "lyricization," or the processes whereby "the stipulative functions of particular genres collapsed into one big idea of poems as lyric." Jackson, "Who Reads Poetry?," 183.

16. Such an ideal perhaps mirrors as well as negates Cleanth Brooks and Robert Penn Warren's assumption that generic classifications are "arbitrary and irrational" and should give way to "poetry as a thing in itself." Jackson and Prins, introduction to *Lyric Theory Reader*, 5. In placing Roumain's work alongside, or in conversation with, the historical schematic of New Criticism, I do not intend to privilege New Critical models; rather, I seek to illuminate an alternate path for lyricization that accounts for composition and interpretive practices that take place outside Euro-American academic and publishing networks.

17. Ilya Selvinski, "On Soviet Poetry," 107.

18. On the importance of the Fourth International for the transnational black left, see Stephens, *Black Empire*.

19. Gourgouris, "Communism and Poetry," 47. See also Badiou, *Age of the Poets*.

20. Glick, *Black Radical Tragic*, 53.

21. Moten, *Black and Blur*, 2. On the role of aesthetics in shaping ideas about the relationships among history, race, and identity and group formation, see also A. Reed, *Freedom Time*; and Pinto, *Difficult Diasporas*.

22. According to interviews conducted by Fowler, the American Communists were initially "suspicious" of Roumain and his companion Christian Beaulieu due to their elite social status. Roumain began organizing in secret in Haiti upon his return, and he wrote to the CPUSA in December 1932 to report on what he had accomplished. Roumain's activities in the United States and Haiti were watched closely by both governments. In December 1932, after learning of the arrest of a national of the Dominican Republic named Pequero, Roumain sent a telegram to New York asking the CPUSA not to send mail until further notice, and he fled from his Port-au-Prince home. After several days, and with the borders of Port-au-Prince blocked, Roumain turned himself in. He was sent to prison in January 1933 and released a month later. He continued to organize the Parti Communiste Haïtien after his release and was arrested again in October 1934 for "communist conspiracy." This time he was sentenced to three years in prison. Fowler, *Knot in the Thread*, 143–47.

23. Balthaser, *Anti-Imperialist Modernism*, 127.

24. Bradley, letter to Jean Toomer, 13 May 1935.

25. Ibid.

26. Balthaser, *Anti-Imperialist Modernism*, 129.

27. Ibid., 128.

28. Hirschman, *All That's Left*, 19. The Jacques Roumain Cultural Brigade also collaborated with Paul Laraque, head of the Association of Haitian Writers Abroad in New York. In addition to *Boumba (Canoe)*, Boadiba and Hirschman published *Open Gate*, an anthology of Haitian translations. Hirschman's description of organizing the Jacques Roumain Cultural Brigade suggests continuities between Old and New Left anti-imperialist activism: he describes the work of the brigade in relation to the activism of the Communist Labor Party, the Left-Write collective of writers and intellectuals that convened in resistance to Ronald Reagan's election, and other efforts by U.S. activists to shed light on U.S. imperial policies in Central America.

29. Hughes, "Free Jacques Roumain," 1.

30. Balthaser, *Anti-Imperialist Modernism*, 128.

31. Bradley, letter to Langston Hughes, 7 February 1935.

32. Hughes, "Free Jacques Roumain," 1.

33. Fowler, *Knot in the Thread*, 134.

34. Patterson, *Race*, 126.

35. Castronovo, *Beautiful Democracy*, 72.

36. Quoted in Denning, *Cultural Front*, 439.

37. Focusing on the example of Hughes, in "The *Coup* of Langston Hughes's Picasso Period," Ryan Kernan demonstrates how Hughes was a historical figure for understanding theories of translation, one who conceptualized translation as a process that "engendered and perpetuated world literature."

38. A. Reed, *Freedom Time*, 8.

39. Smethurst, *New Red Negro*, 24, 26–27.

40. Throughout *New Red Negro*, Smethurst offers multiple historical and formal perspectives on strategic re-creations of the folk voice in interwar African American poetry.

According to Alan Wald, the political makeup of spirituals, blues, and jazz became contested terrain in cultural practice and criticism. "For the Left, rural Black southern folk culture was coded as the authentic voice of the proletarianized peasantry; memories of resistance to slavery and signs of the subversion of Jim Crow racial capitalism were found lurking under every metaphor and simile." Wald, *Exiles*, 291.

41. Bradley, letter to Jean Toomer, 20 February 1936.
42. Smethurst, *New Red Negro*, 28.
43. Taggard, draft of "To Paul Robeson."
44. Glick, *Black Radical Tragic*, 128.
45. Denning discusses the success and importance of Robeson's recording of Earl Robinson's "Ballad for Americans," dubbing it an "unofficial anthem" of the Popular Front movement in *Cultural Front*, 115–16.
46. Taggard, *Long View*, 55.
47. Edwards, "Langston Hughes," 700.
48. Edwards, *Practice of Diaspora*, 9. See also Kernan, "Coup"; Patterson, *Race*; and Kutzinski, *Worlds of Langston Hughes*.
49. Lee, *Ethnic Avant-Garde*, 75.
50. See Kaussen, "Slaves, *Viejos*, and the *Internationale*," for a convincing reading of Edouard Glissant's theories of *creolization* in terms of recent analyses of proletarian internationalism, especially Michael Hardt and Antonio Negri's *Empire*. Kaussen's analyses are a useful counterpoint to scholarship that opposes notions of hybridity in the Caribbean to Marxian discourses.
51. James, *Black Jacobins*, x.
52. Glick, *Black Radical Tragic*, 151.
53. Moten, *Black and Blur*, 2–3.
54. Fowler, *Knot in the Thread*, 77.
55. Ibid., 73.
56. Roumain, *When the Tom-Tom Beats*, 35–36.
57. Ibid.
58. Moten, "Blackness and Nothingness," 738.
59. Roumain, *When the Tom-Tom Beats*, 36.
60. Ibid., 43.
61. Moten, *Black and Blur*, 7.
62. The song sung and discussed in Roumain's story calls out for a "total annihilation" in a way that evokes Frantz Fanon's "zone of nonbeing." Fanon, *Black Skin*, xii. For a reading of how a conception of the dialectic emerges from Fanon's thought, see Ciccariello-Maher, *Decolonizing Dialectics*.
63. Roumain, *When the Tom-Tom Beats*, 38 (emphasis original).
64. James, *Black Jacobins*, x.
65. Roumain, "When the Tom-Tom Beats," 2.
66. Roumain, *Œuvres complètes*, 25.
67. Roumain, "When the Tom-Tom Beats," 2; Roumain, *Œuvres complètes*, 44.
68. Roumain, *When the Tom-Tom Beats*, 21; Roumain, *Œuvres complètes*, 47.
69. Glick, *Black Radical Tragic*, 3.
70. Roumain, *When the Tom-Tom Beats*, 20.

71. Roumain, *Œuvres complètes*, 47.

72. Moten, *Black and Blur*, 13. Moten's reading of James's Caribbeanness is also useful for understanding Roumain's formation of his own identity. This antifoundational approach harkens Moten's citation of Cedric Robinson in the epigraph to *In the Break*: "black radicalism cannot be understood within the particular context of its genesis."

73. This process might be understood in terms of Edouard Glissant's notion of "errantry" or "errant thought," which "silently emerges from the destructuring of compact national entities that yesterday were still triumphant and, at the same time, from difficult, uncertain births of new forms of identity that call to us." Glissant, *Poetics of Relation*, 18.

74. Roumain, *When the Tom-Tom Beats*, 21.

75. Roumain, *Œuvres complètes*, 47.

76. Moten, *Black and Blur*, 7. This moment of poetic exchange between Roumain and Hughes might also be read in terms of what Christina Sharpe identifies as "care." See Sharpe, *In the Wake*, 130–34.

77. Roumain, untitled speech given at Harlem YMCA, 11, 7.

78. Ibid., 7.

79. Endore, *Babouk*, 182.

80. Roumain, untitled speech given at Harlem YMCA, 11.

81. Throughout the thirties and forties, Locke wrote essays analyzing how effectively African American poetry synthesized "race consciousness" with a "more generalized social-mindedness." See Locke, "Poetry—or Propaganda," 70. Locke also served on the Committee for the Release of Jacques Roumain.

82. Locke, "Eleventh Hour," 9.

83. Ibid., 11.

84. Roumain, "Is Poetry Dead," 23.

85. James, *Black Jacobins*, ix

86. Moten notes how poetry is "marked by an excess of tranquility, a lyric and dialectical drive that bring the noise of such emotion." Moten, *Black and Blur*, 11. James's ideas about the dialectical relationship between history and poetry, which parallel Roumain's own, perhaps precipitate a different order of "poetic knowledge" than what Aimé Césaire described in his 1945 essay "Poetry and Knowledge," which opens, "Poetic knowledge is born in the great silence of scientific knowledge" (134).

87. Roumain, "Is Poetry Dead?," 22.

88. Here, Roumain's view of the relationship between poetry and history bears a resemblance to Theodor Adorno's arguments for the political possibilities of modernist autonomous art in his essays "Commitment" and "On Lyric Poetry and Society." For Adorno, political autonomous art derives its significance from both a given reality *and* its nonidentity with that very reality. In "On Lyric Poetry and Society," Adorno delineates the relationship between an artwork's aesthetic qualities and the social truths it reveals. In that essay, he presumes to make his audience "uncomfortable" by offering a sociological explanation of lyric poetry. He suggests that art performs the work of ideological demystification by "giv[ing] voice to what ideology hides, . . . whether intentionally or not," while also describing it as sui generis, created as a "reaction to the reification of the world" and therefore defined by its resistance to the world. Adorno, *Notes to Literature*, 39–40.

89. Roumain, "Is Poetry Dead?," 22.

90. Ibid.
91. Ibid.
92. See, for example, Bernes, Clover, and Spahr, "Self-Abolition of the Poet."
93. Chandler, *X*, 115.
94. Roumain, *Masters of the Dew*, 23.
95. Kaussen, "Slaves," 133–34, 136.
96. See especially Stephens, *Black Empire*.
97. Clayton, *Poetry in Pieces*, 18.
98. A. Reed, *Freedom Time*, 97.
99. Noland, *Voices of Negritude*, 3–8.
100. Badiou, *Age of the Poets*, 105.
101. Robinson, *Black Marxism*, 171.
102. Britton, "Common Being," 168.
103. Roumain, *When the Tom-Tom Beats*, 73, 75; Roumain, *Œuvres complètes*, 55–57.
104. Roumain, *When the Tom-Tom Beats*, 77, 79.
105. Roumain, *Œuvres complètes*, 58.
106. Roumain, *When the Tom-Tom Beats*, 81.
107. Roumain, *Œuvres complètes*, 59.
108. Roumain, *When the Tom-Tom Beats*, 83.
109. Roumain, *Œuvres complètes*, 59–60.
110. Roumain, *Masters of the Dew*, 90.
111. Roumain, *When the Tom-Tom Beats*, 75, 77. Roumain, *Œuvres complètes*, 57.
112. Roumain, *When the Tom-Tom Beats*, 75. Roumain, *Œuvres complètes*, 57.
113. Roumain, *When the Tom-Tom Beats*, 81. Roumain, *Œuvres complètes*, 59. This is potentially similar to how Moten theorizes Aunt Hester's scream in Fredrick Douglass's *Narrative* as a "prefigurative working out" of a mode of rematerialization that might be associated with communism. Following Marx's conception of communism as a "discovery procedure" rather than simply a found or achieved state of being, Moten intimates that black radicalism "might be performed in and as that arrival at becoming-social in the vexed and vexing exchange of role." Moten, *In the Break*, 253.
114. Hughes, draft of translation of "Sales nègres," ca. 1945. In Hughes's archive at Yale, the translation of "Sales nègres" is accompanied by a letter indicating that he had sent the translation to *Phylon*, but it was returned.
115. Roumain, *Œuvres complètes*, 66.
116. Glick, *Black Radical Tragic*, 52.
117. Harney and Moten, "Mikey the Rebelator," 141.
118. Rampersad, *Life of Langston Hughes*, 109.
119. Hughes, "Poem for Jacques Roumain," 25.
120. Rampersad, *Life of Langston Hughes*, 102.
121. Cullen, *Collected Poems*, 266.
122. Richard Wright and Aimé Césaire, to give two prominent examples, made public their decisions to leave the Communist Party in their respective published pieces "I Tried to Be a Communist" (1944) and "Letter to Maurice Thorez" (1956). See Tolliver, *Of Vagabonds and Fellow Travelers*, for an examination of how these resignations signal the predominance

of African diasporic freedom struggles as a revolutionary vanguard that superseded the Euro-American workers movement.

123. Wright, "I Tried to be a Communist," 49. Luce's "The American Century" appeared in the 17 February 1941 issue *Life*. For Wallace's rejoinder that the twentieth century is the "People's Century" or the "Century of the Common Man," see Wallace, *Democracy Reborn*, 193.

124. Hughes, drafts and typescripts of "A Poem for Jacques Roumain."

125. Hughes, "Poem for Jacques Roumain," 25.

126. Roumain, untitled speech given at Harlem YMCA, 8 (emphasis mine). Chandler connects black historical experiences of placeless-ness to questions of intellectual freedom: "there is not now nor has there ever been a free zone or quiet place from which the discourse of the so-called Africanist figures, intellectuals, writers, thinkers, or scholars might issue." Chandler, *X—The Problem of the Negro as a Problem for Thought*," 14.

127. Kelley, *Freedom Dreams*, xii. The phrase "somewhere in advance of nowhere" is taken from the title of Cortez's 1996 poetry volume.

128. Harney and Moten, "Michael Brown," 81.

Chapter Five

1. Millet, "Biographical Note."
2. Here I refer to Kenner, *The Pound Era*.
3. Menand, "Pound Error." More recently, Mark Steven's *Red Modernism* tries to read Pound's modernist epics in relation to theories of communism. While he accounts for Pound's engagements with Lenin and Marx, he does not go so far as to suggest that Pound's politics were Marxist.
4. Huyssen, *Other Cities*, 14.
5. Mao and Walkowitz, "New Modernist Studies," 737. Mao and Walkowitz use "expansionist" to describe the shifting contours of the field of modernist studies starting in about 1999. Fredric Jameson posits that "talk about 'alternate' or 'alternative' modernities" is a means "to overlook the other fundamental meaning of modernity which is that of worldwide capitalism itself. The standardization projected by capitalist globalization in this third or late stage of the system casts considerable doubt on all these pious hopes for cultural variety in a future world colonized by a universal market order." Jameson, *Singular Modernity*, 12–13.

From this vantage, Paul K. Saint-Amour's supposition that the weakening of modernism in theory has led to its strengthening as a field takes a different tenor. Saint-Amour observes that, in contemporary modernist studies, the field's "key term [modernist] has stopped playing bouncer and started playing host." Saint-Amour, *Tense Future*, 42. Such an "open door" view of modernism, however, obscures the fact that critics continue to make evaluative judgments with roots in old models. Perhaps more to the point of this chapter, it seemingly recenters the very types of academic institutions (universities as well as professional organizations and conferences) that Millet criticized for their complicity with capitalist structures of power. Perhaps most in line with Millet's conception of modernism is Jessica Berman's description of how "modernism brings to the fore narrative's role in helping us imagine justice," though in her specific historical milieu, "modernism" would not have been the operative word. Modernism, for

Berman, "stands in for a dynamic set of relationships, practices, problematics, and cultural engagements with modernity rather than a static canon of works, a given set of formal devices, or a specific range of beliefs." Berman, *Modernist Commitments*, 7.

6. Calverton, "Need for Revolutionary Criticism," 5.

7. Genter, *Late Modernism*; Filreis, *Counter-revolution of the Word*.

8. Millet, typescript of "Footnote on Modern Poetry."

9. Millet equally criticized the conservative New Critics and the *Partisan Review* intellectuals for their involvements with academic and publication institutions. See especially Millet, "Modern Poetry: For or Against?"

10. On how literary studies has been adapted for the aims of antiracist liberal capitalism, see Melamed, *Represent and Destroy*.

11. Ali, *Dilemmas of Lenin*, 1

12. Nelson, *Revolutionary Memory*, 67.

13. Gregory Barnhisel illuminates this literary historical development in *Cold War Modernists*.

14. Pound, *Pisan Cantos*, 96.

15. See the arguments of Martin, *Rise and Fall of Meter*, and Kappeler, "Shaping Free Verse."

16. Rahv, "Proletarian Literature," 619.

17. Martin, *Rise and Fall of Meter*, 130; Kappeler, "Shaping Free Verse." Martin's and Kappeler's assessments destabilize conventional definitions of the difference between meter and rhythm that relate meter to predetermined forms (for example, ballad meter) and relate rhythm to natural processes or cycles (for example, the human heartbeat or seasonal patterns).

18. Millet, "Is Poetry Dead?," 21.

19. This schematic is adapted from Wald, *American Night*, 251.

20. Millet, "Pioneer Pied Piper," 4–5, 23.

21. Robinson, letter to Martha Millet, n.d.

22. Gold, "One Columnist," 7. In "The Storyteller" (1936), Walter Benjamin called the fairy tale "the first tutor of mankind," teaching children "to meet the forces of the mythical world with cunning and with high spirits." See Benjamin, *Illuminations*, 102. Frankfurt School film theorist Siegfried Kracauer wrote in his foundational essay "The Mass Ornament" (1927) that "genuine fairy tales . . . are not stories about miracles but rather announcements of the miraculous advent of justice." See Kracauer, *Mass Ornament*, 80. Both of these descriptions are based in the workings of narrative, particularly the ability of children to fight and win against the demonic and despotic.

23. See Martin, "Imperfectly Civilized"; and Michael Cohen, *Social Lives of Poems*.

24. Newman, *Ballad Collection*, 189.

25. See Gramsci, "The Concept of the National-Popular," in *The Gramsci Reader*, 364–70.

26. Millet, "Pioneer Pied Piper," 5.

27. On the ballad as format, see McGill, "What Is a Ballad?"

28. Newman, *Ballad Collection*, 189.

29. Wald, *Exiles*, 18.

30. Richard A. and JoAnne C. Reuss make this point in their study of American folk music and left-wing politics. See Reuss and Reuss, *American Folk Music*, 81–114.

31. Quoted in Denning, *Cultural Front*, 259.

32. W. Kaufman, *Woody Guthrie's Modern World Blues*, 118. Roshanak Kheshti argues that the ballad-collector archetype "emerges through a lineage of listening that constructs pathways of connectivity through a 'structure of feeling' or affective ties of affinity organized and standardized by the world music culture industry. The archetype's class and race matter as the historical form through which the aurality of the contemporary world music listener had been materialized." Kheshti, *Modernity's Ear*, 38.

33. Lomax, *Adventures of a Ballad Hunter*, 27.

34. Mickenberg, *Learning from the Left*, 68.

35. Millet, "Phillip Freneau," 20.

36. Wolff, "Use Traditional Tunes," 7.

37. Millet, "Henry Wadsworth Longfellow," 19.

38. Sorby, *Schoolroom Poets*, 11.

39. Millet, "Henry Wadsworth Longfellow," 19.

40. Quoted ibid., 19.

41. Wald notes that Sinclair's novels reflect her "continuous attempt to recapture the idealistic spirit of the antifascist crusade and recast it in a form that could outlast the desecration of the original dream." Wald, *Trinity of Passion*, 258.

42. Sinclair, *Changelings*, 31.

43. Ibid., 37.

44. Ibid., 304–5.

45. Potamkin, "Mother Goose on the Breadline," 7.

46. Hicks, "Those Who Quibble," 23.

47. Pound, *Literary Essays*, 3. Many communist cultural critics heard no music at all in modernist poetry, even when it was written from the left. Hicks complained in his vehement criticism of volume 1 of Horace Gregory's *New Letters in America* that too many of the selections were not pleasurable to listen to, and he wanted to know "why most of the younger poets are so determined that what they write shall not be pleasing to the ear. Hicks, "Those Who Quibble," 23.

48. "Is Poetry Dead?," 9.

49. Wald, *Exiles*, 131.

50. Lalley, "Good and Effective Poetry," 21.

51. Dudgeon, "Mr. Dudgeon Gets High," 369.

52. M. Clark, "Perils of Poetry," 361. Clark also commented on the "maladjusted egos" of modernist writers.

53. James Farrell identified these tendencies within the left as the opposed poles of a "Marxism" that is "mechanical" versus a "revolutionary sentimentalism." A "feature of this critical tendency," Farrell suggested, "is the devising of a more or less arithmetical scale of the social values of a work of literature in terms of whether or not it expresses hope or despair." Farrell, *Note on Literary Criticism*, 173–74.

54. Quoted in Wald, *Exiles*, 20.

55. Millet, "Is Poetry Dead?," 21.

56. "Rhythm" might be seen here as a key nodal point for distinguishing communist from fascist formations where they have historically been conflated.

57. Golston, *Rhythm and Race*, 42–43.

58. Millet's ideas about rhythm echo Gummere's definition of poetry as "rhythmic utterance, rhythmic speech, with mainly emotional origin." Gummere, *Beginnings of Poetry*, 30. The connection between Millet's and Gummere's ideas demonstrates that left writers were not just reacting to the tenets of modernist poetry but also reworking earlier influential claims. While many poets on the left adopted the ideas about poetic rhythm outlined by critics such as Gummere, especially the notion that rhythm was the essence of poetry and gave poetry its emotional force, they idealized rhythm for different ends.

59. Wilson, "Is Verse Dying Technique?," 16.

60. Jameson, *Archaeologies of the Future*.

61. Denning, *The Cultural Front*, xiv.

62. See especially Archibald MacLeish's glowing *New Masses* review, "The Tradition of the People."

63. Wilson, "Is Verse a Dying Technique?," 30.

64. Niven, *Carl Sandburg*, 491.

65. Sandburg 20 January 1935 letter to MacLeish, in Sandburg, *Letters*, 309.

66. Sandburg 20 January 1935 to Cowley, ibid., 309–10.

67. Sandburg to 14 February 1935 letter to Ueland, ibid., 312.

68. Sandburg, *People, Yes*, i.

69. Davidson, "Life by Water," 7–8. Rachel Blau DuPlessis reads Niedecker's poems in terms of the "implacability" of the ballad stanza, in *Blue Studios*, 141–43. Ruth Jennison deftly portrays Niedecker's Marxist commitments in chapter 4 of *The Zukofsky Era*.

70. Niedecker, *Collected Works*, 101.

71. Ibid., 95.

72. Laughlin, preface to *New Directions*, xi.

73. Niedecker, *Collected Works*, 89.

74. DuPlessis argues that the feminist and anticapitalist ethics of Niedecker's work in forms such as the nursery rhyme is a way to distance herself from "the glut and fattiness of mainstream poetries." DuPlessis, *Blue Studios*, 143.

75. Filreis, *Counter-revolution of the Word*, 32.

76. Wald, *American Night*, 250.

77. Vials, *Haunted by Hitler*, 49.

78. For an account of Millet's relationship to conventional modernist aesthetics, see Filreis, *Counter-revolution of the Word*, 3–7, 18–28

79. Pearce, *Continuity of American Poetry*, 5.

80. O'Sheel, "Introductory Note," n.p.

81. Quoted in Wald, *American Night*, 253.

82. Langston Hughes, "The Bitter River," in Yoseloff, *Seven Poets*, 42–43.

83. Norman Rosten, "Prelude," in Yoseloff, *Seven Poets*, 94.

84. Martha Millet, "Unforgotten Village," in Yoseloff, *Seven Poets*, 83.

85. Ibid.

86. Adorno and Horkheimer, *Dialectic of Enlightenment*, 29.

87. Martha Millet, "Historian," in Yoseloff, *Seven Poets*, 87.

88. In a notable incident, Millet's poem response to Emmett Till's murder, "Mississippi," was publicly criticized in *Masses and Mainstream* for deemphasizing class struggle. This criticism is detailed in Aptheker, "Letter," 58–59.

89. Gold, "Six Open Letters," 4.

90. "Ezra Pound, Silvershirt," 15–16. In a 12 March 1936 letter to Pound, Louis Zukofsky admonished *New Masses* for printing the cover; but he also scolded Pound for writing Somerville: "If you're dead set on completely losing whatever readers you still have in America, keep it up," Zukofsky wrote, citing the large audience that *New Masses* enjoyed in the midthirties. Zukofsky to Pound, in Pound and Zukofsky, *Pound/Zukofsky*, 177.

91. Rosten, "Should Ezra Pound Be Shot?," 6. Rosten also included a biting poem, "Garland for Mr. Pound," in Yoseloff, *Seven Poets*, 94–95.

92. Kindley, *Poet-Critics*, 9.

93. Millet, typescript of "Footnote on Modern Poetry," 6; Millet, typescript of "Poets and Poverty," 14.

94. Millet, typescript of "Poets and Poverty," 36.

95. Millet, typescript of "The Ezra Pound Myth," 66.

96. See Chen and Kreiner, "Free Speech."

97. Maxwell Bodenheim, "The Game," in Yoseloff, *Seven Poets*, 21.

98. Barnhisel, *Cold War Modernists*, 3.

99. Ibid., 48.

100. I capitalize "New York Intellectuals" in order to reference a specific group of left-wing, anti-Stalinist writers and critics based in New York during the mid-twentieth century rather than intellectuals in New York more generally.

101. Brooks, *Modern Poetry and the Tradition*, 44.

102. Wald, *New York Intellectuals*, 221.

103. Rahv, "Proletarian Literature," 619–21. Barbara Foley discusses the contradictions in Rahv's essay in *Radical Representations*, 3–43.

104. Rahv, "Proletarian Literature," 627.

105. Although the suppositions of "Avant-Garde and Kitsch" are generally associated with developments in the visual arts, the aesthetic values and modes of critique they establish are integral to understanding the 1940s literary scene. For instance, Daniel Tiffany demonstrates the importance of Greenberg's theory of kitsch for understanding the history of poetry, in *My Silver Planet*.

106. Greenberg, "Avant-Garde and Kitsch," 39.

107. The descriptor "high modernism" was coined retroactively to describe the version of modernism circulating during the Cold War, which emphasized aesthetic achievement and innovation. See Jameson, *Postmodernism*, 55–66.

108. Harvey Teres discusses *Partisan Review* critics' interest in Henry James's novels, in *Renewing the Left*, 108–9.

109. Millet, "Modern Poetry," 43.

110. Ibid., 41.

111. West, *No Lonesome Road*, 129.

112. Millet, typescript of "The Ezra Pound Myth," 132.

113. Johnson, "Trump on Retweeting."

114. Wark, "Not Yet."

115. Millet, "The Quick and the Dead," 3.

116. Fearing, *Collected Poems*, 92.

117. Ibid., 93–94.

Epilogue

1. The film version of *The Cradle Will Rock* takes obvious liberties with history. Rivera's mural was destroyed in 1933, Blitzstein's opera premiered in 1937, and the Federal Theatre Project was abolished in 1938.
2. Adorno and Horkheimer, *Dialectic of Enlightenment*, xv.
3. Wald, *Writing from the Left*, 73.
4. Wilson, "The Literary Class War," 539.
5. Hughes, *Collected Poems*, 46.
6. Hughes, *Collected Poems*, 174.
7. Rukeyser, *Collected Poems*, 430.

Bibliography

Adorno, Theodor. *Notes to Literature.* Vol. 2. Edited by Rolf Tiedeman. Translated by Shierry Weber Nicholsen. New York: Columbia University Press, 1992.

Adorno, Theodor, and Max Horkheimer. *The Dialectic of Enlightenment.* Translated by Edmund Jephcott. Stanford: Stanford University Press, 2002.

Agee, James, and Walker Evans. *Let Us Now Praise Famous Men.* 1941. Reprint, Boston: Houghton Mifflin, 2001.

Ali, Tariq. *The Dilemmas of Lenin: Terrorism, War, Empire, Love, Revolution.* New York: Verso, 2017.

Allewaert, Monique. *Ariel's Ecology: Plantations, Personhood, and Colonialism in the American Tropics.* Minneapolis: University of Minnesota Press, 2013.

Allred, Jeff. *American Modernism and Depression Documentary.* New York: Oxford University Press, 2009.

Altieri, Charles. *The Art of Twentieth-Century American Poetry: Modernism and After.* Malden, MA: Wiley Blackwell, 2006.

Anker, Elizabeth S. *Fictions of Dignity: Embodying Human Rights in World Literature.* Ithaca, NY: Cornell University Press, 2012.

Appel, Benjamin. *The People Talk: American Voices from the Great Depression.* 1940. Reprint, New York: Simon and Schuster, 1982.

Aptheker, Herber. "Letter." *Masses and Mainstream.* December 1955, 58–59.

Arsić, Branka. *Bird Relics: Grief and Vitalism in Thoreau.* Cambridge, MA: Harvard University Press, 2016.

Ashton, Jennifer. "Labor and the Lyric: The Politics of Self-Expression in Contemporary American Poetry." *American Literary History* 25, no. 1 (2013): 217–30.

Athanasiou, Athena, and Judith Butler. *Dispossession: The Performative in the Political.* Malden, MA: Polity Press, 2013.

Badiou, Alain. *The Age of the Poets.* Edited and translated by Bruno Bosteels. New York: Verso, 2014.

Baldwin, Kate. *Beyond the Color Line and the Iron Curtain: Reading Encounters between Black and Red, 1922–1963.* Durham, NC: Duke University Press, 2002.

Balthaser, Benjamin. *Anti-Imperialist Modernism: Race and Transnational Radical Culture from the Great Depression to the Cold War.* Ann Arbor: University of Michigan Press, 2016.

Barnard, Rita. *The Great Depression and the Culture of Abundance: Kenneth Fearing, Nathanael West, and Mass Culture in the 1930s.* New York: Cambridge University Press, 1995.

Barnhisel, Gregory. *Cold War Modernists: Art, Literature, and American Cultural Diplomacy.* New York: Columbia University Press, 2015.

Barthes, Roland. *Camera Lucida: Reflections on Photography.* Translated by Richard Howard. New York: Hill and Wang, 1994.

Batchen, Geoffrey. *Each Wild Idea: Writing, Photography, History*. Cambridge, MA: MIT Press, 2002.

Beals, Carleton. *The Crime of Cuba*. New York: Lippincott, 1933.

Benjamin, Walter. "Author as Producer." Translated by Edmund Jepchott and Kingsley Shorter. In *The Work of Art in the Age of Its Technological Reproducibility and Other Writings on Media*. Edited by Michael W. Jennings, Brigid Doherty, and Thomas Y. Levin, 73–95. Cambridge, MA: Harvard University Press, 2008.

———. *Berlin Childhood around 1900*. Cambridge, MA: Harvard University Press, 2006.

———. *Illuminations: Essays and Reflections*. Edited by Hannah Arendt. New York: Schocken Books, 1969.

———. *The Work of Art in the Age of Mechanical Reproduction*. 3rd ed. New York: Penguin, 1994.

Bennett, Jane. *Vibrant Matter: A Political Ecology of Things*. Durham, NC: Duke University Press, 2010.

Berke, Nancy. *Women Poets on the Left: Lola Ridge, Genevieve Taggard, Margaret Walker*. Gainesville: University Press of Florida, 2002.

Berlant, Lauren. *Cruel Optimism*. Durham, NC: Duke University Press, 2011.

Berman, Jessica. *Modernist Commitments: Ethics, Politics, and Transnational Modernism*. New York: Columbia University Press, 2011.

Bernes, Jasper. *The Work of Art in the Age of Deindustrialization*. Stanford, CA: Stanford University Press, 2017.

Bernes, Jasper, Joshua Clover, and Juliana Spahr. "The Self-Abolition of the Poet." *Jacket 2*, 2 January 2014. http://jacket2.org/commentary/self-abolition-poet.

Blair, Sara. "About Time: Photographs and the Reading of History." *PMLA* 125, no. 1 (2010): 161–71.

———. *Harlem Crossroads: Black Writers and the Photograph in the Twentieth Century*. Princeton, NJ: Princeton University Press, 2007.

Blanton, C. D. *Epic Negations: The Dialectical Poetics of Late Modernism*. Oxford: Oxford University Press, 2015.

Boggs, Colleen Glenney. *Animalia Americana: Animal Representations and Biopolitical Subjectivity*. New York: Columbia University Press, 2013.

Botkin, B. A., ed. *Lay My Burden Down: A Folk History of Slavery*. Chicago: University of Chicago Press, 1945.

Boyer, Anne. "No." *Poetry Foundation Harriet Blog*, 13 April 2017. https://www.poetryfoundation.org/harriet/2017/04/no.

Bradley, Francine. Letter to Jean Toomer, 20 February 1936. Box 1, Folder 33, Jean Toomer Papers, Beinecke Library, Yale University, New Haven, CT.

———. Letter to Jean Toomer, 13 May 1935. Box 1, Folder 33, Jean Toomer Papers, Beinecke Library, Yale University, New Haven, CT.

———. Letter to Langston Hughes, 7 February 1935. Box 22, Folder 454, Langston Hughes Papers, Beinecke Library, Yale University, New Haven, CT.

Briante, Susan. "Defacing the Monument: Rukeyser's Innovations in Docupoetics." *Jacket 2*, 21 April 2014. http://jacket2.org/article/defacing-monument.

Brinkman, Bartholomew. "Modern American Archives and Scrapbook Modernism." In *The Cambridge Companion to Modern American Poetry*, edited by Walter Kalaidjian, 23–36. New York: Cambridge University Press, 2015.

———. *Poetic Modernism in the Culture of Mass Print*. Baltimore: Johns Hopkins University Press, 2016.

Britton, Celia M. 2006. "'Common Being' and Organic Community in Jacques Roumain's *Gouverneurs de la rosée*." *Research in African Literatures* 37, no. 2 (2006): 164–75.

Brooks, Cleanth. *Modern Poetry and the Tradition*. 1935. Reprint, New York: Oxford University Press, 1965.

Buck-Morss, Susan. *Hegel, Haiti, and Universal History*. Pittsburgh, PA: University of Pittsburgh Press, 2009.

Burnshaw, Stanley. Letter to Harriet Monroe, 6 February 1931. *Poetry, A Magazine of Verse* Records, Special Collections Research Center, University of Chicago, Chicago, IL.

———. "Notes on Revolutionary Poetry." *New Masses*, 20 February 1934, 20–22.

Buuck, David, and Juliana Spahr. *An Army of Lovers*. San Francisco: City Lights, 2013.

Caldwell, Erskine, and Margaret Bourke-White. *You Have Seen Their Faces*. 1937. Reprint, Athens: University of Georgia Press, 1995.

Calverton, V. F. "Leftward Ho!" *Modern Quarterly* 6 (Summer 1932): 26–32.

———. "The Need for Revolutionary Criticism." *The Left: A Quarterly Review of Radical and Experimental Art* 1, no. 1 (1931): 5.

Cameron, Sharon. *Lyric Time: Dickinson and the Limits of Genre*. Baltimore: Johns Hopkins University Press, 1981.

Campbell, Russell. *Cinema Strikes Back: Radical Filmmaking in the United States 1930–1942*. Ann Arbor: University of Michigan Press, 1982.

Cartier-Bresson, Henri. Letter to Langston Hughes, 7 August 1935. Box 42, Folder 732, Langston Hughes Papers, Beinecke Library, Yale University, New Haven, CT.

Casarino, Cesare. *Modernity at Sea: Melville, Marx, Conrad in Crisis*. Minneapolis: University of Minnesota Press, 2002.

Castronovo, Russ. *Beautiful Democracy: Aesthetics and Anarchy in a Global Era*. Chicago: University of Chicago Press, 2009.

———. *Necrocitizenship: Death, Eroticism, and the Public Sphere in the Nineteenth-Century United States*. Durham, NC: Duke University Press, 2001.

Caws, Mary Ann. *The Art of Interference: Stressed Readings in Verbal and Visual Texts*. Princeton, NJ: Princeton University Press, 1989.

Césaire, Aimé. "Poetry and Knowledge." 1945. In *Refusal of the Shadow: Surrealism and the Caribbean*, edited and translated by Michael Richardson and Krzystof Fijalkowski, 134–36. New York: Verso, 1996.

Chambers, Whittaker. "Can You Make Out Their Voices." *New Masses* 6, no. 10 (March 1931): 7–15.

Chandler, Nahum Dimitri. *X—The Problem of the Negro as a Problem for Thought*. New York: Fordham University Press, 2014.

Chasar, Mike. *Everyday Reading: Poetry and Popular Culture in Modern America*. New York: Columbia University Press, 2012.

Chen, Chris, and Tim Kreiner. "Free Speech, Minstrelsy, and the Avant-Garde." *Los Angeles Review of Books*, 10 October 2015. https://lareviewofbooks.org/article/free-speech-minstrelsy-and-the-avant-garde/.

———. "The Politics of Form and Poetics of Identity in Postwar American Poetry." *Routledge Companion to Literature and Economics*, edited by Matt Seybold and Michelle Chihara, 27–40. New York: Routledge, 2018.

Chen, Ken. "Authenticity Obession, Or Conceptualism as Minstrel Show." *Asian American Writers' Workshop*, 11 June 2015. https://aaww.org/authenticity-obsession.

Cherniack, Mark. *The Hawk's Nest Incident: America's Worst Industrial Disaster*. New Haven, CT: Yale University Press, 1986.

Ciccariello-Maher, George. *Decolonizing Dialectics*. Durham, NC: Duke University Press, 2017.

Clark, Mildred H. "The Perils of Poetry." *New Republic*, 27 April 1938, 360–61.

Clark, T. J. *Farewell to an Idea: Episodes from a History of Modernism*. New Haven, CT: Yale University Press, 1999.

Clayton, Michelle. *Poetry in Pieces: Cesar Vallejo and Lyric Modernity*. Berkeley: University of California Press, 2011.

Clover, Joshua. "Autumn of the System: Poetry and Financial Capital." *JNT: Journal of Narrative Theory* 41, no. 1 (2011): 34–52.

Clover, Joshua, Christopher Nealon, and Juliana Spahr. "Poetry and Politics Roundtable." *Evening Will Come: A Monthly Journal of Poetics* 6 (June 2011). http://www.thevolta.org/ewc6-politicsroundtable-p1.html.

Cohen, Lizabeth. *Making a New Deal: Industrial Workers in Chicago, 1919–1939*. 2nd ed. Cambridge: Cambridge University Press, 2008.

Cohen, Michael. "Paul Laurence Dunbar and the Genres of Dialect." *African American Review* 41, no. 2 (2007): 247–57.

———. *The Social Lives of Poems in Nineteenth Century America*. Philadelphia: University of Pennsylvania Press, 2015.

Cohen, Milton. *Beleaguered Poets and Leftist Critics: Stevens, Cummings, Frost, and Williams in the 1930s*. Tuscaloosa: University of Alabama Press, 2010.

Coiner, Constance. *Better Red: The Writing and Resistance of Tillie Olsen and Meridel LeSueur*. Urbana: University of Illinois Press, 1995.

Cortez, Jayne. *Somewhere in Advance of Nowhere*. New York: Serpent's Tail, 1996.

Costello, Bonnie. "Lyric Poetry and the First-Person Plural: 'How Unlikely.'" In *Something Understood: Essays and Poetry for Helen Vendler*, edited by Stephen Burt and Nick Halpern, 193–206. Charlottesville: University of Virginia Press, 2009.

Cowley, Malcolm. *Exile's Return: A Literary Odyssey of the 1920s*. 1934. Reprint, New York: Penguin, 1994.

———. "The Last of the Lyric Poets." *New Republic*, 27 January 1932, 299–300.

Cullen, Countee. *Collected Poems*. Edited by Major Jackson. New York: Library of America, 2013.

Culler, Jonathan. "Lyric, History, and Genre." *New Literary History* 40, no. 4 (2009): 879–99.

———. *Theory of the Lyric*. Cambridge, MA: Harvard University Press, 2013.

Cunard, Nancy. *Negro: An Anthology*. Paris: Hours Press, 1934.

Damon, Maria. *Postliterary America: From Bagel Shop Jazz to Micropoetries*. Iowa City: University of Iowa Press, 2011.

Damon, Maria, and Ira Livingston, eds. *Poetry and Cultural Studies: A Reader*. Urbana: University of Illinois Press, 2009.

Davidson, Michael. *Ghostlier Demarcations: Modern Poetry and the Material Word*. Berkeley: University of California Press, 1997.

———. "Life by Water: Lorine Niedecker and Critical Regionalism." In *Radical Vernacular: Lorine Niedecker and the Politics of Place*, edited by Elizabeth Willis, 3–20. Iowa City: University of Iowa Press, 2008.
Dawahare, Anthony. *Nationalism, Marxism, and African American Literature between the Wars: A New Pandora's Box*. Jackson: University Press of Mississippi, 2001.
Dayton, Tim. *Muriel Rukeyser's "The Book of the Dead."* Columbia: University of Missouri Press, 2003.
Dean, Jodi. *Crowds and Party*. New York: Verso, 2016.
DeCarava, Roy, and Langston Hughes. *The Sweet Flypaper of Life*. 1955. Reprint, New York: David Zwirner Books, 2018.
Deleuze, Gilles, and Félix Guattari. *What Is Philosophy?* Translated by Graham Burchell and Hugh Tomlinson. New York: Verso, 1994.
Dell, Floyd. Letter to Genevieve Taggard, n.d. Box 2, Folder 48, Midwest Manuscripts Collection, Newberry Library, Chicago, IL.
Denning, Michael. *The Cultural Front: The Laboring of American Culture in the Twentieth Century*. New York: Verso, 1996.
———. *Culture in the Age of Three Worlds*. New York: Verso, 2004.
Dimock, Wai-chee. *Residues of Justice: Literature, Law, Philosophy*. Berkeley: University of California Press, 1997.
———. *Through Other Continents: American Literature across Deep Time*. Princeton, NJ: Princeton University Press, 2008.
Dos Passos, John. *The 42nd Parallel*. 1938. Reprint, New York: Houghton Mifflin, 2000.
Dudgeon, W. J. "Mr. Dudgeon Gets High." *New Republic*, 2 February 1938, 369.
DuPlessis, Rachel Blau. *Blue Studios: Poetry and Its Cultural Work*. Tuscaloosa: University of Alabama Press, 2006.
"Editors' Note on 'Romanticism and Communism.'" *New Masses*, 25 September 1934, 20.
Edwards, Brent Hayes. "Dossier on Black Radicalism: Introduction: The 'Autonomy' of Black Radicalism." *Social Text* 19, no. 2 (2001): 1–13.
———. "Langston Hughes and the Futures of Diaspora." *American Literary History* 19, no. 3 (2007): 689–711.
———. *The Practice of Diaspora: Literature, Translation, and the Rise of Black Internationalism*. Cambridge, MA: Harvard University Press, 2003.
Ellis, John. C. *John Grierson: Life, Contributions, Influence*. Carbondale: Southern Illinois University Press, 2000.
Endore, Guy. *Babouk*. New York: Monthly Review Press, 1991.
"Ezra Pound, Silvershirt." *New Masses*, 17 March 1936, 15–16.
Fanon, Frantz. *Black Skin, White Masks*. Rev. ed., New York: Grove, 2008.
Farrell, James T. *A Note on Literary Criticism*. 1936. Edited by Alan Wald. New York: Columbia University Press, 1992.
Fearing, Kenneth. *The Collected Poems of Kenneth Fearing*. New York: Random House, 1940.
Feder, Rachel. "The Experimental Dorothy Wordsworth." *Studies in Romanticism* 53, no. 4 (2014): 541–60.
Federal Writers Project, Regional Staff. *These Are Our Lives*. 1939. Reprint, Chapel Hill: University of North Carolina Press, 2016.

Feinsod, Harris. *The Poetry of the Americas: From Good Neighbors to Countercultures.* Oxford: Oxford University Press, 2017.

Filreis, Alan. *Counter-revolution of the Word: The Conservative Attack on Modern Poetry, 1945–1960.* Chapel Hill: University of North Carolina Press, 2008.

———. *Modernism from Right to Left: Wallace Stevens, the Thirties, and Literary Radicalism.* Cambridge: Cambridge University Press, 1994.

Flanagan, Hallie, and Margaret Ellen Clifford. *Can You Hear Their Voices: A Play for Our Time.* Poughkeepsie, NY: Experimental Theatre of Vassar College, 1931.

Foley, Barbara. *Radical Representations: Politics and Form in U.S. Proletarian Fiction, 1929–1941.* Durham, NC: Duke University Press, 1993.

Folsom, Michael. "Introduction." *Mike Gold: A Literary Anthology.* Edited by Michael Folsom. 7–20. New York: International, 1972.

Foster, Stephen. "The Love Campaign." *Dynamo* 2, no. 1 (1935): 24–29.

Fowler, Carolyn. *A Knot in the Thread: The Life and Work of Jacques Roumain.* Washington, DC: Howard University Press, 1980.

Freeman, Jonathan. Introduction to *Proletarian Literature in the United States: An Anthology*, edited by Granville Hicks, Michael Gold, Isidor Schneider, Joseph North, Paul Peters, and Alan Calmer, 9–28. New York: International, 1935.

———. "They Find Strength." *New Masses*, 10 March 1936, 23–25.

Friedman, Susan Stanford. "Definitional Excursions: The Meanings of Modern/Modernity/Modernism." *Modernism/modernity* 8, no. 3 (2001): 493–513.

Frost, Elisabeth. *The Feminist Avant-Garde in American Poetry.* Iowa City: University of Iowa Press, 2003.

Funaroff, Sol. *The Spider and the Clock.* New York: International, 1938.

Gander, Catherine. *Muriel Rukeyser and Documentary: The Poetics of Connection.* Edinburgh: Edinburgh University Press, 2013.

Garvey, Ellen Gruber. *Writing with Scissors: American Scrapbooks from the Civil War to the Harlem Renaissance.* New York: Oxford University Press, 2012.

Genter, Robert. *Late Modernism: Art, Culture, and Politics in Cold War America.* Philadelphia: University of Pennsylvania Press, 2010.

Girard, Melissa. "'Jeweled Bindings': Modernist Women's Poetry and the Limits of Sentimentality." In *The Oxford Handbook of Modern and Contemporary Poetry*, edited by Cary Nelson, 96–119. New York: Oxford University Press, 2012.

Glick, Jeremy Matthew. *The Black Radical Tragic: Performance, Aesthetics, and the Unfinished Haitian Revolution.* New York: NYU Press, 2016.

Glissant, Édouard. *Poetics of Relation.* Translated by Betsy Wing. Ann Arbor: University of Michigan Press, 2010.

Goble, Mark. *Beautiful Circuits: Modernism and the Mediated Life.* New York: Columbia University Press, 2010.

Gold, Mike. "Go Left, Young Writers." *New Masses*, January 1929, 3.

———. Introduction to *We Gather Strength*, 7–9. New York: Liberal Press, 1933.

———. *Jews without Money: A Novel.* 1930. Reprint, New York: Public Affairs, 2009.

———. *Mike Gold: A Literary Anthology.* Edited by Michael Folsom. New York: International, 1972.

———. "One Columnist Who Fails to Cry in His Beer over 'Snow White.'" *Daily Worker*, 7 April 1938, 7.

———. "Six Open Letters." *New Masses*, September 1931, 3–5.
Golston, Michael. *Rhythm and Race in Modernist Poetry and Science*. New York: Columbia University Press, 2008.
Gomez, Manuel, ed. *Poems for Workers: An Anthology*. Chicago: Daily Worker Publishing, n.d.
Gore, Dayo. *Radicalism at the Crossroads: African American Women Activists in the Cold War*. New York: NYU Press, 2011.
Gourgouris, Stathis. "Communism and Poetry." *Gramma: Journal of Theory and Criticism* 8 (2000): 43–54.
Gramsci, Antonio. *The Gramsci Reader: Selected Writings, 1916–1935*. Edited by David Forgacs. New York: NYU Press, 2000.
Green, Chris. *The Social Life of Poetry: Appalachia, Race, and Radical Modernism*. New York: Palgrave Macmillan, 2009.
Greenberg, Clement. "Avant-Garde and Kitsch." *Partisan Review* 6, no. 5 (1939): 34–49.
Gregory, Horace. *Chorus for Survival*. New York: Covici-Friede, 1935.
Gronbeck-Tedesco, John A. *Cuba, the United States, and Cultures of the Transnational Left, 1930–1975*. New York: Cambridge University Press, 2015.
Gummere, Francis Barton. *The Beginnings of Poetry*. New York: Macmillan, 1901.
Guridy, Frank Andre. *Forging Diaspora: Afro-Cubans and African-Americans in a World of Empire and Jim Crow*. Chapel Hill: University of North Carolina Press, 2010.
Halberstam, Jack. "The Wild Beyond: With and for the Undercommons." In *The Undercommons: Fugitive Planning and Black Study*, by Stefano Harney and Fred Moten, 2–13. New York: Minor Compositions, 2013.
Hardt, Michael, and Antonio Negri. *Empire*. Cambridge, MA: Harvard University Press, 2000.
Harney, Stefano, and Fred Moten. "Michael Brown." *Boundary 2* 42, no. 4 (2015): 81–87.
———. "Mikey the Rebelator." *Performance Research* 20, no. 4 (2015): 141–45.
Harrington, Joseph. "Docupoetry and Archive Desire." *Jacket 2*, 27 October 2011. http://jacket2.org/article/docupoetry-and-archive-desire.
Hayes, Alfred. "Untitled response to Edwin Rolfe." *Partisan Review* 2, no. 7 (1935): 47.
Hays, Lee. "Wants a Communist Poetry." *New Masses*, 11 January 1938, 21.
Hicks, Granville. "Those Who Quibble, Bicker, Nag, and Deny." *New Masses*, 28 September 1937, 22–23.
Higashida, Cheryl. *Black Internationalist Feminism: Women Writers of the Black Left: 1945–1995*. Urbana: University of Illinois Press, 2011.
Higashida, Cheryl, Gary Holcomb, and Aaron Lecklider, eds. "Sexing the Left." Special issue, *English Language Notes* 53, no. 1 (2015).
Hirschman, Jack. *All That's Left*. San Francisco: City Lights, 2008.
Hofer, Jen. "If You Hear Something Say Something, Or If You're Not at the Table You're on the Menu." *Entropy*, 18 December 2015. https://entropymag.org/if-you-hear-something-say-something-or-if-youre-not-at-the-table-youre-on-the-menu.
Hong, Cathy Park. "Delusions of Whiteness in the Avant-Garde." *Lana Turner* 7 (2014): 248–53.
Howard, June. *Publishing the Family*. Durham: Duke University Press, 2001.
Hughes, Langston. *The Collected Poems of Langston Hughes*. Edited by Arnold Rampersad and David Roessel. New York: Vintage Classics, 1995.

———. Draft of translation of "Sales nègres" by Jacques Roumain, ca. 1945. Box 426, Folder 9471, Langston Hughes Papers, Beinecke Library, Yale University, New Haven, CT.

———. Drafts and typescripts of "A Poem for Jacques Roumain (Late Poet of Haiti)." Box 383, Folder 6827, Langston Hughes Papers, Beinecke Library, Yale University, New Haven, CT.

———. *Essays on Art, Race, Politics, and World Affairs*. Edited by Christopher C. De Santis. Columbia: University of Missouri Press, 2002.

———. "Free Jacques Roumain: A Letter from Langston Hughes." *Dynamo* 2, no. 1 (1935): 1.

———. *I Wonder as I Wander*. 1956. Reprint, New York: Hill and Wang, 1993.

———. *The Plays to 1942: "Mulatto" to "The Sun Do Move."* Edited by Leslie Catherine Sanders and Nancy Johnston. Columbia: University of Missouri Press, 2002.

———. "A Poem for Jacques Roumain (Late People's Poet of Haiti)." *New Masses*, 2 October 1945, 25.

———. *The Simple Omnibus*. New York: Aeonian Press, 1961.

———. Typescript of "Kilby Prison: Scottsboro Boys." Box 313, Folder 5098, Langston Hughes Papers, Beinecke Library, Yale University, New Haven, CT.

Hughes, Langston, and Zell Ingram. "The Official Daily Log Book—Jersey to the West Indies—Lang & Zel—Via Narimova." 1931. Box 492, Folder 12437, Langston Hughes Papers, Beinecke Library, Yale University, New Haven, CT.

Hunter, Walt. *Forms of a World: Contemporary Poetry and the Making of Globalization*. New York: Fordham University Press, 2019.

Hurston, Zora Neale. *Mules and Men*. 1935. Reprint, New York: Harper Collins, 2009.

Huyssen, Andreas. *Other Cities, Other Worlds: Urban Imaginaries in a Globalizing Age*. Durham, NC: Duke University Press, 2008.

"Is Poetry Dead?" *New Masses*, 21 December 1937, 9.

Izenberg, Oren. *Being Numerous: Poetry and the Ground of Social Life*. Princeton, NJ: Princeton University Press, 2011.

Jackson, Virginia. *Dickinson's Misery: A Theory of Lyric Reading*. Princeton, NJ: Princeton University Press, 2005.

———. "Please Don't Call It History." *Non Site* 2 (September 2011). http://nonsite.org/the-tank/being-numerous.

———. "Who Reads Poetry?" *PMLA* 123, no. 1 (2008): 181–87.

Jackson, Virginia, and Yopie Prins. Introduction to *The Lyric Theory Reader: A Critical Anthology*, edited by Virginia Jackson and Yopie Prins, 1–8. Baltimore: Johns Hopkins University Press, 2014.

———, eds. *The Lyric Theory Reader: A Critical Anthology*. Baltimore: Johns Hopkins University Press, 2014.

Jacobs, Karen. "Files in Amber: Documentary Objects as Subjects in Carrie Mae Weems." *English Language Notes* 50, no. 1 (2012): 55–66.

James, C. L. R. *Black Jacobins*. 2nd ed. New York: Vintage, 1989.

Jameson, Fredric. *Archaeologies of the Future: The Desire Called Utopia and Other Science Fictions*. New York: Verso, 2005.

———. "Cognitive Mapping." In *Marxism and the Interpretation of Culture*, edited by Cary Nelson, and Lawrence Grossberg, 347–57. Urbana: University of Illinois Press, 1988.

———. *The Geopolitical Aesthetic: Cinema and Space in the World System*. Bloomington: Indiana University Press, 1995.
———. *The Political Unconscious: Narrative as a Socially Symbolic Act*. Ithaca, NY: Cornell University Press, 1982.
———. *Postmodernism; or, The Cultural Logic of Late Capitalism*. Durham, NC: Duke University Press, 1991.
———. *A Singular Modernity: Essay on the Ontology of the Present*. New York: Verso, 2002.
Janowitz, Anne. *Lyric and Labour in the Romantic Tradition*. Cambridge: Cambridge University Press, 1998.
Jennison, Ruth. "29 / 73 / 08: Poetry, Crisis, and a Hermeneutic of Limits." *Mediations* 28, no. 2 (2015): 37–46.
———. "Radical Politics and Experimental Poetics in the 1930s." *The Cambridge Companion to American Literature of the 1930s*, edited by William Solomon. 72–91. New York: Cambridge University Press, 2018.
———. *The Zukofsky Era: Modernity, Margins, and the Avant-Garde*. Baltimore: Johns Hopkins University Press, 2012.
Jeon, Joseph. *Racial Things, Racial Forms: Objecthood in Avant-Garde Asian American Poetry*. Iowa City: University of Iowa Press, 2012.
Johnson, Jenna. "Trump on Retweeting Questionable Quote: 'What Difference Does It Make Whether It's Mussolini.'" *Washington Post*, 28 February 2016.
Johnson, W. L. R. *The Idea of Lyric: Lyric Modes in Ancient and Modern Poetry*. Berkeley: University of California Press, 1983.
Kadlec, David. "X-ray Testimonials in Muriel Rukeyser." *Modernism/modernity* 5, no. 1 (1998): 23–47.
Kahana, Jonathan. *Intelligence Work: The Politics of American Documentary*. New York: Columbia University Press, 2013.
Kalaidjian, Walter. *American Culture between the Wars: Revisionary Modernism and Postmodern Critique*. New York: Columbia University Press, 1993.
———. *The Edge of Modernism: American Poetry and the Traumatic Past*. Baltimore: Johns Hopkins University Press, 2006.
Kaplan, Louis. *American Exposures: Photography and Community in the Twentieth Century*. Minneapolis: University of Minnesota Press, 2005.
Kappeler, Erin Joyce. "Shaping Free Verse: American Prosody and Poetics, 1880–1920." PhD diss., Tufts University, 2014.
Kaufman, Robert. "Lyric Commodity Critique, Benjamin Adorno Marx, Baudelaire Baudelaire Baudelaire." *PMLA* 123, no. 1 (2008): 207–15.
Kaufman, Will. *Woody Guthrie's Modern World Blues*. Norman: University of Oklahoma Press, 2017.
Kaussen, Valerie. "Slaves, *Viejos*, and the *Internationale*: Modernity and Global Contact in Jacques Roumain's *Gouverneurs de la rosée*." *Research in African Literatures* 35, no. 4 (2004): 121–41.
Kazin, Alfred. *On Native Grounds: An Interpretation of Modern American Prose Literature*. New York: Harcourt Brace, 1942.
Keller, Lynn. *Thinking Poetry: Readings in Contemporary Women's Exploratory Poetics*. Iowa City: University of Iowa Press, 2010.

Kelley, Robin D. G. *Freedom Dreams: The Black Radical Imagination.* Boston: Beacon, 2002.

Kenner, Hugh. *The Pound Era.* Berkeley: University of California Press, 1973.

Kernan, Ryan James. "The *Coup* of Langston Hughes's Picasso Period: Excavating Mayakovsky in Langston Hughes's Verse." *Comparative Literature* 66, no. 2 (2014): 227–46.

Kheshti, Roshanak. *Modernity's Ear: Listening to Race and Gender in World Music.* New York: NYU Press, 2015.

Kindley, Evan. *Poet-Critics and the Administration of Culture.* Cambridge, MA: Harvard University Press, 2017.

Kinnahan, Linda. *Lyric Interventions: Feminism, Experimental Poetry, and Contemporary Discourse.* Iowa City: University of Iowa Press, 2004.

Kohlmann, Benjamin. *Committed Styles: Modernism, Politics, and Left-Wing Literature in the 1930s.* Oxford: Oxford University Press, 2014.

Kozol, Wendy. "Madonnas of the Fields: Photography, Gender, and 1930s Farm Relief." *Genders* 2 (Summer 1988): 1–23.

Kracauer, Sigfried. *The Mass Ornament: Weimar Writings.* Edited and Translated by Thomas Y. Levin. Cambridge, MA: Harvard University Press, 1995.

Kreiner, Timothy. "The Long Downturn and Its Discontents: Language Writing and the New Left." PhD diss., University of California–Davis, 2013.

Kuiken, Kir. *Imagined Sovereignties: Toward a New Political Romanticism.* New York: Fordham University Press, 2014.

Kutzinski, Vera. *The Worlds of Langston Hughes: Modernism and Translation in the Americas.* Ithaca, NY: Cornell University Press, 2012.

Lalley, R. W. "Good and Effective Poetry." *New Masses,* 11 January 1938, 21.

Lange, Dorothea, and Paul Taylor. *An American Exodus: A Record of Human Erosion.* New York: Reynal and Hitchcock, 1939.

Laughlin, James. Preface to *New Directions in Prose and Poetry,* vol. 2, edited by James Laughlin. vii–xii. Norfolk: New Directions, 1937.

Lechlitner, Ruth. "Poetry." *Partisan Review,* April 1935, 50–51.

———. *Tomorrow's Phoenix.* New York: Alcestis, 1937.

Lee, Steven. *The Ethnic Avant-Garde: Writers, Artists, and the Magic Pilgrimage to the Soviet Union.* New York: Columbia University Press, 2015.

Lessing, Doris. *The Golden Notebook.* 1962. Reprint, New York: Harper Classics, 1999.

Lieberman, Robbie. *"My Song Is My Weapon": People's Songs, American Communism, and the Politics of Culture, 1930–50.* Urbana: University of Illinois Press, 1995.

Lobo, Julius. "From 'The Book of the Dead' to 'Gauley Bridge': Muriel Rukeyser's Documentary Poetics and Film at the Crossroads of the Popular Front." *Journal of Modern Literature* 35, no. 3 (2012): 77–102.

Locke, Alain. "The Eleventh Hour of Nordicism: Retrospective Review of the Literature of the Negro for 1934." *Opportunity,* January 1935, 8–12.

———. "Poetry—or Propaganda?" *Race* 1 (Summer 1936): 70–76, 87.

Lomax, John. *Adventures of a Ballad Hunter.* Austin: University of Texas Press, 2017.

Lowenfels, Walter. *Some Deaths.* Highlands, NC: Nantahala Foundation, 1964.

Lowney, John. *History, Memory, and the Literary Left: Modern American Poetry, 1935–1968.* Iowa City: University of Iowa Press, 2006.

Löwy, Michael, and Robert Sayre. *Romanticism Against the Tide of Modernity*. Translated by Catherine Porter. Durham: Duke University Press, 2002.
Luce, Henry. "The American Century." *Life Magazine*, 17 February 1941, 61–65.
Maas, Willard. "Lost between Wars." *Poetry: A Magazine of Verse* 52 (May 1938): 102.
MacKenzie, Donald. *An Engine, Not a Camera: How Financial Models Shape Markets*. Cambridge, MA: MIT Press, 2006.
MacLeish, Archibald. *Conquistador*. Boston: Houghton Mifflin, 1933.
———. *The Land of the Free*. 1938. Reprint, New York: Da Capo, 1977.
———. "The Tradition of the People." *New Masses*, 1 September 1936, 25–27.
Maddow, Ben [David Wolff]. "Document and Poetry." *New Masses*, 22 February 1938, 23–24.
———. "Film into Poem." *New Theatre*, November 1936, 23.
Magi, Jill. "Poetry in Light of Documentary." *Chicago Review* 59, nos. 1–2 (2014): 248–75.
Manovich, Lev. *The Language of New Media*. Cambridge, MA: MIT Press, 2001.
Mao, Douglas, and Rebecca Walkowitz. "The New Modernist Studies." *PMLA* 123, no. 3 (2008): 737–48.
Martin, Meredith. "Imperfectly Civilized: Ballads, Nations, and Histories of Form." *English Literary History* 82, no. 2 (2015): 345–63.
———. *The Rise and Fall of Meter: Poetry and English National Culture, 1860–1930*. Princeton, NJ: Princeton University Press, 2006.
Marx, Karl, and Friedrich Engels. *The Marx-Engels Reader*. Edited by Robert C. Tucker. 2nd ed. New York: Norton, 1978.
Maxwell, William J. "Global Poetics and State-Sponsored Transnationalism: A Reply to Jahan Ramazani." *American Literary History* 18, no. 2 (2006): 360–64.
———. *New Negro, Old Left: African-American Writing and Communism between the Wars*. New York: Columbia University Press, 1999.
McGill, Meredith. "What Is a Ballad? Reading for Genre, Format, and Medium." *Nineteenth Century Literature* 71, no. 2 (2016): 156–75.
Melamed, Jodi. *Represent and Destroy: Rationalizing Violence in the New Racial Capitalism*. Minneapolis: University of Minnesota Press, 2011.
Meltzer, Milton and Langston Hughes. *A Pictorial History of the Negro in America*. New York: Crown Publishers, 1956.
Menand, Louis. "The Pound Error: The Elusive Master of Illusion." *New Yorker*, 9–16 June 2008. https://www.newyorker.com/magazine/2008/06/09/the-pound-error.
Metres, Philip, and Mark Nowak. "Poetry as Social Practice in the First Person Plural: A Dialogue on Documentary Poetics." *Iowa Journal of Cultural Studies* 12/13 (2010): 9–22.
Mickenberg, Julia L. *Learning from the Left: Children's Literature, the Cold War, and Radical Politics in the United States*. New York: Oxford University Press, 2006.
Miéville, China. *October: The Story of the Russian Revolution*. London: Verso, 2018.
Millet, Martha. "Biographical Note." n.d. Martha Millet Papers, Kislak Center for Special Collections, Rare Books and Manuscripts, University of Pennsylvania, Philadelphia, PA.
———. *Dangerous Jack: A Fantasy in Verse*. New York: Sierra Press, 1953.
———. "Henry Wadsworth Longfellow." *New Pioneer*, October 1938, 19.
———. "Is Poetry Dead?" *New Masses*, 26 January 1938, 21.
———. "Modern Poetry: For or Against?" *Masses and Mainstream*, March 1955, 35–44.

———. "Philip Freneau: An American Poet of All the Peoples." *New Pioneer*, October 1938, 20.

———. "Pioneer Pied Piper." *New Pioneer*, May 1933, 4–5, 23.

———. "The Quick and the Dead." *Trace* 18 (1956): 3–9.

———, ed. *Rosenbergs: Poems of the United States*. New York: Sierra Press, 1957.

———. *Thine Alabaster Cities: A Poem for Our Times*. Brooklyn: n.p., 1952.

———. Typescript of "The Ezra Pound Myth." n.d. Martha Millet Papers, Kislak Center for Special Collections, Rare Books and Manuscripts, University of Pennsylvania, Philadelphia, PA.

———. Typescript of "Footnote on Modern Poetry." n.d. Martha Millet Papers, Kislak Center for Special Collections, Rare Books and Manuscripts, University of Pennsylvania, Philadelphia, PA.

———. Typescript of "Kid with a Kazoo," 1958–1959. Martha Millet Papers, Kislak Center for Special Collections, Rare Books and Manuscripts, University of Pennsylvania, Philadelphia, PA.

———. Typescript of "The Last of the Lemmings," 1967. Martha Millet Papers, Kislak Center for Special Collections, Rare Books and Manuscripts, University of Pennsylvania, Philadelphia, PA.

———. Typescript of "Poets and Poverty." n.d. Martha Millet Papers, Kislak Center for Special Collections, Rare Books and Manuscripts, University of Pennsylvania, Philadelphia, PA.

Mills, Nathaniel. *Ragged Revolutionaries: The Lumpenproletariat and African American Marxism in Depression-Era Literature*. Amherst: University of Massachusetts Press, 2017.

Mirzoeff, Nicholas. *The Right to Look: A Counterhistory of Visuality*. Durham, NC: Duke University Press, 2011.

Mitchell, W. J. T. *Picture Theory: Essays on Verbal and Visual Representation*. Chicago: University of Chicago Press, 1995.

Morton, Timothy. *Dark Ecology: For a Logic of Future Coexistence*. New York: Columbia University Press, 2016.

———. *Ecology without Nature: Rethinking Environmental Aesthetics*. Cambridge, MA: Harvard University Press, 2009.

———. *Hyperobjects: Philosophy and Ecology after the End of the World*. Minneapolis: University of Minnesota Press, 2013.

Moten, Fred. *Black and Blur (consent not to be a single being)*. Durham, NC: Duke University Press Books, 2017.

———. "Blackness and Nothingness (Mysticism in the Flesh)." *South Atlantic Quarterly* 112, no. 4 (2013): 737–80.

———. *In the Break: The Aesthetics of the Black Radical Tradition*. Minneapolis: University of Minnesota Press, 2003.

———. "On Marjorie Perloff." *Entropy*, 28 December 2015. https://entropymag.org/on-marjorie-perloff/.

Mullen, Edward J. *Langston Hughes in the Hispanic World and Haiti*. Hamden, CT: Archon Books, 1977.

Muñoz, José Esteban. *Cruising Utopia: The Then and There of Queer Futurity*. New York: NYU Press, 2009.

Naison, Mark D. *Communists in Harlem During the Depression*. Urbana: University of Illinois Press, 1983.
Nealon, Christopher. *The Matter of Capital: Poetry and Crisis in the American Century*. Cambridge, MA: Harvard University Press, 2011.
———. "Reading on the Left." *Representations* 108, no. 1 (2009): 22–50.
Negri, Antonio. *Marx beyond Marx: Lessons on the Grundrisse*. London: Pluto, 1992.
Neigh, Janet. "The Transnational Frequency of Radio Connectivity in Langston Hughes's 1940s Poetics." *Modernism/modernity* 20, no. 2 (2013): 265–85.
Neihardt, John. *Black Elk Speaks*. New York: William and Morrow, 1932.
Nelson, Cary. "Lyric Politics." In *Collected Poems*, by Edwin Rolfe, edited by Cary Nelson and Jefferson Hendricks, 1–56. Urbana: University of Illinois Press, 1997.
———. *Repression and Recovery: Modern American Poetry and the Politics of Cultural Memory, 1910–1945*. Madison: University of Wisconsin Press, 1989.
———. *Revolutionary Memory: Recovering the Poetry of the American Left*. New York: Routledge, 2001.
Newman, Steve. *Ballad Collection, Lyric, and the Canon*. Philadelphia: University of Pennsylvania Press, 2007.
Nickels, Joel. *The Poetry of the Possible: Spontaneity, Modernism, and the Multitude*. Minneapolis: University of Minnesota Press, 2012.
Niedecker, Lorine. *Collected Works*. Edited by Jenny Penberthy. Berkeley: University of California Press, 2002.
Nielsen, Aldon Lyn. *Black Chant: Languages of African-American Postmodernism*. New York: Cambridge University Press, 1997.
Niven, Penelope. *Carl Sandburg: A Biography*. New York: Macmillan, 1991.
Nixon, Rob. *Slow Violence and the Environmentalism of the Poor*. Cambridge, MA: Harvard University Press, 2011.
Noland, Carrie. *Voices of Negritude in Modernist Print: Aesthetic Subjectivity, Diaspora, and the Lyric Regime*. New York: Columbia University Press, 2015.
North, Michael. *Camera Works: Photography and the Twentieth-Century Word*. New York: Oxford University Press, 2005.
Nowak, Mark. "Documentary Poetics." *Poetry Foundation Harriet Blog*, 17 April 2010. https://www.poetryfoundation.org/harriet/2010/04/documentary-poetics.
Olsen, Tillie. *Yonnondio: From the Thirties*. 1974. Reprint, Lincoln: University of Nebraska Press, 2004.
Olson, Charles. *Selected Writings of Charles Olson*. Edited by Robert Creeley. New York: New Directions, 1966.
Orvell, Miles. *The Real Thing: Imitation and Authenticity in American Culture, 1880–1940*. Chapel Hill: University of North Carolina Press, 1989.
O'Sheel, Shaemas. "Introductory Note." In *Seven Poets in Search of an Answer*, edited by Thomas Yoseloff, 7–11. New York: Bernard Ackerman, 1944.
Patchen, Kenneth. *Before the Brave*. New York: Random House, 1936.
Patterson, Anita Haya. *Race, American Literature, and Transnational Modernisms*. New York: Cambridge University Press, 2008.
Pearce, Roy Harvey. *The Continuity of American Poetry*. Princeton, NJ: Princeton University Press, 1961.

Perloff, Marjorie. "Janus-Faced Blockbuster." *Symploke* 8, nos. 1–2 (2000): 205–13.
Pinto, Samantha. *Difficult Diasporas: The Transnational Feminist Aesthetic of the Black Atlantic.* New York: NYU Press, 2013.
Pitts, Rebecca. "Tough, Reasonable, Witty." Review of *Calling Western Union*, by Genevieve Taggard. *New Masses*, 27 October 1936, 22.
Posmentier, Sonya. *Cultivation and Catastrophe: The Lyric Ecology of Modern Black Literature.* Baltimore: Johns Hopkins University Press, 2017.
Potamkin, Harry Alan. "Mother Goose on the Breadline." *New Pioneer*, May 1931, 7.
Pound, Ezra. *Literary Essays of Ezra Pound.* New York: New Directions, 1954.
———. *The Pisan Cantos.* 1948. Reprint, New York: New Directions, 2003.
Pound, Ezra, and Louis Zukofsky. *Pound/Zukofsky: Selected Letters of Ezra Pound and Louis Zukofsky.* New York: New Directions, 1987.
Prins, Yopie. "Break, Break, Break into Song." In *Meter Matters: Verse Cultures of the Long Nineteenth Century*, edited by Jason Hall, 105–35. Columbus: Ohio State University Press, 2011.
———. "Historical Poetics, Dysprosody, and the Science of English Verse." *PMLA* 123, no. 1 (2008): 229–34.
———. *Victorian Sappho.* Princeton, NJ: Princeton University Press, 1999.
———. "'What Is Historical Poetics?'" *Modern Language Quarterly* 77, no. 1 (2016): 13–40.
Rabinowitz, Paula. "Class Ventriloquism: Women's Letters, Lectures, Lyrics—and Love." In *Red Love across the Pacific: Political and Sexual Revolutions of the Twentieth Century*, edited by Ruth Barraclough, Heather Bowen-Struyk, and Paula Rabinowitz, 201–20. New York: Palgrave, 2015.
———. *Labor and Desire: Women's Revolutionary Fiction in Depression America.* Chapel Hill: University of North Carolina Press, 1991.
———. *They Must Be Represented: The Politics of Documentary.* New York: Verso, 1994.
Rahv, Phillip. "An Open Letter to Young Writers." *Rebel Poet* 16 (September 1932): 3–4.
———. "Proletarian Literature: A Political Autopsy." *Southern Review* 4, no. 3 (1939): 616–28.
Ramazani, Jahan. *A Transnational Poetics.* Chicago: University of Chicago Press, 2009.
Rampersad, Arnold. *The Life of Langston Hughes.* Vol. 1. Oxford: Oxford University Press, 2002.
Rancière, Jacques. *Aesthesis: Scenes from the Aesthetic Regime of Art.* Translated by Zakir Paul. New York: Verso, 2013.
———. *Staging the People: The Proletarian and His Double.* Translated by David Fernbach. New York: Verso, 2011.
Reed, Anthony. *Freedom Time: The Poetics and Politics of Black Experimental Writings.* Baltimore: Johns Hopkins University Press, 2014.
Reed, Brian. *Phenomenal Reading: Essays on Modern and Contemporary Poetics.* Tuscaloosa: University of Alabama Press, 2012.
Reid, Tiana. "The Shape of Poetics to Come: On Taking Up the Task of Criticism." *American Quarterly* 70, no. 1 (2018): 139–50.
Renda, Mary. *Taking Haiti: Military Occupation and the Culture of U.S. Imperialism.* Chapel Hill: University of North Carolina Press, 2001.
Reuss, Richard A., and JoAnne C. Reuss. *American Folk Music and Left-Wing Politics, 1927–1957.* Lanham, MD: Scarecrow, 2001.

Robinson, Cedric. *Black Marxism: The Making of the Black Radical Tradition*. Chapel Hill: University of North Carolina Press, 1983.
Robinson, Earl. Letter to Martha Millet, n.d. Martha Millet Papers, Kislak Center for Special Collections, Rare Books and Manuscripts, University of Pennsylvania, Philadelphia, PA.
Rolfe, Edwin. *Collected Poems*. Edited by Cary Nelson and Jefferson Hendricks. Urbana: University of Illinois Press, 1997.
Ronda, Margaret. "'Not Much Left': Wageless Life in Millennial Poetry." *Post 45*, October 2011. http://post45.research.yale.edu/2011/10/not-much-left-wageless-life-in-millenial-poetry/.
———. "'Not One': The Poetics of Multitude in Great Recession-Era America." In *Created Unequal: Class and the Making of American Literature*, edited by Andrew Lawson, 245–64. New York: Routledge, 2014.
———. *Remainders: American Poetry at Nature's End*. Stanford, CA: Stanford University Press, 2018.
Rosenberg, Leah. "'Watch How Dem Touris' Like Fe Look': Tourist Photography and Claude McKay's Jamaica." In *On Writing with Photography*, edited by Karen Redrobe Beckman and Lilliane Weissberg, 41–-68. Minneapolis: University of Minnesota Press, 2013.
Rosler, Martha. "In, Around, and Afterthoughts." In *The Contest of Meaning*, edited by Richard Bolton, 303–42. Cambridge, MA: MIT Press, 1989.
Rosten, Norman. "Should Ezra Pound Be Shot?" *New Masses*, 25 December 1945, 6.
Rotha, Paul. Letter to Muriel Rukeyser, 22 March 1965. Box I:4, Folder 8, Muriel Rukeyser Papers, Library of Congress, Washington, DC.
Roumain, Jacques. "Is Poetry Dead?" *New Masses*, 7 January 1941, 22–23.
———. *Masters of the Dew*. Translated by Mercer Cook and Langston Hughes. New York: Harcourt, 1978.
———. *Œuvres complètes*. Edited by Léon-Francois Hoffman. Paris: Signataires de L'Accord Archivos ALLCA XX, 2003.
———. Untitled speech given at Harlem YMCA, 15 November 1939. Vertical file, Schomburg Collection, New York Public Library, New York, NY.
———. "When the Tom-Tom Beats." Translated by Langston Hughes. *Dynamo* 2, no. 1 (1935): 2.
———. *When the Tom-Tom Beats: Selected Prose and Poetry*. Translated by Ronald Sauer with Joanne Fungaroli. Washington, DC: Azul, 1995.
Rowe, John Carlos. *The New American Studies*. Minneapolis: University of Minnesota Press, 2002.
Rukeyser, Muriel. "Adventures of Children." *Coronet*, September 1939, 23–38.
———. *The Book of the Dead*. Morgantown: West Virginia University Press, 2017.
———. *The Collected Poems of Muriel Rukeyser*. Edited by Janet E. Kaufman and Anne F. Herzog. Pittsburgh: University of Pittsburgh Press, 2006.
———. Foreword. In *Berenice Abbott: Photographs*. New York: Horizon, 1970. 9–12.
———. "Gauley Bridge." *Films*, Summer 1940, 51–64.
———. *The Life of Poetry*. Ashfield, MA: Paris, 1996.
———. "Sights and Sounds." *New Masses*, 26 October 1937, 27.

———. "Story Outline for Gauley Bridge." Box II:14, Muriel Rukeyser Papers, Library of Congress, Washington, DC.

———. "We Aren't Sure . . . We're Wondering." *New Masses*, 26 April 1938, 26–28.

———. "Words and Images." *New Republic*, 2 August 1943, 140–42.

Saint-Amour, Paul K. *Tense Future: Modernism, Total War, Encyclopedic Form*. Oxford: Oxford University Press, 2015.

Sandburg, Carl. *The Letters of Carl Sandburg*. Edited by Herbert Mitgang. New York: Harcourt Brace, 1968.

———. *The People, Yes*. 1936. Reprint, New York: Harcourt, 2015.

Sanders, Ed. *Investigative Poetry*. San Francisco: City Lights, 1976.

Scandura, Jani. *Down in the Dumps: Place, Modernity, American Depression*. Durham, NC: Duke University Press, 2008.

Schmitt, Carl. *Political Romanticism*. 1919. Translated by Guy Oakes. New Brunswick, NJ: Transaction, 1928.

Schneider, Isidor. "Proletarian Poetry." In *American Writers' Congress*, edited by Henry Hart, 114–20. New York: International, 1935.

See, Sarita. "Gambling with Debt: Lessons from the Illiterate." *American Quarterly* 64, no. 3 (2012): 495–513.

Sekula, Allan. "The Traffic in Photographs." *Art Journal* 41, no. 1 (1981): 15–25.

Selvinski, Ilya. "On Soviet Poetry." *International Literature* 3 (1935): 106–10.

Sharpe, Christina: *In the Wake: On Blackness and Being*. Durham: Duke University Press, 2016.

Shepherd, Reginald. *Lyric Postmodernisms: An Anthology of Contemporary Innovative Poetries*. Denver: Counterpath, 2008.

Shockley, Evie. *Renegade Poetics: Black Aesthetics and Formal Innovation in African American Poetry*. Iowa City: University of Iowa Press, 2011.

Sinclair, Jo [Ruth Seid]. *The Changelings*. New York: McGraw-Hill, 1955.

Smethurst, James Edward. *The New Red Negro: The Literary Left and African American Writing, 1930–1944*. New York: Oxford University Press, 1999.

Smith, Rachel Greenwald. "Six Propositions on Compromise Aesthetics." *The Account*, accessed 6 November 2017, http://theaccountmagazine.com/?article=six-propositions-on-compromise-aesthetics.

Smith, Shawn Michelle. *Photography on the Color Line: W. E. B. DuBois, Race, and Visual Culture*. Durham, NC: Duke University Press, 2004.

Socarides, Alexandra. *Dickinson Unbound: Paper, Process, Poetics*. New York: Oxford University Press, 2012.

Sorby, Angela. *Schoolroom Poets: Childhood, Performance, and the Place of American Poetry*. Durham: University of New Hampshire Press / University Press of New England, 2005.

Southern Tenant Farmers Union and Workers Defense League. *The Disinherited Speak: Letters from Sharecroppers*. New York: Workers Defense League, 1936.

Spahr, Clemens. *A Poetics of Global Solidarity: Modern American Poetry and Social Movements*. New York: Palgrave Macmillan, 2015.

Spahr, Juliana. *DuBois's Telegram: Literary Resistance and State Containment*. Cambridge, MA: Harvard University Press, 2018.

———. *Well Then There Now*. Boston: Black Sparrow, 2011.
Spahr, Juliana, and Claudia Rankine, eds. *American Women Poets of the 21st Century: Where Lyric Meets Language*. Middletown, CT: Wesleyan University Press, 2002.
———. Introduction to *American Women Poets of the 21st Century: Where Lyric Meets Language*, 1–17. Middletown CT: Wesleyan University Press, 2002.
Staub, Michael. *Voices of Persuasion: Politics of Representation in 1930s America*. Cambridge: Cambridge University Press, 1994.
Stein, Sally. "Peculiar Grace: Dorothea Lange and the Testimony of the Body." In *Dorothea Lange: A Visual Life*, edited by Elizabeth Partridge, 57–89. Washington, DC: Smithsonian Institution Press, 1994.
Stephens, Michelle A. *Black Empire: The Masculine Global Imaginary of Caribbean Intellectuals in the United States, 1914–1962*. Durham, NC: Duke University Press Books, 2005.
Steven, Mark. *Red Modernism: American Poetry and the Spirit of Communism*. Baltimore: Johns Hopkins University Press, 2017.
Stewart, Susan. *Crimes of Writing: Problems in the Containment of Representation*. Durham, NC: Duke University Press, 1991.
———. *On Longing: Narratives of the Miniature, the Gigantic, the Souvenir, the Collection*. Durham, NC: Duke University Press, 1984.
———. *Poetry and the Fate of the Senses*. Chicago: University of Chicago Press, 2002.
Stott, William. *Documentary Expression and Thirties America*. Chicago: University of Chicago Press, 1986.
Strimple, Nick. *Choral Music in the Twentieth Century*. Pompton Plains, NJ: Amadeus, 2002.
Swayne, Steve. *Orpheus in Manhattan: William Schuman and the Shaping of America's Musical Life*. New York: Oxford University Press, 2011.
Swensen, Cole, and David St. John. *American Hybrid: A Norton Anthology of Contemporary Innovative Poetries*. New York: Norton, 2008.
Szalay, Michael. *New Deal Modernism: American Literature and the Invention of the Welfare State*. Durham, NC: Duke University Press, 2000.
Taggard, Genevieve. Annotated typed copies of *The Poems of Emily Dickinson*, ca. 1942. Genevieve Taggard Papers, Manuscripts and Archive Division, New York Public Library, New York, NY.
———. *Calling Western Union*. New York: Harper Brothers, 1936.
———. *Collected Poems, 1918–1938*. New York: Harper Brothers, 1938.
———. Draft of "In the Plural." n.d. Genevieve Taggard Papers, Manuscripts and Archive Division, New York Public Library, New York, NY.
———. Draft of "To Paul Robeson." n.d. Genevieve Taggard Papers, Manuscripts and Archive Division, New York Public Library, New York, NY.
———. Drafts in preparation for *Long View*, n.d. Genevieve Taggard Papers, Manuscripts and Archive Division, New Yorks Public Library, New York, NY.
———. *The Life and Mind of Emily Dickinson*. New York: Knopf, 1930.
———. *Long View*. New York: Harper Brothers, 1942.
———. Notes on Christopher Caudwell's *Illusion and Reality*, n.d. Genevieve Taggard Papers, Manuscripts and Archive Division, New York Public Library. New York, NY.

———. "The Poetry of the Future." n.d. Genevieve Taggard Papers, Manuscripts and Archive Division, New York Public Library, New York, NY.

———. "Romanticism and Communism." *New Masses*, 25 September 1934, 18–20.

Tejada, Roberto. *National Camera: Photography and Mexico's Image Environment*. Minneapolis: University of Minnesota Press, 2009.

———. "Vanishing Acts." *English Language Notes* 50, no. 1 (2012): 5–8.

Terada, Rei. "After the Critique of Lyric." *PMLA* 123, no. 1 (2008): 195–200.

Teres, Harvey. *Renewing the Left: Politics, Imagination, and the New York Intellectuals*. Oxford: Oxford University Press, 1996.

Thomas, Katherine Elwes. *The Real Personages of Mother Goose*. Boston: Lothrop, Lee, and Shepard Company, 1930.

Thompson, Krista. *An Eye for the Tropics: Tourism, Photography, and Framing the Caribbean Picturesque*. Durham, NC: Duke University Press, 2007.

Thurston, Michael. *Making Something Happen: American Political Poetry between the Wars*. Chapel Hill: University of North Carolina Press, 2001.

Tiffany, Daniel. "Cheap Signaling: Class Conflict and Diction in Avant-Garde Poetry." *Boston Review*, 15 July 2014. http://bostonreview.net/poetry/daniel-tiffany-cheap-signaling-class-conflict-and-diction-avant-garde-poetry.

———. *My Silver Planet: A Secret History of Poetry and Kitsch*. Baltimore: Johns Hopkins University Press, 2014.

Tolliver, Cedric. *Of Vagabonds and Fellow Travelers: African Diaspora Literary Culture and the Cultural Cold War*. Ann Arbor: University of Michigan Press, 2019.

Toscano, Albert, and Jeff Kinkle. *Cartographies of the Absolute*. New Alesford, UK: Zero Books, 2015.

Tucker, Herbert. "Dramatic Monologue and the Overhearing of Lyric." In *Lyric Poetry beyond New Criticism*, edited by Chaviva Hosek and Patricia Parker, 229–43. Ithaca, NY: Cornell University Press, 1985.

Vadde, Aarthi. *Chimeras of Form: Modernist Internationalism beyond Europe, 1914–2016*. New York: Columbia University Press, 2016.

Van Nyhuis, Alison. "Revolution and Modern American Poetry: Genevieve Taggard's *Calling Western Union*." *Revista Canaria de Estudios Ingleses* 52 (2006): 29–35.

Vendler, Helen. "The Unweary Blues." Review of *The Collected Poems of Langston Hughes*. *New Republic*, 6 March 1995, 37–42.

Vials, Chris. *Haunted by Hitler: Liberals, the Left, and the Fight against Fascism in the United States*. Amherst: University of Massachusetts Press, 2014.

Von Eschen, Penny. *Race against Empire: Black Americans and Anticolonialism, 1937–1957*. Ithaca, NY: Cornell University Press, 1997.

Wald, Alan M. *American Night: The Literary Left in the Era of the Cold War*. Chapel Hill: University of North Carolina Press, 2012.

———. *Exiles from a Future Time: The Forging of the Mid-Twentieth-Century Literary Left*. Chapel Hill: University of North Carolina Press, 2002.

———. *The New York Intellectuals: The Rise and Decline of the Anti-Stalinist Left*. Chapel Hill: University of North Carolina Press, 1987.

———. *The Revolutionary Imagination: The Poetry and Politics of John Wheelwright and Sherry Mangan*. Chapel Hill: University of North Carolina Press, 1983.

———. *Trinity of Passion: The Literary Left and the Antifascist Crusade*. Chapel Hill: University of North Carolina Press, 2014.

———. *Writing from the Left: New Essays on Radical Culture and Politics*. New York: Verso, 1994.

Waligora-Davis, Nicole. *Sanctuary: African-Americans and Empire*. Oxford: Oxford University Press, 2011.

Wallace, Henry. *Democracy Reborn*. Edited by Russell Lord. New York: Reynal and Hitchcock, 1944.

Wang, Dorothy. *Thinking Its Presence: Form, Race, and Subjectivity in Contemporary Asian American Poetry*. Stanford, CA: Stanford University Press, 2013.

Wark, McKenzie. "'Not Yet': On the Novels of Kenneth Fearing." *Brooklyn Rail*, 2 April 2007, https://www.brooklynrail.org/2007/4/books/not-yet-on-the.

Washington, Mary Helen. *The Other Black List: The African American Literary and Cultural Left in the 1950s*. New York: Columbia University Press, 2013.

Wechsler, Shoshana. "A Mat(t)er of Fact and Vision: The Objectivity Question and Muriel Rukeyser's 'Book of the Dead.'" *Twentieth Century Literature* 45, no. 2 (1999): 121–37.

West, Don. *No Lonesome Road: Selected Poems and Prose*. Edited by Jeff Biggers and George Borsi. Urbana: University of Illinois Press, 2010.

Wheeler, Lesley. *Voicing American Poetry: Sound and Performance from the 1920s to the Present*. Ithaca, NY: Cornell University Press, 2008.

Wheelwright, John. "Muriel Rukeyser—*U.S. 1*." In *Muriel Rukeyser's "The Book of the Dead,"* by Tim Dayton, 139–42. Columbia: University of Missouri Press, 2003.

White, Gillian. *Lyric Shame: The "Lyric" Subject of Contemporary American Poetry*. Cambridge, MA: Harvard University Press, 2014.

Williams, William Carlos. "Muriel Rukeyser's *U.S. 1*." *New Republic*, 9 March 1938, 141.

———. *Spring and All*. 1923. Reprint, New York: New Directions, 2011.

Wilson, Edmund. *Axel's Castle: A Study in the Imaginative Literature in 1870–1930*. New York: Scribner, 1931.

———. "Is Verse a Dying Technique?" In *The Triple Thinkers: Twelve Essays on Literary Subjects*, 15–30. New York: Oxford University Press, 1948.

———. "The Literary Class War." In *The Shores of Light*, 534–39. New York: Farrar, Strauss, and Young, 1952.

Wolff, William. "Use Traditional Tunes for New Union Songs." *Daily Worker*, 16 November 1939, 7.

Wright, Richard. "I Tried to Be a Communist." *Atlantic Monthly*, September 1944, 48–56.

Yoseloff, Thomas, ed. *Seven Poets in Search of an Answer*. New York: Ackerman, 1944.

Yu, Timothy. *Race and the Avant-Garde: Experimental and Asian Poetry since 1965*. Stanford, CA: Stanford University Press, 2009.

Zaturenska, Marya. Letter to Harriet Monroe, 13 August 1935. Box 43, Folder 1, *Poetry, A Magazine of Verse* Records, Special Collections Research Center, University of Chicago Libraries, Chicago, IL.

Zukofsky, Louis. *Anew: Complete Shorter Poetry*. New York: New Directions, 2011.

Text Credits

Every effort has been made to identify, contact, and acknowledge copyright holders. I am grateful to acknowledge permission to reprint the following works:

Excerpts from "Wait," "Open Letter to the South," "Always the Same," "Johannesburg Mines," "House in the World," and "Negro Ghetto," from *The Collected Poems of Langston Hughes*, by Langston Hughes, edited by Arnold Rampersad with David Roessel, Associate Editor, copyright © 1994 by the estate of Langston Hughes, used by permission of Alfred A. Knopf, an imprint of the Knopf Doubleday Publishing Group, a division of Penguin Random House LLC. All rights reserved.

Excerpts from "When the Tom-Tom Beats," translated by Langston Hughes, and "For Jacques Roumain (Late Poet of Haiti)," by Langston Hughes, reprinted by permission of Harold Ober Associates Incorporated.

Excerpts from "The Road," "Gauley Bridge," "The Face of the Dam: Vivian Jones," "Mearl Blankenship," "George Robinson: Blues," "Alloy," "Absalom," "The Book of the Dead," "Ann Burlak," and "Poem (I lived in the first century of world wars)," by Muriel Rukeyser; and archival materials from the Muriel Rukeyser Papers, Library of Congress, used with permission of William Rukeyser.

Excerpts from "Night Letter to Walt Whitman," "Adding Up America—You Try," "At Last the Women Are Moving," "Definition of Song," "Lark," and "Funeral in May" from *Calling Western Union*, by Genevieve Taggard; excerpts from "Prologue" and "This Is Our Time," from *Long View*, by Genevieve Taggard; and archival materials from the Genevieve Taggard Papers, New York Public Library, used with permission of Judith Benet Richardson.

Excerpt from Marya Zaturenska, letter to Harriet Monroe, August 13, 1935, Box 43, Folder 1, *Poetry: A Magazine of Verse* Records, used with permission of the Special Collections Research Center, University of Chicago Library.

Excerpt from Floyd Dell, letter to Genevieve Taggard, in the Dell Papers at the Newberry Library, used by permission of Jerri Dell, literary executor, Floyd Dell Estate.

Excerpts from the English translations of "Langston Hughes," "Ebony Wood," and "Talk and Nothing More," in *When the Tom-Tom Beats: Selected Prose and Poems*, by Jacques Roumain, translated by Ronald Sauer with Joanne Fungaroli, used by permission of Ronald Sauer.

Excerpts from archival materials in the Martha Millet Papers at the Kislak Center, University of Pennsylvania, used by permission of Alex Garlin.

Excerpt from Earl Robinson, letter to Martha Millet, in the Martha Millet Papers at the Kislak Center, University of Pennsylvania, used by permission of Perry Robinson.

Excerpts from "American Rhapsody (I)," "American Rhapsody (III)," and "Bulletin," by Kenneth Fearing, reprinted by permission of Russell and Volkening as agents for the author. Copyright © 1994 by Jubal Fearing and Phoebe Fearing.

Excerpts from "Credo," "Homage to Karl Marx," and "To My Contemporaries," from *Collected Poems* by Edwin Rolfe, edited by Cary Nelson and Jefferson Hendricks, copyright © 1997, used with permission of the University of Illinois Press.

Index

Note: Page numbers in *italic* type indicate illustrations.

Abbott, Berenice, *Photographs*, 78–79
abstraction, 183–84, 212, 213
Adorno, Theodor: *The Dialectic of Enlightenment* (with Horkheimer), 208–9, 219–20; "On Lyric Poetry and Society," 245n88
African Americans: antiracism and, 15, 21, 107; capitalism and, 83, 169; Caribbean/U.S. travel networks and, 31–32; Communist Party and, 144–45, 175, 242n11, 246–47n122; Gauley Bridge and, 83–84; Haiti and, 31–32; photography and, 30; Popular Front and, 144–45, 153–56; racial violence and, 15, 53–55, 116, 178, 199, 206, 221–22; racism and, 27, 32, 84, 148, 182, 183, 206, 210, 212; Scottsboro Boys case and, 55–60, 57; southern workers and, 52; vernacular speech and, 58; white nationalism and, 206; working-class alliances, 83. *See also* black culture; black radical tradition
Agee, James, 68, 69, 72; *Let Us Now Praise Famous Men*, 20–21, 23, 30–31, 62–63, 67, 71, 92
Ajanta Buddhist painter-monks, 100
Ali, Tariq, *On Lenin*, 183
Alloy (W. Va.), 65, 69
allusiveness, 183–84, 212
Álvarez Bravo, Manuel, 29; *Los agachados*, 60, 61, *61*
American New Criticism. *See* New Criticism
American Poets in the Twenty-First Century: A New Poetic, 70–71
American School of the Air (radio program), 190

American Writers' Congress, 105, 111, 145
Anker, Elizabeth, 137
anticapitalism, 21, 181, 183; poetics and, 106, 107, 110–11
anticommunism, 19, 181, 205, 211, 216–17, 219; traditional literary forms and, 184
antifascism, 23, 150, 156; activism and, 182; Communist Party USA and, 175; Haiti as symbol of, 144–47, 169; international coalition and, 145; poetic anthology and, 9, 146, 203–9; Popular Front and, 131, 193; verse genres and, 169, 176, 205, 207, 217–18
anti-imperialism, 3, 148, 151, 192
antimodernism, 197–98, 199, 206, 224n28
antiracism, 15, 21, 107
anti-Semitism, 182, 210
apolitical art, 15, 183
Appalachian ballads, 191
Appel, Benjamin, *The People Talk*, 86
Army of Lovers, An (Buuck and Spahr), 1
artistic impersonality, 212
art-propaganda distinction, 212–13
Association Démocratique Hatïenne, 175
atom bomb, 215
Auden, W. H., 16, 93
authenticity, 71, 95, 153
avant-garde, 7, 46, 182, 217, 226n45, 228n24; antilyricism and, 106; experimental tradition and, 18; film technique and, 74; internationalism and, 156; kitsch vs., 213–14; race and, 20, 118, 168, 211–12

Badiou, Alain, 148; "Poetry and Communism," 169
"Ballad for Americans" (LaTouche and Robinson), 155, 187, 244n45

ballads, 58, 61, 131, 138, 146, 156, 184, 187–91, 193; collectors of, 190, 191; meter of, 202; political significance of, 188–90, 205; rhythms of, 188, 191; traditional stanza of, 187, 188
Balthaser, Benjamin, 145, 149, 150
Barnhisel, Greg, 212
Barthes, Roland, 39, 45
Batchen, Geoffrey, 32
Beals, Carleton, 149; *The Crime of Cuba*, 36, 37
Beaulieu, Christian, 243n22
Benjamin, Walter, 69, 78, 99; "The Author as Producer," 69, 72; "The Storyteller," 53, 248n22; "The Task of the Translator," 153
Benton, Thomas, 149
Berke, Nancy, 129
Berman, Jessica, 247–48n5
Bhopal mine disaster. *See* Gauley tunnel disaster
bilingualism, 156
Bird, Caroline, 5
black culture, 153–60, 244n40; avant-garde and, 20, 118, 168, 211–12; "Black Belt Thesis," and, 154; blues and, 71, 83–84, 154, 162; folk forms and, 153, 154, 155, 156, 244–45n40; poetic culture, 154, 164–65, 168; proletarian aesthetic and, 164–65, 173–74; white poets' appropriation of, 154–55
Black Lives Matter movement, 15
black radical tradition, 4, 13, 144–46, 148, 154, 155, 178; art and, 167, 168; internationalism and, 145, 146, 153, 156, 169; lyricism and, 146, 168, 169; personification-lyricization relationship, 157–62
black rebellions, 27, 170, 173. *See also* Haitian Revolution
black studies, 146
Blair, Sara, 45, 61
Blanton, C. D., 113–14
Blecher, Miriam, 154
Blitzstein, Marc, 132; *The Cradle Will Rock*, 132, 219; *No for an Answer*, 132
blues, 71, 83–84, 154

Boadiba (Haitian poet), 150; *Open Gate* (with Hirschman), 243n28
Bodenheim, Maxwell, 206, 212; "The Game," 212
Boggs, Colleen Glenney, 90
Bollingen Prize for Poetry, 181
Bontemps, Arna, 33
Bonus Army, 50
Book of the Dead (ancient Egypt), 69, 88, 89
Book of the Dead, The (Rukeyser), 1–2, 4, 22, 65–102; "Absalom" section, 65–67, 87, 88–89; "Alloy" section, 85; art-politics-media relationship and, 72; "The Book of the Dead" section, 90–91; "Cornfields" section, 89; critical reception of, 69–70, 75, 82, 85, 86; "The Dam" section, 94; definitions of poetry and, 72–73; "The Disease: After-Effects" section, 89–90; documentary basis of, 65–68, 72, 80; documentary film adaptation plan for, 22, 69, 92–102; "Face of the Dam: Vivian Jones" section, 80–81, 84, 85, 97; "Gauley Bridge" section, 78, 83–84, 89, 100, 234n58; "George Robinson: Blues" section, 80, 83–85, 96; "Juanita Tinsley" section, 95, 96; lyricism and, 72; "Mearl Blankenship" section, 80, 81–82, 84, 95–97, 99, 101; photography and, 75, 77–78; "Power" section, 85, 98–99; racial differences and, 82–83; reading of, 68–69; responses to, 72–74; "Road" section, 75; Shirley Jones character, 69, 97; silica dust and, 65, 68, 69, 83; source texts of, 69; "Vivian Jones" section, 80–81, 82; voice and, 85–91; Williams description of, 91–92; X-ray plate image, 82–83, 87
Boumba (Canoe) (newsletter), 150
Bourke-White, Margaret, 75; *You Have Seen Their Faces*, 77
Bradley, Francine, 151, 169
Brinkman, Bartholomew, 46
British General Post Office (GPO) film unit, 93

Brooks, Cleanth, 242n16; "Metaphysical Poets and Propaganda Art," 212, 214; *Modern Poetry and the Tradition*, 212
Brooks, Gwendolyn, 224n17
Browder, Earl, 175
Buddhist painter-monks, 100
Bulosan, Carlos, "The Romance of Magno Rubio," 3
Bureau of d'Ethnologie (Haiti), 169
Burke, Kenneth, 153
Burnshaw, Stanley, 140; "Notes on Revolutionary Poetry," 9, 227n68
Buuck, David, *An Army of Lovers* (with Spahr), 1

Caldwell, Erskine, *You Have Seen Their Faces*, 77
Calverton, V. F., 19, 183
Camera obscura, 75
Campbell, E. Simms, 33
capitalism, 3, 7, 67, 68, 72, 82, 183; "cognitive mapping" of, 48, 50–51, 54; lyric linked with, 105, 106, 107, 109, 110; 1930s crisis in, 49, 82; presumptive end of, 145–46; race and, 83, 169; relationship of poetry to, 15–16, 17, 105, 106, 107, 167; rhythm linked with, 208–9. *See also* anticapitalism
Caribbean: African American travel networks, 31–32; Afro Marxists and, 146 (*see also* Roumain, Jacques); black liberation struggle in, 168; Communist documentary accounts of, 36, 37; Hughes travels in, 27, 28, 31–32; U.S. imperialism in, 36, 144, 149, 156, 167
Cartier-Bresson, Henri, 29, 36, 37, 60
Casarino, Cesare, 139
Castronovo, Russ, 153
Césaire, Aimé: "Letter to Maurice Thorez," 247–48n122; "Poetry and Knowledge," 226n43
Cezanne, Paul, 100
CHAIN (journal), 70
Chambers, Whittaker, *Can You Make Out Their Voices*, 77

Chandler, Nahum Dimitri, 144, 167, 242n7
chants, 58, 138
Chaplin, Charlie, 142
Chasar, Mike, 46, 225n42
Chicago Defender (newspaper), 151
Child, Francis, 188
children's verse, 185–95; formal traits of, 196. *See also* Nursery rhymes
China Strikes Back (film), 93, 94
choral forms. *See* Song
Christophe, Henri, 38–39
cinema. *See* Films
"cine-poem," 93–94
Citadel La Ferrière (Haiti), 38–39, 42
Clark, T. J., 227n66
class struggle, 144, 166, 184–85. *See also* working class
Clayton, Michelle, 168
Clifford, Mary Ellen, *Can You Hear Their Voices*, 77
Clinton-Baddeley, V. C., *Words for Music*, 133
Clover, Joshua, 237n11
cognitive mapping aesthetic, 48–49
Cohen, Michael, 59; *The Social Lives of Poems*, 42, 224n22, 225n30
Cold War, 3, 4, 21, 176, 181, 193, 206; lyric and, 106, 141–42; Millet and, 210, 212, 215; modernism and, 183, 210, 251n107
collective expression, 126–28, 130, 135–37; rhythm and, 185; translation and, 156; "We" voice and, 108, 121, 127, 131, 135, 136; "You" voice and, 126, 127, 131
Comintern, 5, 154
Committee for the Release of Jacques Roumain, 149, 150, 151, 154, 162, 169
common people. *See* working class
Communism, 4, 181–95, 221; ballad and, 189–90; Caribbean intellectuals and, 168; children's writers and, 185–95; Haitian party, 145, 149, 243n27; *Internationale* as anthem of, 57, 174, 219; as international movement, 3, 18, 22–23, 144–45, 147–48, 169, 174, 181; in 1940s, 175; relationship of art to, 167, 168, 169, 184 (*see also*

Communism (*continued*)
  Communist poetic culture); Roumain and, 143, 149, 164, 169; Third Period ideology of, 11, 109, 131; Third Period shift to Popular Front and, 5, 105, 131, 185. *See also* anticommunism; Marxism
Communist Party of Haiti, 145, 149, 243n22
Communist Party USA, 2, 36, 37, 213, 216–17; affiliates of, 140; African Americans and, 144–45, 175, 242n11, 246–47n122; defections from, 246–47n122, 247n123; fellow travelers and, 164; founding member of, 181; Pound's attacks on, 210–11; Roumain and, 149, 175, 243n22. *See also* Depression-era poetic culture; *New Masses*; Popular Front
Communist poetic culture, 2–5, 7–11, 13–18, 113, 154, 187, 191, 193, 220; constraints of, 184, 212; critics of, 213; favored forms of, 131; form-content relationship of, 198; lyric and, 106, 112, 117, 119, 144–45, 148, 168, 169, 173, 184; media forms and, 10, 107; Objectivist poetics and, 140; race and, 144–45; rhythm and, 184–85, 199; Rolfe and, 107, 109–10, 117–23; Romanticism and, 118, 119; Taggard and, 107–8, 117–23; writing formulas of, 109–10, 184, 186, 189, 190, 193, 201. *See also* leftist poetics; Proletarian aesthetics
Composers Collective, 131
Confessional poetry, 107
Conroy, Jack, 105, 110, 184
Cook, Mercer, 168
Copland, Aaron, 131; "Lark," 133
Cornell, Julien, *The Trial of Ezra Pound*, 211–12
Coronet (magazine), "Adventures of Children" photo-text, 79–80, 79
Cortez, Jayne, 178
Costello, Bonnie, 129
Couch, W. T., 86
Cowley, Malcolm, 2, 105, 153, 200; *Exile's Return*, 124
CPUSA. *See* Communist Party USA
Cradle Will Rock, The (Blitzstein), 132, 219

Cradle Will Rock, The (Robbins film), 219–20, 252n1
Crane, Hart, 17
Crisis (journal), 151, 156
Crocodile (Soviet journal), 110–11
Crosby, Harry, 124
Cuba, 27–28, 31, 32, 36, 37
Cullen, Countee, "Elegy (In Memoriam: Jacques Roumain)," 175
Cummings, E. E., *Buffalo Bill*, 133, 134
Cunard, Nancy, *Negro* (anthology), 151, 156

Daily Worker (newspaper), 115, 116, 187, 191
Davidson, Michael, 202
Dean, Jodi, 4
death trope, 124–26
DeCarava, Roy, *Sweet Flypaper of Life* (with Hughes), 62
Deleuze, Gilles, 224n25
Dell, Floyd, 132
Denning, Michael, 71, 87, 144, 199, 224n15, 241n5; *The Cultural Front*, 6, 8
Depression-era poetic culture, 2–23, 87, 126; canonical poets of, 22; current literary discussions and, 220–21; death trope and, 124–25; documentary and, 65–66, 67, 69–70, 71–72, 74, 75–77, 79, 86; genres and, 58, 130, 144, 213; ideas and, 94; key formal innovation of, 126; leftist prescriptions and, 191–96; lyric and, 13–15, 106, 108–9, 110, 113, 118, 119; Objectivism and, 140, 202; photojournalism and, 49, 71, 75; political and literary crises and, 8–9, 14; proletarian "grotesque" and, 87 (*see also* Proletarian aesthetics); protest verse and, 129–30, 185, 203; radical poetics and, 2–3, 6, 13, 19–21, 124, 126, 131, 138; rhythm and, 199–200; scholarship on, 220; shift in media forms and, 53; syntax and, 108; voice and, 86–87, 127, 131, 136. *See also* Communist poetic culture; political poetry
Dessalines, Jean-Jacques, 38–39, 159, 161
Deutsch, Babette, 154
dialectic, 113–14

dialectical materialism, 167
Dialectic of Enlightenment (Adorno and Horkheimer), 208–9, 219–20
dialect poems, 33, 154
Dickinson, Emily, 128, 132
didactic verse, 146
Dies Committee, 219
Dimock, Wai-Chee, 120, 122–23
Disinherited Speak, The (sharecroppers' letters), 86
documentary, 21–22, 27–29, 70–75; Agee and, 67, 71; associative elements of, 71; coining of term, 73; genre-mixing forms, 67, 75–78; Lange and, 67; lists, 51–52; portraiture, 80; propaganda, 74; reemergence in 1970s of, 71; Rukeyser and, 85, 91, 93–95; voice-over narration and, 74, 93, 94, 95, 96
documentary films, 70, 73; *Book of the Dead* project, 22, 69, 92–100; "Gauley Bridge" project, 92, 94–102
documentary photography, 10, 22, 33–64, 91, 231n92, 234n65; African American writers and, 30; cultural relevance of, 70; Depression-era, 62, 65–66, 67, 75–76, 79, 80, 88; Hughes and, 28–30, 32, 33, 35, 36, 39–44, 40, 41, 42, 43, 47, 49, 54, 56, 59, 60, 62–63; meaning and, 59; phonographic content of, 59–60; photojournalism and, 49, 71, 75; relationship between poetry and, 30, 34, 47, 62–64, 67, 76–77; as revealing inward reality, 75; temporality of, 30; "vernacular," 32–33
documentary poetry, 19, 22, 52–53, 67, 70–73; critics of, 85; defining elements of, 70–71; first use of term, 72; Hughes and, 61–62; Rukeyser and, 70, 94; voice and, 87
Dos Passos, John, 86
DuBois, W. E. B., 210
Duncan, Robert, 16
Dunham, Harry, 93
Durant, Kenneth, 18–20
Duvalier, Jean Claude, 150

Dynamo (magazine), 110, 111, 112, 120, 150–56; "Free Jacques Romain" letter, 150–52, 152, 155

economic depression. *See* Depression-era poetic culture/ Financial crisis (2008)
Edwards, Brent Hayes, 155–56, 242n11
Egyptian *Book of the Dead*, 69, 88, 89
Eliot, T. S., 109, 197, 210, 227n68; high modernism and, 214; "The Love Song of J. Alfred Prufock," 198; Marxist dialectic and, 113–14; *The Waste Land*, 114
Ellison, Ralph, 84
Endore, Guy, *Babouk*, 163–64
Equal Rights (magazine), 128, 129
ethnography, 86
Evans, Walker, 36, 37, 76; *Let Us Now Praise Famous Men* photography, 30–31, 62–63
experimental writing, 6, 15, 18, 106, 107, 203
expressiveness, 8, 184

fairy tales, 248n22
Fanon, Frantz, *The Wretched of the Earth*, 174, 244n62
Farm Security Administration (FSA), 66, 75, 88
Farrell, James, 249n53
fascism, 105, 143, 144, 176, 183, 200, 209; marching rhythm and, 199; Pound and, 181–82, 210–11, 216, 251n90. *See also* antifascism
Faulkner, William, 214
Fearing, Kenneth, 111, 154, 216–18; "American Rhapsody" sequence, 11, 217; "Bulletin," 217–18; "Denouement," 4, 112; "Lullaby," 133, 134
Feder, Rachel, 44
Federal Theatre Project, 219, 220, 252n1
Feinsod, Harris, *Poetry of the Americas*, 241n5
fellow travelers, 164
feminist thought, 204, 233n22, 250n74; communism and, 183, 225n29; documentary poetics and, 70, 71, 72; experimental writing and, 15; lyric and, 107; Taggard and, 128–30

Filipino migrant workers, 3
Film (periodical), 93
"film poems," 74
films, 10, 22, 202, 219–20; cinema verité, 71; editing of, 100; poetic forms and, 93–94, 100–101. *See also* documentary films
Filreis, Alan, 204–5
financial crisis (2008), 3, 15
First World War, 8
Flaherty, Robert, *Moana*, 73
Flanagan, Hallie, 219; *Can You Hear Their Voices*, 77
folk culture, 71, 86, 215; black, 153–56, 244n40; genres, 108, 131, 138, 147, 188, 190
folk songs, 71, 187, 190, 202
"folk voice," 52, 60, 61–62, 156
Folsom, Mary and Franklin ("Dank"), 187
Form, 226n45
formalism: experimental, 106; New Critical, 15, 183, 210, 212–13, 214
Foster, Stephen, 110–12
Fourth International, 147
Fowler, Carolyn, 152–53, 157–58
fragmentation, 183–84, 212
free expression, 212, 213
Freeman, Joseph, 9, 109, 110, 112–13
free market. *See* Capitalism
free verse, 133, 193, 197
French Revolution, 150
Freneau, Philip, 191
Frontier Films, 93, 101
"Frustrated Poetry Renaissance, The" (symposium), 164
Funaroff, Sol, 115, 154; *The Spider and the Clock*, 109–10; "What the Thunder Said: A Fire Sermon," 114

Garcia Lorca, Federico, 156
Gauley tunnel disaster (W. Va.), 1–2, 4, 80, 83–84, 89, 97, 99, 232n1; miners' silicosis, 60, 61, 65, 66, 68, 69, 75, 83, 91, 95, 96, 101, 205, 234n58
gaze, 33
genre, 12, 130, 138, 153–54
Ginsberg, Allen, 70

Giovannitti, Arturo, 224n17
Girard, Melissa, 129
Glick, Jeremy Matthew, 148, 155, 157, 161, 174, 242n9
Glissant, Édouard, 12; notion of "erranty," 245n73
globalization, 144, 169, 175, 178
Goble, Mark, 53, 230n47
Gold, Mike, 62, 109, 117, 187; "Go Left, Young Writers!" column, 11; *Jews without Money*, 87–88; on Pound's right-wing politics, 210–11; on Rolfe's poetry, 109, 110, 113; on Whitman, 119
Golden, Jules (fictional), 193–94
Golston, Michael, 199
Gourgouris, Stathis, 14, 148
Gramsci, Antonio, 188
Grapes of Wrath (film), 136
Graphics Workshop, 99–100
Great Depression (1930s). *See* Depression-era poetic culture
Green, Ernest, 206
Greenberg, Clement, "Avant-Garde and Kitsch," 213–14, 217, 251n105
Gregory, Horace, 154; *Chorus for Survival*, 109–10; *New Letters in America*, 249n47
Grierson, John, 73, 74
Gronbeck-Tedesco, John A., 37
Gruening, Martha, 149
Guattari, Félix, 224n25
Gulette, George, 196–97
Gummere, Francis Barton, 188, 190, 250n58
Guthrie, Woody, 132, 190

Haiti: African American travel to, 31–32; as antifascist trope, 144–47, 169; Communist Party, 145, 149, 243n22; cultural left interest in, 163; Hughes photograph albums and scrapbooks of, 27–30, 32, 33–34, 40, 41, 42, 43, 44–46, 52, 59, 61; Hughes poetry and, 53; nationalist movement, 145; Roumain and, 143, 144, 148, 149, 150–52, 154, 169, 176; symbolism of, 151; U.S. occupation of, 27–28, 32, 34,

38, 39, 149–50, 156; U.S. popular images of, 33, 39
Haitian Revolution (1791), 38, 39, 149, 165, 230n40, 242n9; historiography of, 144, 148, 157, 159, 161
Halberstam, Jack, 23
Harlem YMCA, 143, 154, 162–64, 165, 169, 247n126
Harney, Stefano: "Mikey the Rebelator" (with Moten), 174, 178; *The Undercommons* (with Moten), 23
Harrington, Joseph, 70
Hayes, Alfred, 18, 111, 112; "Into the Streets May 1st," 131; "Joe Hill" (with Robinson), 187
Hays, Lee, 2
Hegelian universalism, 106
Helsinki Peace Conference (1955), 210
Hicks, Granville, 130, 196, 247n49
high culture, 1, 8, 9, 182, 213
high modernism, 6, 11, 110, 196, 212, 213, 214, 217, 251n107
High School of Music and Art (N.Y.C.), 134–35
Himket, Nazim, 169
Hirschman, Jack, 150; *Open Gate* (with Boadiba), 243n28
historical poetics, 3, 8, 11–13, 70, 220, 225n37; definitions of, 12
history, 70, 74, 85; counternarratives and, 190; Marxist concept of, 106, 156; representation of, 19, 99–100, 191, 192
Hitchcock, Alfred, *The Thirty-Nine Steps*, 236n102
Hitler-Stalin Pact (1939), 5, 136, 175, 176, 183, 212
Holmes, Oliver Wendell, "The Stereoscope and the Stereograph," 40
Horkheimer, Max, *The Dialectic of Enlightenment* (with Adorno), 208–9, 219–20
Howe, Susan, 70
Hughes, Langston, 27–64, 148; antifascist poetry and, 206–7; Caribbean travels of, 27–28, 31; documentary modernist tradition and, 51–52, 62, 67; dramatic monologues and, 52; early 1930s works of, 46–51; first-person plural and, 48; focus on feet and, 28, 61; folk voice of, 52, 61–62, 156; in France, 161; intersection between photography and writing and, 34–35; "I" voice of, 48, 52–53, 119–20; leftist politics and, 28–29, 30, 33–34, 51–52, 54, 59, 67, 155–56, 176, 228n2; *Los agachados* image and, 60, 61, 61; multiple media used by, 58; photographic albums and scrapbooks of, 28–29, 30, 33, 35, 37, 39–46, 40, 41, 42, 43, 47, 49, 54, 59–60, 62, 63–64; photographic-poetic mode of, 55–56, 59; poetic techniques and, 51–52, 55, 206–7; Roumain friendship with, 148, 154, 156–62, 175–77; Roumain translations by, 159–60, 167–68, 173; Scottsboro Boys and, 55–60, 57; *Seven Poets* anthology and, 206–7; travel journal of, 32; visual experimentation and, 34, 51; vitalization of poetry by, 197; "white shadow" conceit of, 34; works: "Addressed to Alabama," 51; "Always the Same," 27–28, 51, 53–55; "The Bitter River," 206–7; "Christ in Alabama," 55; "Come to the Waldorf Astoria," 51; "Danse Africaine," 163; "Free Jacques Romain," 150–52, 152; "Goodbye Christ," 55; "Good Morning, Revolution," 51; "House in the World," 34, 36, 37–38; "I, Too," 221; *I Wonder as I Wander*, 27, 28, 32; Jesse B. Simple sketches, 61; "Johannesburg Mines," 7–8; "Kids Who Die," 52; "Kilby Prison: Scottsboro boys" (article), 55–56; "Let America Be America Again," 52; "Negro Ghetto," 62; "The Negro Speaks of Rivers," 153; "A New Song," 52; "Open Letter to the South," 51, 52, 54–55; "The People without Shoes," 28; *A Pictorial History of the Negro in America* (with Meltzer), 62; "Pictures More than Pictures" (essay), 60; "A Poem for Jacques Roumain (Late Poet of Haiti),"

Hughes (*continued*)
175, 176–77; "Poor Homes" (photograph), 37; *Popo and Fifina: Children of Haiti*, 33; "Roar, China," 52; *Scottsboro Limited* (play), 30, 55, 56–59; "Sharecroppers," 224n28; "Southern Gentlemen, White Prostitutes, Mill-Owners, and Negroes" (essay), 55; *Sweet Flypaper of Life* (with DeCarava), 62; "Wait," 46–51, 52, 54–55, 171, 221–22; "White Shadow" (later "House in the World"), 34, 36; "White Shadows in a Black Land" (essay), 28, 32, 34, 38; "Writers, Words, and the World" (speech), 54
humanism, 72
Hurston, Zora Neale, 39; *Mules and Men*, 86

Ibarro, Felipe, 87
imagism, 129
imperialism, 27–28, 32, 34, 36, 38, 39, 144–51, 176; Hughes poetic "mapping" of, 48; opponents of, 3, 148, 151, 192; U.S. occupation of Haiti as, 27–28, 32, 34, 38, 39, 149–50, 156
industrial disaster. *See* Gauley tunnel disaster
Ingram, Zell, 27, 35
International Brigades, 156
Internationale (anthem), 57, 174, 219
internationalism, 241–42n5, 242n7; antifascist coalition and, 145; black left and, 145, 146, 153, 156; communist movement and, 3, 22–23, 144–45, 147–48, 169, 174, 181; Roumain and, 22, 143–78. *See also* globalization
International Literature (journal), "On Soviet Poetry," 147
International Workers Order, 62
International Writers Association for the Defense of Culture, 54
investigative poetics, coining of term, 70
Izenberg, Oren, 12, 85, 225n37

Jackson, Virginia, 113, 141; *Being Numerous*, 12; *Dickinson's Misery*, 12; *The Lyric Theory Reader*, 12
James, C.L.R., 144, 146, 165, 174; *The Black Jacobins*, 144, 148, 157, 159, 161–62, 165
James, Henry, 214
Jameson, Fredric, 48, 199, 234n67, 247n5
Janowitz, Anne, 110, 118
jazz, 154
Jefferson School (N.Y.C.), 214
Jennison, Ruth, 16, 19, 140, 223n9
Jerome, V. J., 154
Jewish culture, 215
Jim Crow, 27, 32, 84, 148
"Joe Hill" (folk song), 187
John Reed Club, 47, 228n2
Johnson, W. R., 136, 137
Jones, Shirley, 69, 97

Kadlec, David, 82–83
Kahana, Jonathan, 234n65
Kalaidjian, Walter, 75, 110
Kaplan, Louis, 76
Kappeler, Erin, 184
Kaufman, Robert, 132–33
Kazin, Alfred, *On Native Grounds*, 8
Keats, John, 109
Kelley, Robin D. G., 178; *Freedom Dreams*, 13, 226n43
Kenner, Hugh, 215; *The Pound Era*, 210
Key West (Fla.), 139
Kheshti, Roshanak, 249n32
Kinkle, Jeff, 48
kitsch, 16, 213–14, 217, 251n105
Kohlmann, Benjamin, 227–28n68
Komorowski, Conrad, 149
Krakauer, Siegfried, "The Mass Ornament," 248n22
Kramer, Aaron, 206

Labor Defender (magazine), 181
labor movement, 3, 17, 187, 197, 199; songs of, 131, 154, 184, 190, 191
Lange, Dorothea, 75, 76; *American Exodus*, 77; *Migrant Mother* (photographs), 66

language: bilingualism and, 156; black vernacular and, 58; experimentalism and, 15, 71, 203; photography and, 62, 63; syntax and, 108, 117, 120, 123; translation and, 153–54, 156; word embodiment and, 63. *See also* Voice
Language writing, 6, 15, 18, 106–7, 226n51
Laraque, Paul, 243n28
LaTouche, John, "Ballad for Americans" (with Robinson), 155, 187, 244n45
Laughlin, James, 200, 203
Lay My Burden Down (oral history), 86
League of American Writers, "Frustrated Poetry Renaissance" symposium, 164
Lechlitner, Ruth, 105–6, 120; "The Body Politic," 105
Ledbetter, Huddie William (Lead Belly), 132
Lee, Canada, 175
Lee, Steven, 156
Left: A Quarterly Review of Radical and Experimental Art, 19, 183
leftist literary studies, 3, 6, 10, 17, 23
leftist poetics, 2, 17, 18, 20–21, 58, 119, 184–213, 224n28; documentary rhetoric and, 71; folk songs and, 187; nineteenth-century ideals and, 192; poetic forms and, 131, 146; rhyme and, 195–96; rhythm and, 58, 196, 199, 204, 212; Taggard's legacy and, 130–31; traditional genres and, 138; works for children, 33, 185–96. *See also* Communist poetic culture
leftist politics, 4, 16, 17, 197; Hughes and, 28, 153, 155–56, 228n2; lyric and, 105–6, 110; Roumain and, 143, 144, 146; Taggard and, 20, 108. *See also* antifascism; Communism; Popular Front
leftist scholars, 70, 71
Left Pass (fictional magazine), 111–12
Leopardi, Giacamo, 158
Lessing, Doris, *The Golden Notebook*, 6–7
liberalism, 3, 15, 86, 105, 183, 220; lyric tradition and, 107, 137, 155–56; politics of, 155–56
Lidice (Czech village), Nazi destruction of, 207–8

Life (magazine), 49
linguistics. *See* Language
literary modernism. *See* Modernism
Locke, Alain, 149, 164–65, 245n81
Lomax, John, 190–91
Longfellow, Henry Wadsworth, 192; "Song of Hiawatha," 192–93
Los agachados image, 60, 61, 61
Louisiana State University, 213
L'Ouverture, Toussaint, 38–39, 149, 161
"Love Campaign, The" (Soviet satire), American adaptation of, 110–12
Lowell, Amy, 128
Lowenfels, Walter, 17
Lowney, John, 234n58
Luce, Henry, "The American Century," 175
lynchings, 116, 206
lyric, 2, 13–15, 72, 80, 82, 87, 105–78; antilyric and, 71, 106; authenticity and, 153; black radicalism and, 146, 168, 169; choral and, 136; Cold War and, 106, 141–42; Communist poetic culture and, 106, 112, 117, 119, 144–45, 148, 168, 169, 173, 184; critiques of, 15, 105–6, 146–47; defenses of, 146–47; definitions of, 10, 74, 106, 107, 111, 147, 237n8; Depression era and, 106, 108–9, 110, 113, 118, 119; folk forms and, 108, 147, 156; future of poetry and, 137–42; historical change and, 106, 144; historical epoch of, 168; histories of, 147–48; idealization of poetry and, 138; idea of, 12, 74, 141; liberalism and, 107, 137, 155–56; "lyric shame" and, 141, 142; manifest content of, 112; mode of address and, 126; mode of semblance and, 132–33; modernist models of, 168; narrative vs., 148, 157; narrow definition of, 111; orality of, 108, 137–39; personification and, 157–62; refiguration of, 108, 119; rejection of terms of, 14; Rolfe and, 141–42; Romantic conception of, 107, 108, 110, 112, 119, 125, 142, 168; Roumain and, 143–44, 146, 156–62, 169; shared assumptions about, 105–6; shift in expression of, 108, 125–30; social

lyric (*continued*)
  implications of, 14, 107; as solitary expression, 106; song and, 108, 130–32, 134, 135, 141; subjectivity and, 108, 128–29, 133, 138–39, 168; Taggard and, 22, 107–8, 109, 119, 126, 128, 141; women writers and, 129
"lyric effect," 107–8
"lyric ideal," 22, 108
Lyric Theory Reader, The (Jackson and Prins), 12

Maas, Willard, 73–74, 93
MacKenzie, Donald, 50, 231n68
MacLeish, Archibald, 29, 86, 200; *Conquistador*, 93; *The Land of the Free*, 75–77
Maddow, Ben, 29; definition of poetry, 72–73; "Film into Poem," 93–94
Magi, Jill, 70, 71, 72
Mallarmé, Stéphane, 145–46, 166
Manovich, Lev, 53
Mao, Douglas, 182
marginalization, 19, 23, 86
Markham, Edwin, 132
Martin, Meredith, 184; *The Rise and Fall of Meter*, 225n42
Marx, Karl, 75, 108, 114–15; *The Communist Manifesto*, 113
Marxism, 140, 214, 225n29, 247n53; Afro-Caribbean, 146; concept of history, 106, 156; dialectic, 113–14; hermeneutics, 15; international, 181; literary tradition, 183, 213; lyricism, 109, 114
Mason, Charlotte Osgood, 27
mass culture, 213
mass political mobilizations, 15, 132, 205–6, 221
Matthiessen, F. O., 211
Maxwell, William J., 58
Mayakovsky, Vladimir, 166
May Day: parades, 126, 181, 184–85, 197, 198; song competition, 131
Mbembe, Achille, 158
McCarthyism, 181, 211
McKay, Claude, 33

Mechanics of Love, The (film poem), 74
media culture, 10, 22, 53, 58, 69, 71, 72, 75. *See also* Films; Radio
Mellino, Miguel, "The *Langue* of the Damned: Fanon and the Remnants of Europe," 174
Meltzer, Milton, *A Pictorial History of the Negro in America* (with Hughes), 62
Meter, 134, 192–93; scansion and, 133–34
Metropolitan Museum of Art (N.Y.C.), 69
Mickenberg, Julia L., 191
Miéville, China, 101–2
Mill, John Stuart, 110, 237n8
Miller, Arthur, 211
Millet, Joseph, 181
Millet, Martha, 5, 23, 181–93, *182*, 203–11, 218, 248n9; antifascist poems and, 203–9; children's poems and, 185–87, 193, 202; Cold War and, 210, 212, 215; Communist Party background of, 181; folk forms and, 215; literary studies and, 215–16; modernist forms and, 181–84, 197–98, 205–6, 214–15, 247n5; political writing and, 210–11, 215–16; rhythm and, 23, 185, 186, 196–99, 209, 215, 250n58; works: *Dangerous Jack*, 205, 210, 215; "Ezra Pound Myth" (unpublished), 181, 182, 183–84, 210, 211–12, 215, 217; "Footnote on Modern Poetry" (unpublished), 183; "Historian," 209; *Kid with Kazoo*, 187; *Last of the Lemmings: An Allegory*, 187; "The Love Song of J. Anonymous Proletariat," 198; "Mississippi," 250n88; "Modern Poetry: For or Against?," 181, 214–15; "Pioneer Pied Piper," 186, 187–88, *188*, 189, 190, 208; "Poets and Poverty" (unpublished), 211; *Rosenbergs: Poems of the United States* (co-editor), 210, 217; "Silicosis in Our Town," 205; *Thine Alabaster Cities: A Poem for Our Time*, 186, 210; "Unforgotten Village," 207–8
Mirzoeff, Nicholas, 39
Mitchell, Broadus, 149
Moana (Flaherty film), 73

modernism, 8, 14, 16, 21, 23, 54, 247–48n5; antimodernists and, 197–98, 199, 206; avant-garde and, 7; contested definitions of, 204; documentary culture and, 62, 71; globalization and, 169; high, 6, 11, 110, 212, 213, 214, 217, 251n107; historical and theoretical reexaminations of, 19, 204; Hughes's scrapbooks and, 46; legacies of, 18–19; literary forms and, 118, 168, 220; media and, 53; Millet critique of, 181–84, 197–98, 205–6, 214–15, 247n5; New Critics and, 18, 19, 212; Pound and, 181, 182, 184, 196, 210, 211, 217, 247n3; rhythm and, 184, 196, 206; stylistic techniques and attitudes, 183–84, 212; two views of, 18, 20

Monroe, Harriet, 140

Moten, Fred, 27, 59, 63, 146, 167, 246n113; analysis of James's *Black Jacobins*, 148, 157, 159, 161, 162; *In the Break*, 64; "Mikey the Rebelator" (with Harney), 174, 178; *The Undercommons*, (with Harney) 23

Mother Goose, 195–96, 200, 202–4

multimedia, 69, 72, 75

Muñoz, José Esteban, 109

Murphy, George B., Jr., 149

Museum of Modern Art (N.Y.C.), 214

music: blues, 71, 83–84, 154; choral, 133–37; left-wing, 131; poetry's relationship with, 108, 134, 137, 140. *See also* song

Mussolini, Benito, 216

Mydan, Carl, Ozarks cabin photo, 79

Narcissus (film poem), 74

narrative: database vs., 53; lyric vs., 148, 157; voice-over, 74, 93, 94, 95, 96

National Maritime Union, 181

National Public Radio, 182

Native American culture, 192–93

nature, 120–21

Naumberg, Nancy, 65, 75

nazis: destruction of Lidice by, 207–8; refugees from, 20

Nazi-Soviet Pact. *See* Hitler-Stalin Pact

Nealon, Christopher, 67; *The Matter of Capital: Poetry and Crisis in the American Century*, 15, 16, 17

Negri, Antonio, 108

Negritude poetry, 168

Negro (Cunard anthology), 151, 156

Neihardt, John, *Black Elk Speaks*, 86

Nelson, Cary, 19, 20, 49, 107; "Lyric Politics," 141–42; *Repression and Recovery*, 17, 223n7

Neoliberal politics, 19

New American Poetry, 15, 18

New Criticism, 6, 14, 17–19, 224n17, 227–28n68, 242n16, 248n9; apolitical formalism, 15, 183, 210, 212–13, 214; critics of, 70, 183, 211, 215, 216; definition of lyric and, 10, 74, 106, 107, 147, 237n8; emergence in 1930s of, 106, 183, 184; as fascist/racist ideology, 183; lyric speaker, 106, 148; modernist version of, 18–19, 212; postwar influence of, 107, 209, 210; tenets of, 183

New Deal photography, 62, 66, 75–76, 80, 88, 234n48

New Directions (publication), 200, 203

New Historicism, 225n37

new journalism, 71

New Masses (CPUSA magazine), 2, 34, 77, 81, 93, 110, 118, 119, 140, 204, 227n68; editorial on rhythm, 184; Gold "Go Left, Young Writers!" column, 11; Hughes's elegy for Roumain, 175; popularization of poetry, 193; on Pound's politics, 210–11, 251n90; review of Taggard poem, 130; Roumain "Is Poetry Dead?" essay, 145–46, 164, 196–97, 198 ; Taggard essay, 118, 198–99

New Pioneer (children's magazine), 185–86, 187, 188, 190–93, 196, 202; "American History Told in Pictures" series, 191

New Republic (magazine), 105, 197

New River Gorge, 65, 69, 75

New Song, A (anthology), 62

New York Intellectuals, 212, 213, 214, 251n100

New York Times, 221
Niedecker, Lorine, *New Goose* ("Mother Goose" rhymes), 200, 202–4, 250n74
nineteenth-century poetry, 191, 192–93
1930s. *See* Communist Party USA; Depression-era poetic culture; New Deal; Popular Front
Nobel Prize, 214
Noland, Carrie, 135, 168
nonfiction poem. *See* documentary poetry
Norman, Charles, *The Case of Ezra Pound*, 211
Nowak, Mark, 85
nursery rhymes, 16, 196, 202, 203, 204, 224n28, 250n74

Objectivist poetics, 16, 118, 140, 202; subjective and, 71, 74
Occupy movement, 15, 221
Office of War Information (OWI), Graphics Workshop, 99–100
O'Hara, Frank, 20
Oliver, Mary, 1
Olsen, Tillie, 71; "I Want You Women Up North to Know," 87; *Yonnondio*, 71, 87
Olson, Charles, 70; "Projective Verse," 72
Oppen, George, 202
Opportunity (periodical), 164
oral history, 86
oral recitation, 108, 137–39
O'Sheel, Shaemas, 9, 146, 204, 205–6
Oxford Anthology of Modern American Poetry (2000), 19–20

parataxis, 15, 107
Parti Communiste Haïtien, 145, 149, 243n22
Partisan (John Reed Club magazine), 47, 49
Partisan Review, 18, 110, 120, 213, 214, 248n9; forum on poetry, 106
Patchen, Kenneth, *Before the Brave*, 109–10, 117
Patterson, Anita Haya, 153
People of the Cumberland (film), 101
Perloff, Marjorie, 19–20
personal voice. *See* voice

personification, 157–62
Phillips, William, 213
photography. *See* documentary photography; films
photojournalism, 49, 71, 75
Pictorial History of the Negro in America, A (Hughes and Meltzer), 62
Pitts, Rebecca, 130
Poems for Workers (publication), 110
poetic culture: black, 164–65, 168; death trope and, 124–26; investigative poetics and, 70; nineteenth-century, 191, 192–93; political action and, 222; social and political function of, 166–67; two American camps of, 18; utilitarian function of, 9–10; white appropriation of black, 154. *See also* Communist poetic culture; documentary poetry; leftist poetics; lyric; modernism; political poetry; voice
Poetry (magazine), 73–74, 140
"poets' international," 144
political poetry, 1–12, 21, 22, 23, 107, 136, 137, 143, 144, 220; accessibility of, 197; backlash against, 213; contested definitions of, 204; documentary and, 65–67; experimental poetics and, 107; historical lyric and, 142; Hughes and, 51–52, 54, 55–60; marginalization and, 23; Millet and, 185–93, 212, 215; New Critical opposition to, 183; new lyric ideal and, 108, 112, 118; rhyme use and, 205–6; rhythm use and, 58, 198–99; Rolfe's assessment of, 120; Romanticism and, 119; Rukeyser and, 85, 86; social engagement and, 2, 70, 109–10, 192; subjectivity and, 136; Taggard and, 124–25, 128, 138; voice and, 87. *See also* Communist poetic culture; Leftist poetics
political speech, 89–90
Pollock, Jackson, 214; *The She-Wolf*, 214
Popular Front, 23, 72, 83, 147; "Ballad for Americans" as anthem of, 155, 244n45; debates on genre and, 200–201, 202, 203, 205; language and, 153–54, 156; poetic culture and, 19, 146, 185, 187, 191, 192,

193–95, 200–201, 202, 203, 210; poetic propaganda and, 210; political issues of, 192, 193–94, 199–200, 209; "the people" rhetoric of, 136; race and, 144–45, 153, 154, 155; rhythm and, 196; Roumain as symbol to, 144, 145, 149, 150, 151, 156; song and, 131, 132, 155; Third Period shift to, 5, 105, 131, 185
popular genres: high art boundaries with, 182; Hughes's interest in, 61; political appropriation of, 193; social usefulness of, 56, 58; verse and, 107, 191
portraiture, 75, 77, 80
Postmentier, Sonya, 12
Potamkin, Harry Alan, "Mother Goose on the Breadline," 195–96, 202
Pound, Ezra, 16, 70, 181–84, 210–12; anti-Semitism of, 210; fascist politics of, 181–82, 210–11, 216, 251n90; modernism and, 181, 182, 184, 196, 210, 211, 217, 247n3; *The Pisan Cantos*, 181, 184; poetic legacy of, 181; "A Retrospect," 196; on rhythm, 196; treason trial of, 181, 211; Zukofsky break with, 18
Prins, Yopie, 11–12, 240n92; *The Lyric Theory Reader*, 12; *Victorian Sappho*, 11–12
proletarian aesthetics, 33, 36, 58, 71, 112; black culture and, 164–65, 173–74; early 1940s reactions against, 212, 213; grotesque and, 87; novel and, 144; Whitman and, 119, 120
proletariat. *See* working class
propaganda, 71, 147, 165, 199, 203, 210; art vs., 212–13; documentary, 74
protest verse, 129–30, 185, 203

"Quand bat le tam-tam" ("When the Tom-Tom Beats") (Roumain), 151–62, 164, 169; circulation contexts for, 156; Hughes's English translation of, 156, 159–60

Rabinowitz, Paula, 5, 87, 235n73
race. *See* African Americans: black *headings*
"racialized reading," 29, 154

racism, 182, 183, 206, 210, 211–12; opponents of, 15, 21, 107; segregation and, 27, 32, 84, 148
radical poetics. *See* black radical tradition; Depression-era poetic culture
radio, 10, 29, 108, 137–39, 190, 202
Rahv, Philip, 10, 110, 184; "Open Letter to Young Writers," 105; "Proletarian Literature," 213
Rampersad, Arnold, 38, 175
Rancière, Jacques, 20–21, 31, 217
Ransom, John Crowe, 210, 215
realism, 71, 214
Rebel Poet (magazine), 10, 105, 110, 184
Reece, Florence, 1
Reed, Anthony, 29, 153–54, 168
Reed, Brian, 225n29
representation, 29, 74, 85, 99–100
Resettlement Administration, 75, 76
revolution, 54, 55, 58, 64; idea of, 13; poetic models, 70, 120, 128, 145, 146, 165, 166, 167, 221. *See also* Haitian Revolution
revolutionary romantic, 108, 117, 118, 119, 126
rhyme, 187, 195–96, 205–6
rhythm, 23, 184–218, 250n58; abstract definition of, 199; authentic expression aligned with, 58, 188; concept of, 184; Hughes experiments with, 56; leftist poetic culture and, 184–87, 189, 191, 193, 196–200, 203, 212; mechanizations of, 209, 210; modernism and, 184, 196, 206; poetic function of, 199; political function of, 58, 205–7, 208–9; social idealization of, 58
Richards, I.A., 227n68
Riis, Jacob, *How the Other Half Lives*, 66
Rivera, Diego, 252n1; *Man at the Crossroads*, 219
Robbins, Tim, 219–20
Robeson, Paul, 132, 155, 244n45
Robinson, Cedric, 169, 245n72
Robinson, Earl, 132, 186; "Ballad for Americans" (with LaTouche), 155, 187, 244n45; "Joe Hill" (with Hayes), 187
Rockefeller, Nelson, 219, 220

Rolfe, Edwin, 14, 20, 22, 106, 107–20, 117, 224n17; lyric and, 141–42; on political poetry, 120; reception of poems of, 108, 141; Romantic lyric and, 107, 108, 109–10, 119; significance of poems of, 109; Whitman's forms and, 120; works: *Before the Brave*, 117; "Catalogue of I," 119–20; *Collected Poems*, 141; "Credo," 112–13, 114, 115–16; "First Love," 141; *First Love and Other Poems*, 141; "Georgia Nightmare," 116; "Homage to Karl Marx," 114–15; "Lyric Politics," 142; "Madrid," 142; "The Melancholy Comus," 142; "Testament to a Flowering Race," 113; "To My Contemporaries," 115–17; *To My Contemporaries*, 109, 110–17

Romanticism: bourgeois vs. "revolutionary," 108, 117, 118, 119, 126; communism and, 118, 124; individual subjectivity and, 119; lyric and, 107, 108, 110, 112, 119, 125, 142, 168; modernism and, 18; Taggard's and Rolfe's engagements with, 108, 109, 110, 117–23, 124, 238n40; tropes of nature, 120–21; Wilson's view of, 119

Ronda, Margaret, 237n11

Rosenberg, Leah, 33

Rosenberg case, 210, 217

Rosten, Norman, "Prelude," 206–7

Rotha, Paul, 236n89

Rothstein, Arthur, 76

Roumain, Jacques, 5, 22, 143–78, 242n16, 245n88; antifascism and, 144, 145, 147; Communist Party USA and, 149, 175, 243n22; death and elegies for, 175–77; exile from Haiti of, 143, 148, 176; Harlem YMCA lecture, 143, 154, 162–64, 165, 169, 247n126; historical and political import of, 148–49, 169; historical/ideological context for poems of, 16, 168, 169; Hughes and, 156–62, 167–68, 173, 175, 176–77; memorial service for, 175; on poetry's death and rebirth, 164, 165–67; political activism of, 145, 146, 169; political imprisonment of, 149, 150; as resistance synecdoche, 156–62; Schomburg Center lecture, 173; translation of poetry and, 157–59, 168; tributes to, 175–77; works: "Aprés-Midi," 152; "Bois d'ébèóne" ("Ebony Wood"), 169–74; *Gouverneurs de la rosée* (*Masters of the Dew*), 167–68, 172; *Griefs de l'homme noir* (*Grievances of the Black Man*), 169; "Is Poetry Dead?" (essay and lecture), 145–46, 165–67; "Langston Hughes," 159, 160–62, 164, 169; "Midi," 152; "Miragône," 152; *La proie et l'ombre* (*The Prey and the Shadow*), 157–59; "Propos sans suite" ("Talk and Nothing More"), 157, 160; "Quand bat le tam-tam" ("When the Tom-Tom Beats)", 151–62; 164, 169; "Sales nègres" ("Filthy Negroes"), 173–74

Rukeyser, Muriel, 65–101; alternate forms of representation and, 99–100, 154; Communist critics of, 2; critical responses to, 73–74, 94, 197, 224n17; documentary poetry and, 70, 94; on documentation, 29; film techniques of, 94; foreword to Abbott's *Photographs*, 78–79; Graphic Workshop and, 99–100; later poetic cinematic style of, 94; marginalization of, 71–72; as recipient of Yale Younger Poets Prize (1935), 110; review of MacLeish's *Land of the Free* by, 76–77; works: "Adventures of Children" (photo-text sequence), 79–80, 79; "Alloy," 73; "A Child Asleep," 73; "The Dam," 73; *The Life of Poetry*, 65, 89, 91, 92, 99–100, 101; "Poem (I lived in the first century of World Wars)," 222; "Poem out of Childhood," 112; "Power," 73; *The Speed of Darkness*, 94; *Theory of Flight*, 110; *U.S. 1*, 1–2, 65, 67, 72, 73, 74, 94. See also *Book of the Dead, The*

Russian Revolution (1917), 27, 101–2

Saint-Amour, Paul K., 247n5

Sandburg, Carl, 52, 197; "Cool Tombs," 133, 134; *The People, Yes*, 200–201, 202, 204

Sanders, Ed, 70

Sauer, Ronald F., 150
Scandura, Jani, *Down in the Dumps*, 139
Schmitt, Carl, *Political Romanticism*, 119
Schneider, Isidor, 105, 106, 110
Schomburg Center (N.Y.C.), 173
school programs, 190–91
Schuman, William, 134–36, 139; *Prologue*, 134–35; *This Is Our Time*, 135–36, 137
Scott, Keith Lamont, 221
Scottsboro Boys, 55–60, 57
Seabrook, William, *Magic Island*, 33
Second World War. *See* World War II
See, Sarita, 3
Seeger, Charles, 131
segregation, 27, 32, 84, 148
Sekula, Allan, 50
self, 14, 106, 123
Selvinski, Ilya, "On Soviet Poetry," 147–48
Seven Poets in Search of an Answer (antifascist anthology), 9, 203–10, 212; O'Sheel introduction, 146, 206
Sexton, Jared, 158
Shahn, Ben, 76
Shakespeare, William, *Othello*, 161
sharecroppers letters, 86
Shepard, Albert, 196, 197, 199, 207, 209
Sierra Leone, 53
silicosis deaths, 65, 66, 68, 69, 75, 83, 91, 95, 96, 101, 205, 234n58
Silver Shirt Legion of America, 11
Simple, Jesse B. (Hughes character), 61
Sinclair, Jo (Ruth Seid), *The Changelings*, 193–95
slave rebellion (1791). *See* Haitian Revolution
slavery, 170, 191, 192, 215, 216; abolitionists, 120; oral history, 86
Smethurst, James, 52, 58, 154
Smith, Shawn Michelle, 32
social action, 70
social identity, 107
socialist realism, 212, 214
socially engaged poetics. *See under* political poetry

song, 58, 61, 130–38; black, 54, 71, 155; choral forms, 133–37, 140, 141; folk, 71, 187, 190, 202; labor movement, 131, 191; leftist folk, 187; lyric, 108, 130–32, 141; worker, 131, 154, 184, 190, 191. *See also* ballads
"Song of the Chinese Soldier" (poem), 93, 94
Sorby, Angela, 192
South, U.S.: New Critics and, 215; racism and, 169; sharecroppers and, 86; white labor in, 52. *See also* Jim Crow; slavery
southern agrarians, 211, 215, 216
Southern Review, 184, 213
Soviet Union: Communism, 18; Five-Year Plans, 147; Hitler-Stalin pact (1939), 5, 136, 175, 176, 183, 212; "Love Campaign" satire, 110–12; Revolution of 1917, 27, 101–2; Tass news agency, 19–20; verse, 147, 203, 224n28
Spahr, Clemens, 224n17
Spahr, Juliana, 223n6, 226n51; *An Army of Lovers* (with Buuck), 1; "The Incinerator," 235n88
Spanish Civil War, 20, 176, 192; Hughes poems about, 51, 155–56; Rolfe and, 141, 142; Roumain and, 169
speech. *See* voice
Spicer, Jack, 16
Spingarn, Amy, 28
spirituals, 154
Spivak, Gayatri, 237n11
Stalin, Joseph. *See* Hitler-Stalin pact
Stein, Gertrude, 15, 18
Steven, Mark, *Red Modernism*, 225n29, 247n3
Stevens, Wallace, 73
Stewart, Susan, 87, 230n47
stock market crash (1929), 7, 17
Stott, William, 52–53; *Documentary Expression and Thirties America*, 71
Strimple, Nick, 133
Stryker, Roy, 88
subjective expression, 73, 74, 86, 101, 107, 108–9, 119, 126; lyric and, 108, 128–29, 133, 138–39, 168; objective and, 71, 74, 128–29; politics and, 136

Swayne, Steve, 135
synaptic vs. syntactic, 117
syntax, 108, 117, 120, 123

Taggard, Genevieve, 5, 22, 105–41, 240nn 102,103; autobiographical explication and, 123–24; on black expressive culture, 154–55; choral forms and, 130–37, 140; communist causes and, 19–20, 107–8, 117–23; death trope and, 124–26; framing devices and, 130–31; ideal lyric and, 108–9; on individual's relationship to group, 123–24; interests of, 108; literary importance of, 19–20; lyric experiments and, 22, 107–8, 109, 119, 126, 128, 141; metrical marks and, 133–34; Popular Front culture and, 132; on popular function of poetry, 138; radio and, 108, 137–39; range of genres used by, 130; Romanticism and, 108, 118–19, 120–21; shift to protest poem and, 129–30; vitalization of poetry and, 197; voice and, 121, 126–28, 136; Whitman critique by, 121–23; works: "Adding Up America—You Try," 122–23, 128; "At Last the Women Are Moving," 129–30; *Calling Western Union*, 120, 122, 123–28, 130–31, 132, 136; "Chant for the Great Negro Poet of America Not Yet Born," 155; *Collected Poems*, 126–27; "Definition of Song," 130–31, 132, 137–38; "Feeding the Children," 127; "Funeral in May," 124–28, 130, 132; "Image," 130; "In the Plural" (unpublished draft), 139; "Lark," 130, 132–33, 134; *The Life and Mind of Emily Dickinson*, 128, 132; *Long View*, 128, 134, 135, 136; "Mass Song," 127; "Night Letter to Walt Whitman," 120–22, 127; "Note Book I," 124; "Notes on Writing Words for Music," 133, 134; "Ode in a Time of Crisis," 20; *Prologue* (lyrics), 134–35; "Remembering Vaughan," 130; "Romanticism and Communism" (essay), 118, 119, 124; *This Is Our Time* (lyrics), 135–36, 137; "To Arm You for This Time," 128; "To Paul Robeson," 155; "To the Negro People," 155

Tass (Soviet news agency), 19–20
Tate, Allen, 210, 211
Taylor, Paul, *American Exodus: A Record of Human Erosion*, 77
Tejada, Roberto, 39, 53
Terada, Rei, 14
These Are Our Lives (oral histories), 86
Third International, 225n29
Third Period, 11, 109; shift to Popular Front, 5, 105, 131, 185
third-person voice, 127, 137
Thomas, Jean, *Ballad Makin' in the Mountains of Kentucky*, 191
Thomas, Katherine Elwes, *The Real Personages Mother Goose*, 202
Thompson, Krista, 33
Thoreau, Henry David, 69
Thurston, Michael, 58, 82
Tiffany, Daniel, 217, 251n105
Till, Emmett, 250n88
Toomer, Jean, 149, 154
Toscano, Alberto, 48
train image, 101–2
transcendentalism, 142
trochaic tetrameter, 192–93
"tropicalizing gaze," 33

Ueland, Brenda, 200
Union Carbide Company, 1–2, 4, 65, 66
University of Buffalo, 70
university system, 190

Vallejo, Cesar, 168
Vietnam era, 18, 71
Vincent, Sténio, 143, 149
voice, 85–91; "authentic," 95; choral forms, 136–37; collective, 126, 127–28, 130, 131, 135–36, 137; of common people, 58–59, 131; gendering of, 129; Hughes's "folk," 52, 60, 61–62, 156; Hughes's "I," 48, 52–53, 119–20; 1930s and, 86–87; personal, 59, 107, 126, 127, 129; in Rukeyser's work, 85, 86, 88, 95; subjective, 73, 86; in Taggard's

work, 121, 126–28, 136; third-person, 127, 137; Whitman's "I," 121, 127
voice-over narration, 74, 93, 94, 95, 96

Wald, Alan, 2, 18, 205, 213, 220, 238n40, 243–44n40; *The Revolutionary Imagination*, 223n7, 224n28
Waligora-Davis, Nicole, 39
Walkowitz, Rebecca, 182
Wallace, Henry, "People's Century," 175
Wall Street crash (1929), 7, 27
Wang, Dorothy, 126n45
Warhol, Andy, *Electric Chair*, 217
Wark, McKenzie, 216–17
Warren, Robert Penn, 184, 213, 242n16
Washington, Mary Helen, *The Other Black List*, 224n17
West, Don, 215; "They Take Their Stand (For Some Professional Agrarians)," 215
West Virginia. *See* Gauley tunnel disaster
"we" voice, 108, 121, 127, 131, 135, 136
"What We Talk About When We Talk About Poetry," (short story) 1
Wheelwright, John, 82
"When the Tom-Tom Beats" (Roumain). *See* "Quand bat le tam-tam"
White, Gillian, 6, 106, 141
white nationalism, 206
Whitman, Walt, 52, 53, 108, 120–23, 128, 210; catalogue device, 122–23; Communist Party edition of poems of, 119; early twentieth-century appropriations of, 122, 193–94; free verse and, 193; "I" voice and, 121, 127; legacy of, 108, 122; proletarian aesthetics and, 119, 120; "Song of Myself," 120
Whittier, John Greenleaf, 120

Wilderson, Frank B. III, 158
Williams, William Carlos, 2, 18, 74, 91–92; *Spring and All*, 122
Wilson, Edmund, 8, 220–21; *Axel's Castle*, 119; "Is Verse a Dying Technique?," 134, 199, 200
Wolff, David (pseud.). *See* Maddow, Ben
women writers, 19, 87, 128, 129. *See also* feminist thought; *specific names*
workers. *See* labor movement
working class, 83, 108, 126, 132, 184, 200–201; class struggle and, 144, 166, 184–5; poetic expression and, 188–91, 197, 198, 205, 213, 215; voice of, 58–59, 127, 131, 136. *See also* proletarian aesthetics
workshop poem, 107
work songs, 131, 154, 184, 190, 191
World War I, 8
World War II, 132, 136, 175, 185; build-up to, 7, 163–64, 166–67; Caribbean intellectuals and, 168; German refugees from, 20; Hitler-Stalin Pact and, 5, 136, 175, 176, 183; Lidice destruction and, 207–8
Wright, Richard, 29, 175, 246–47n122; "I Tried to Be a Communist," 247n123; *Twelve Million Black Voices*, 48

Yale Younger Poets Prize (1935), 110
Yoseloff, Thomas, 204–5
Young Communist League, 181, *182*
"you" voice, 126, 127, 131

Zaturenska, Marya, 18
zombie movies, 33
Zukofsky, Louis, 1, 18, 107, 202, 251n90; "To My Wash-Stand," 140

www.ingramcontent.com/pod-product-compliance
Lightning Source LLC
Chambersburg PA
CBHW030525230426
43665CB00010B/770